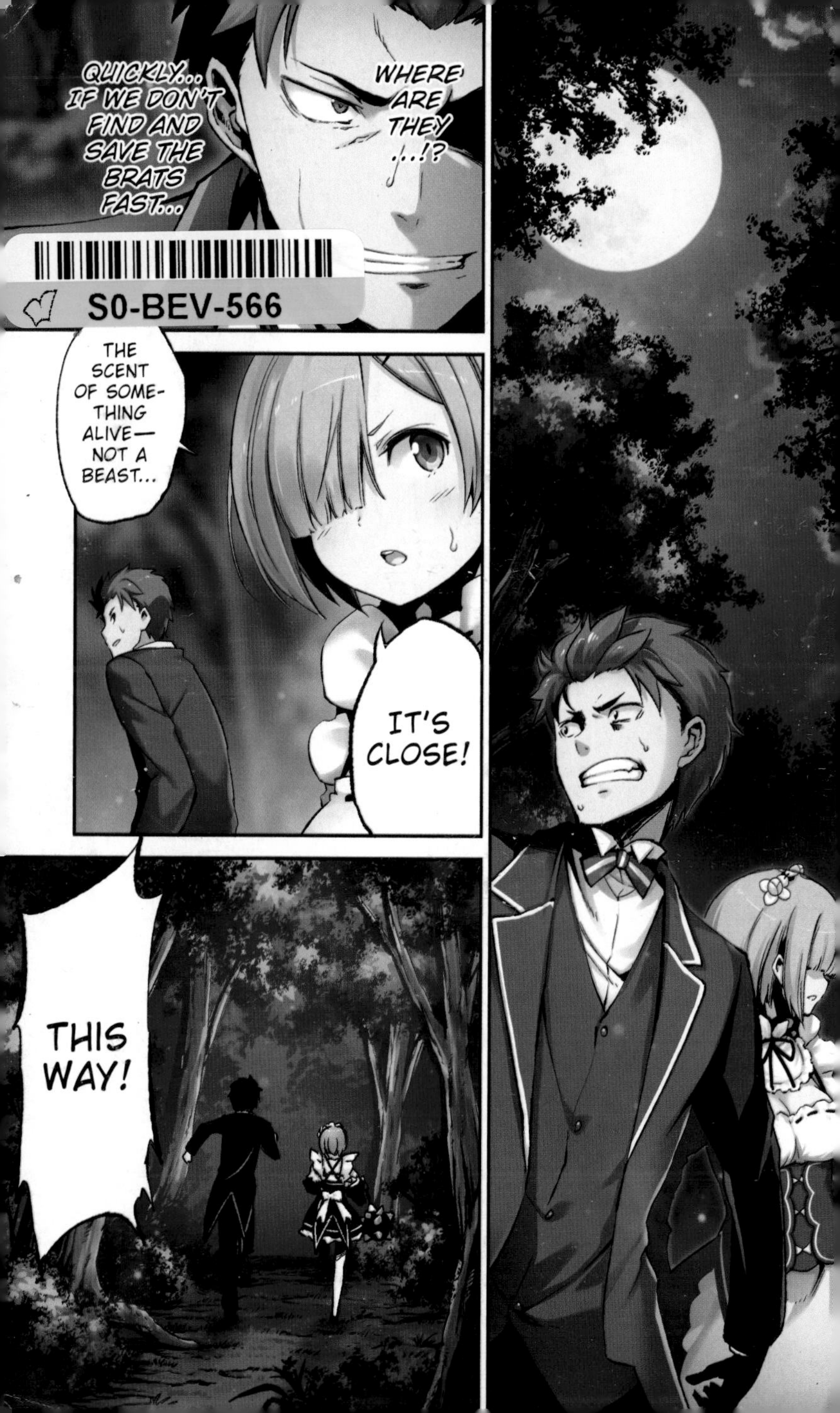
WHERE ARE THEY ...!?
QUICKLY... IF WE DON'T FIND AND SAVE THE BRATS FAST...
THE SCENT OF SOME-THING ALIVE—NOT A BEAST...
IT'S CLOSE!
THIS WAY!

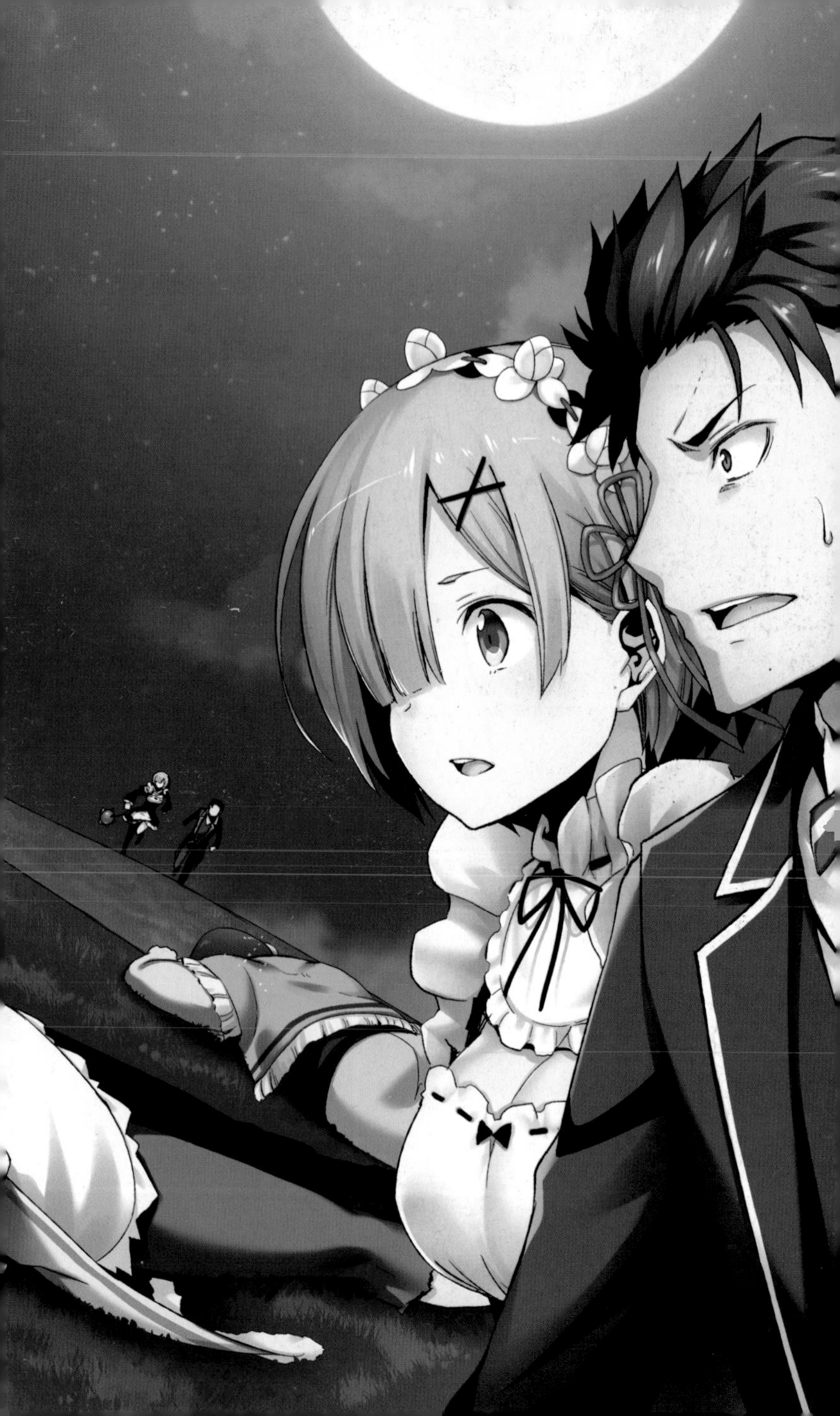

Re:ZeRo
-Starting Life in Another World-
Chapter 2: A Week at the Mansion

Episode 16
Demon Beasts

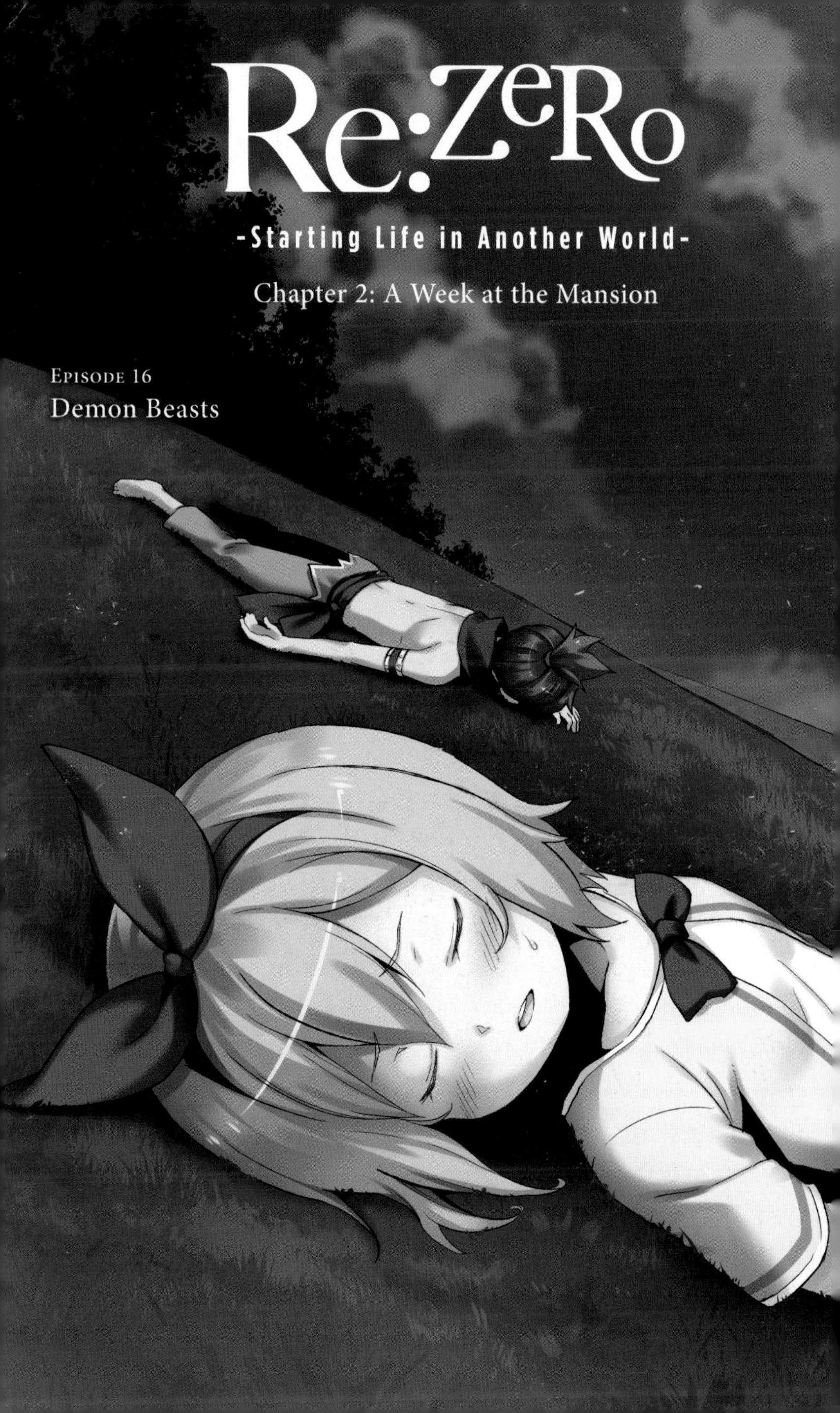

Re:ZERO -Starting Life in Another World-

Chapter 2: A Week at the Mansion

The only ability Subaru Natsuki gets when he's summoned to
another world is time travel via his own death. But to save her,
he'll die as many times as it takes.

Contents

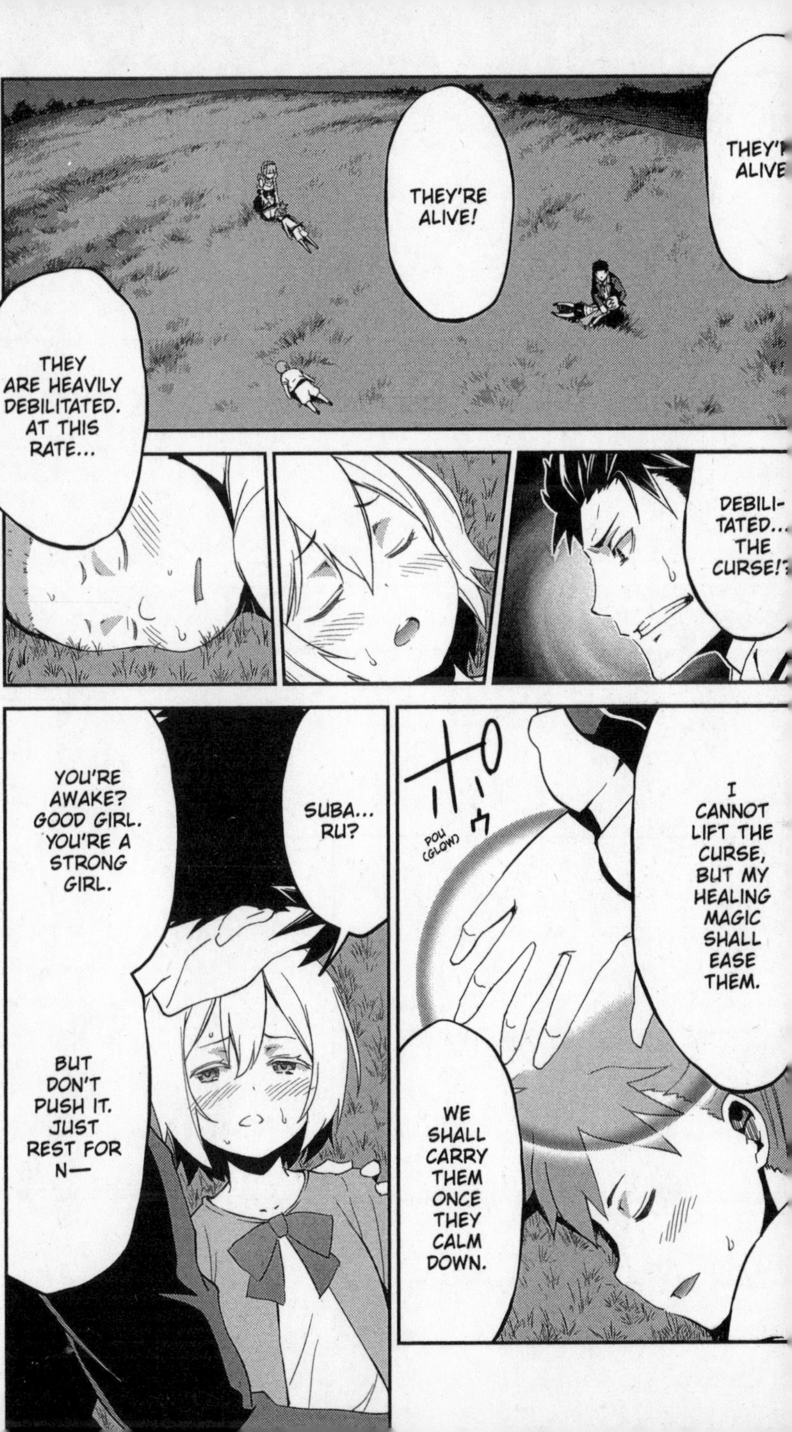
THEY'R ALIVE
THEY'RE ALIVE!
THEY ARE HEAVILY DEBILITATED. AT THIS RATE...
DEBILI-TATED... THE CURSE!?
ポウ
POU (GLOW)
I CANNOT LIFT THE CURSE, BUT MY HEALING MAGIC SHALL EASE THEM.
WE SHALL CARRY THEM ONCE THEY CALM DOWN.
SUBA... RU?
YOU'RE AWAKE? GOOD GIRL. YOU'RE A STRONG GIRL.
BUT DON'T PUSH IT. JUST REST FOR N—

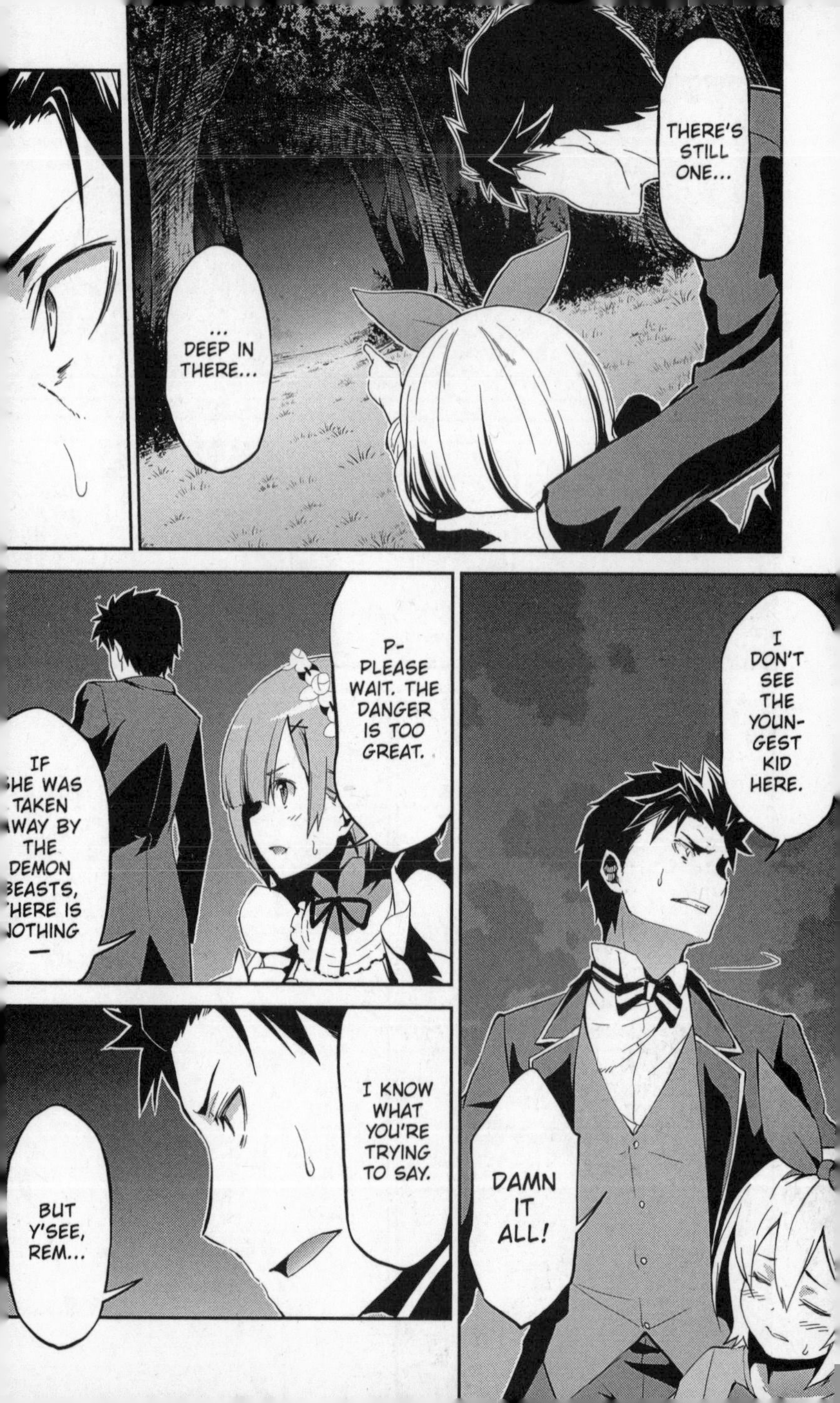
THERE'S STILL ONE...
...DEEP IN THERE...
I DON'T SEE THE YOUN-GEST KID HERE.
DAMN IT ALL!
P-PLEASE WAIT. THE DANGER IS TOO GREAT.
IF SHE WAS TAKEN AWAY BY THE DEMON BEASTS, THERE IS NOTHING—
I KNOW WHAT YOU'RE TRYING TO SAY.
BUT Y'SEE, REM...

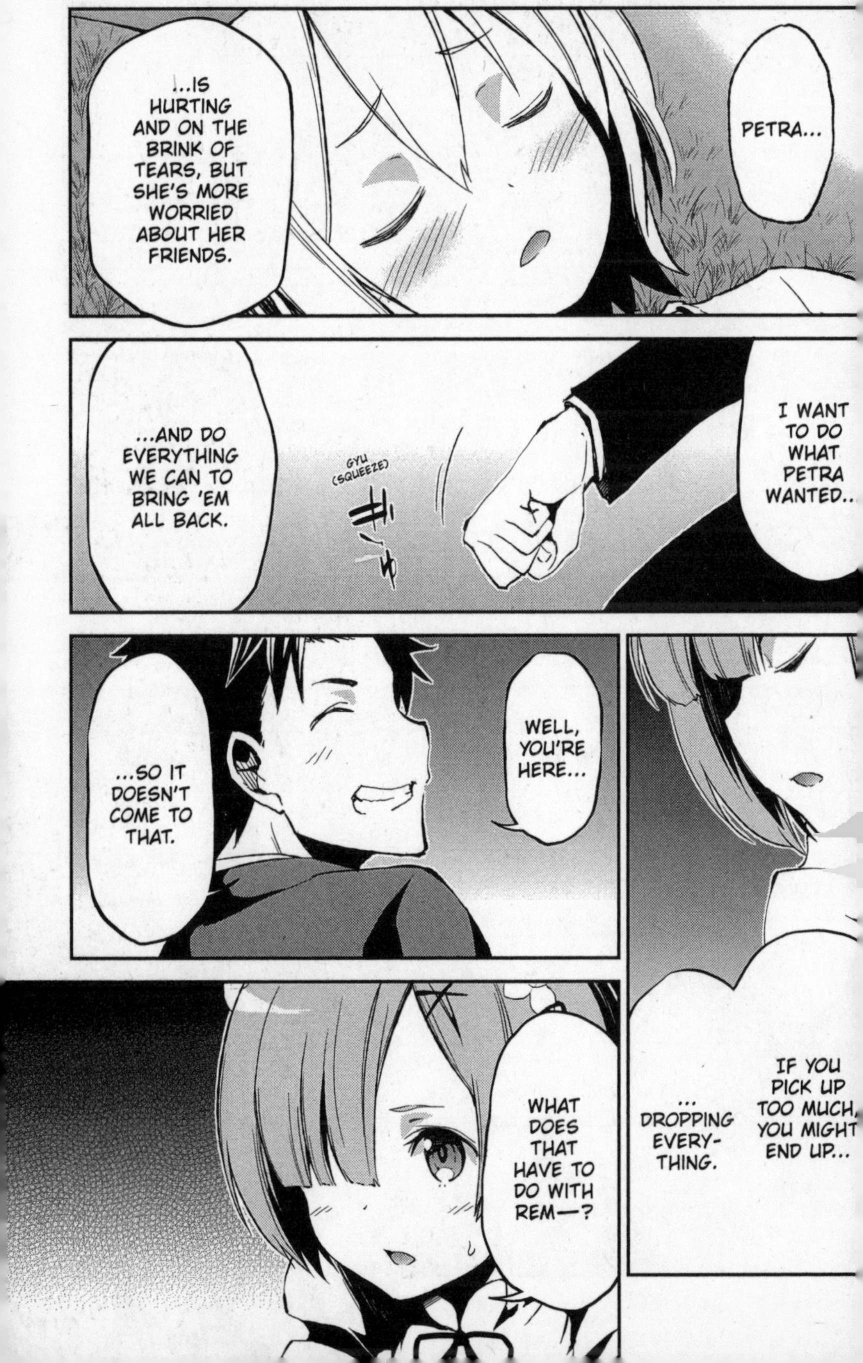
PETRA...
...IS HURTING AND ON THE BRINK OF TEARS, BUT SHE'S MORE WORRIED ABOUT HER FRIENDS.
I WANT TO DO WHAT PETRA WANTED...
GYU (SQUEEZE)
...AND DO EVERYTHING WE CAN TO BRING 'EM ALL BACK.
IF YOU PICK UP TOO MUCH, YOU MIGHT END UP...
...DROPPING EVERY-THING.
WELL, YOU'RE HERE...
...SO IT DOESN'T COME TO THAT.
WHAT DOES THAT HAVE TO DO WITH REM—?

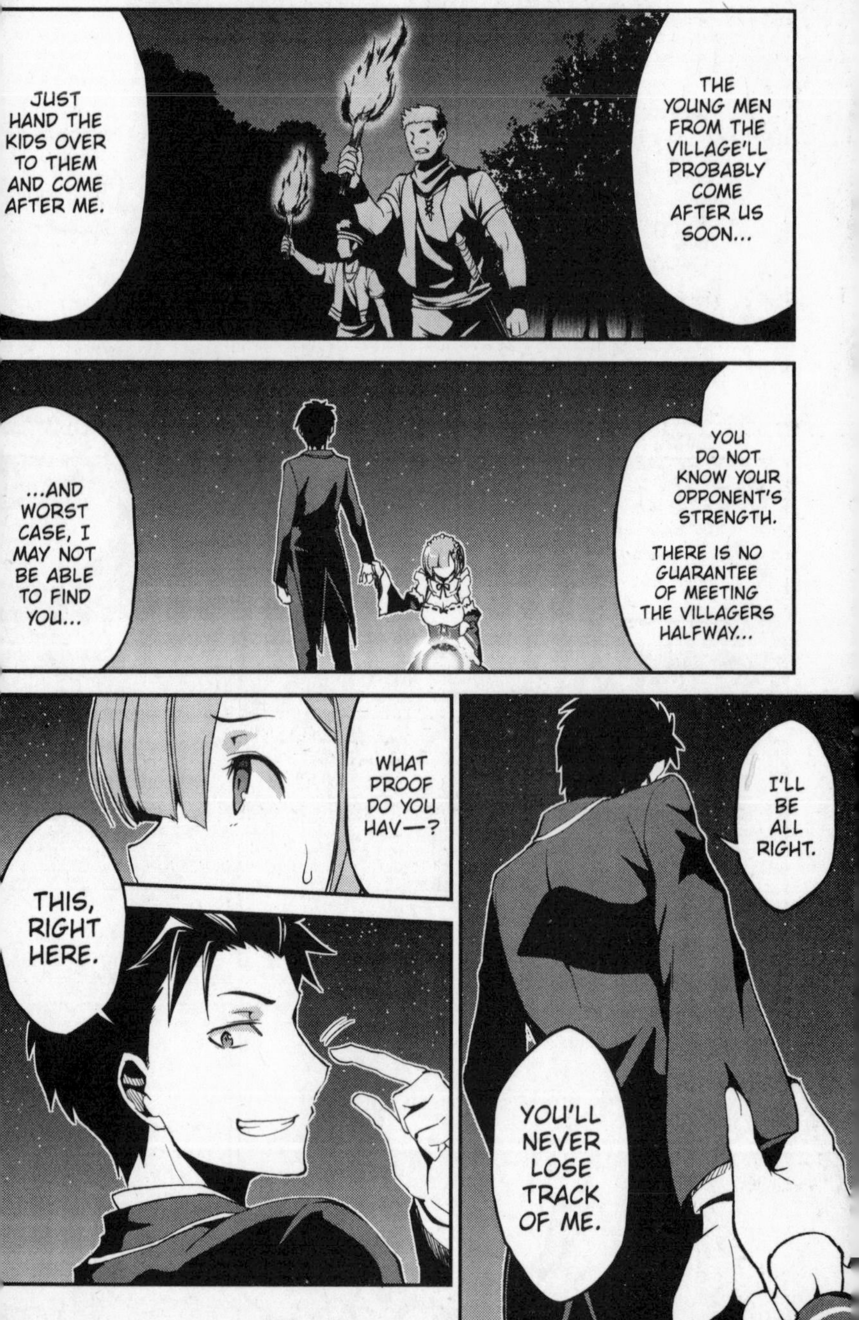
THE YOUNG MEN FROM THE VILLAGE'LL PROBABLY COME AFTER US SOON...
JUST HAND THE KIDS OVER TO THEM AND COME AFTER ME.
YOU DO NOT KNOW YOUR OPPONENT'S STRENGTH.
THERE IS NO GUARANTEE OF MEETING THE VILLAGERS HALFWAY...
...AND WORST CASE, I MAY NOT BE ABLE TO FIND YOU...
I'LL BE ALL RIGHT.
YOU'LL NEVER LOSE TRACK OF ME.
WHAT PROOF DO YOU HAV—?
THIS, RIGHT HERE.

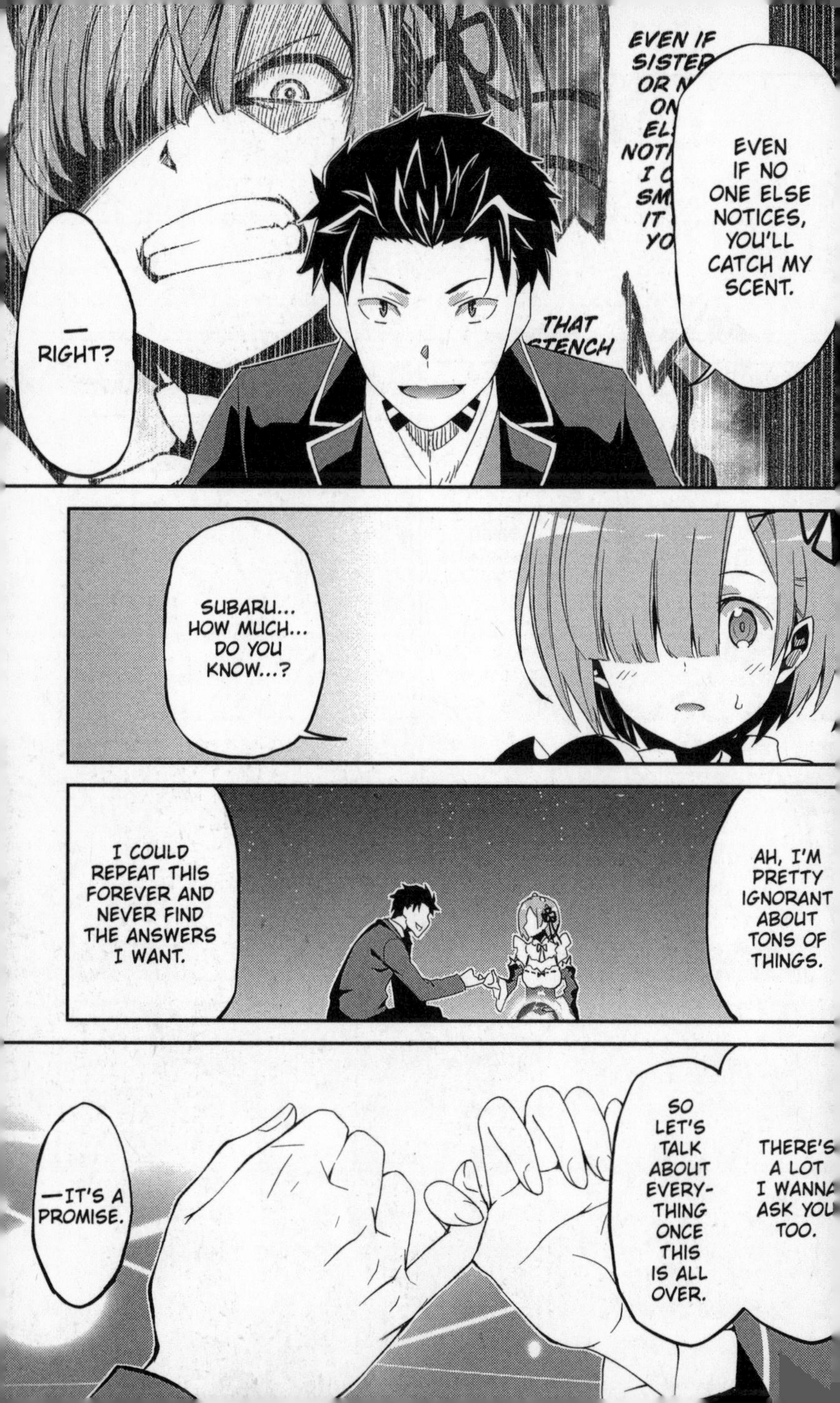
EVEN IF NO ONE ELSE NOTICES, YOU'LL CATCH MY SCENT.
THAT STENCH
—RIGHT?
SUBARU... HOW MUCH... DO YOU KNOW...?
AH, I'M PRETTY IGNORANT ABOUT TONS OF THINGS.
I COULD REPEAT THIS FOREVER AND NEVER FIND THE ANSWERS I WANT.
THERE'S A LOT I WANNA ASK YOU TOO.
SO LET'S TALK ABOUT EVERY-THING ONCE THIS IS ALL OVER.
—IT'S A PROMISE.

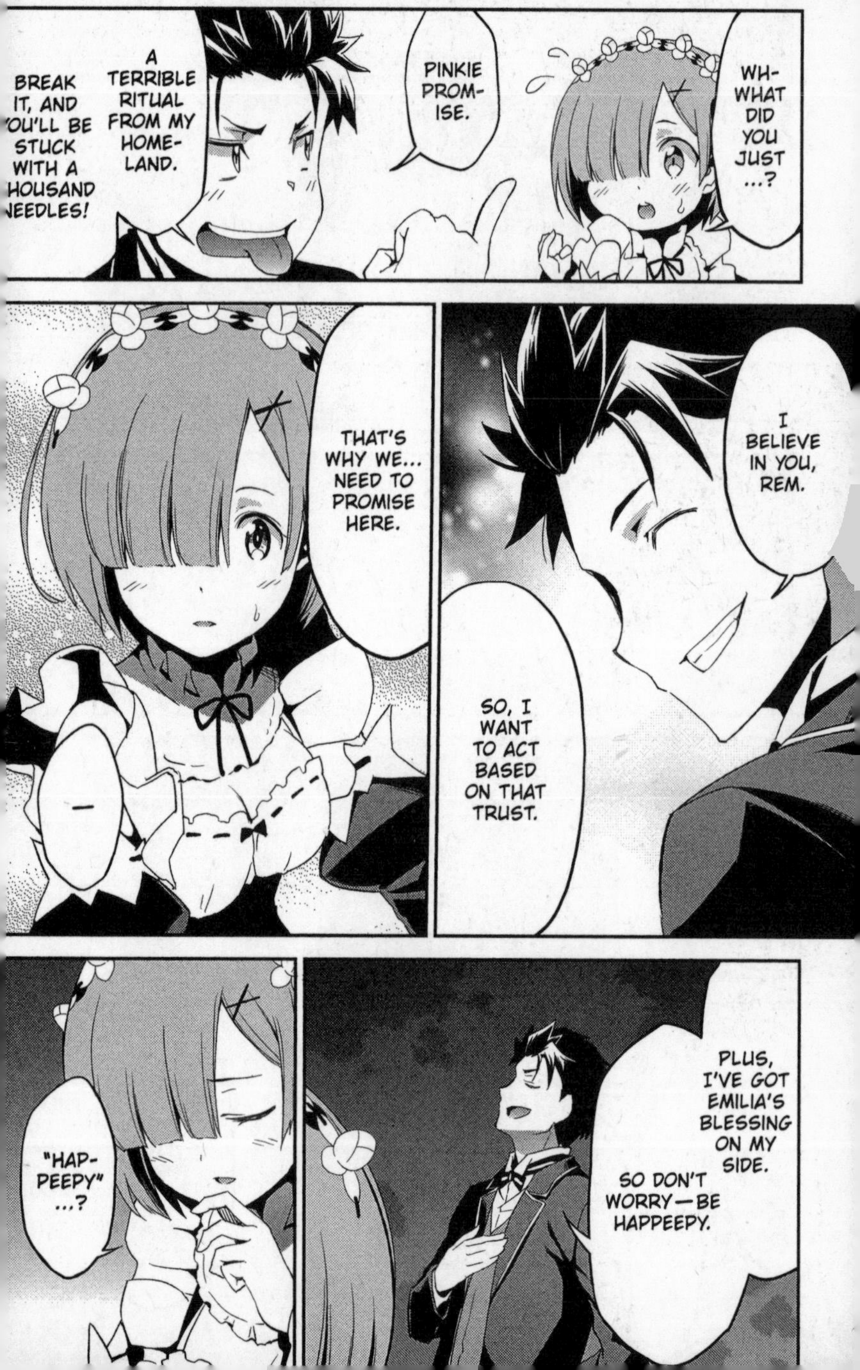
WH-WHAT DID YOU JUST ...?
PINKIE PROMISE.
A TERRIBLE RITUAL FROM MY HOMELAND.
BREAK IT, AND OU'LL BE STUCK WITH A HOUSAND EEDLES!
I BELIEVE IN YOU, REM.
SO, I WANT TO ACT BASED ON THAT TRUST.
THAT'S WHY WE... NEED TO PROMISE HERE.
—
PLUS, I'VE GOT EMILIA'S BLESSING ON MY SIDE.
SO DON'T WORRY—BE HAPPEEPY.
"HAP-PEEPY" ...?

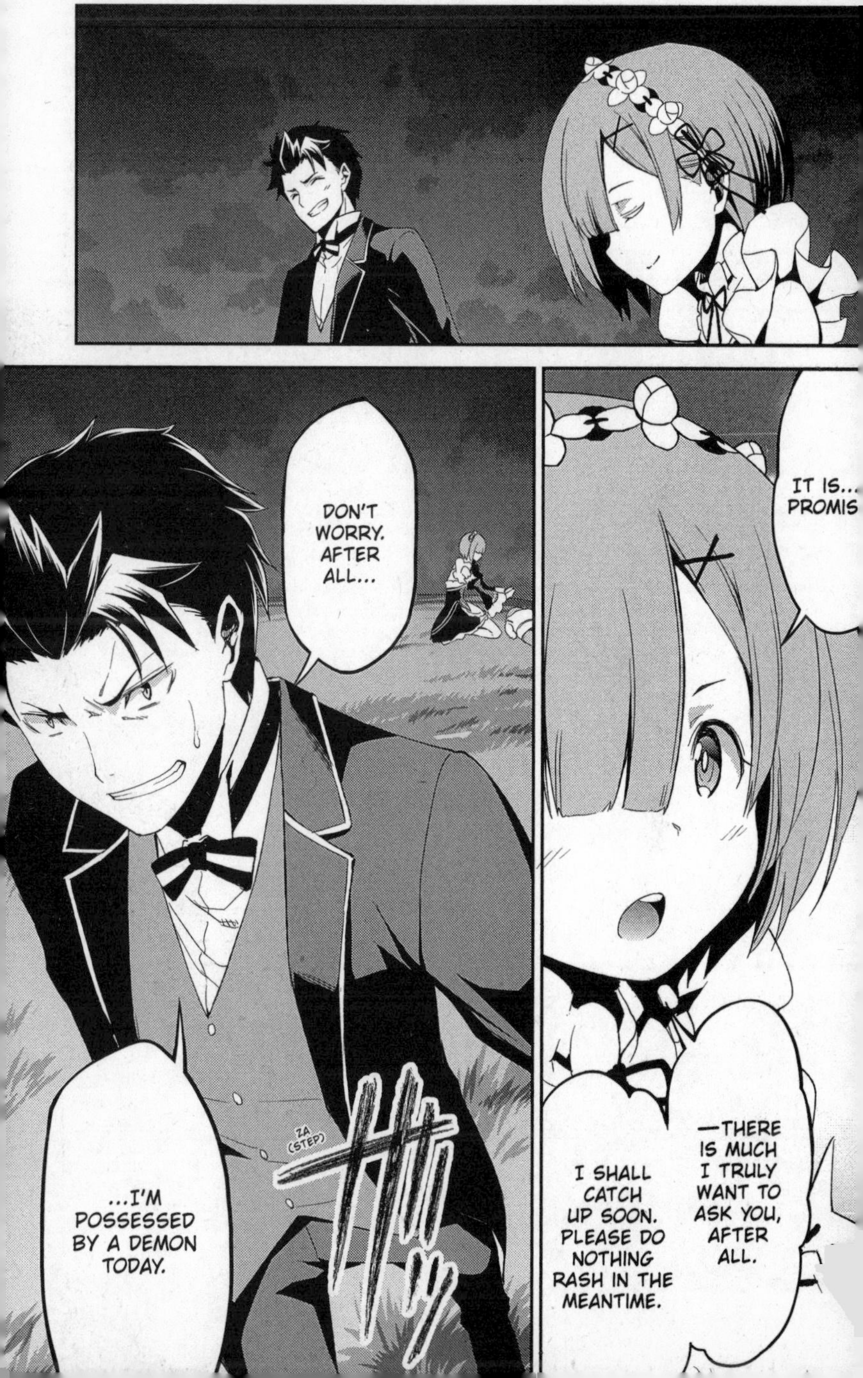
IT IS...
PROMIS
—THERE IS MUCH I TRULY WANT TO ASK YOU, AFTER ALL.
I SHALL CATCH UP SOON. PLEASE DO NOTHING RASH IN THE MEANTIME.
DON'T WORRY. AFTER ALL...
ZA (STEP)
...I'M POSSESSED BY A DEMON TODAY.

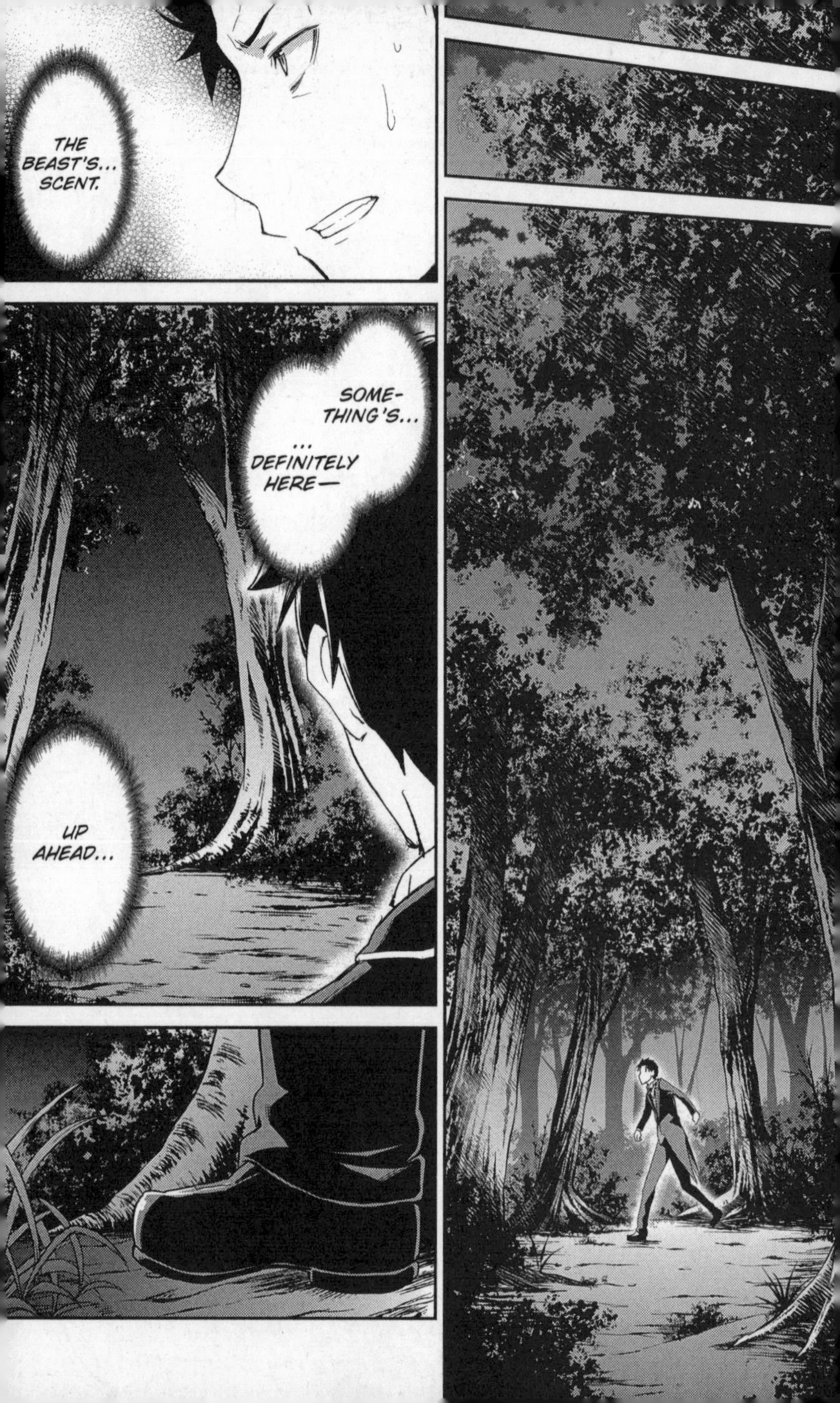
THE BEAST'S... SCENT.
SOME-THING'S...
...DEFINITELY HERE—
UP AHEAD...

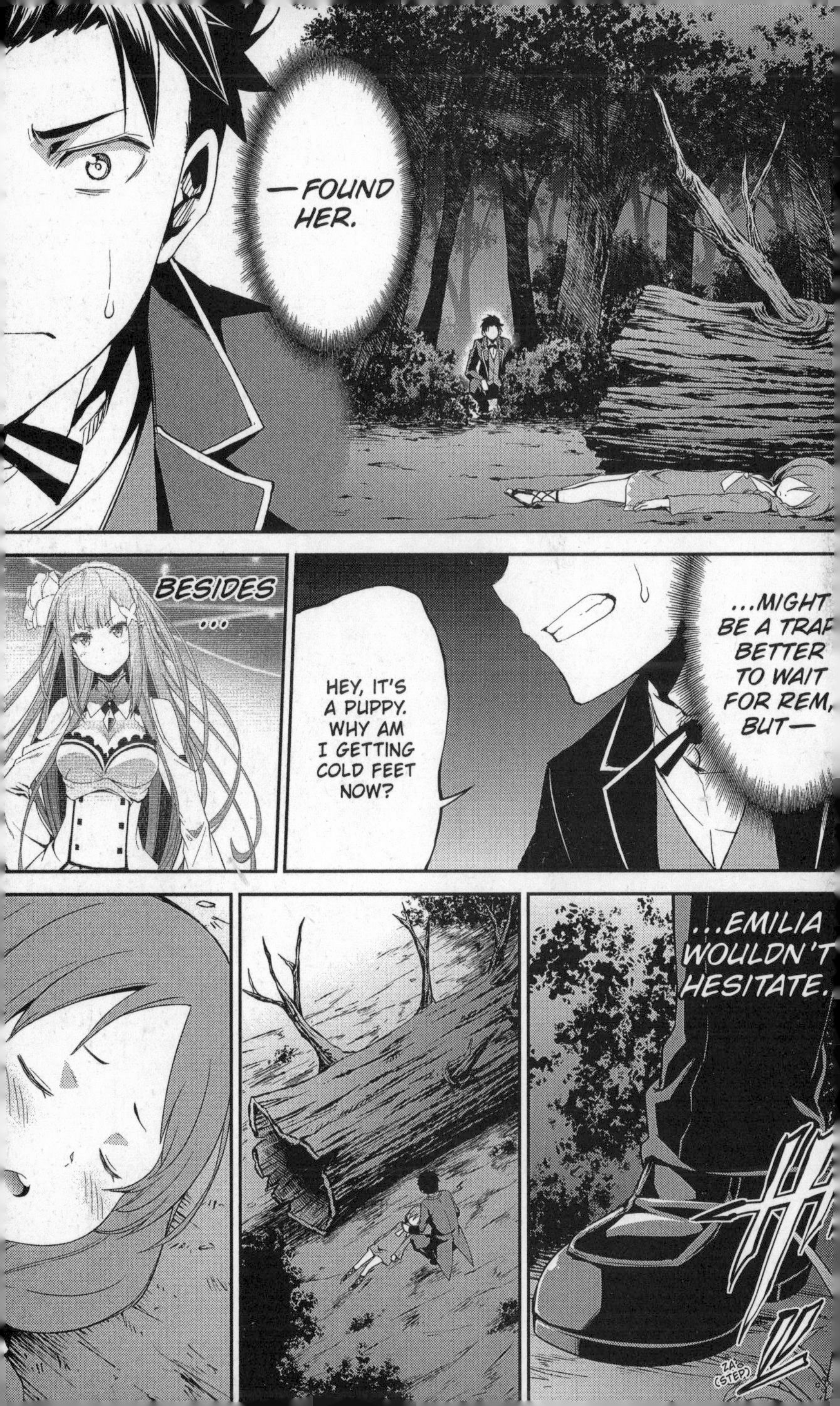
—FOUND HER.
...MIGHT BE A TRAP BETTER TO WAIT FOR REM, BUT—
HEY, IT'S A PUPPY. WHY AM I GETTING COLD FEET NOW?
BESIDES...
...EMILIA WOULDN'T HESITATE.
ZA (STEP)

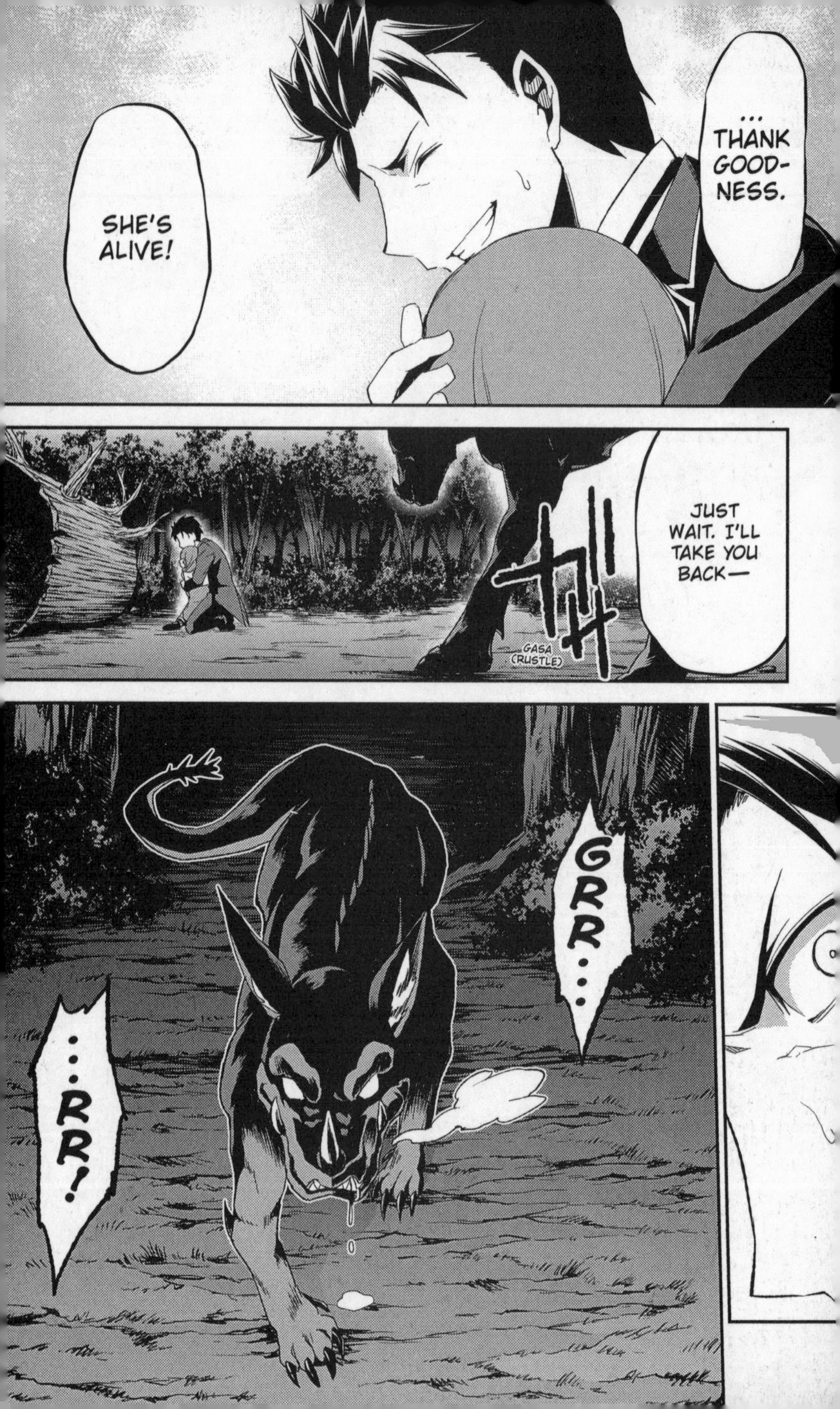
...THANK GOODNESS.
SHE'S ALIVE!
JUST WAIT. I'LL TAKE YOU BACK—
GASA (RUSTLE)
GRR...
...RR!

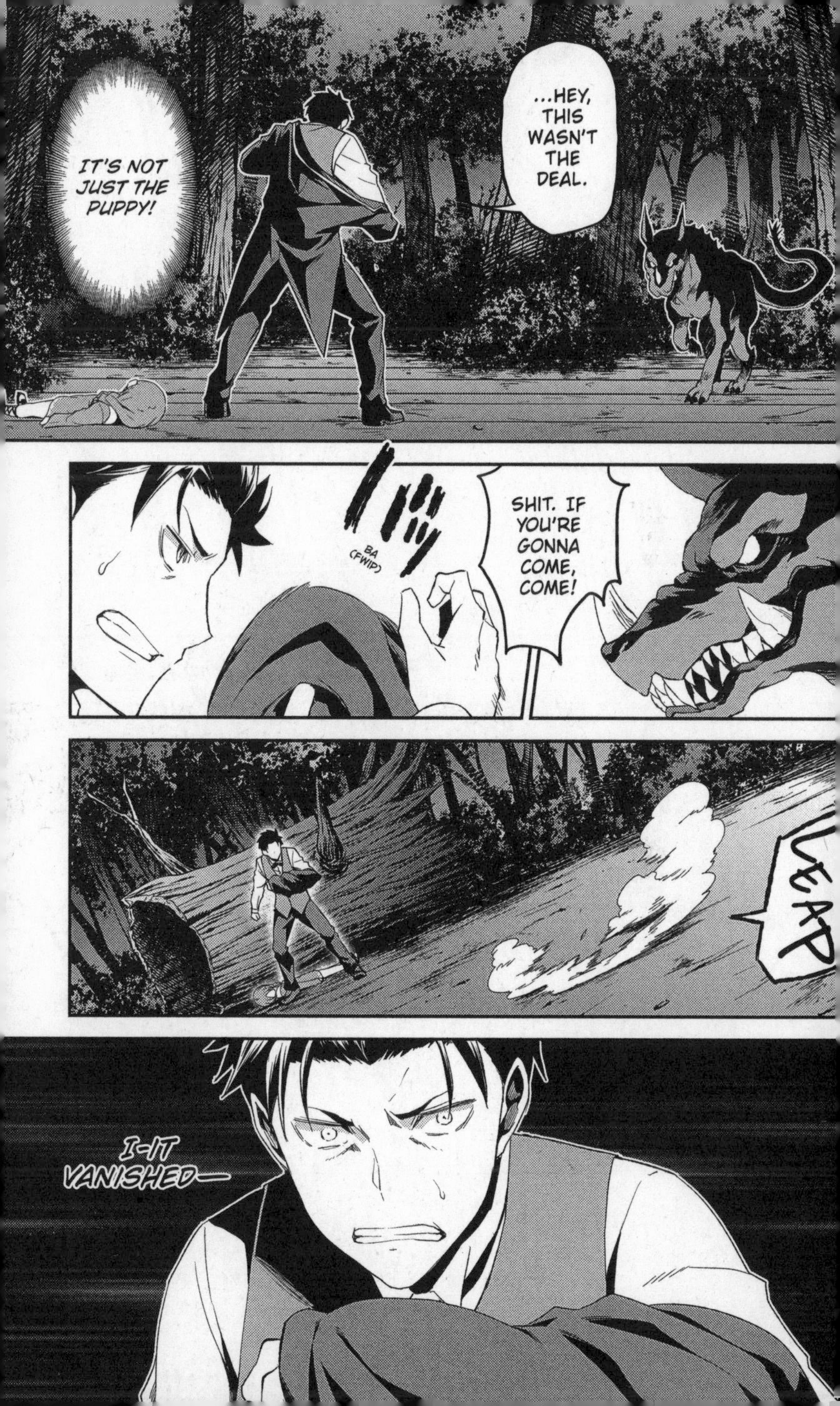
...HEY, THIS WASN'T THE DEAL.
IT'S NOT JUST THE PUPPY!
SHIT. IF YOU'RE GONNA COME, COME!
BA (FWIP)
LEAP
I-IT VANISHED—

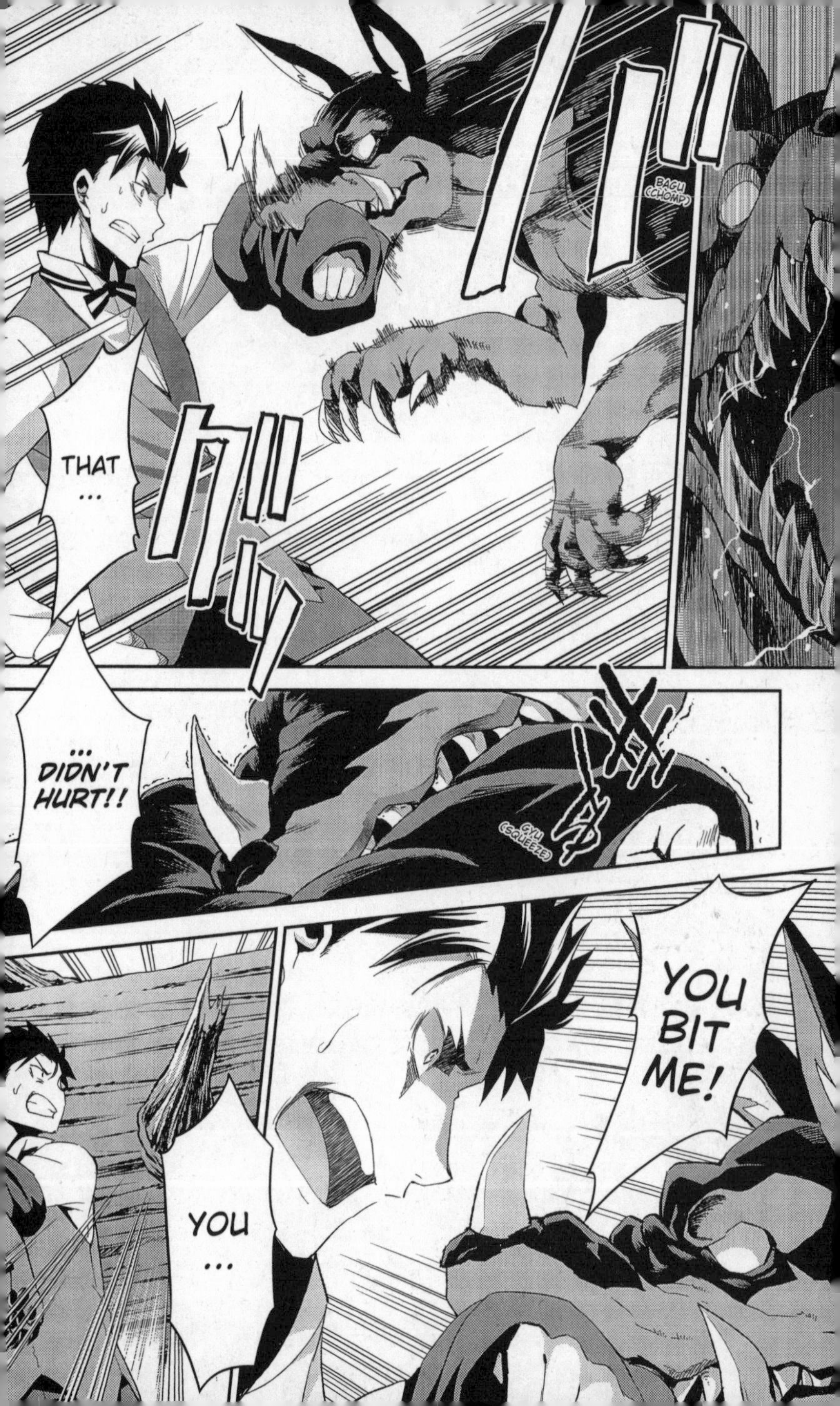
BAGU (CHOMP)
THAT ...
GYU (SQUEEZE)
... DIDN'T HURT!!
YOU BIT ME!
YOU ...

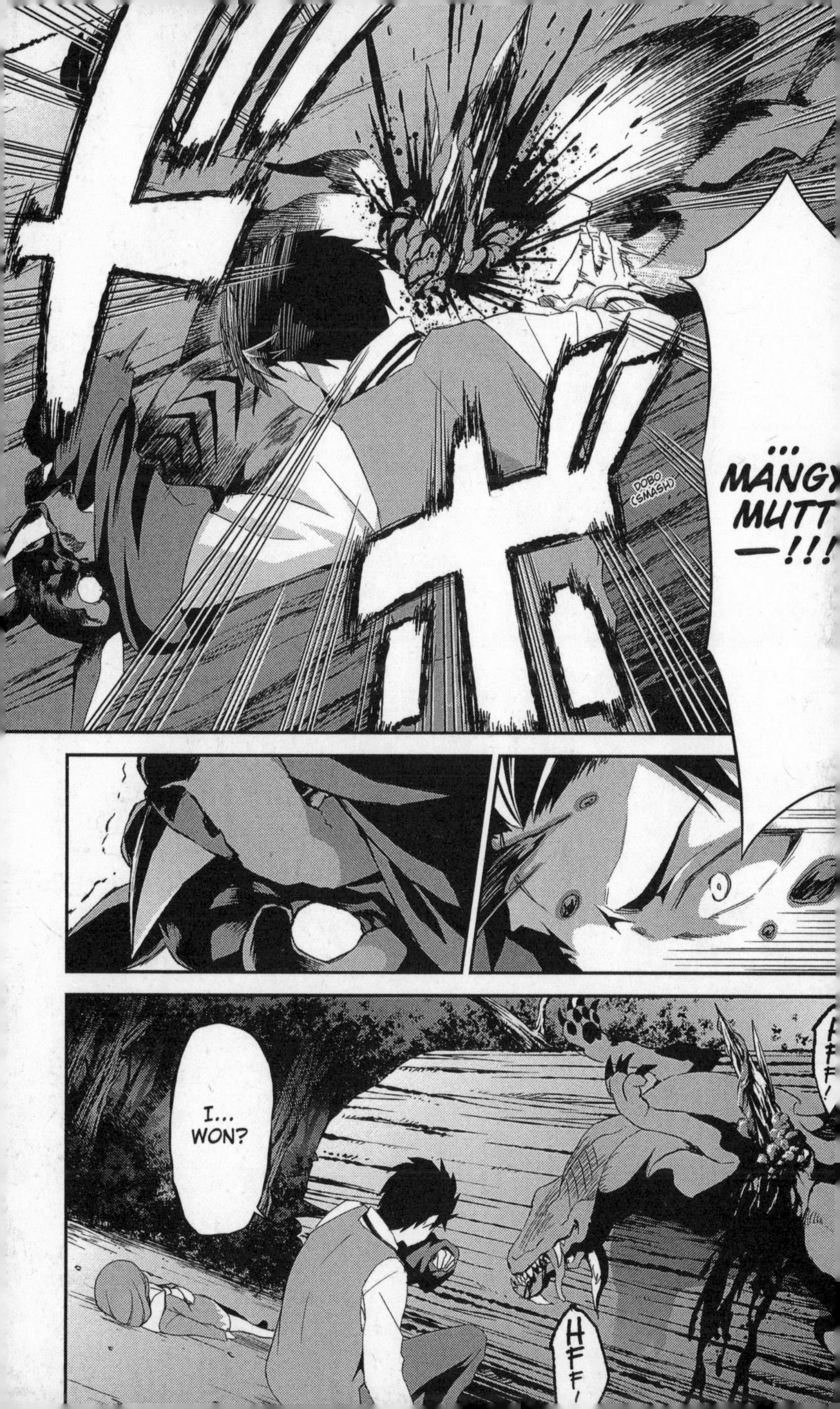

...MÄNGY MUTT —!!!
DOBO (SMASH)
HFFF!
I... WON?
HFF!

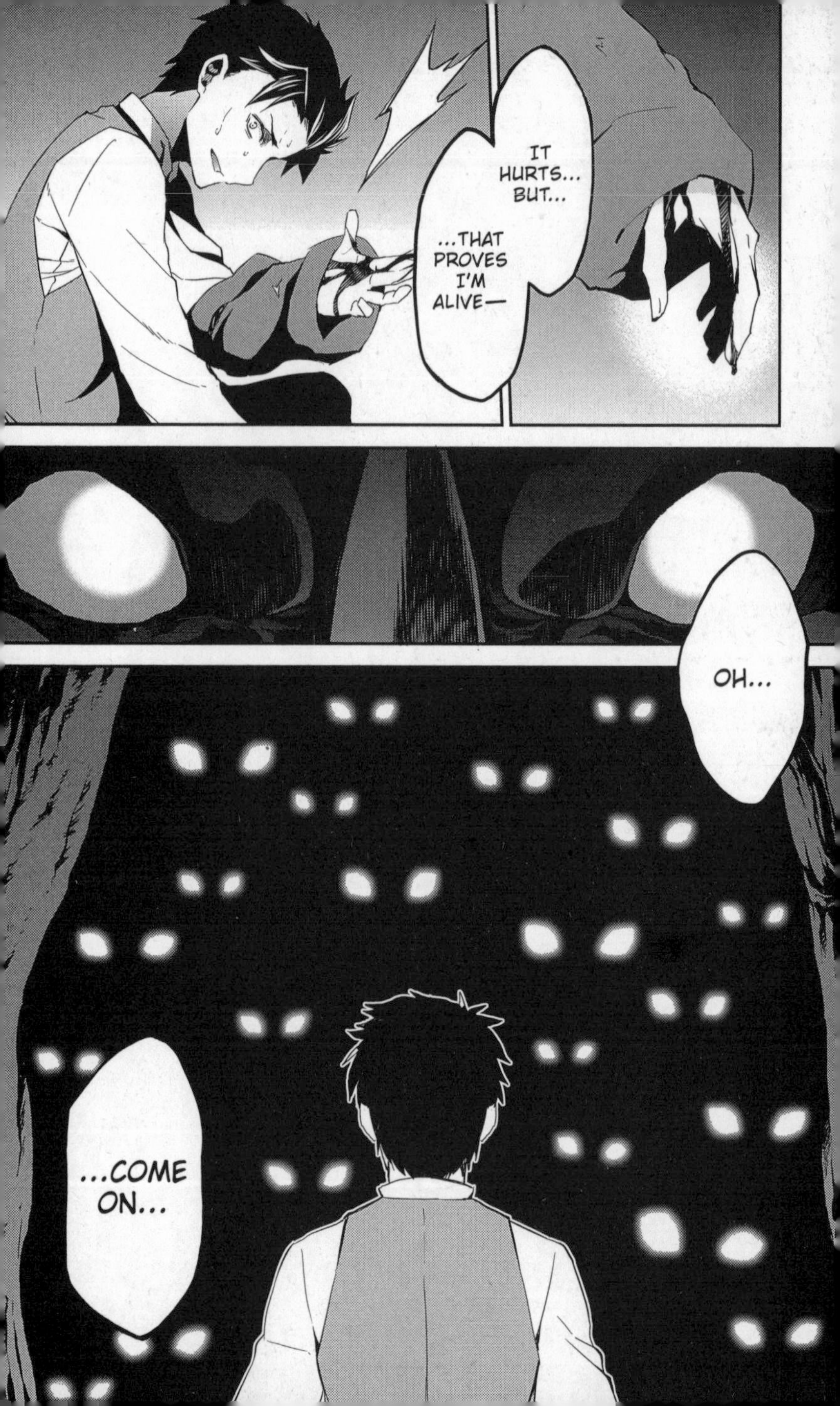
IT HURTS... BUT...
...THAT PROVES I'M ALIVE—
OH...
...COME ON...

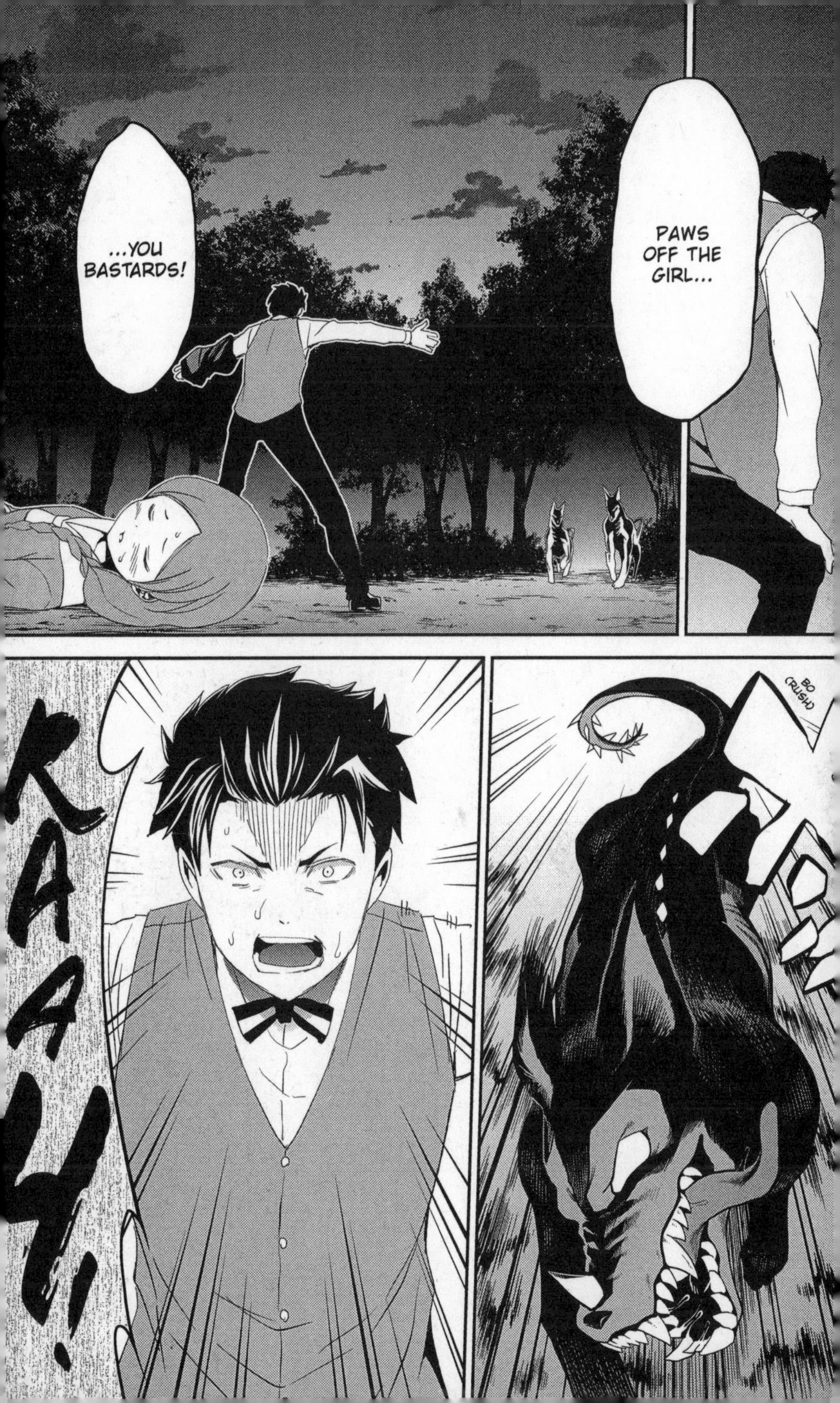
PAWS OFF THE GIRL...
...YOU BASTARDS!
BO (RUSH)
KAAAH!!

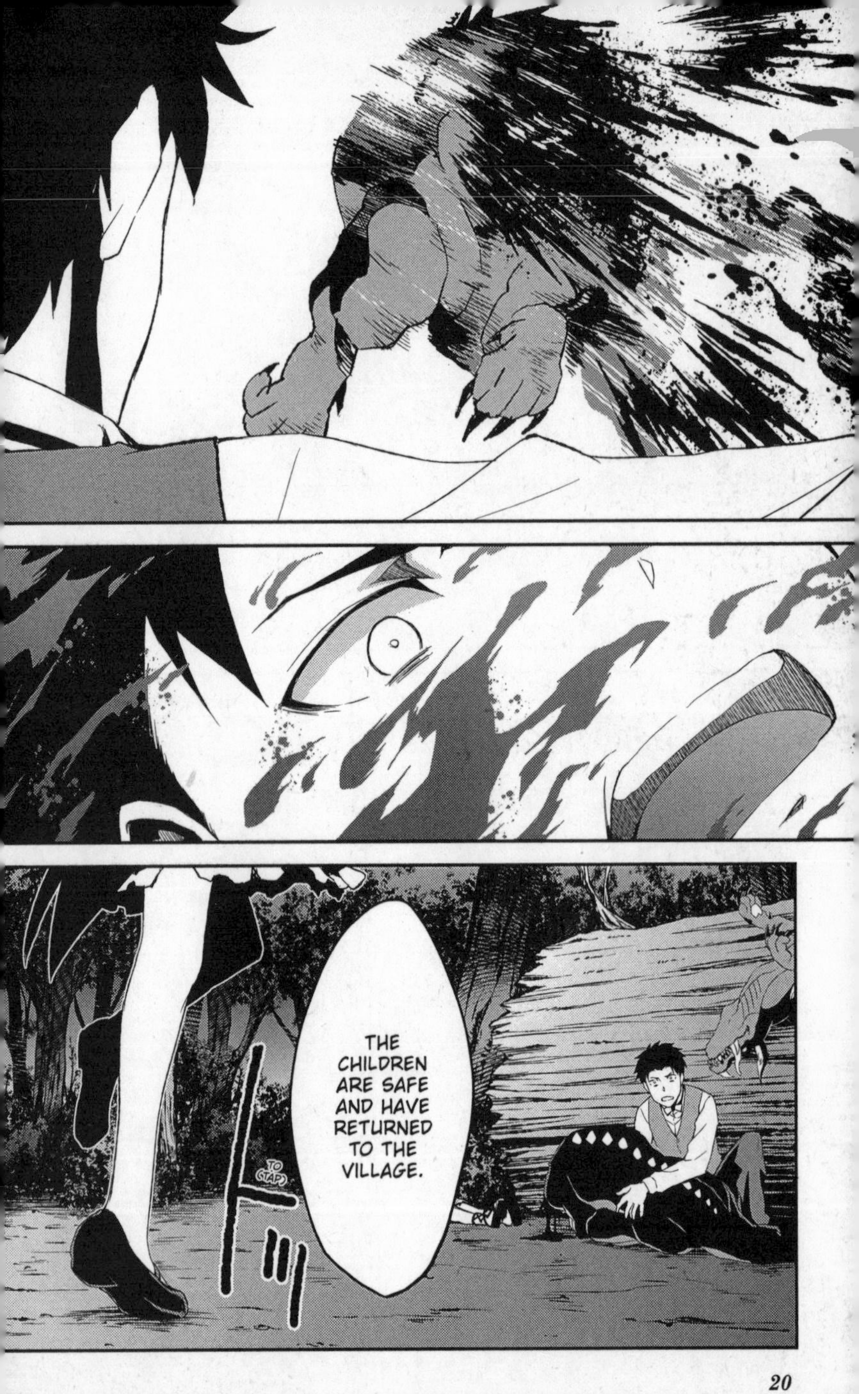
THE CHILDREN ARE SAFE AND HAVE RETURNED TO THE VILLAGE.
TO (TAP)

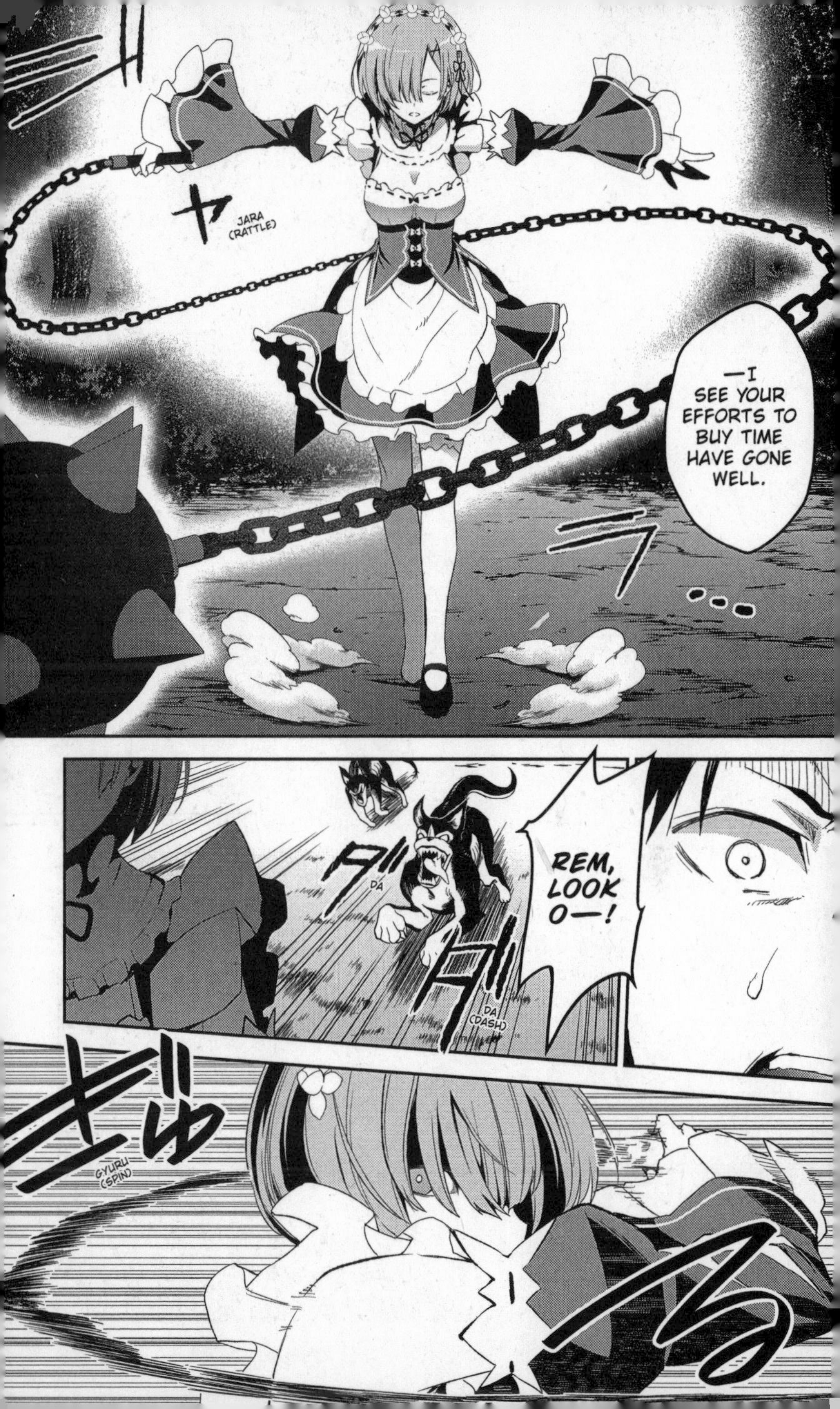
JARA (RATTLE)
—I SEE YOUR EFFORTS TO BUY TIME HAVE GONE WELL.
REM, LOOK O—!
DA
DA (DASH)
GYURU (SPIN)

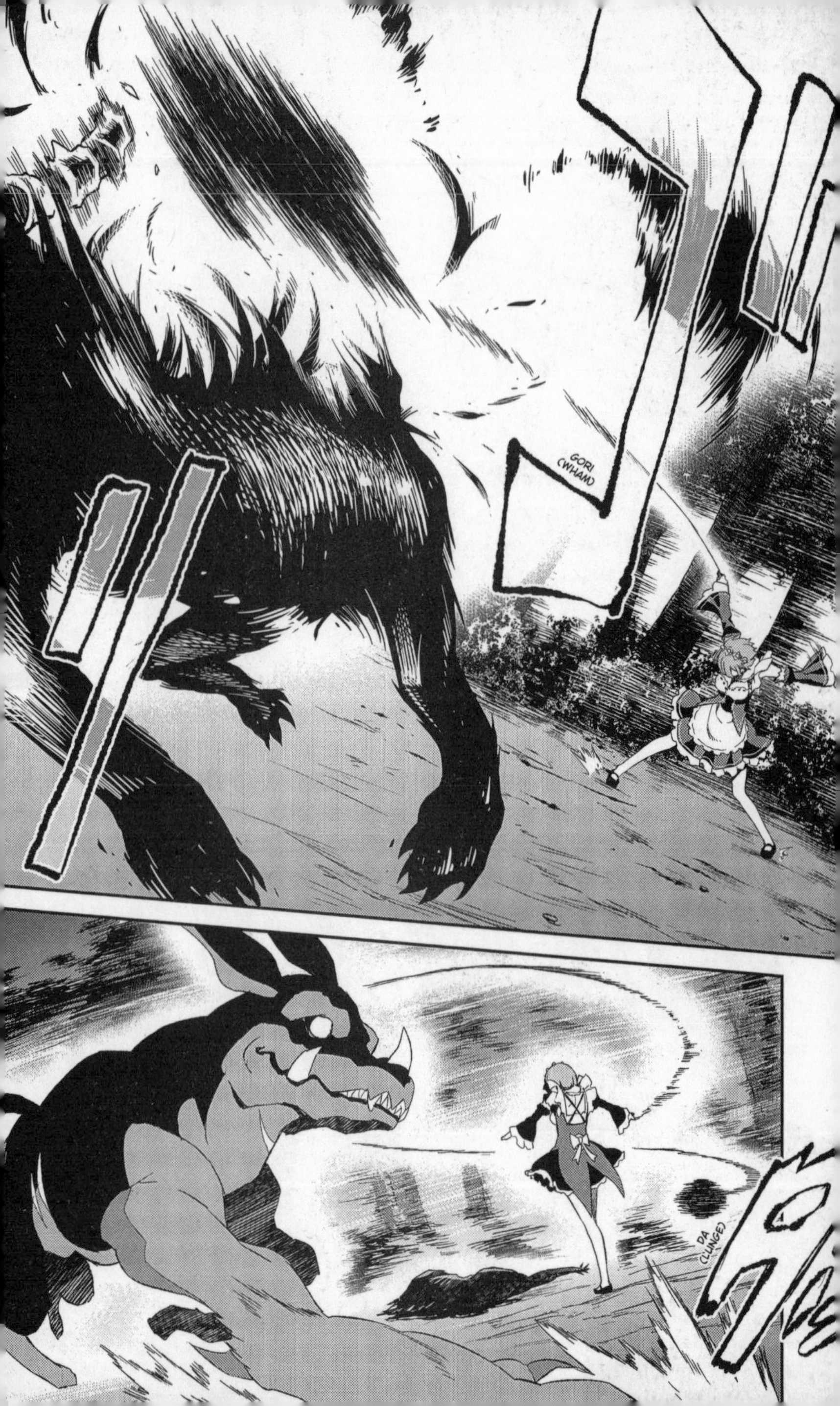
GORI
(WHAM)
DA
(LUNGE)

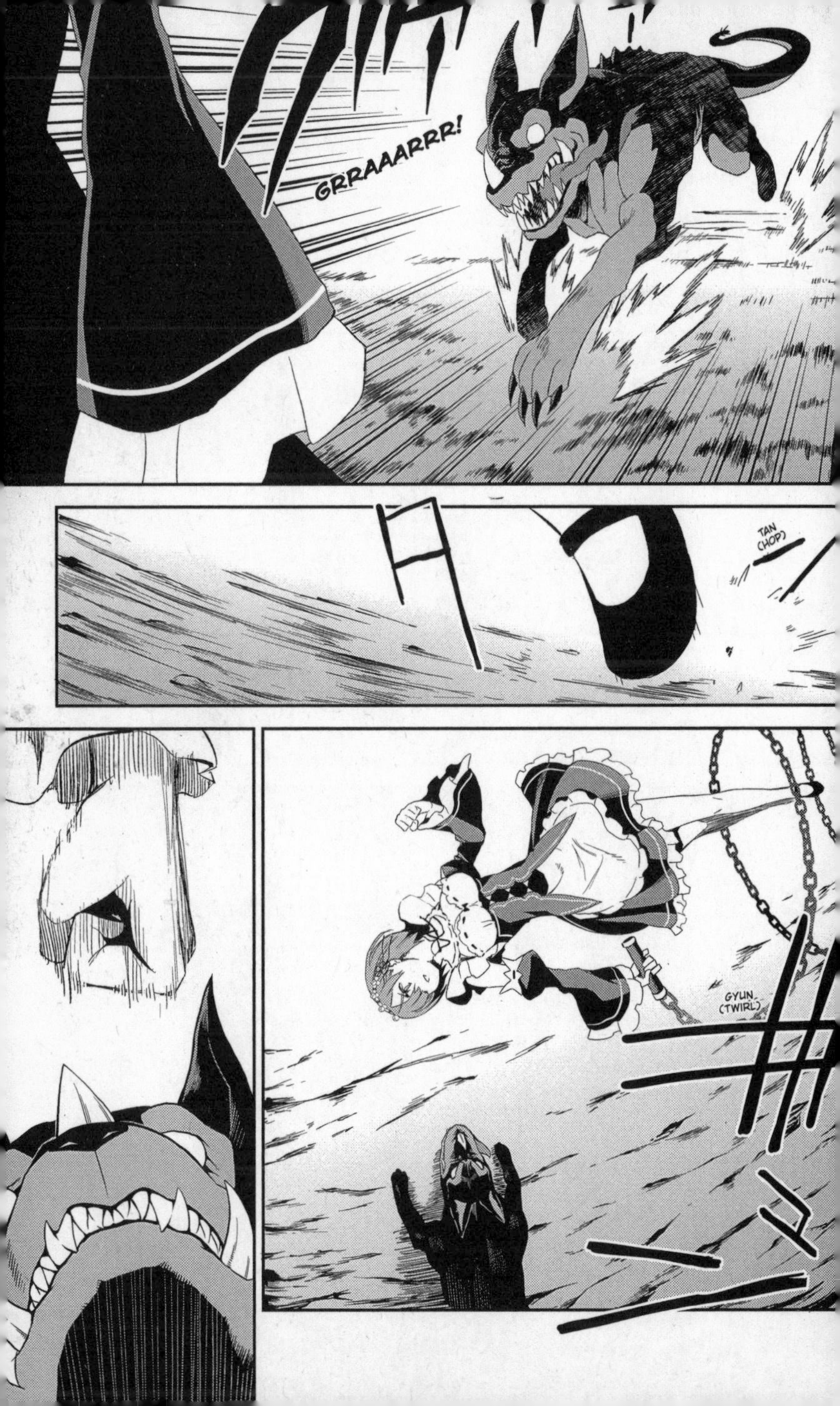
GRRAAARRR!
TAN (HOP)
GYUN (TWIRL)

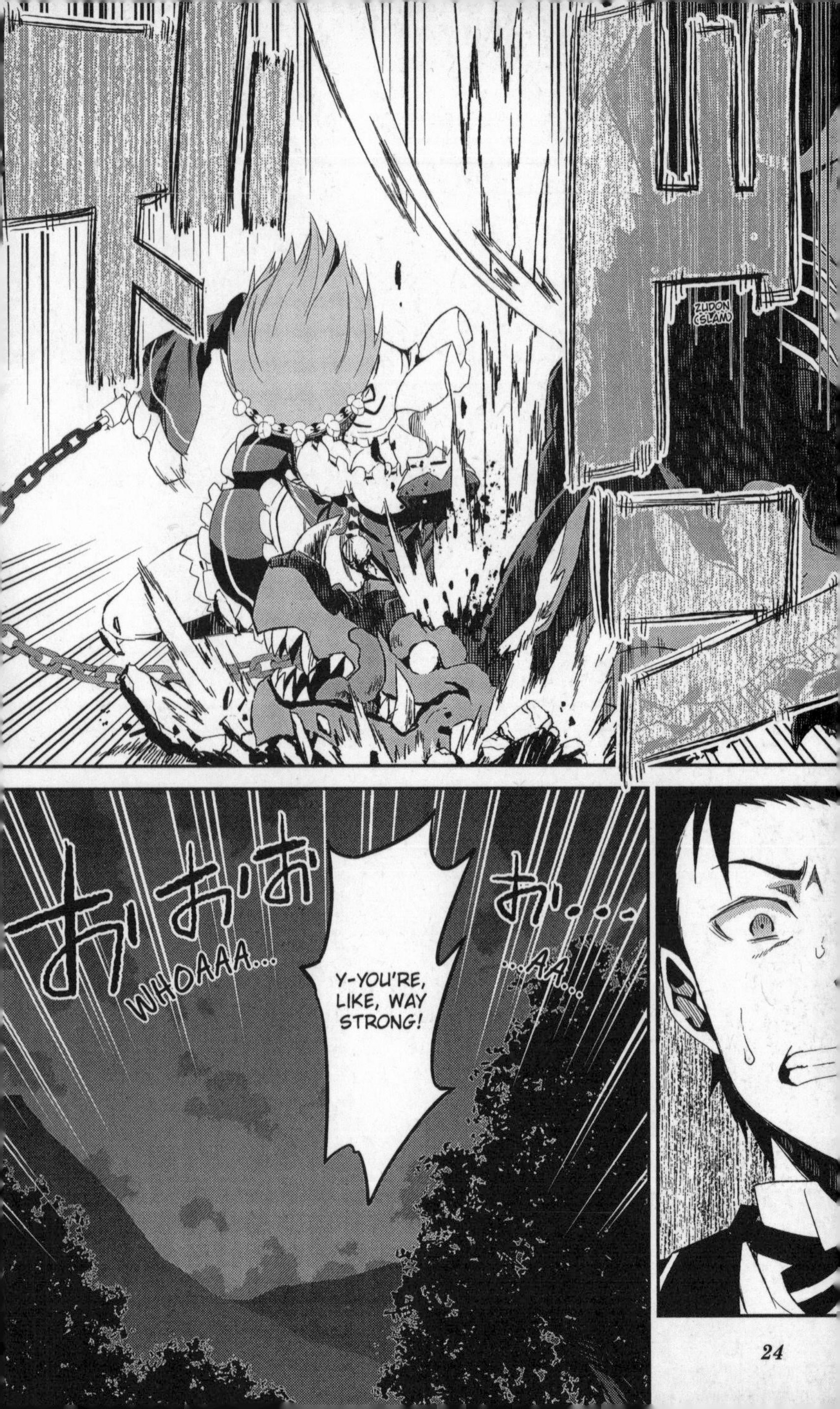
ZUDON ISLAND
おあお
WHOAAA...
Y-YOU'RE, LIKE, WAY STRONG!
あ…
...AA...

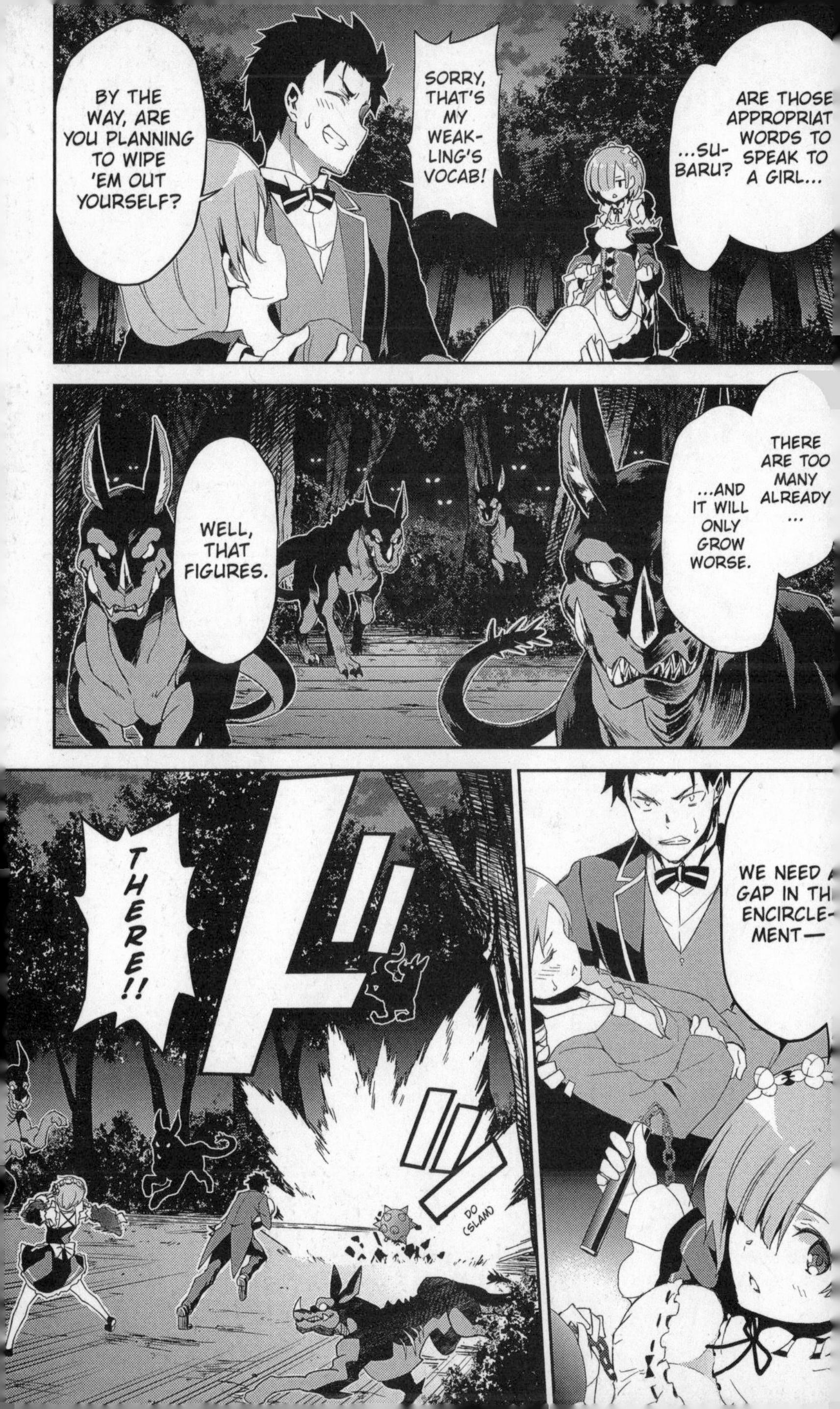
ARE THOSE APPROPRIAT WORDS TO SPEAK TO A GIRL...
...SU-BARU?
SORRY, THAT'S MY WEAK-LING'S VOCAB!
BY THE WAY, ARE YOU PLANNING TO WIPE 'EM OUT YOURSELF?
THERE ARE TOO MANY ALREADY ...
...AND IT WILL ONLY GROW WORSE.
WELL, THAT FIGURES.
WE NEED A GAP IN TH ENCIRCLE-MENT—
THERE!!
DO (SLAM)

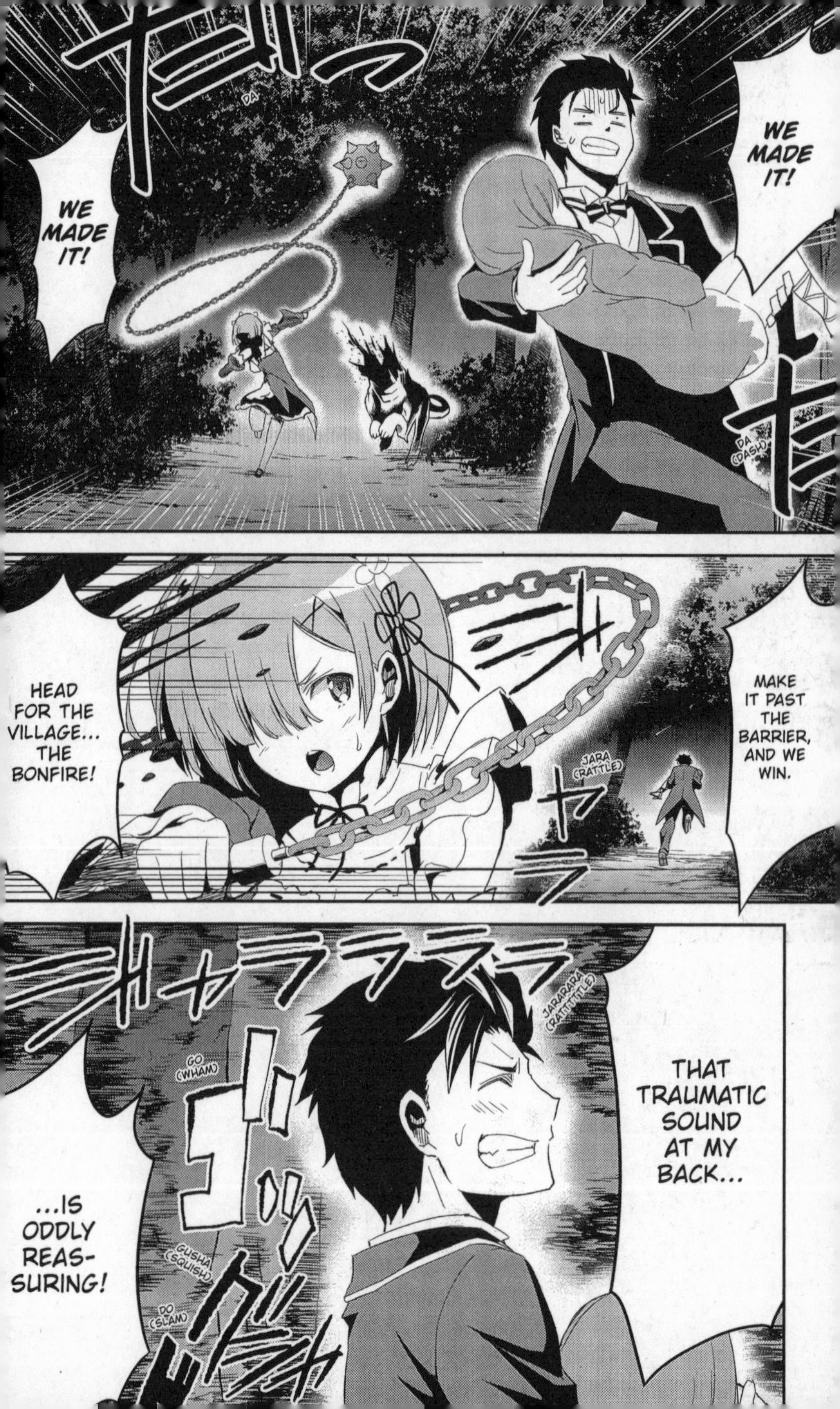

WE MADE IT!
DA
WE MADE IT!
DA (DASH)
MAKE IT PAST THE BARRIER, AND WE WIN.
JARA (RATTLE)
HEAD FOR THE VILLAGE... THE BONFIRE!
JARARARA (RATTTTTLE)
THAT TRAUMATIC SOUND AT MY BACK...
GO (WHAM)
GUSHA (SQUISH)
DO (SLAM)
...IS ODDLY REAS-SURING!

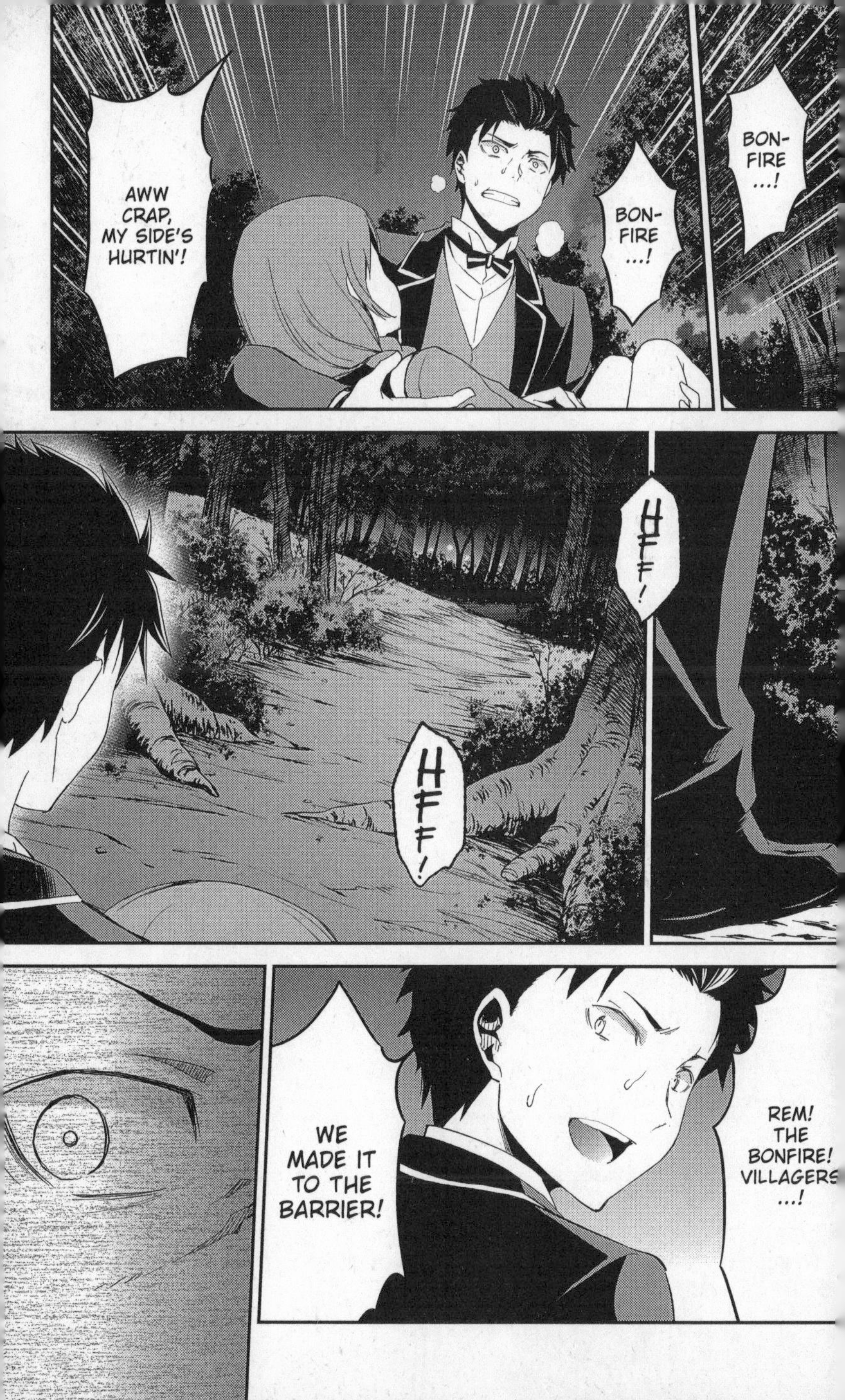
BON-FIRE ...!
BON-FIRE ...!
AWW CRAP, MY SIDE'S HURTIN'!
HFF!
HFF!
REM! THE BONFIRE! VILLAGERS ...!
WE MADE IT TO THE BARRIER!

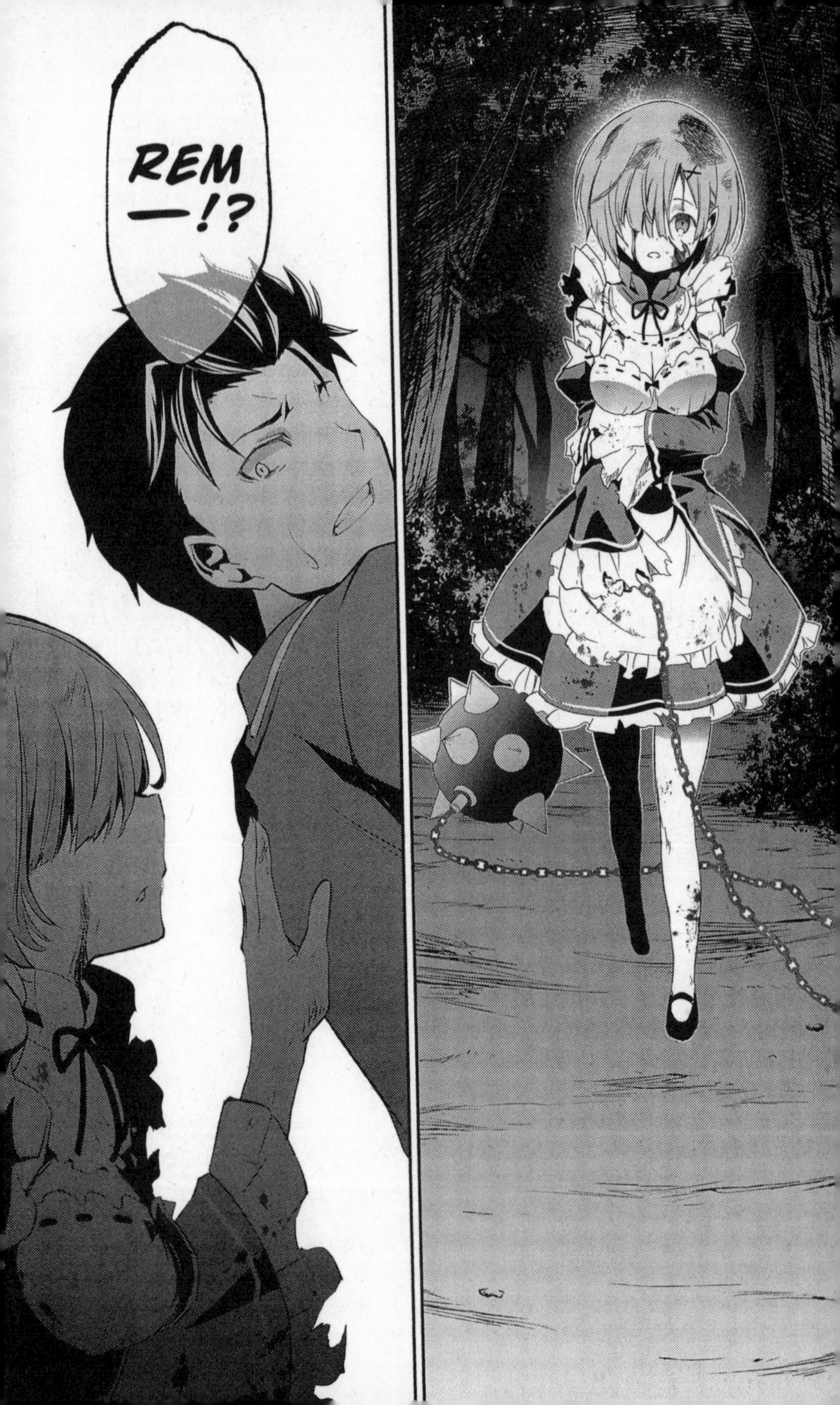
REM —!?

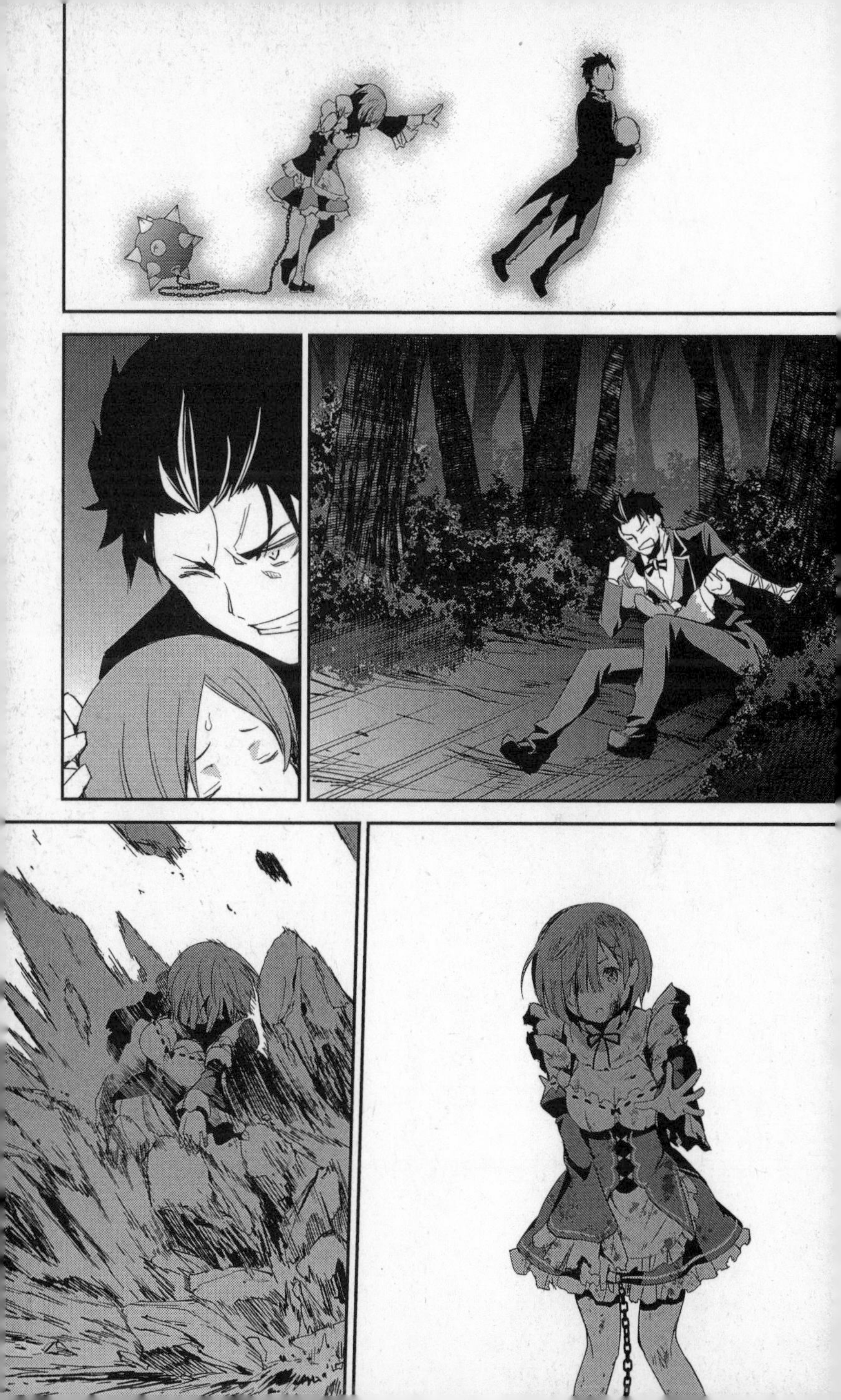

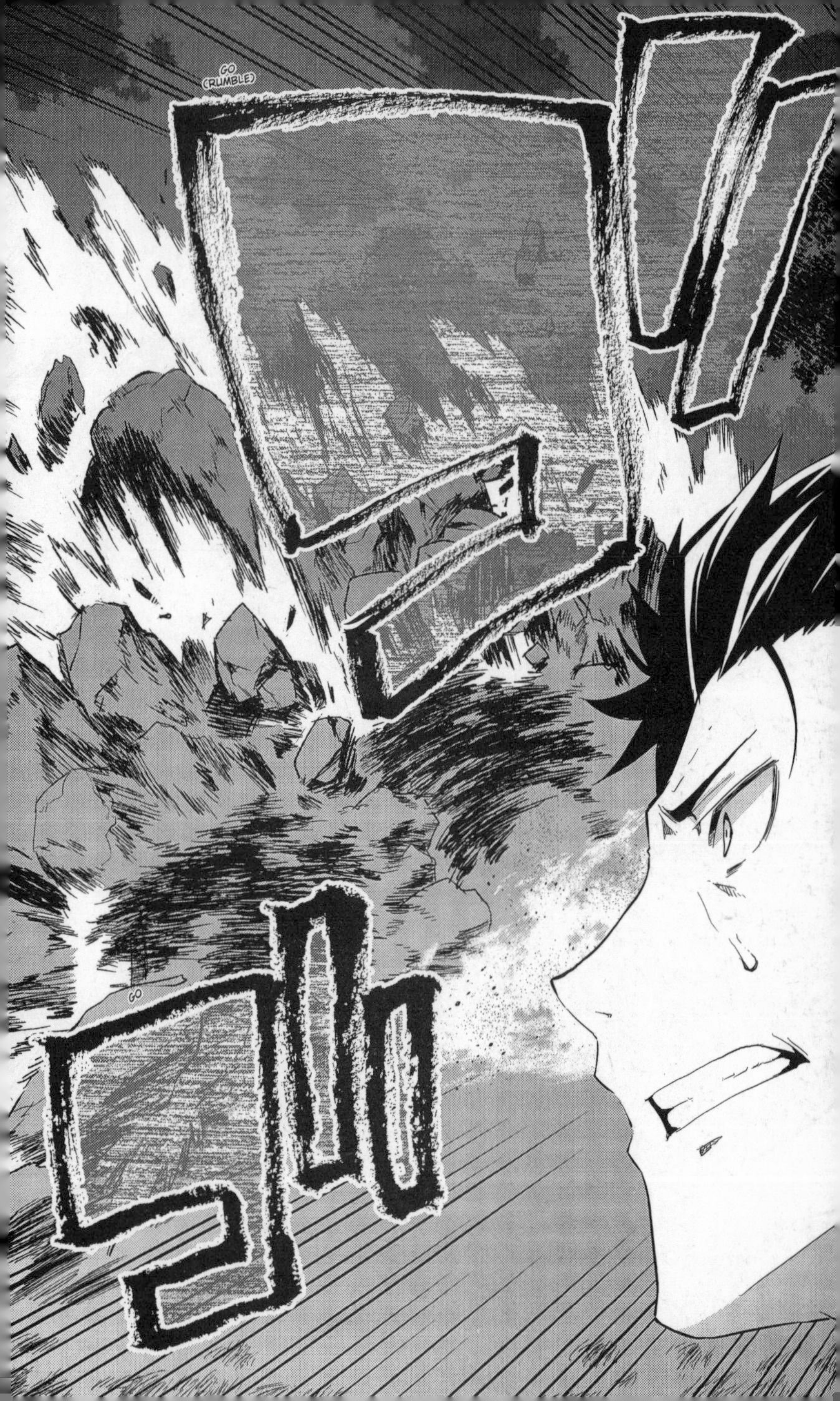
GO
(RUMBLE)
GO

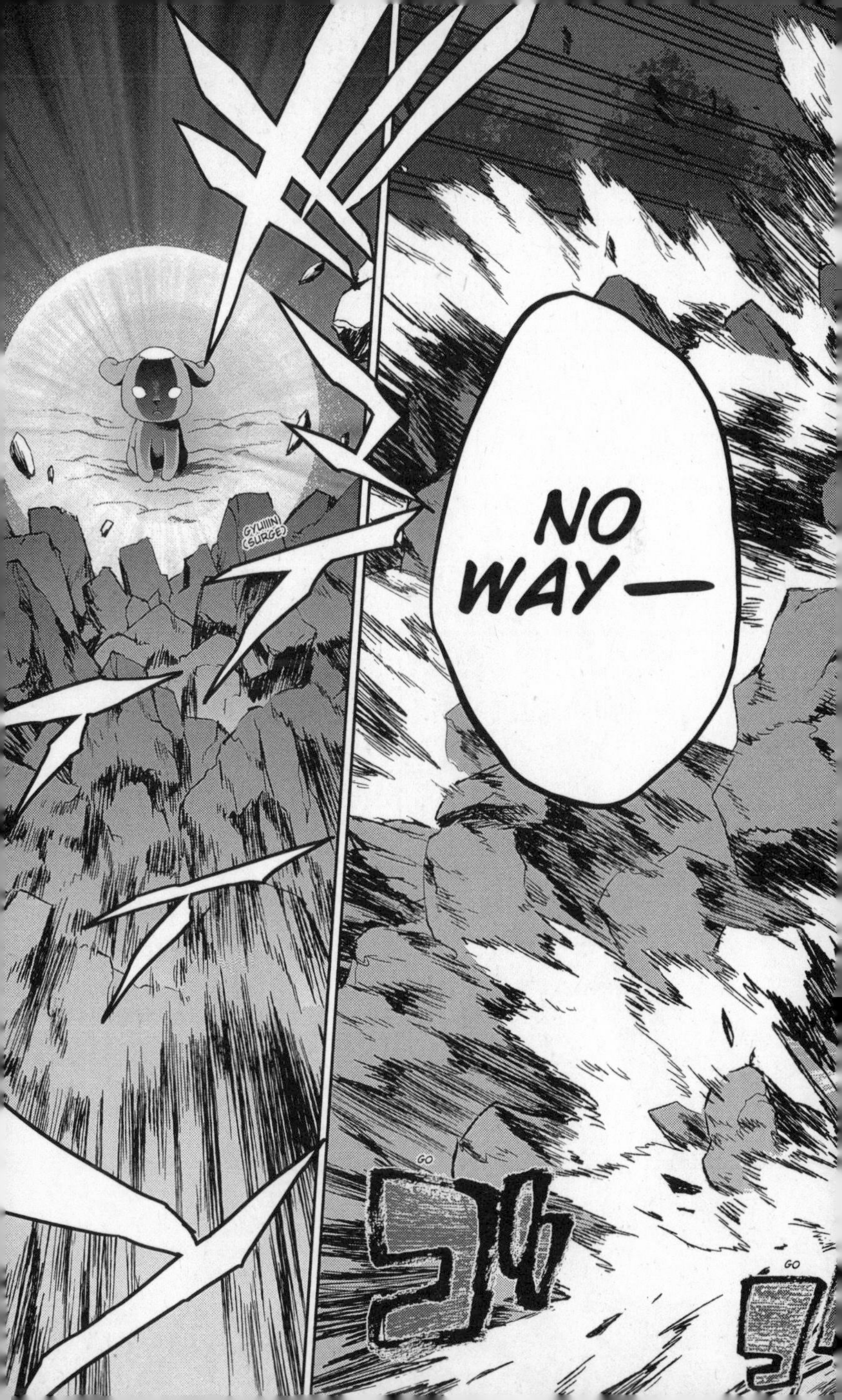
NO WAY—
GO
GO
GYUIIIN
(SURGE)

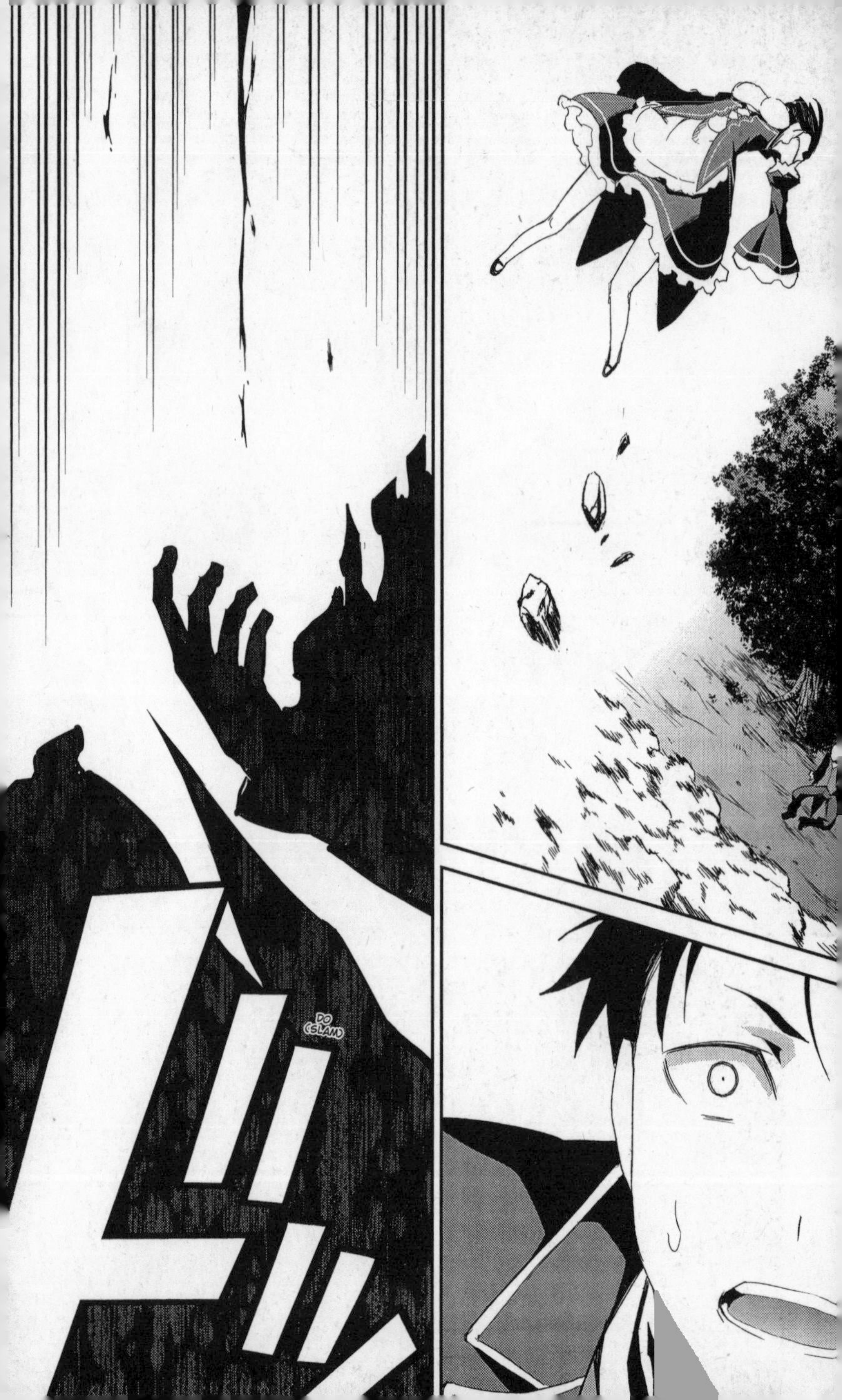
DO (SLAM)

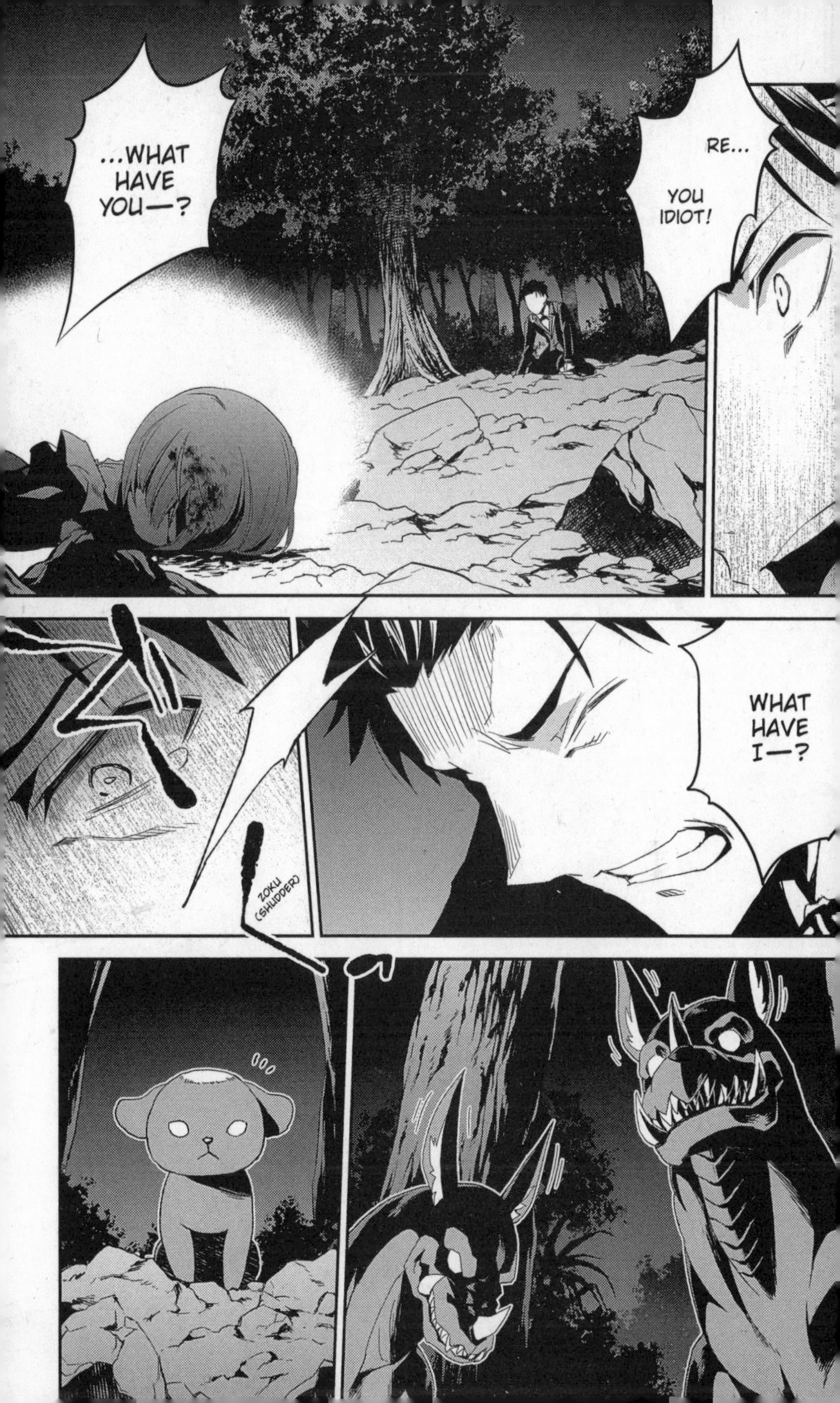
RE...
YOU IDIOT!
...WHAT HAVE YOU—?
WHAT HAVE I—?
ZOKU (SHUDDER)

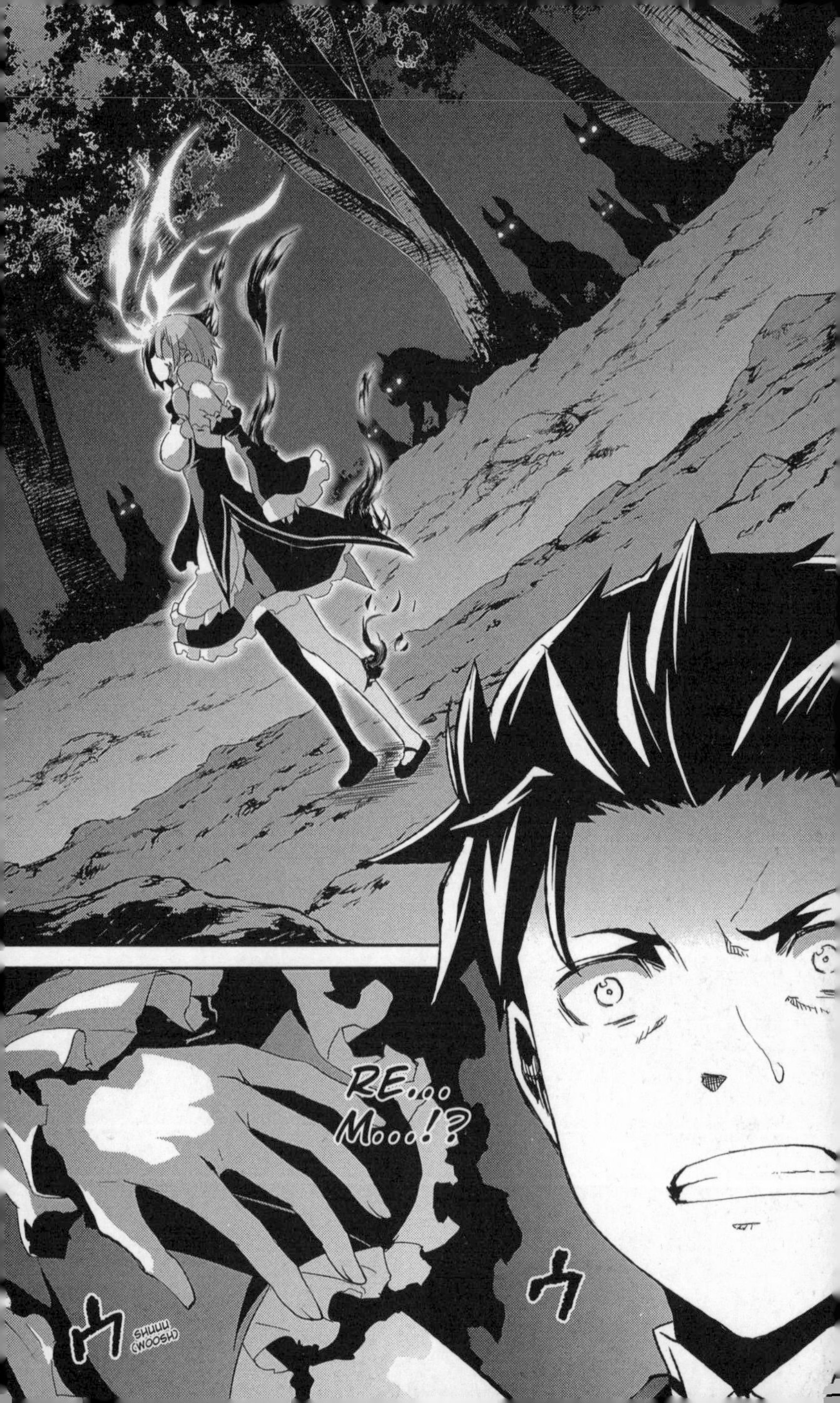
RE...
M...!?
SHUUU
(WOOSH)

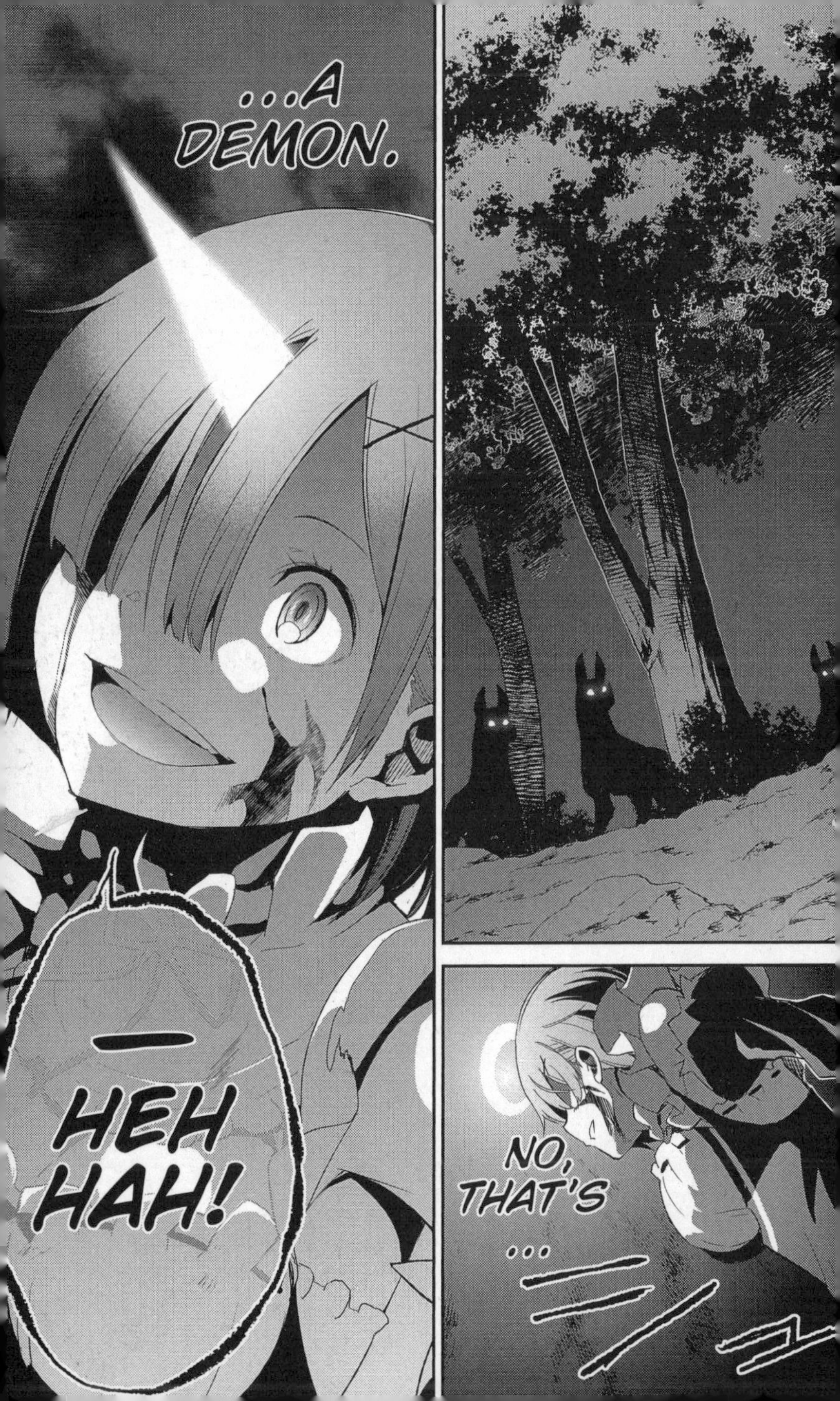
NO, THAT'S ...
...A DEMON.
— HEH HAH!

Re···

Rem

Ri～N!!

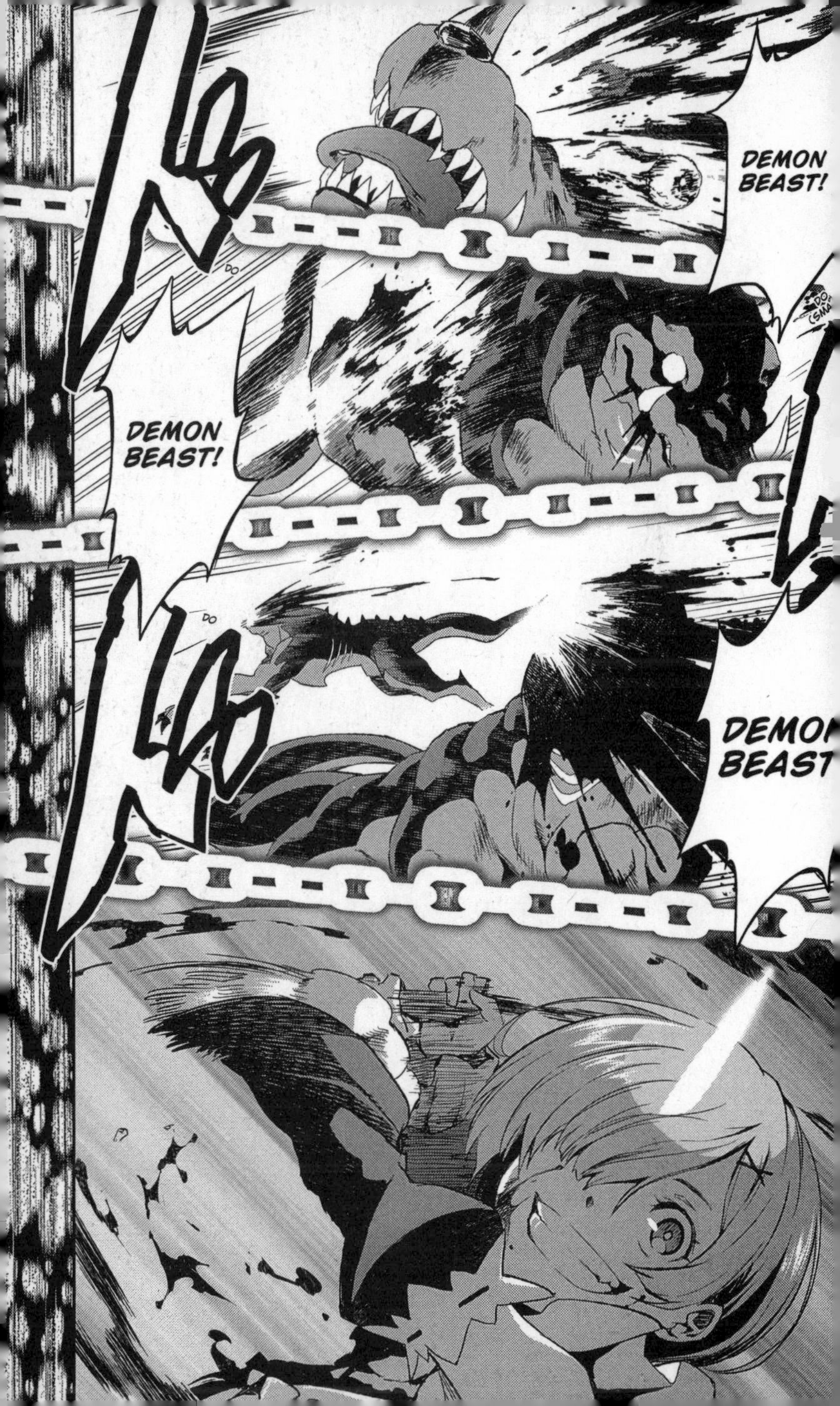
DEMON BEAST!
DO
DEMON BEAST!
DO
DEMON BEAST

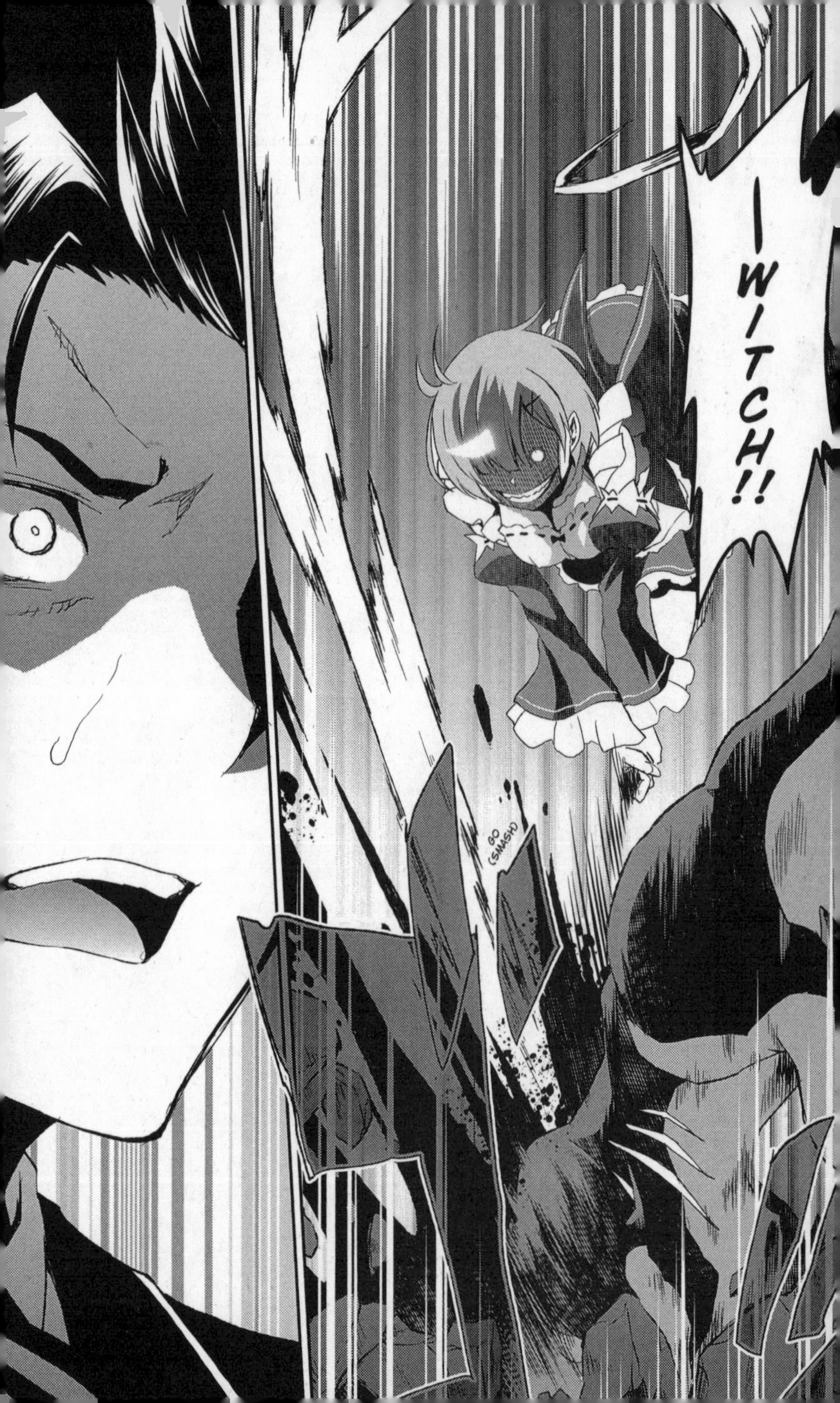
—WITCH!!
GO (SMASH)

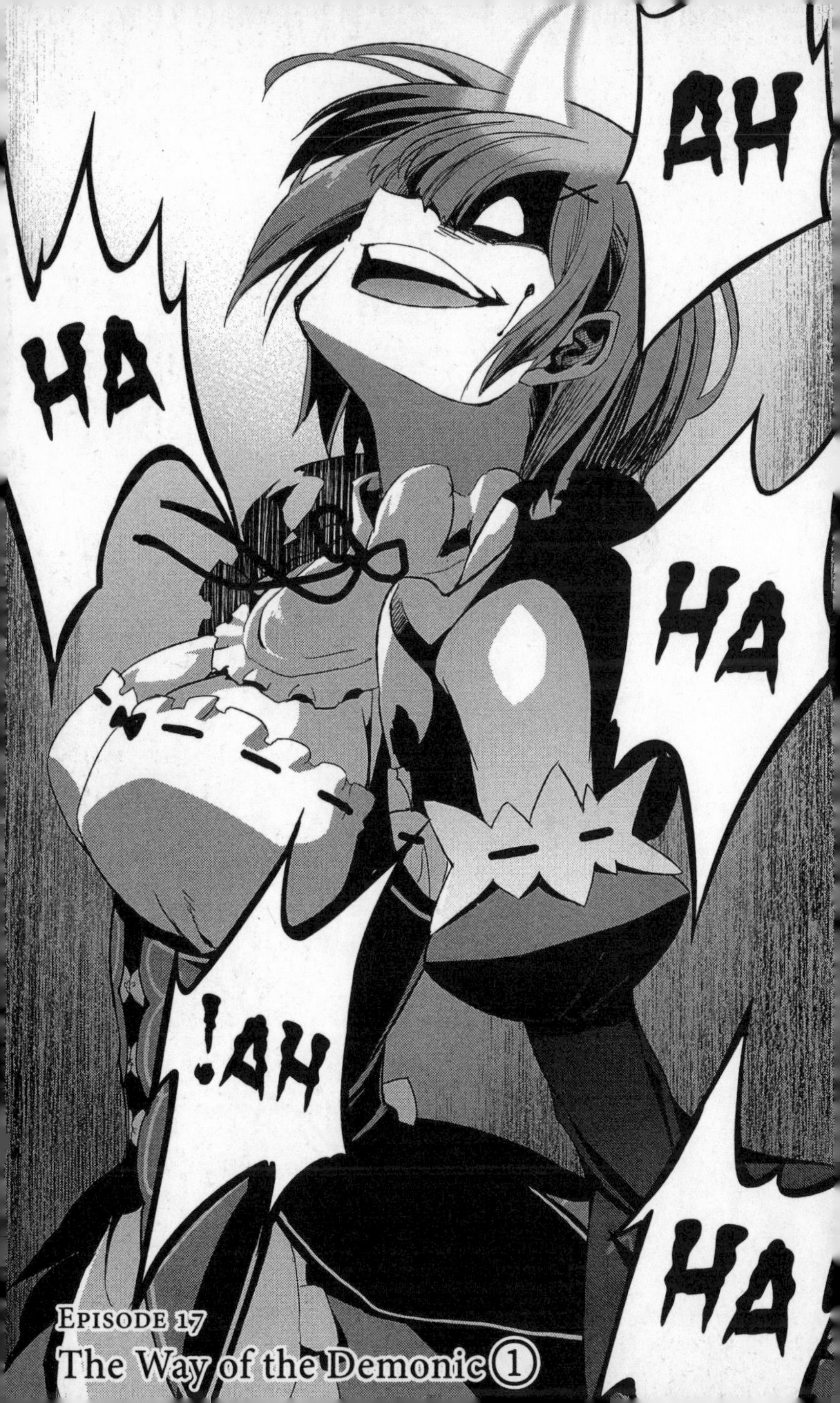
AH
HA
HA
HA
HA!

Episode 17
The Way of the Demonic ①

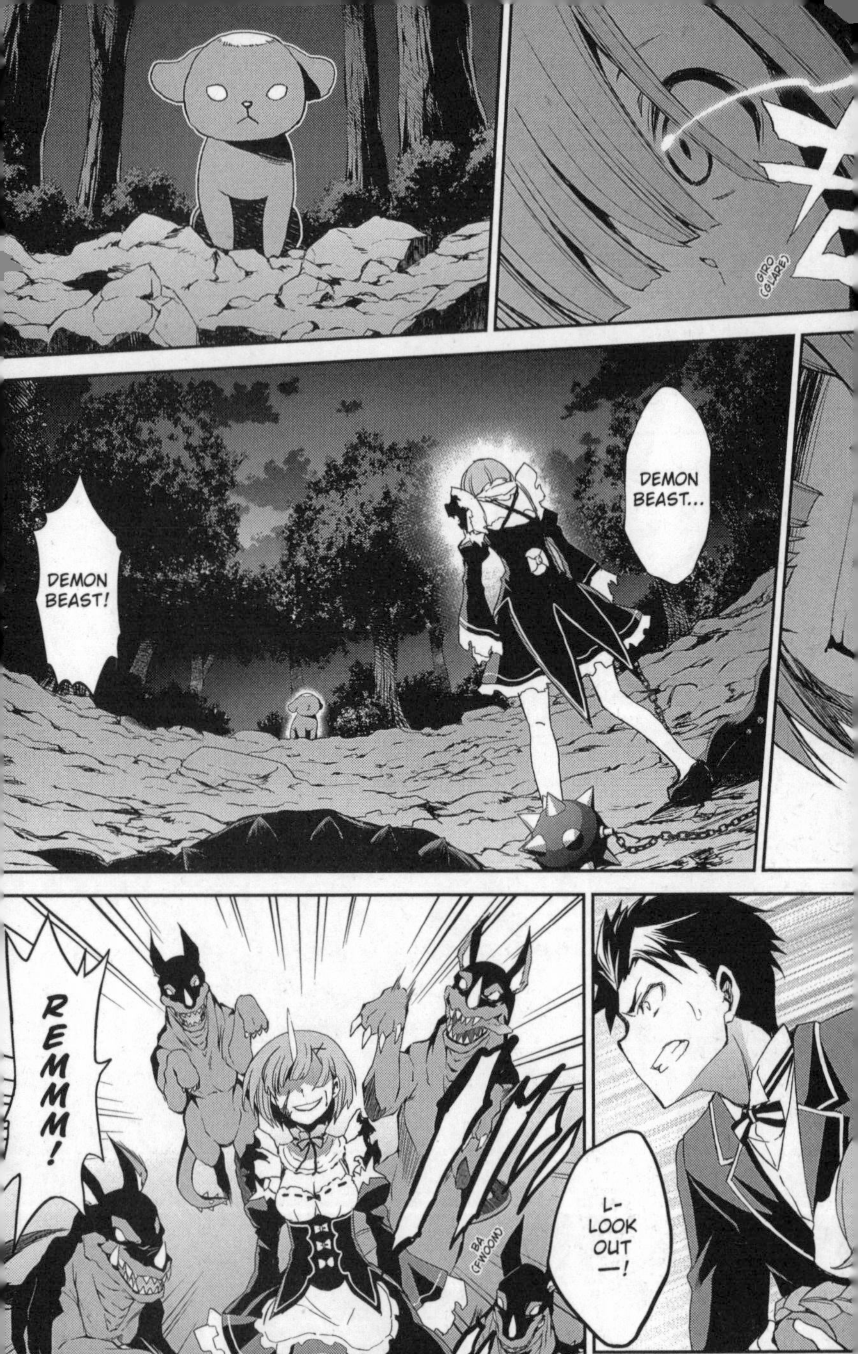
GIRO (GLARE)
DEMON BEAST...
DEMON BEAST!
L-LOOK OUT—!
REMMM!
BA (FWOOM)

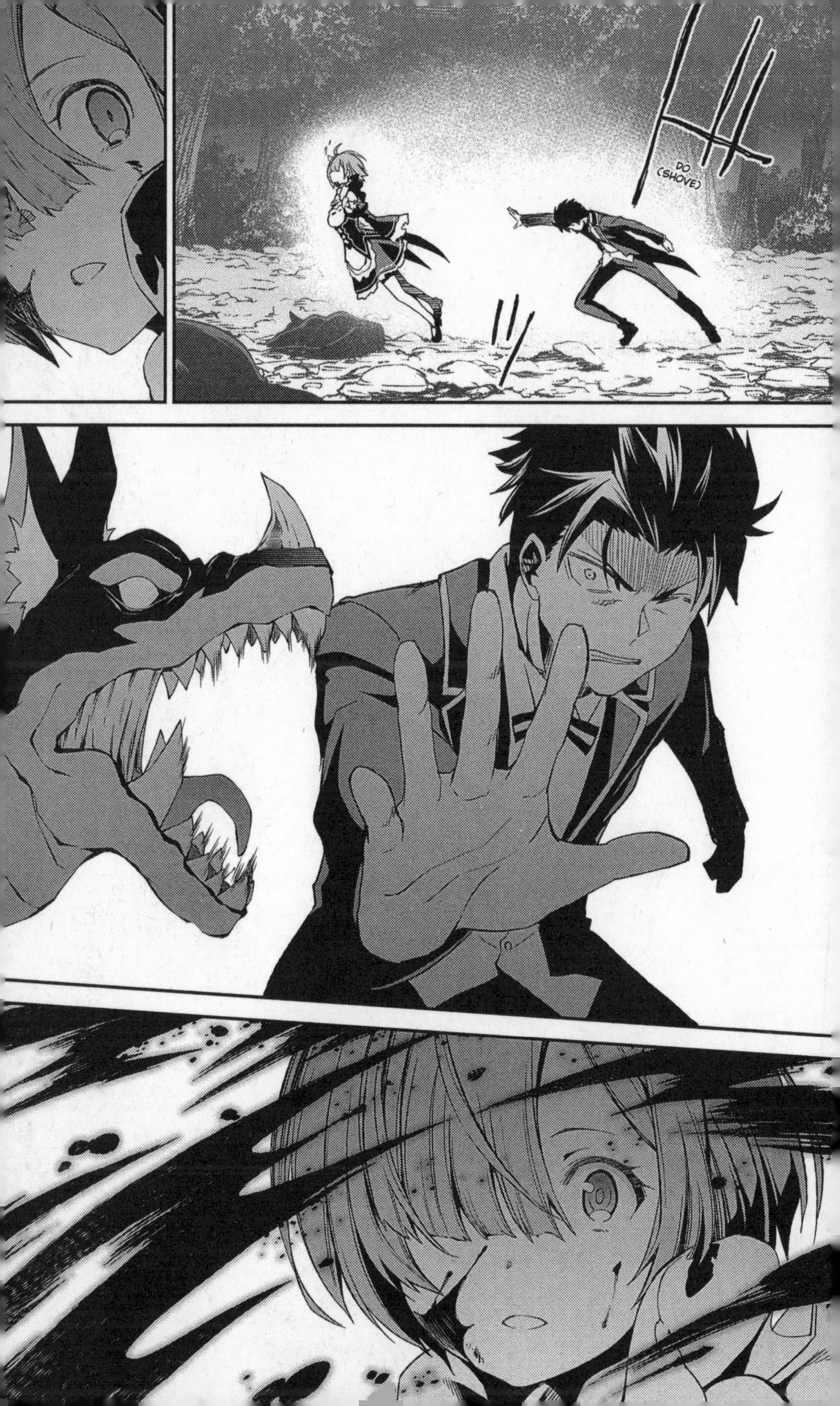
DO
(SHOVE)

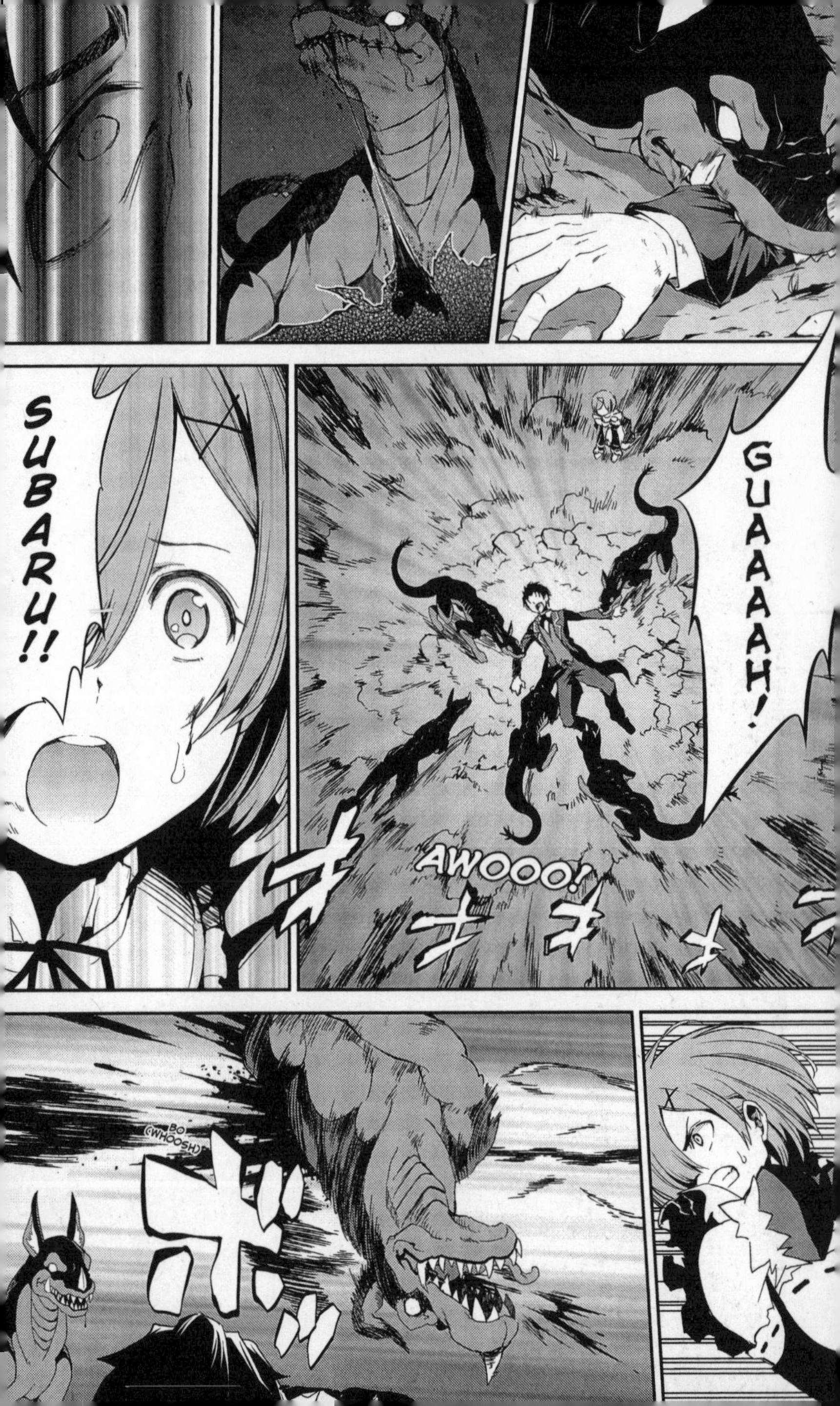
GUAAAAH!
AWOOO!
SUBARU!!
BO (WHOOSH)

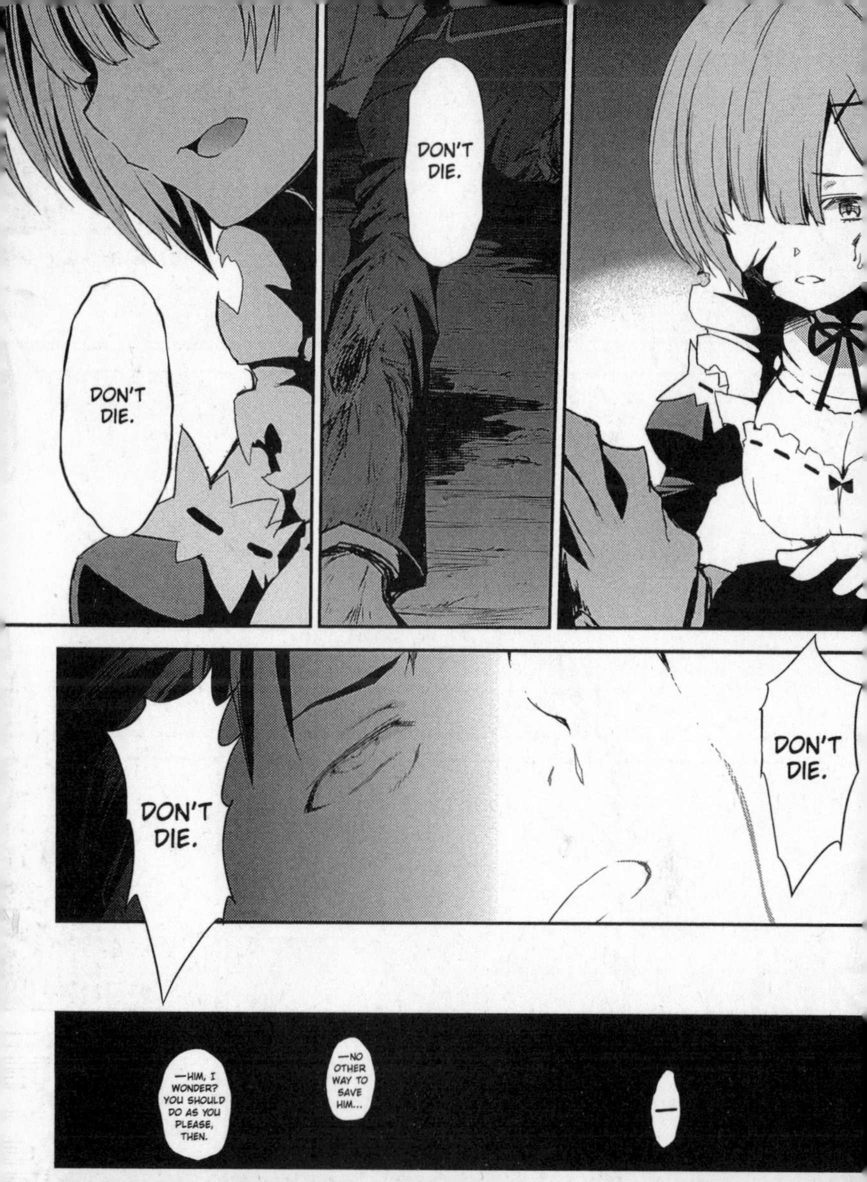
DON'T DIE.
DON'T DIE.
DON'T DIE.
DON'T DIE.
—
—NO OTHER WAY TO SAVE HIM...
—HIM, I WONDER? YOU SHOULD DO AS YOU PLEASE, THEN.

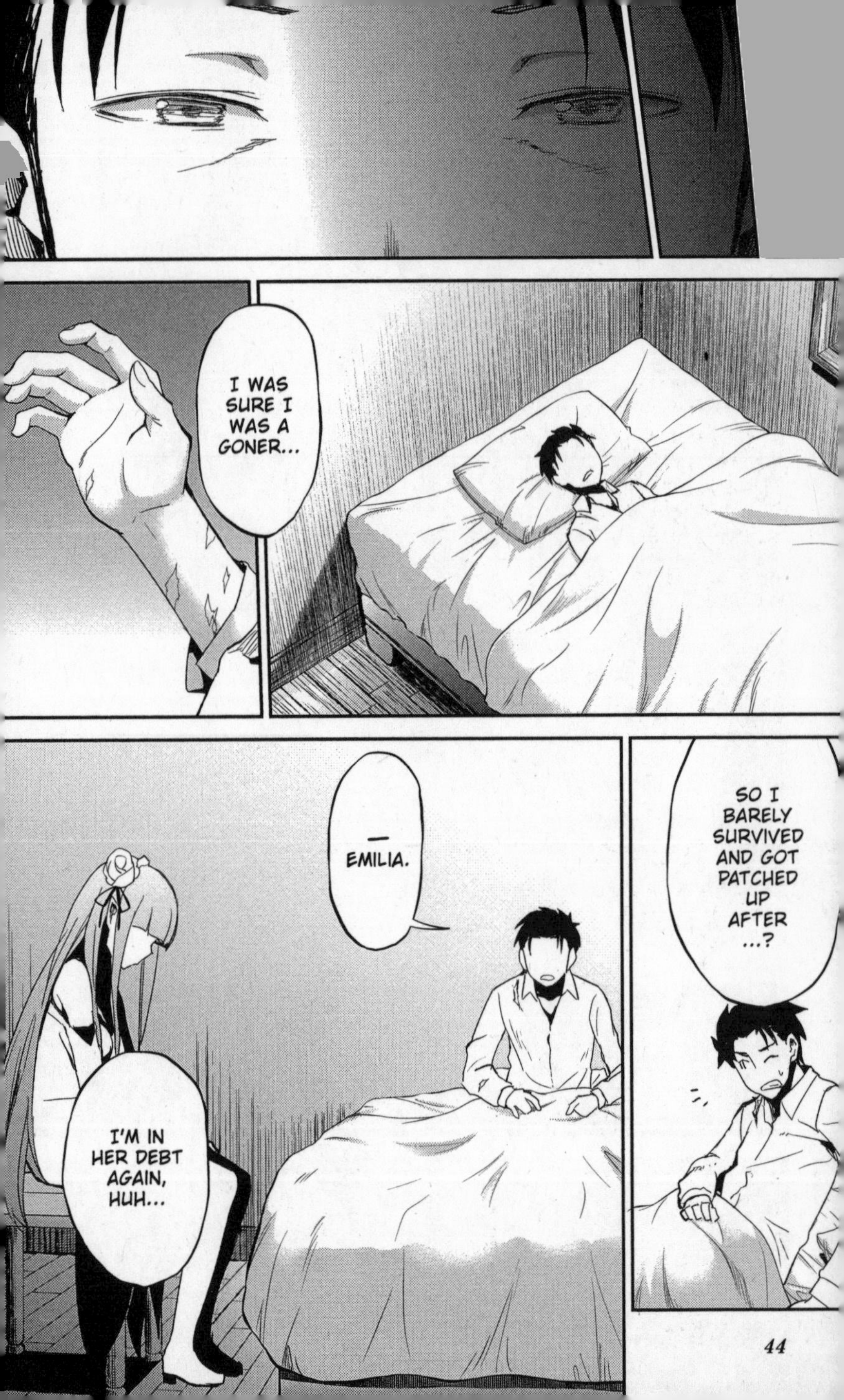
I WAS SURE I WAS A GONER...
SO I BARELY SURVIVED AND GOT PATCHED UP AFTER ...?
— EMILIA.
I'M IN HER DEBT AGAIN, HUH...

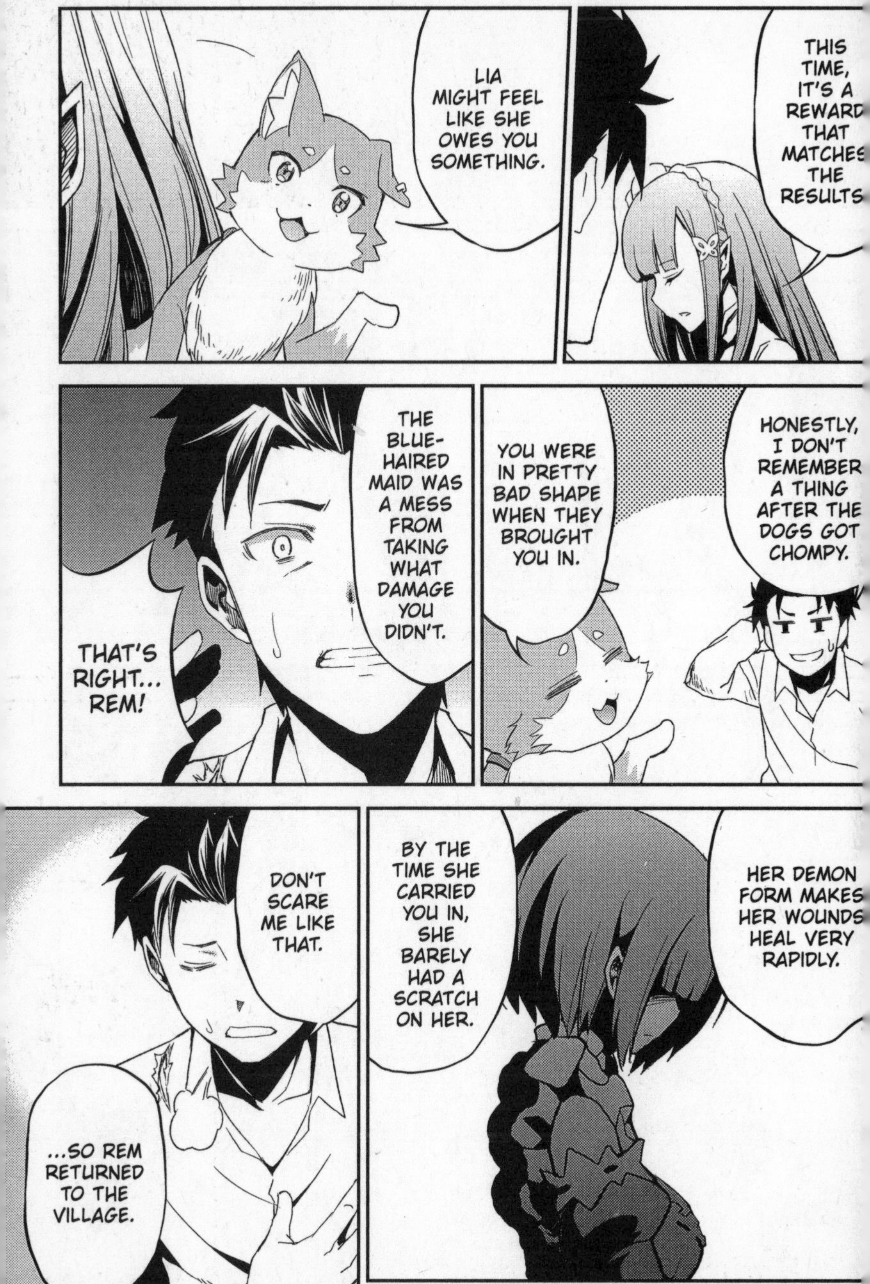
THIS TIME, IT'S A REWARD THAT MATCHES THE RESULTS.
LIA MIGHT FEEL LIKE SHE OWES YOU SOMETHING.
HONESTLY, I DON'T REMEMBER A THING AFTER THE DOGS GOT CHOMPY.
YOU WERE IN PRETTY BAD SHAPE WHEN THEY BROUGHT YOU IN.
THE BLUE-HAIRED MAID WAS A MESS FROM TAKING WHAT DAMAGE YOU DIDN'T.
THAT'S RIGHT... REM!
HER DEMON FORM MAKES HER WOUNDS HEAL VERY RAPIDLY.
BY THE TIME SHE CARRIED YOU IN, SHE BARELY HAD A SCRATCH ON HER.
DON'T SCARE ME LIKE THAT.
...SO REM RETURNED TO THE VILLAGE.

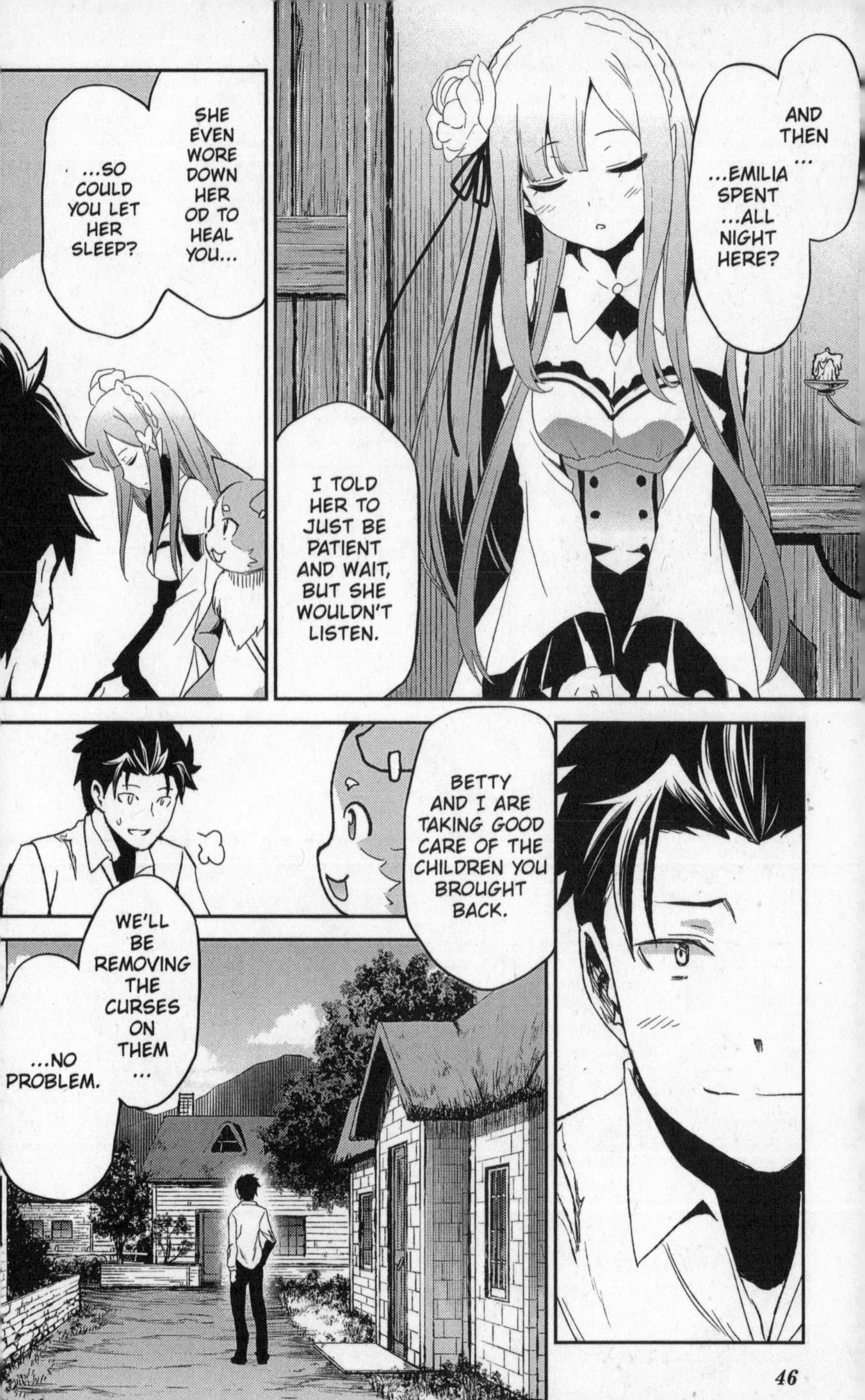
AND THEN ... ...EMILIA SPENT ...ALL NIGHT HERE?
I TOLD HER TO JUST BE PATIENT AND WAIT, BUT SHE WOULDN'T LISTEN.
SHE EVEN WORE DOWN HER OD TO HEAL YOU...
...SO COULD YOU LET HER SLEEP?
BETTY AND I ARE TAKING GOOD CARE OF THE CHILDREN YOU BROUGHT BACK.
WE'LL BE REMOVING THE CURSES ON THEM ...
...NO PROBLEM.

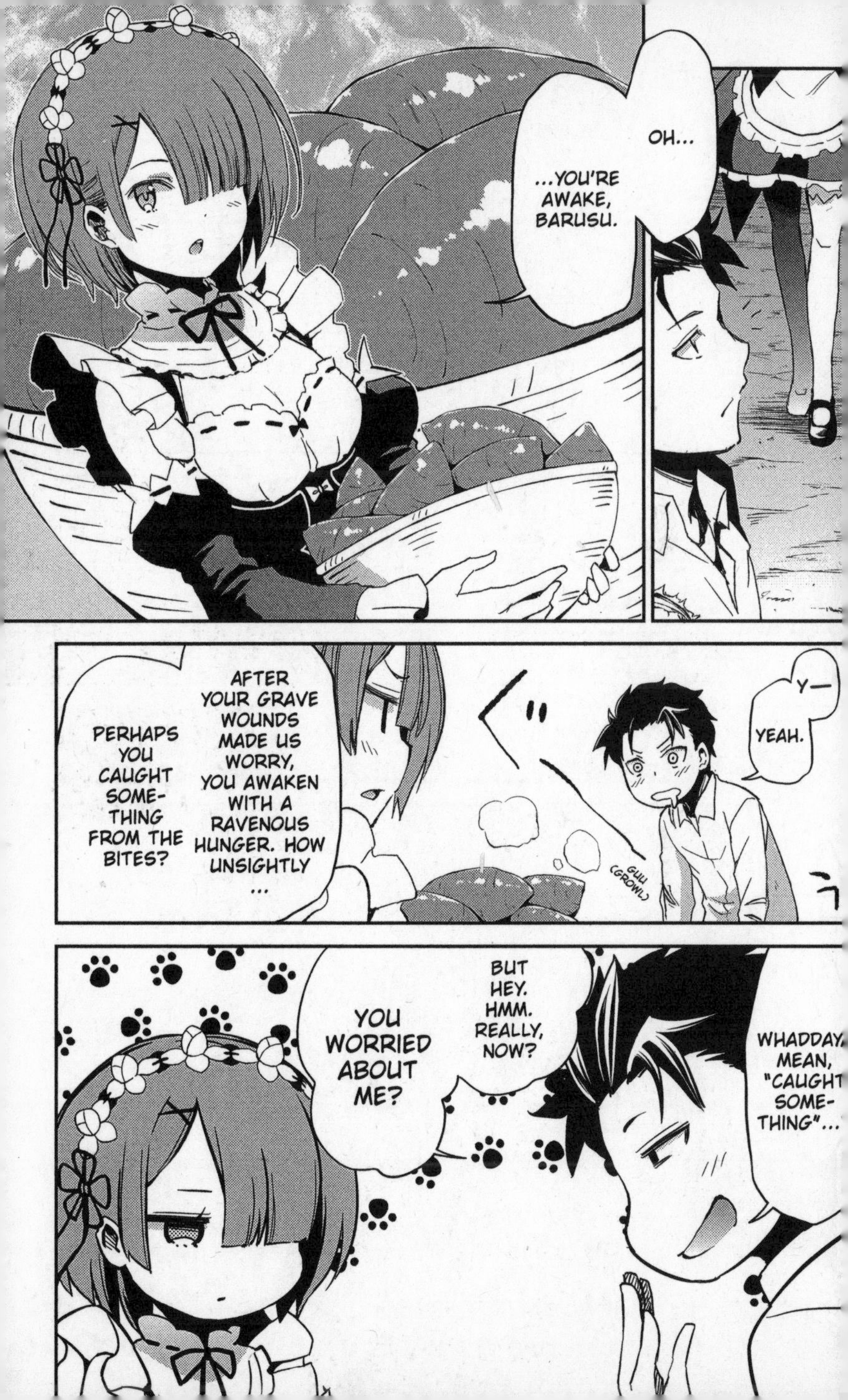
OH...
...YOU'RE AWAKE, BARUSU.
Y—
YEAH.
GUU (GROWL)
AFTER YOUR GRAVE WOUNDS MADE US WORRY, YOU AWAKEN WITH A RAVENOUS HUNGER. HOW UNSIGHTLY...
PERHAPS YOU CAUGHT SOME-THING FROM THE BITES?
WHADDAYA MEAN, "CAUGHT SOME-THING"...
BUT HEY. HMM. REALLY, NOW?
YOU WORRIED ABOUT ME?

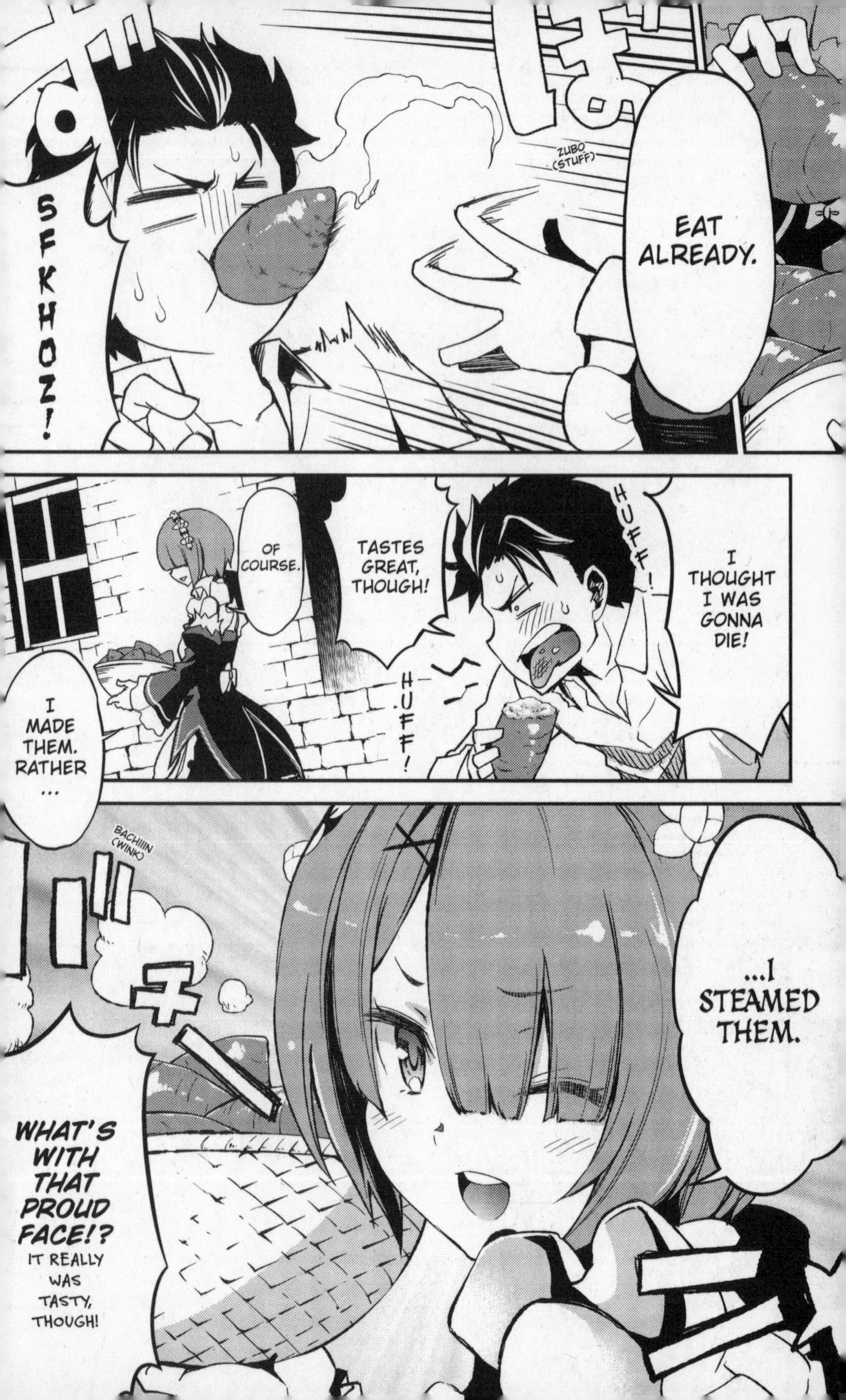
EAT ALREADY.
ZUBO (STUFF)
SFKHOZ!
I THOUGHT I WAS GONNA DIE!
HUFF!
TASTES GREAT, THOUGH!
HUFF!
OF COURSE.
I MADE THEM. RATHER ...
...I STEAMED THEM.
BACHIIIN (WINK)
WHAT'S WITH THAT PROUD FACE!?
IT REALLY WAS TASTY, THOUGH!

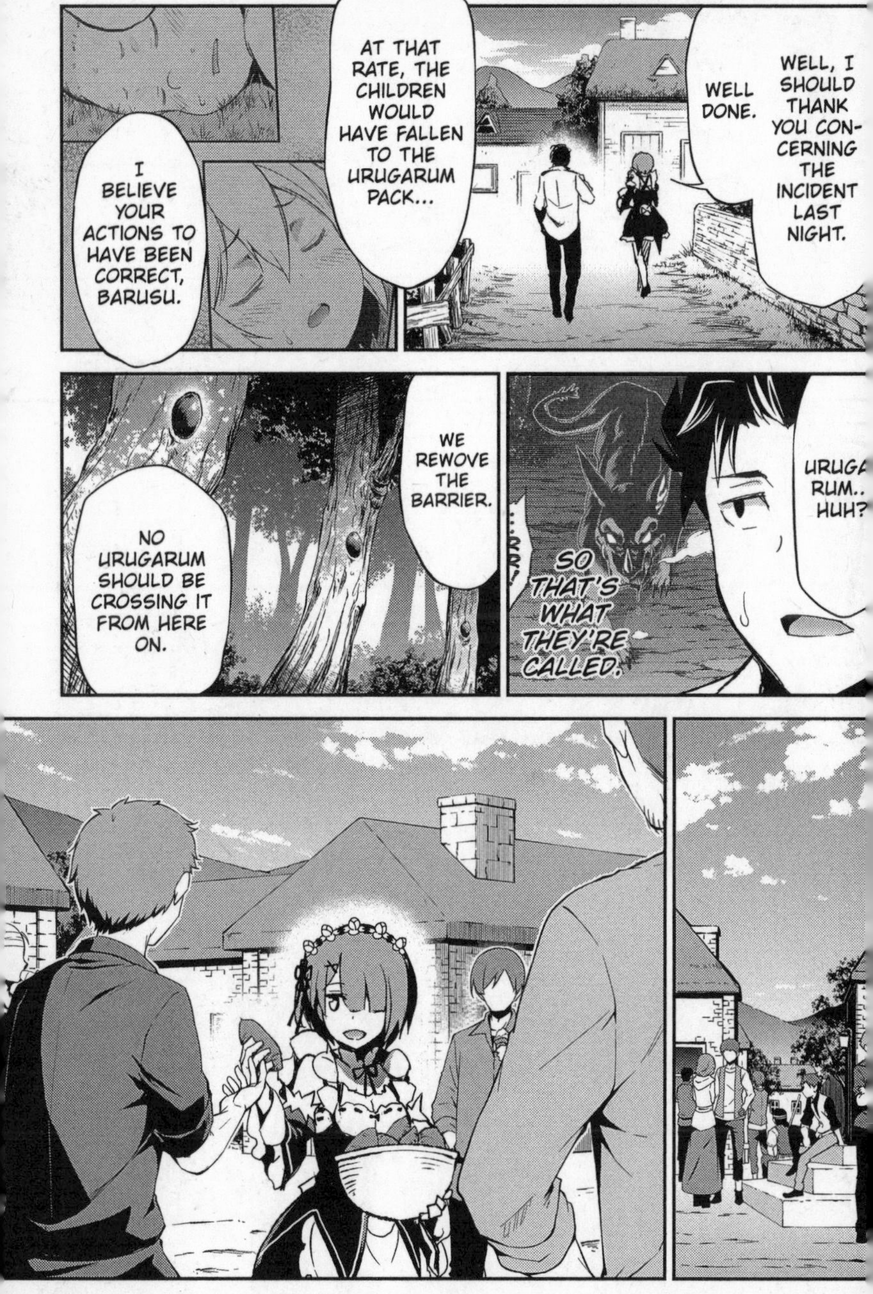
WELL, I SHOULD THANK YOU CON-CERNING THE INCIDENT LAST NIGHT.
WELL DONE.
AT THAT RATE, THE CHILDREN WOULD HAVE FALLEN TO THE URUGARUM PACK...
I BELIEVE YOUR ACTIONS TO HAVE BEEN CORRECT, BARUSU.
URUGA RUM.. HUH?
...RR!
SO THAT'S WHAT THEY'RE CALLED.
WE REWOVE THE BARRIER.
NO URUGARUM SHOULD BE CROSSING IT FROM HERE ON.

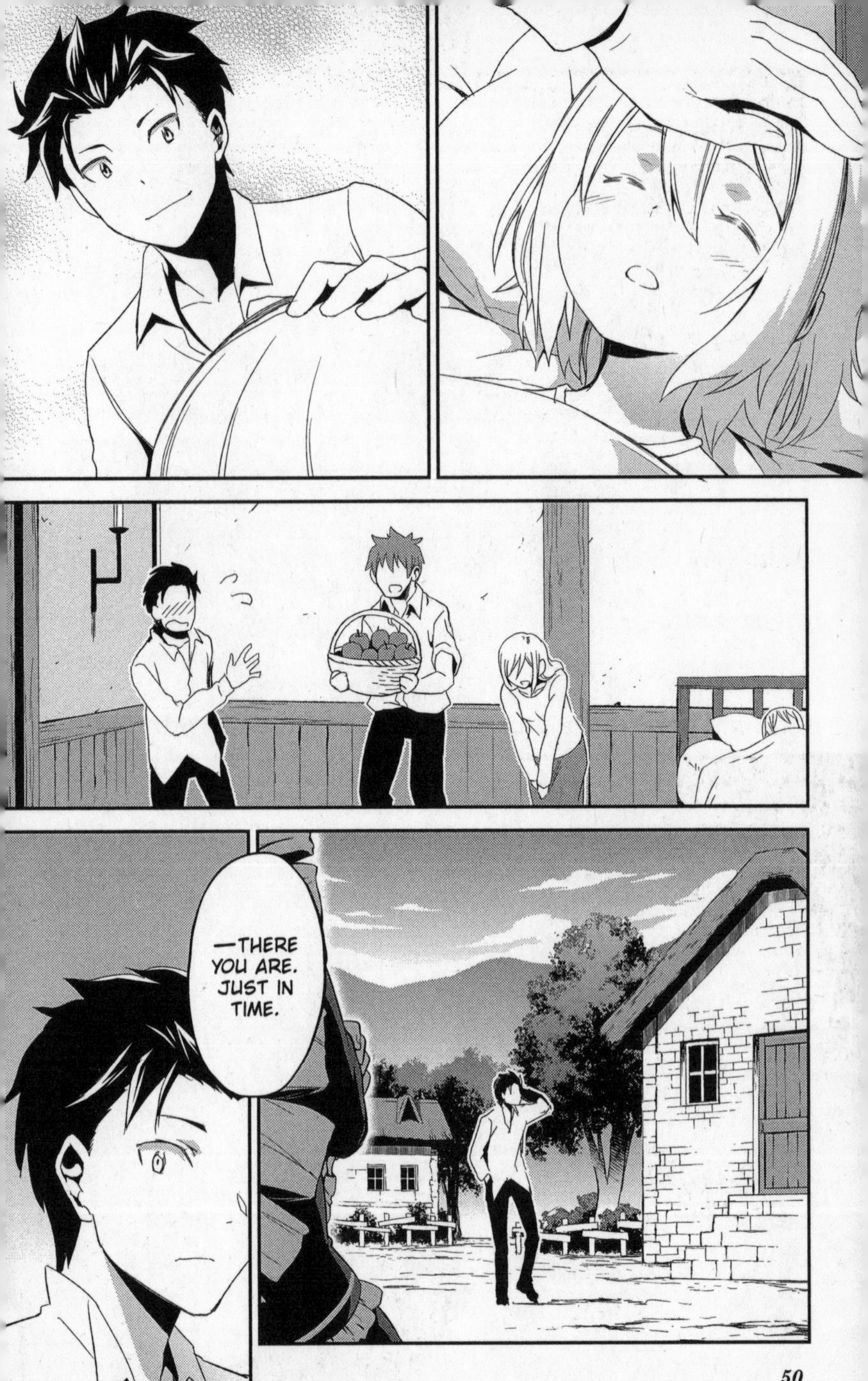
—THERE YOU ARE. JUST IN TIME.

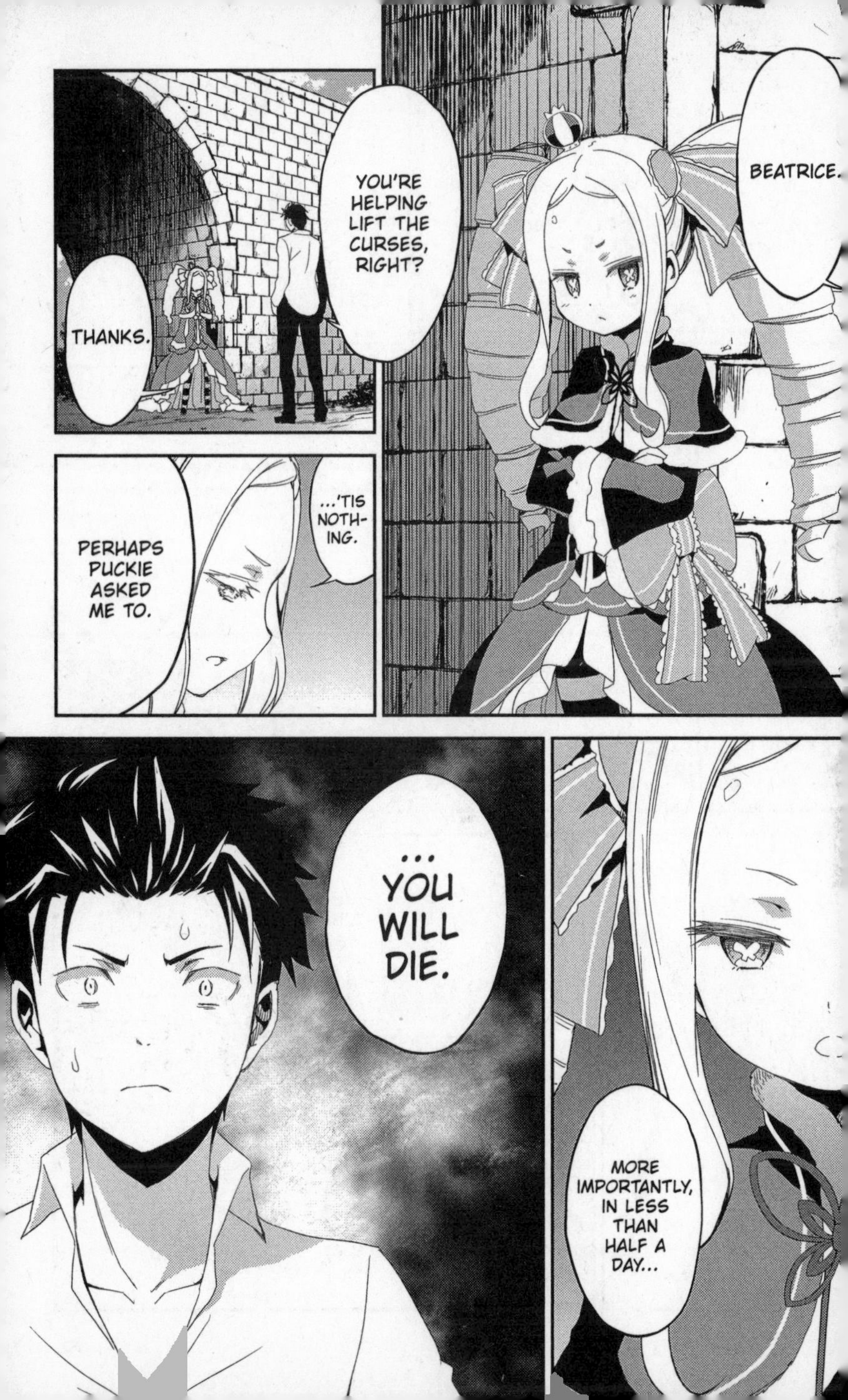
BEATRICE.
YOU'RE HELPING LIFT THE CURSES, RIGHT?
THANKS.
...'TIS NOTH-ING.
PERHAPS PUCKIE ASKED ME TO.
MORE IMPORTANTLY, IN LESS THAN HALF A DAY...
...YOU WILL DIE.

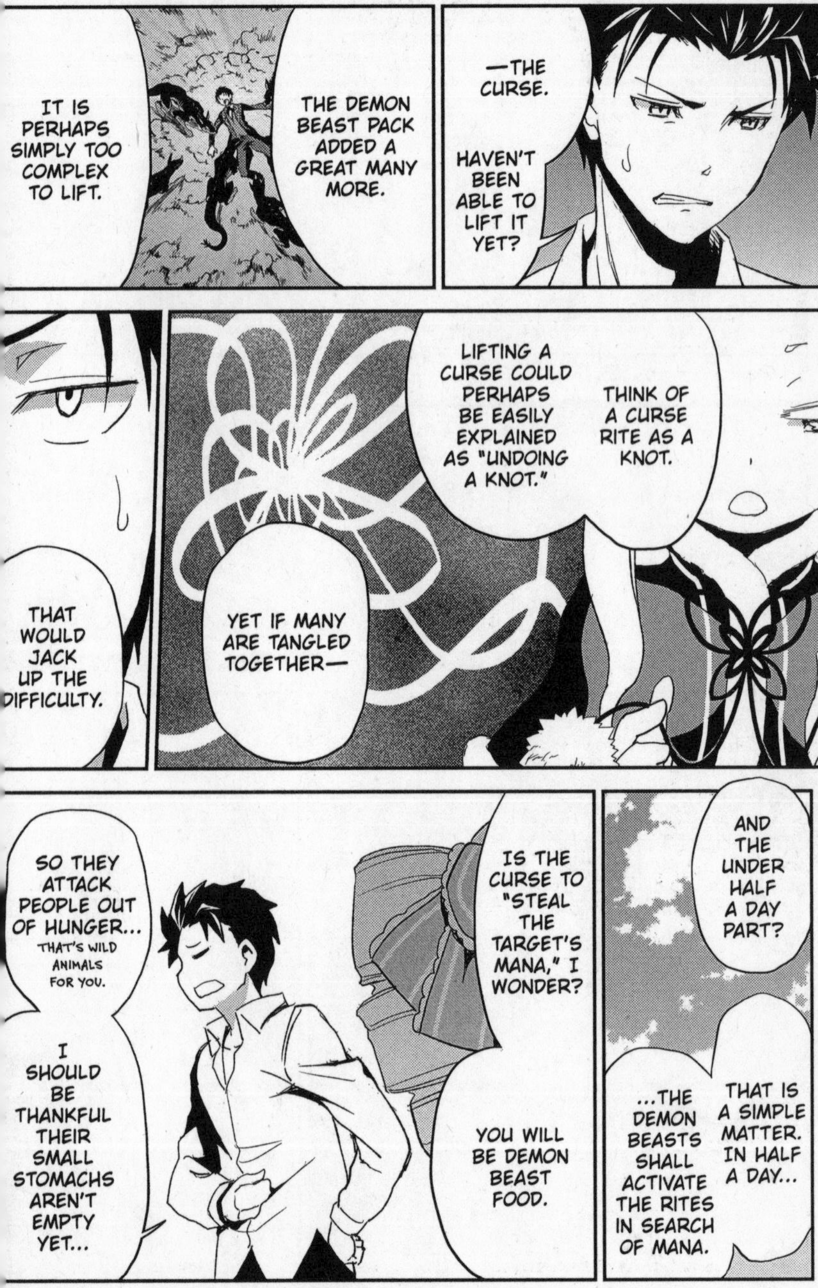
—THE CURSE.
HAVEN'T BEEN ABLE TO LIFT IT YET?
THE DEMON BEAST PACK ADDED A GREAT MANY MORE.
IT IS PERHAPS SIMPLY TOO COMPLEX TO LIFT.
THINK OF A CURSE RITE AS A KNOT.
LIFTING A CURSE COULD PERHAPS BE EASILY EXPLAINED AS "UNDOING A KNOT."
YET IF MANY ARE TANGLED TOGETHER—
THAT WOULD JACK UP THE DIFFICULTY.
AND THE UNDER HALF A DAY PART?
THAT IS A SIMPLE MATTER. IN HALF A DAY...
...THE DEMON BEASTS SHALL ACTIVATE THE RITES IN SEARCH OF MANA.
IS THE CURSE TO "STEAL THE TARGET'S MANA," I WONDER?
YOU WILL BE DEMON BEAST FOOD.
SO THEY ATTACK PEOPLE OUT OF HUNGER... THAT'S WILD ANIMALS FOR YOU.
I SHOULD BE THANKFUL THEIR SMALL STOMACHS AREN'T EMPTY YET...

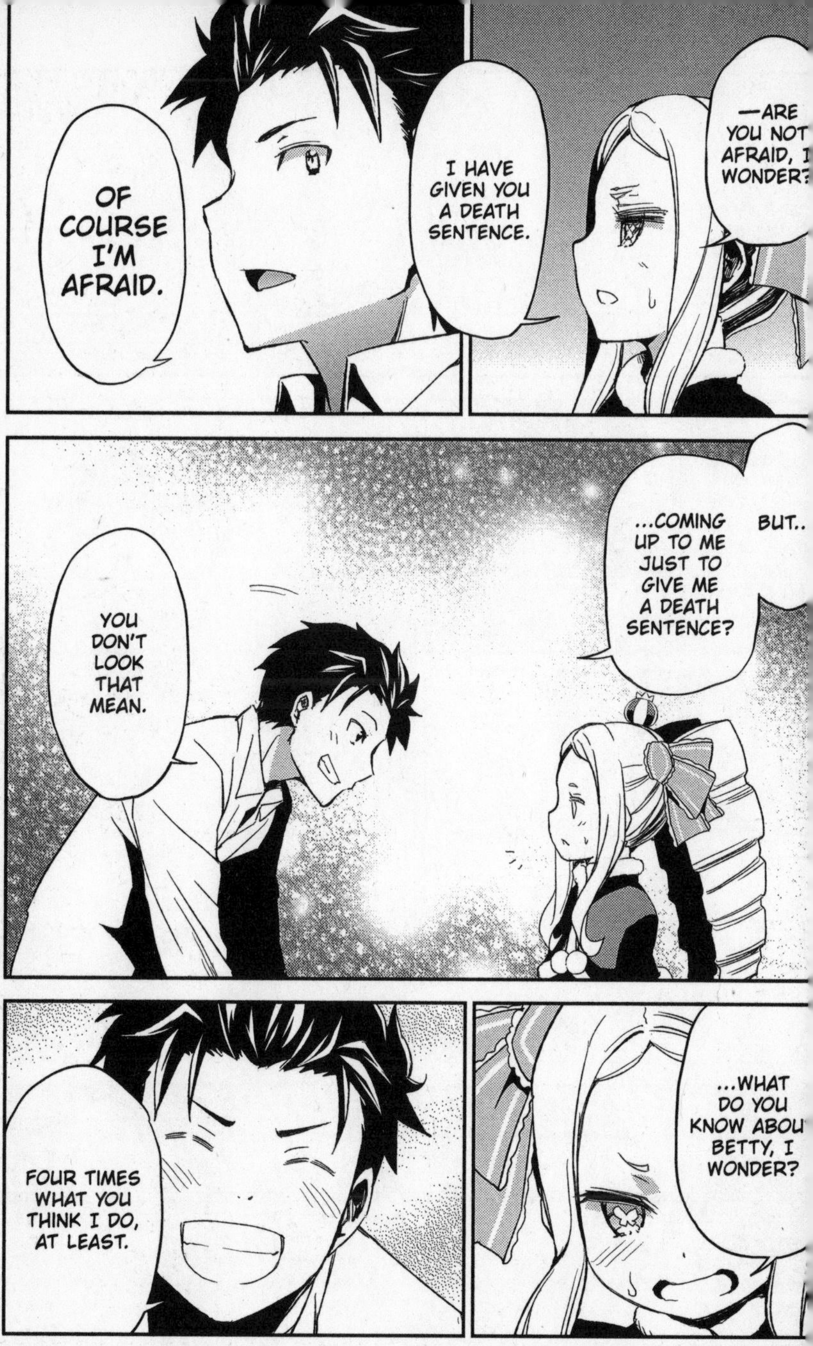
—ARE YOU NOT AFRAID, I WONDER?
I HAVE GIVEN YOU A DEATH SENTENCE.
OF COURSE I'M AFRAID.
BUT...
...COMING UP TO ME JUST TO GIVE ME A DEATH SENTENCE?
YOU DON'T LOOK THAT MEAN.
...WHAT DO YOU KNOW ABOU BETTY, I WONDER?
FOUR TIMES WHAT YOU THINK I DO, AT LEAST.

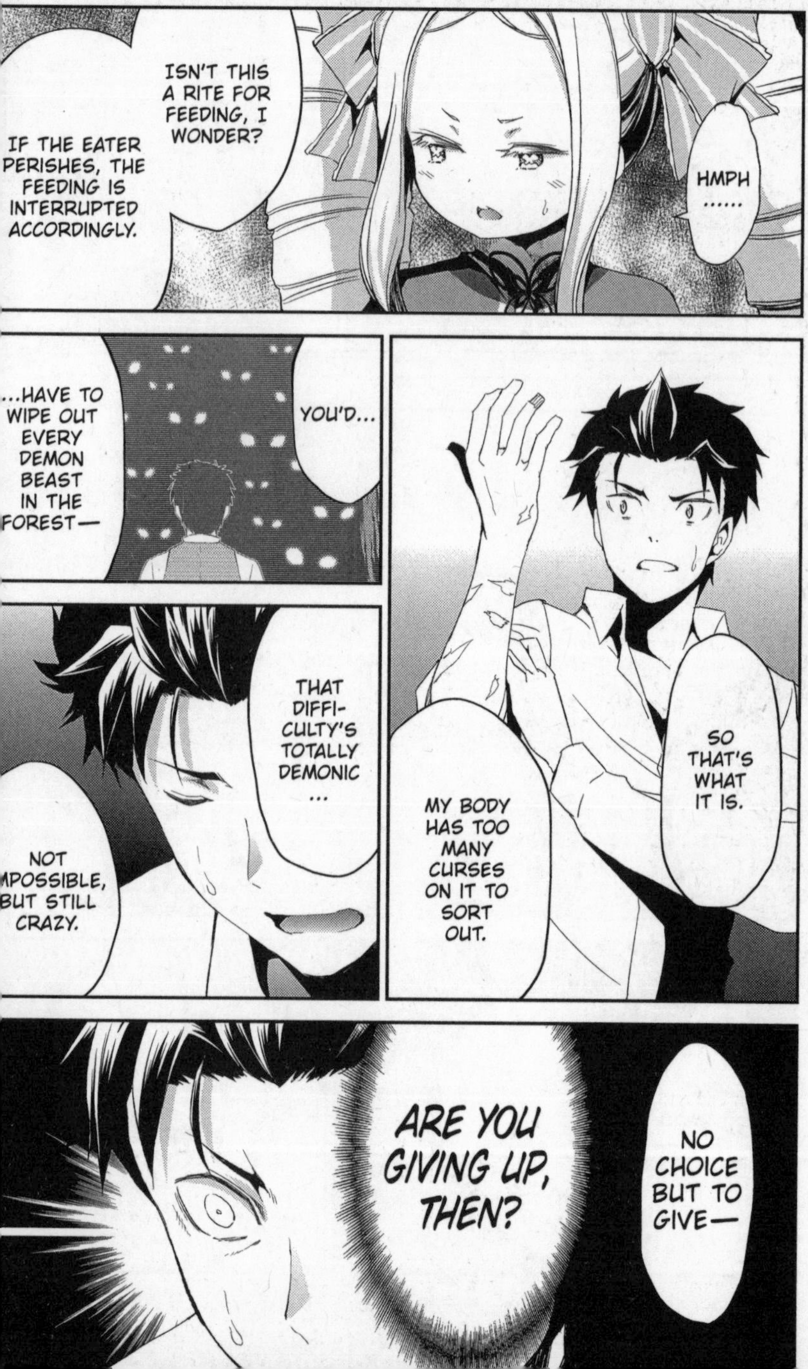
HMPH......
ISN'T THIS A RITE FOR FEEDING, I WONDER?
IF THE EATER PERISHES, THE FEEDING IS INTERRUPTED ACCORDINGLY.
SO THAT'S WHAT IT IS.
MY BODY HAS TOO MANY CURSES ON IT TO SORT OUT.
YOU'D...
...HAVE TO WIPE OUT EVERY DEMON BEAST IN THE FOREST—
THAT DIFFICULTY'S TOTALLY DEMONIC...
NOT MPOSSIBLE, BUT STILL CRAZY.
NO CHOICE BUT TO GIVE—
ARE YOU GIVING UP, THEN?

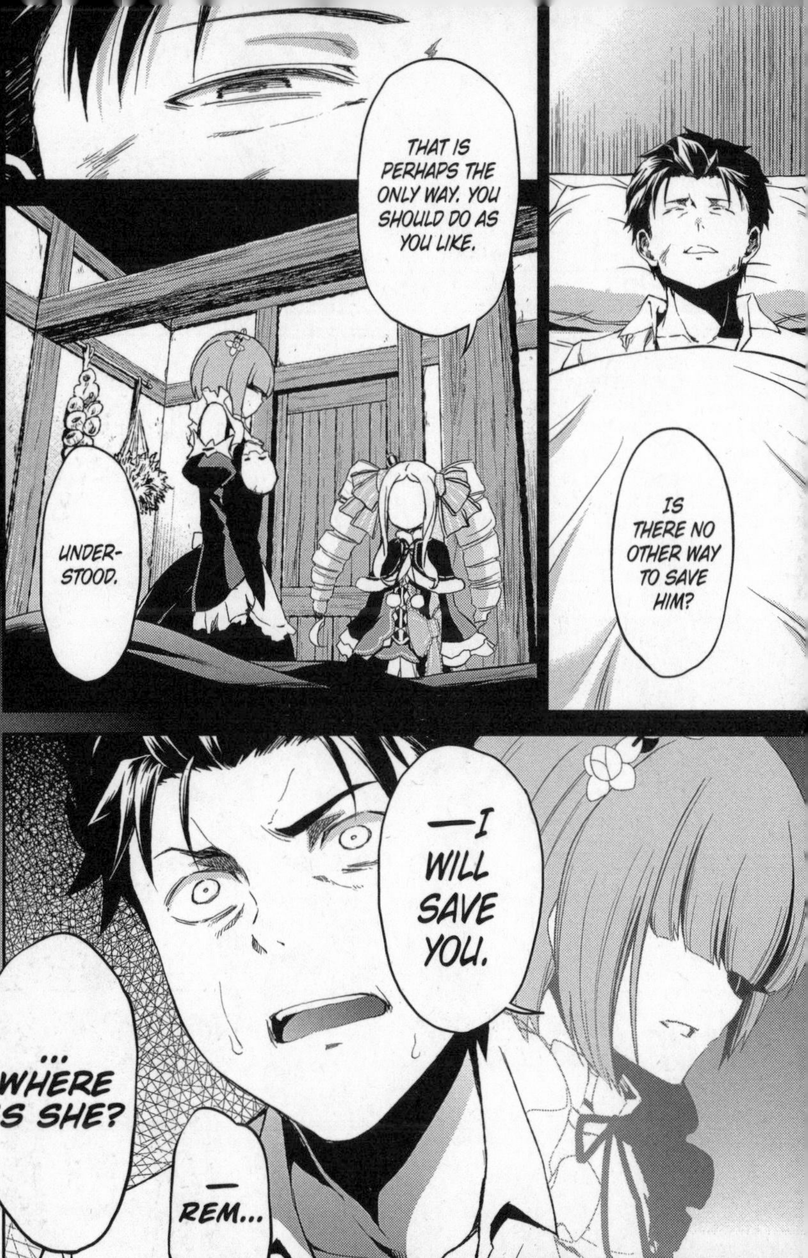
IS THERE NO OTHER WAY TO SAVE HIM?
THAT IS PERHAPS THE ONLY WAY. YOU SHOULD DO AS YOU LIKE.
UNDER-STOOD.
—I WILL SAVE YOU.
...WHERE IS SHE?
—REM...

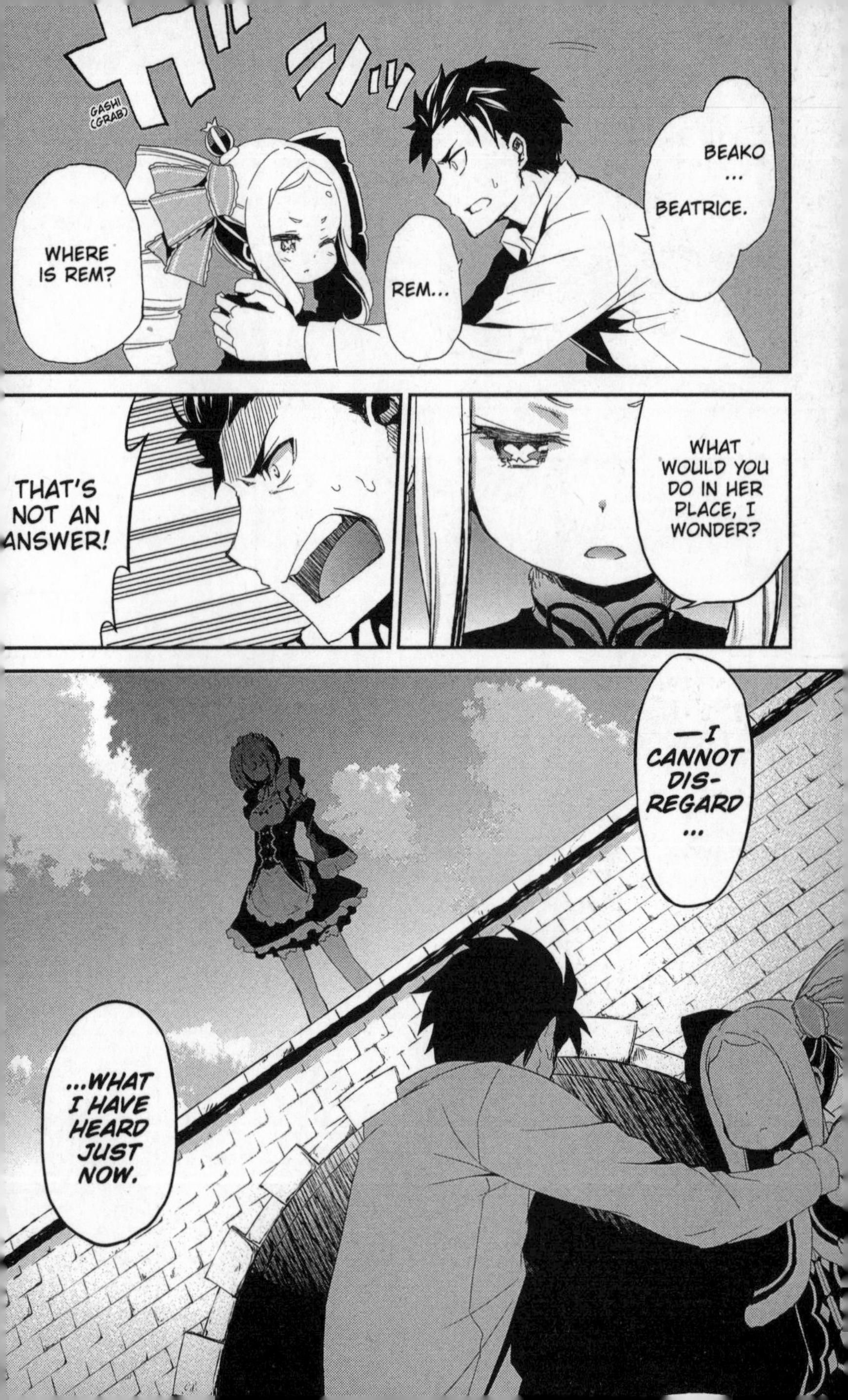

GASHI (GRAB)
BEAKO ... BEATRICE.
REM...
WHERE IS REM?
WHAT WOULD YOU DO IN HER PLACE, I WONDER?
THAT'S NOT AN ANSWER!
—I CANNOT DIS-REGARD ...
...WHAT I HAVE HEARD JUST NOW.

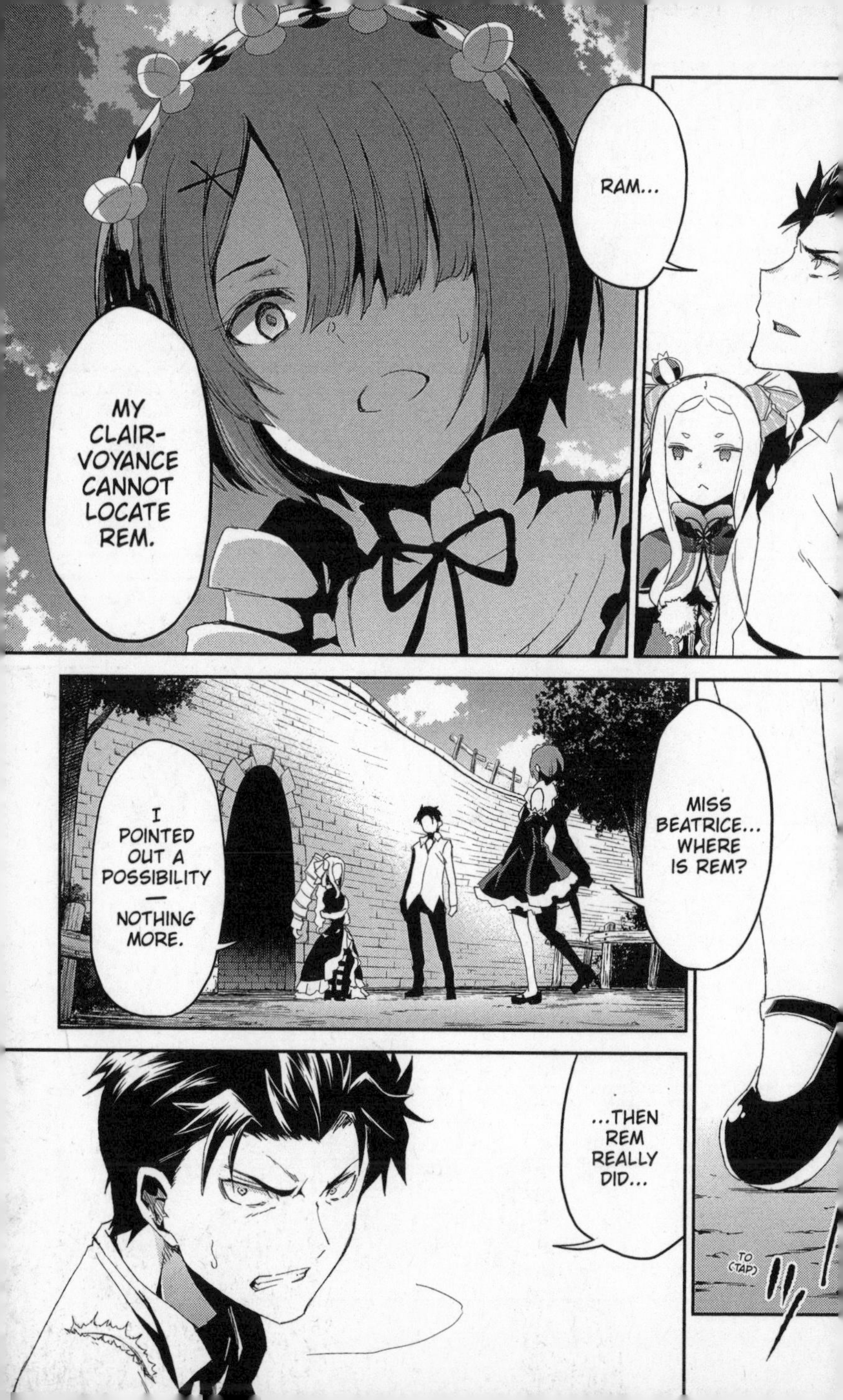
RAM...
MY CLAIR-VOYANCE CANNOT LOCATE REM.
TO (TAP)
MISS BEATRICE... WHERE IS REM?
I POINTED OUT A POSSIBILITY—NOTHING MORE.
...THEN REM REALLY DID...

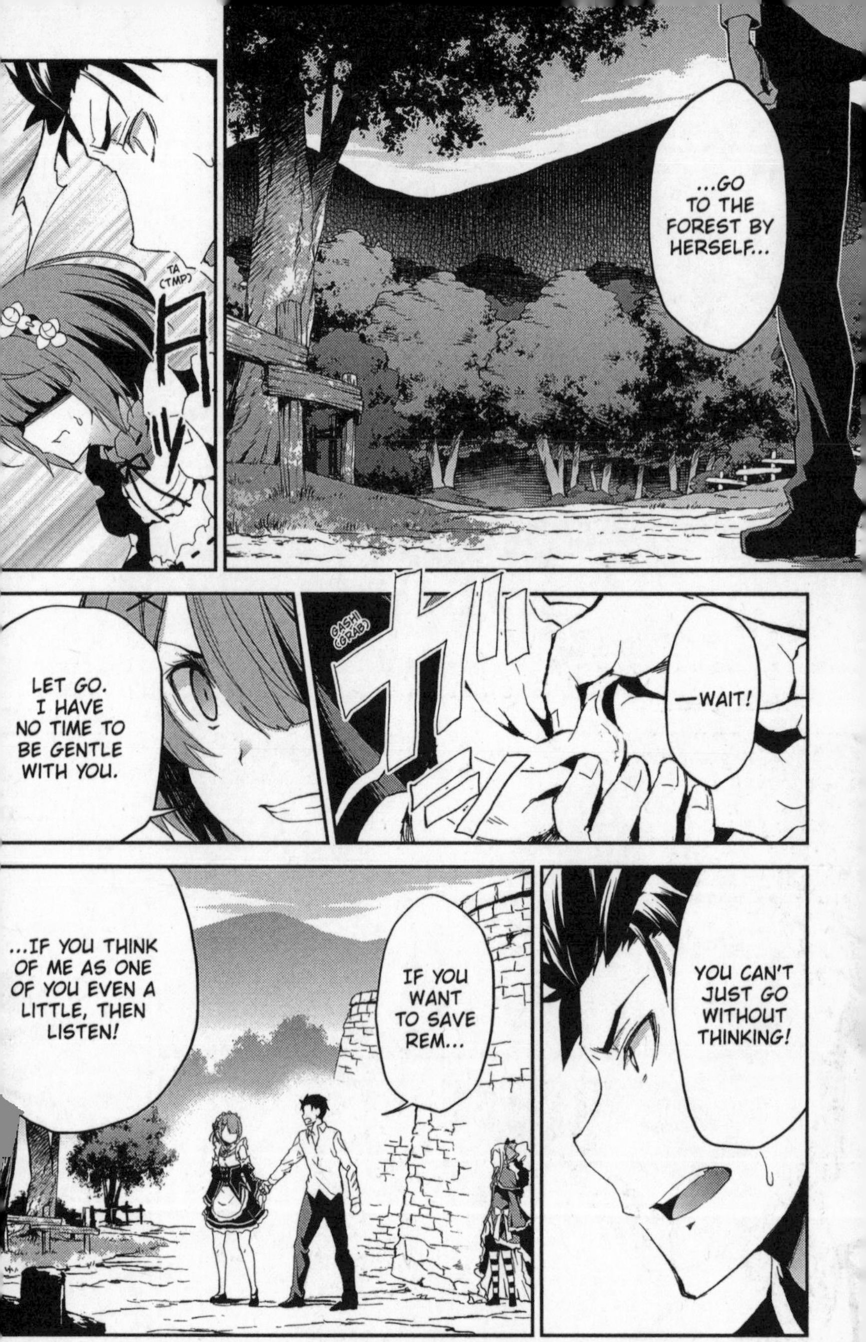
...GO TO THE FOREST BY HERSELF...
TA (TMP)
—WAIT!
GASHI (GRAB)
LET GO. I HAVE NO TIME TO BE GENTLE WITH YOU.
YOU CAN'T JUST GO WITHOUT THINKING!
IF YOU WANT TO SAVE REM...
...IF YOU THINK OF ME AS ONE OF YOU EVEN A LITTLE, THEN LISTEN!

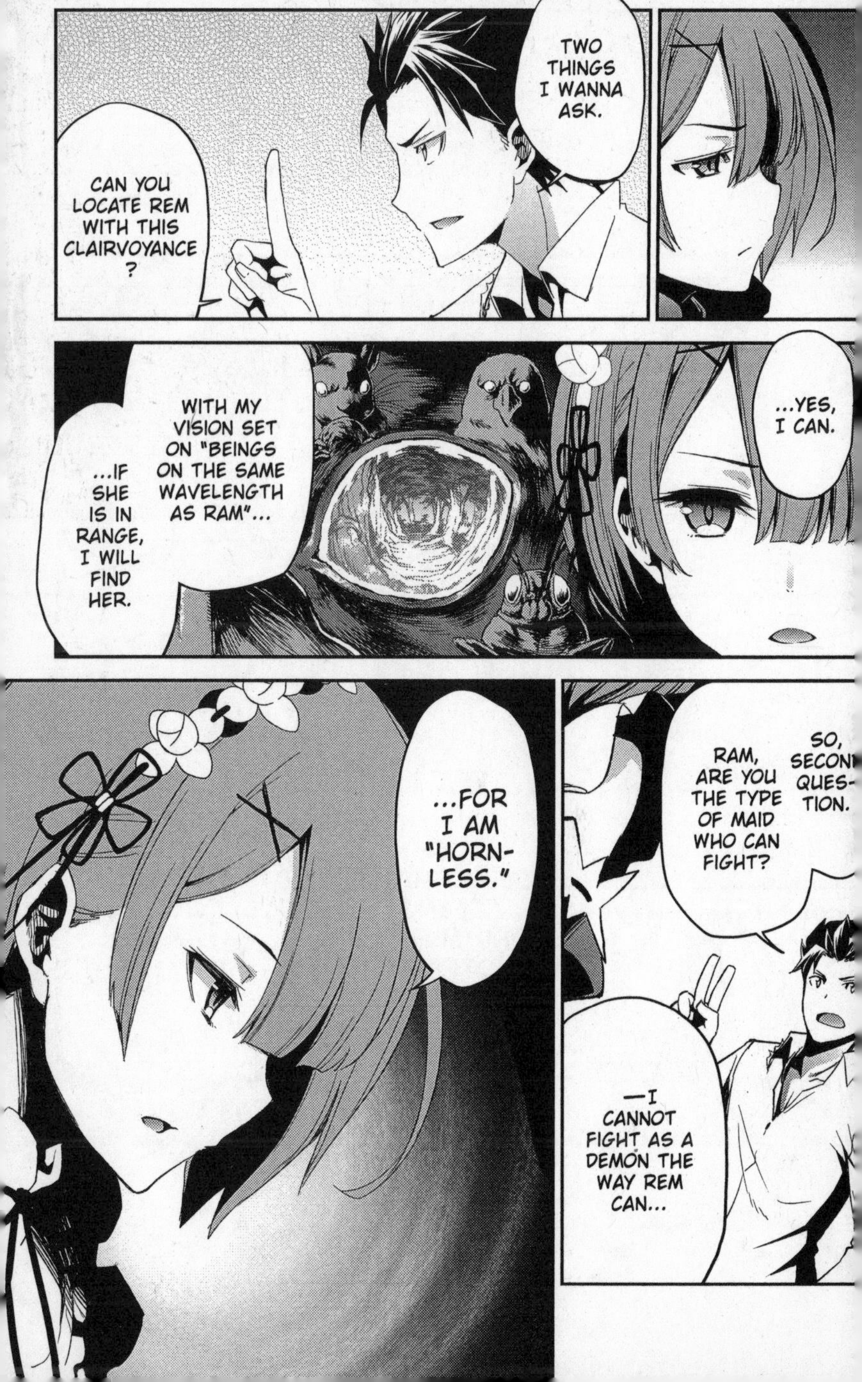
TWO THINGS I WANNA ASK.
CAN YOU LOCATE REM WITH THIS CLAIRVOYANCE?
...YES, I CAN.
WITH MY VISION SET ON "BEINGS ON THE SAME WAVELENGTH AS RAM"...
...IF SHE IS IN RANGE, I WILL FIND HER.
SO, SECOND QUES-TION.
RAM, ARE YOU THE TYPE OF MAID WHO CAN FIGHT?
—I CANNOT FIGHT AS A DEMON THE WAY REM CAN...
...FOR I AM "HORN-LESS."

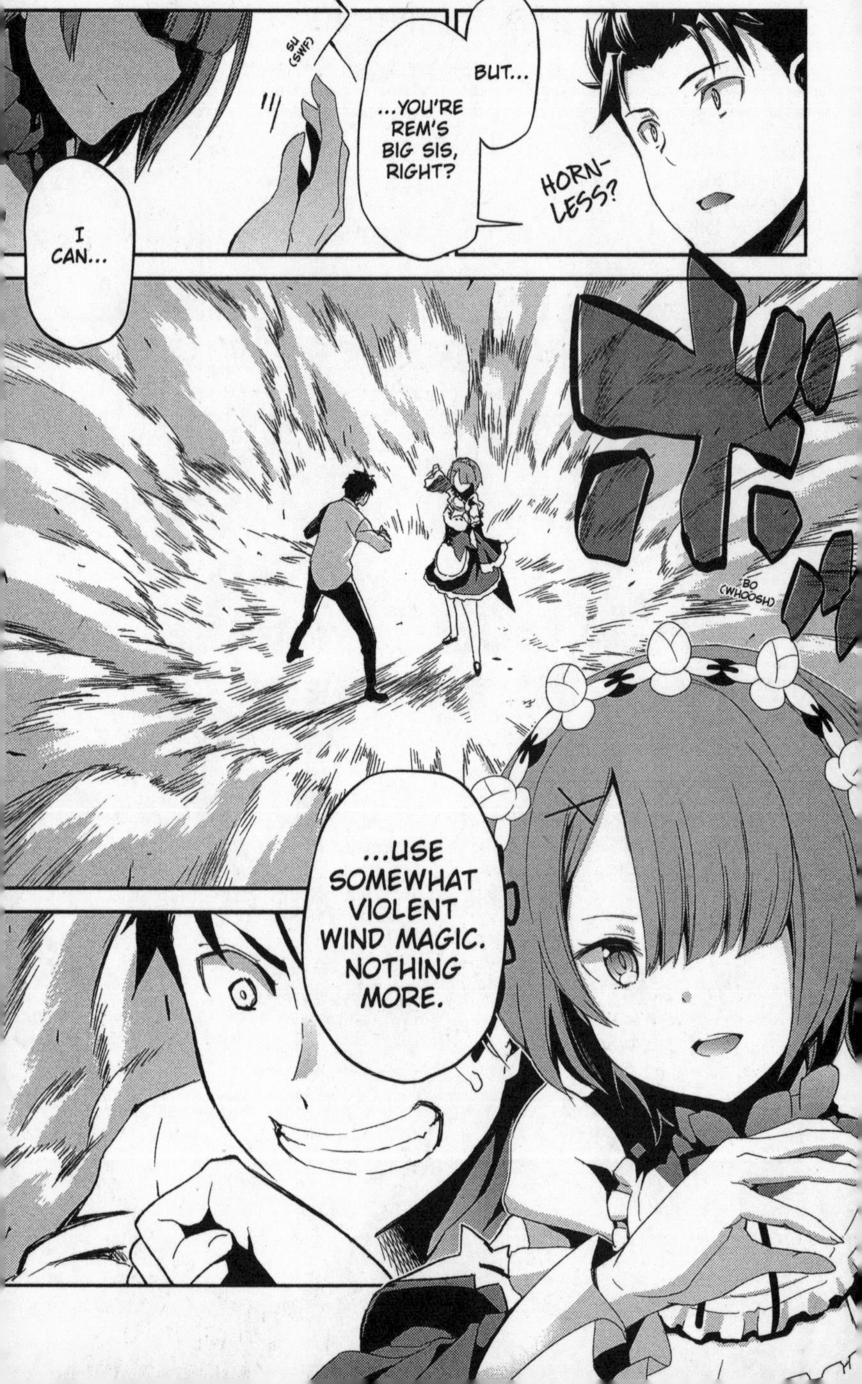
HORN-LESS?
BUT...
...YOU'RE REM'S BIG SIS, RIGHT?
SU (SWF)
I CAN...
BO (WHOOSH)
...USE SOMEWHAT VIOLENT WIND MAGIC. NOTHING MORE.

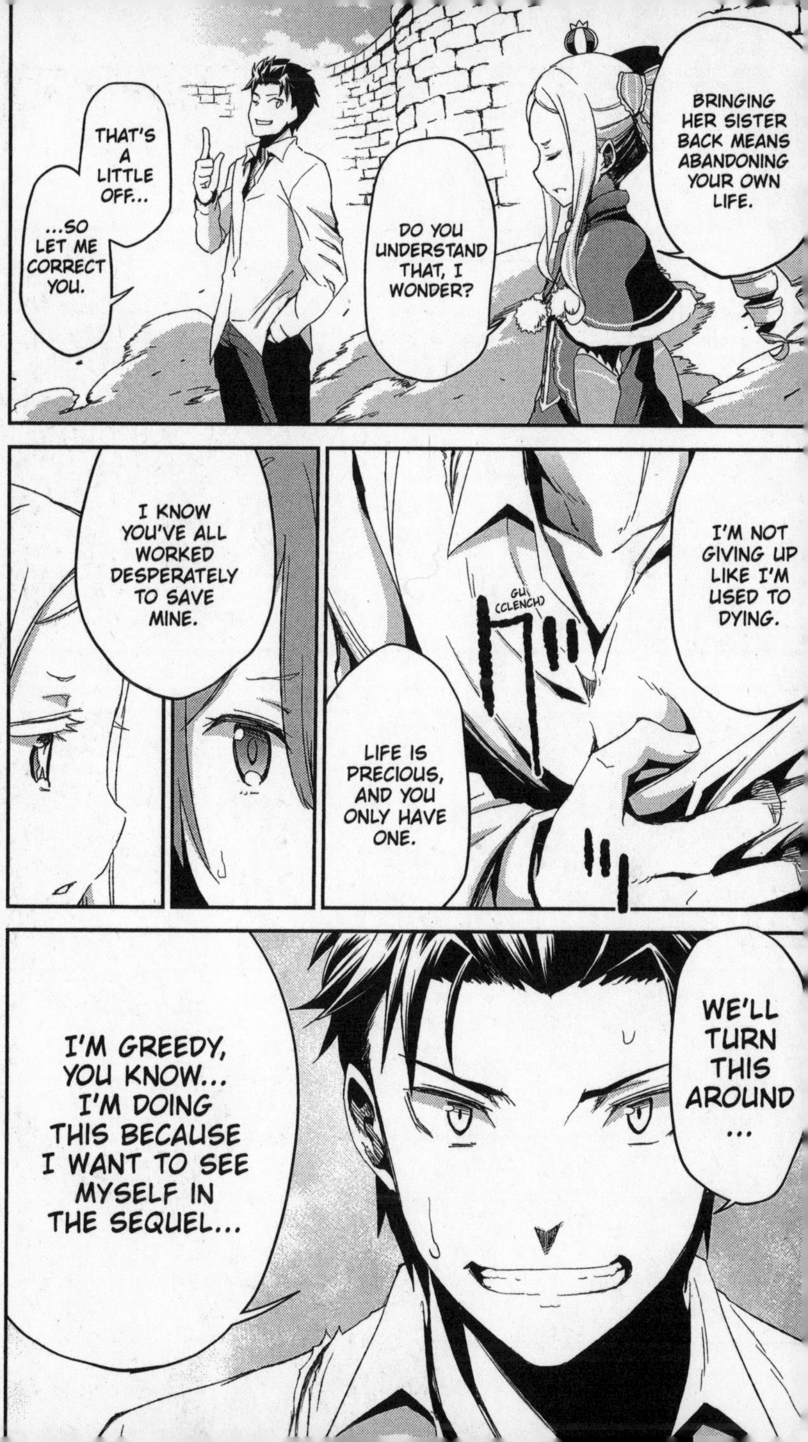
BRINGING HER SISTER BACK MEANS ABANDONING YOUR OWN LIFE.
DO YOU UNDERSTAND THAT, I WONDER?
THAT'S A LITTLE OFF...
...SO LET ME CORRECT YOU.
I'M NOT GIVING UP LIKE I'M USED TO DYING.
GU (CLENCH)
LIFE IS PRECIOUS, AND YOU ONLY HAVE ONE.
I KNOW YOU'VE ALL WORKED DESPERATELY TO SAVE MINE.
WE'LL TURN THIS AROUND...
I'M GREEDY, YOU KNOW... I'M DOING THIS BECAUSE I WANT TO SEE MYSELF IN THE SEQUEL...

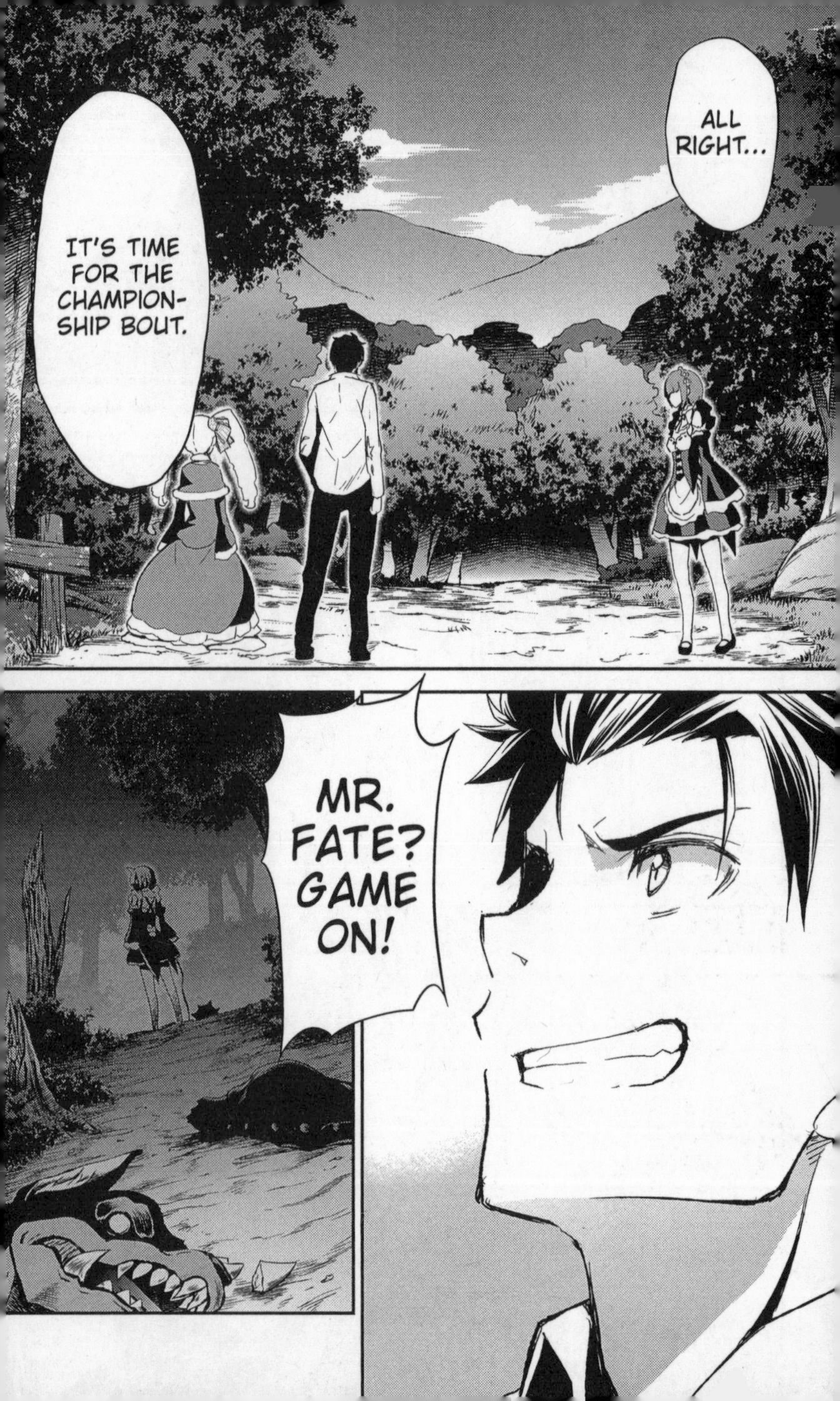
ALL RIGHT...
IT'S TIME FOR THE CHAMPIONSHIP BOUT.
MR. FATE? GAME ON!

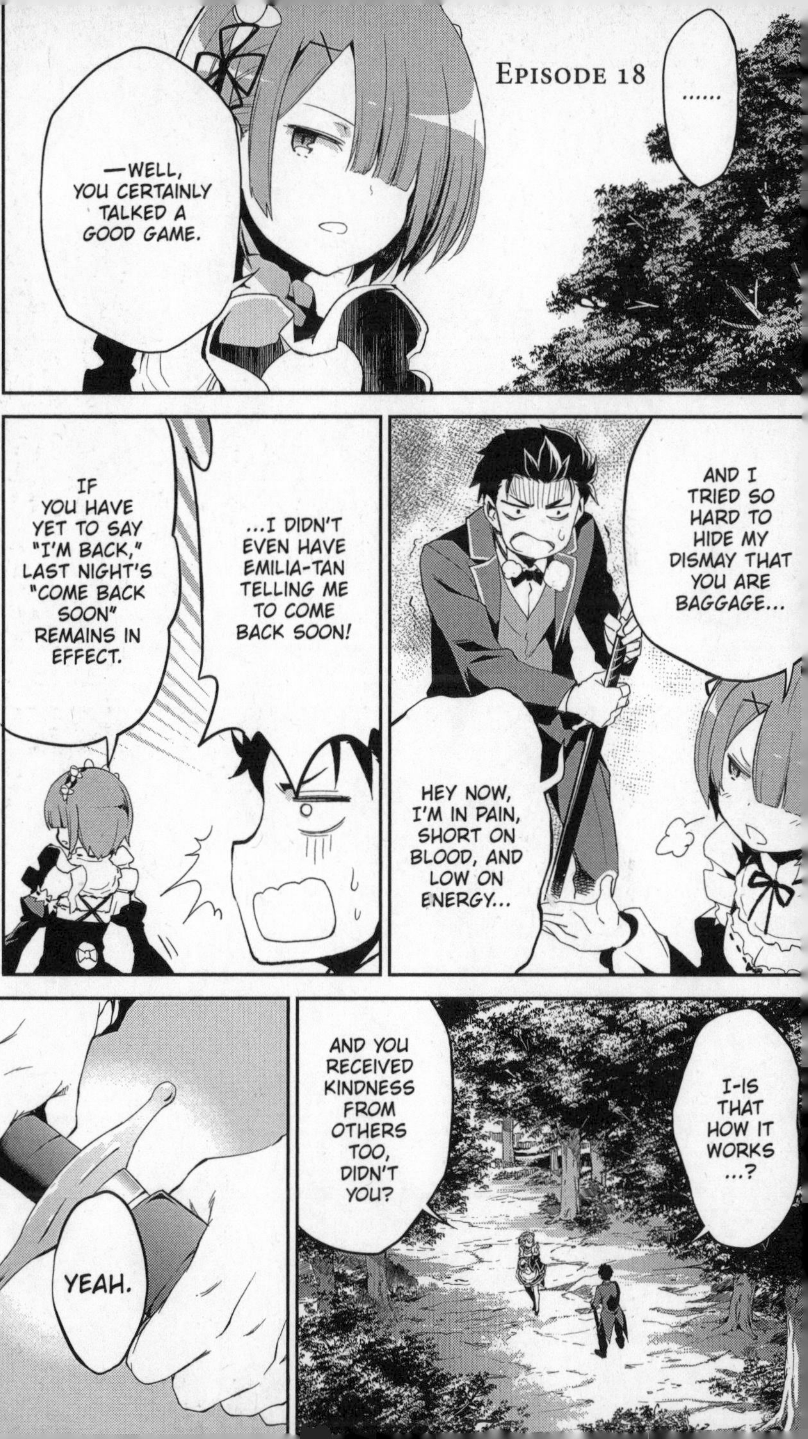
......
EPISODE 18
—WELL, YOU CERTAINLY TALKED A GOOD GAME.
AND I TRIED SO HARD TO HIDE MY DISMAY THAT YOU ARE BAGGAGE...
HEY NOW, I'M IN PAIN, SHORT ON BLOOD, AND LOW ON ENERGY...
...I DIDN'T EVEN HAVE EMILIA-TAN TELLING ME TO COME BACK SOON!
IF YOU HAVE YET TO SAY "I'M BACK," LAST NIGHT'S "COME BACK SOON" REMAINS IN EFFECT.
I-IS THAT HOW IT WORKS ...?
AND YOU RECEIVED KINDNESS FROM OTHERS TOO, DIDN'T YOU?
YEAH.

Episode 18
The Way of the Demonic ②

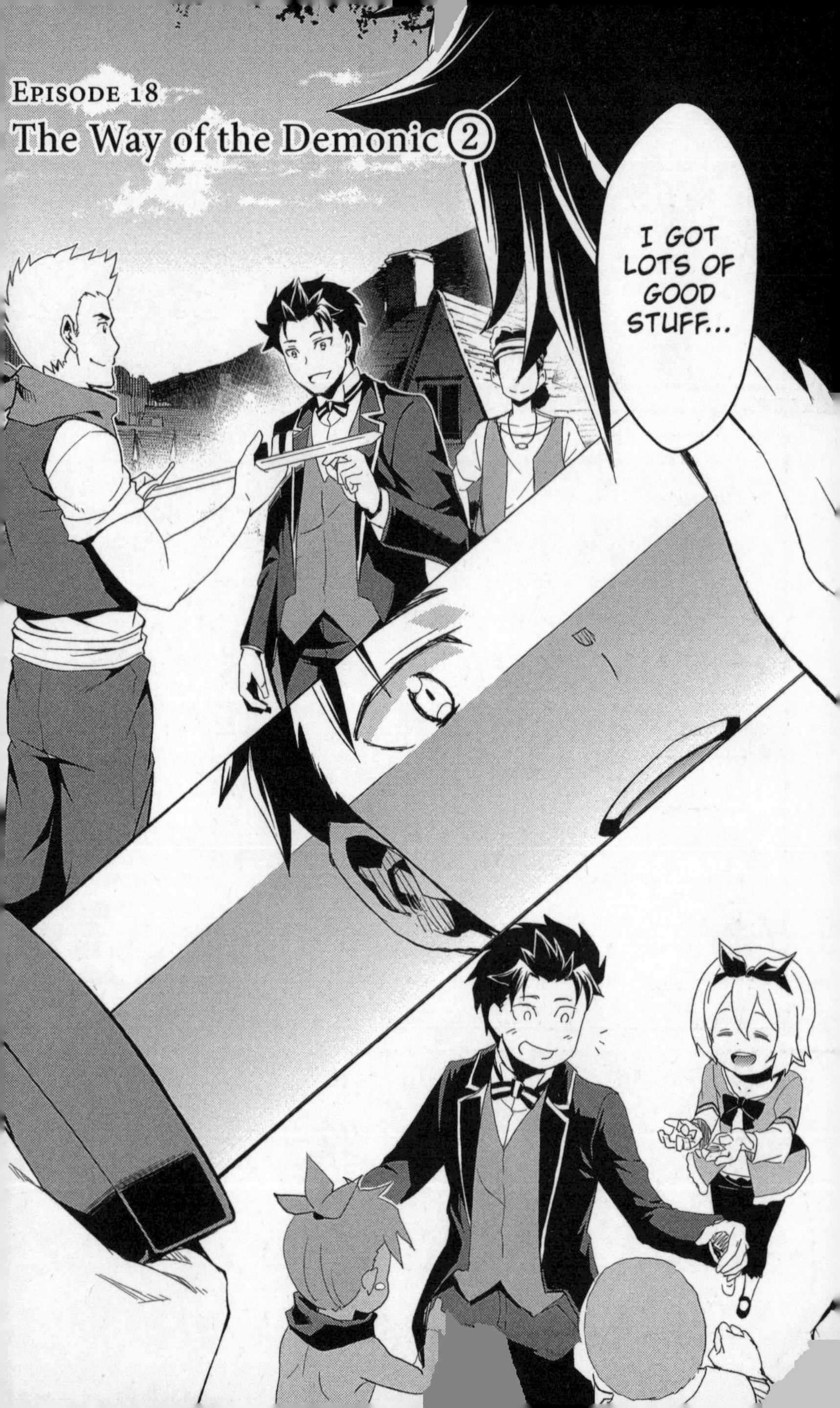
I GOT LOTS OF GOOD STUFF...

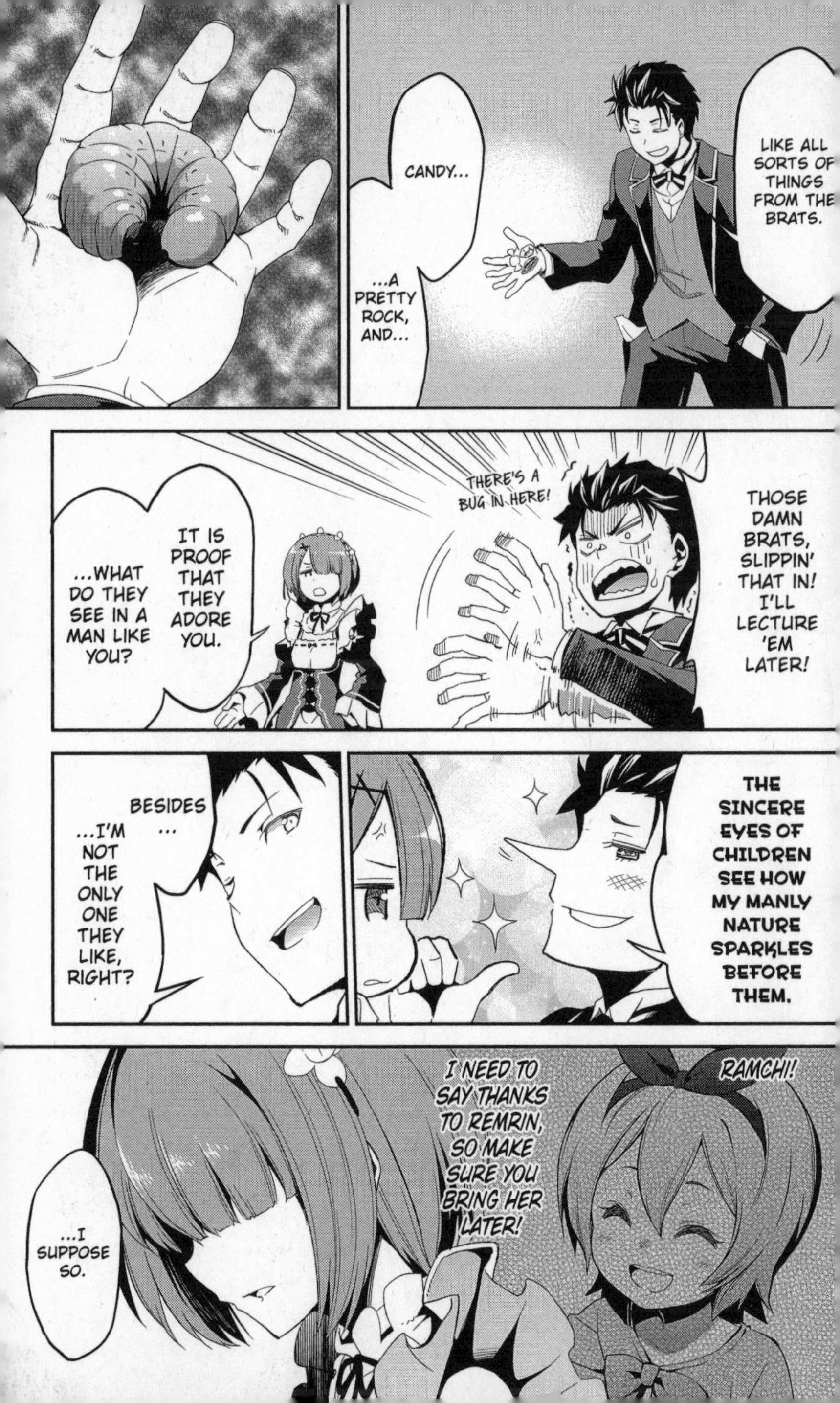
LIKE ALL SORTS OF THINGS FROM THE BRATS.
CANDY...
...A PRETTY ROCK, AND...
THOSE DAMN BRATS, SLIPPIN' THAT IN! I'LL LECTURE 'EM LATER!
THERE'S A BUG IN HERE!
IT IS PROOF THAT THEY ADORE YOU.
...WHAT DO THEY SEE IN A MAN LIKE YOU?
THE SINCERE EYES OF CHILDREN SEE HOW MY MANLY NATURE SPARKLES BEFORE THEM.
BESIDES...
...I'M NOT THE ONLY ONE THEY LIKE, RIGHT?
RAMCHI!
I NEED TO SAY THANKS TO REMRIN, SO MAKE SURE YOU BRING HER LATER!
...I SUPPOSE SO.

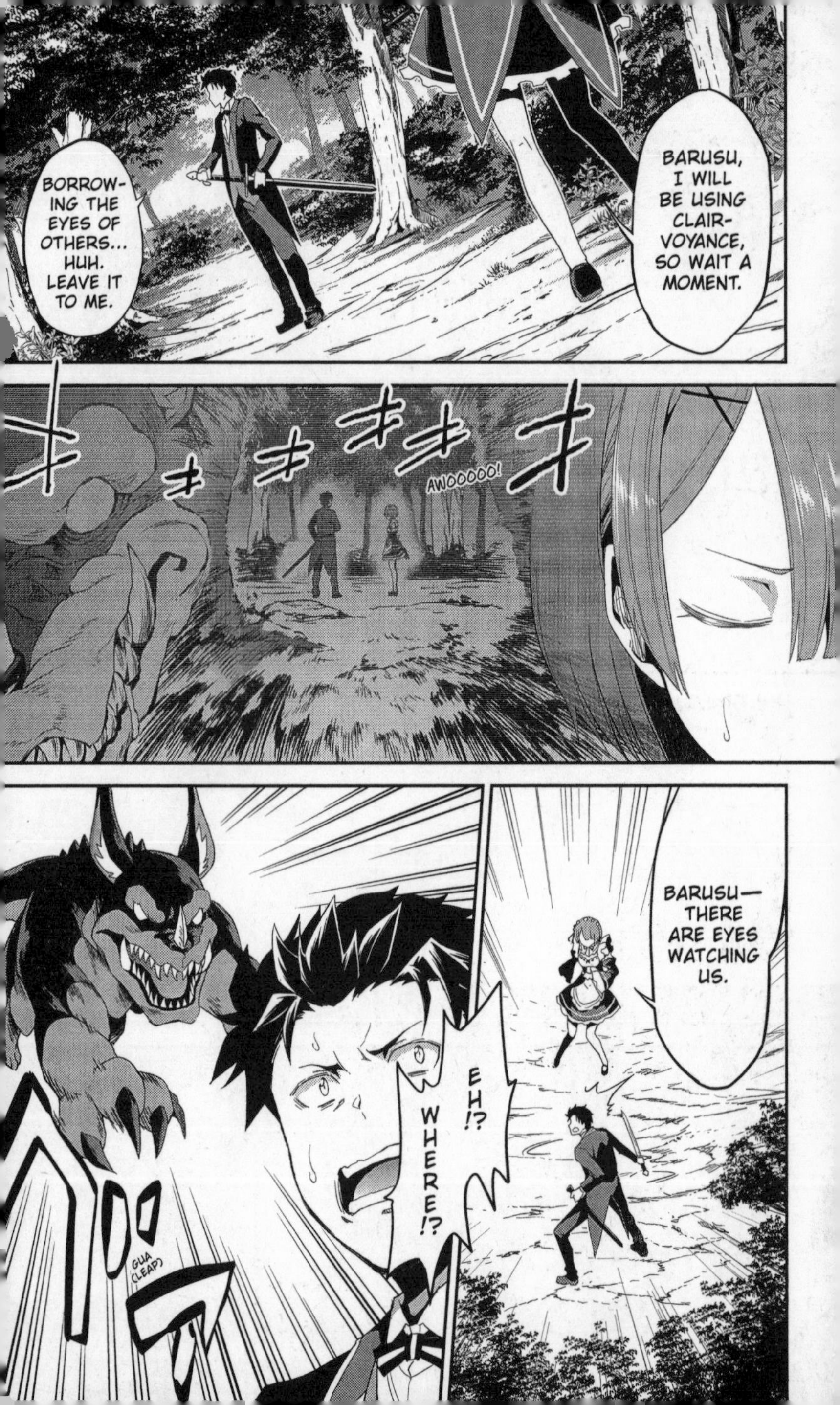
BARUSU, I WILL BE USING CLAIR-VOYANCE, SO WAIT A MOMENT.
BORROW-ING THE EYES OF OTHERS... HUH. LEAVE IT TO ME.
AWOOOOO!
BARUSU— THERE ARE EYES WATCHING US.
EH!? WHERE!?
GUA (LEAP)

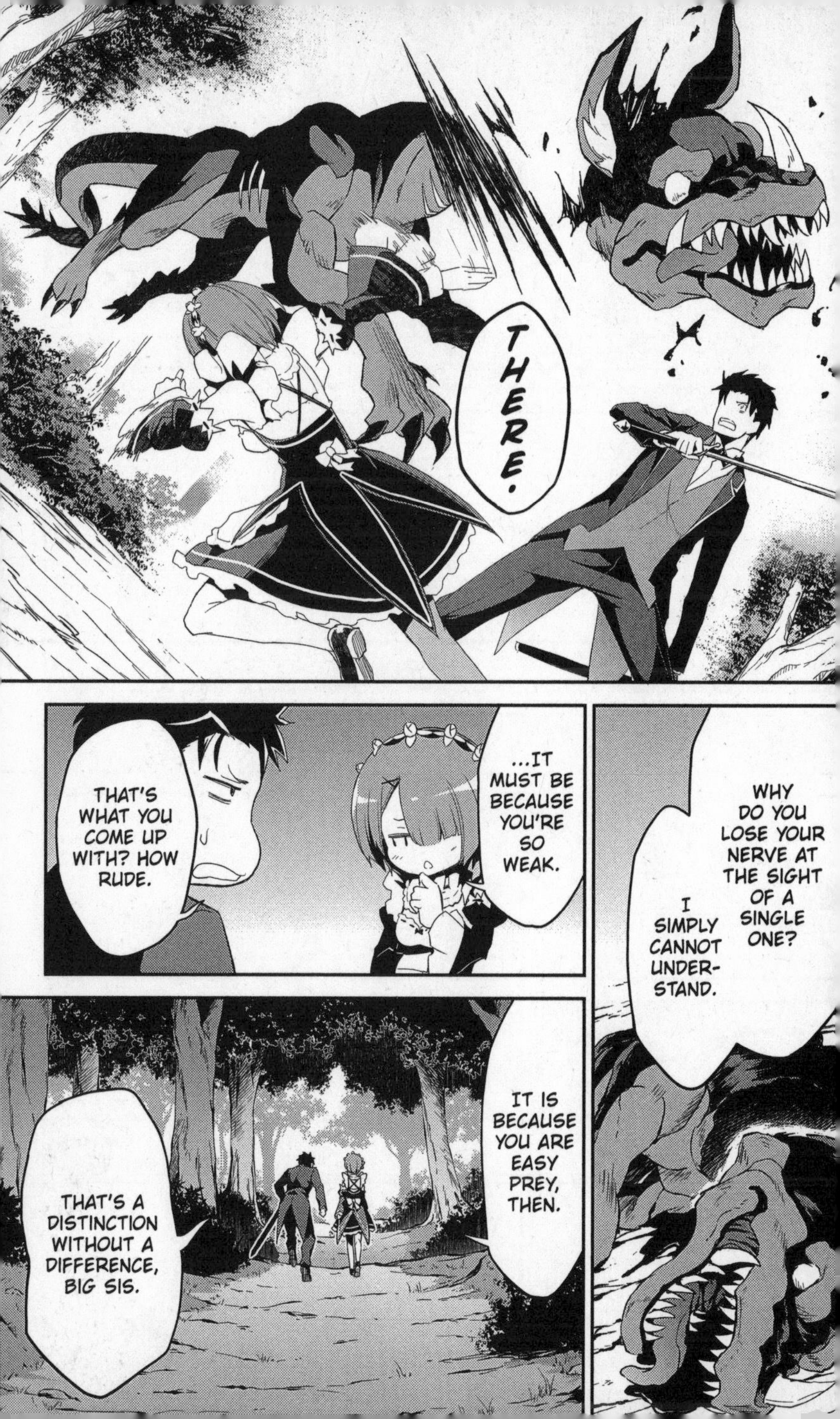
THERE.
WHY DO YOU LOSE YOUR NERVE AT THE SIGHT OF A SINGLE ONE?
I SIMPLY CANNOT UNDER-STAND.
...IT MUST BE BECAUSE YOU'RE SO WEAK.
THAT'S WHAT YOU COME UP WITH? HOW RUDE.
IT IS BECAUSE YOU ARE EASY PREY, THEN.
THAT'S A DISTINCTION WITHOUT A DIFFERENCE, BIG SIS.

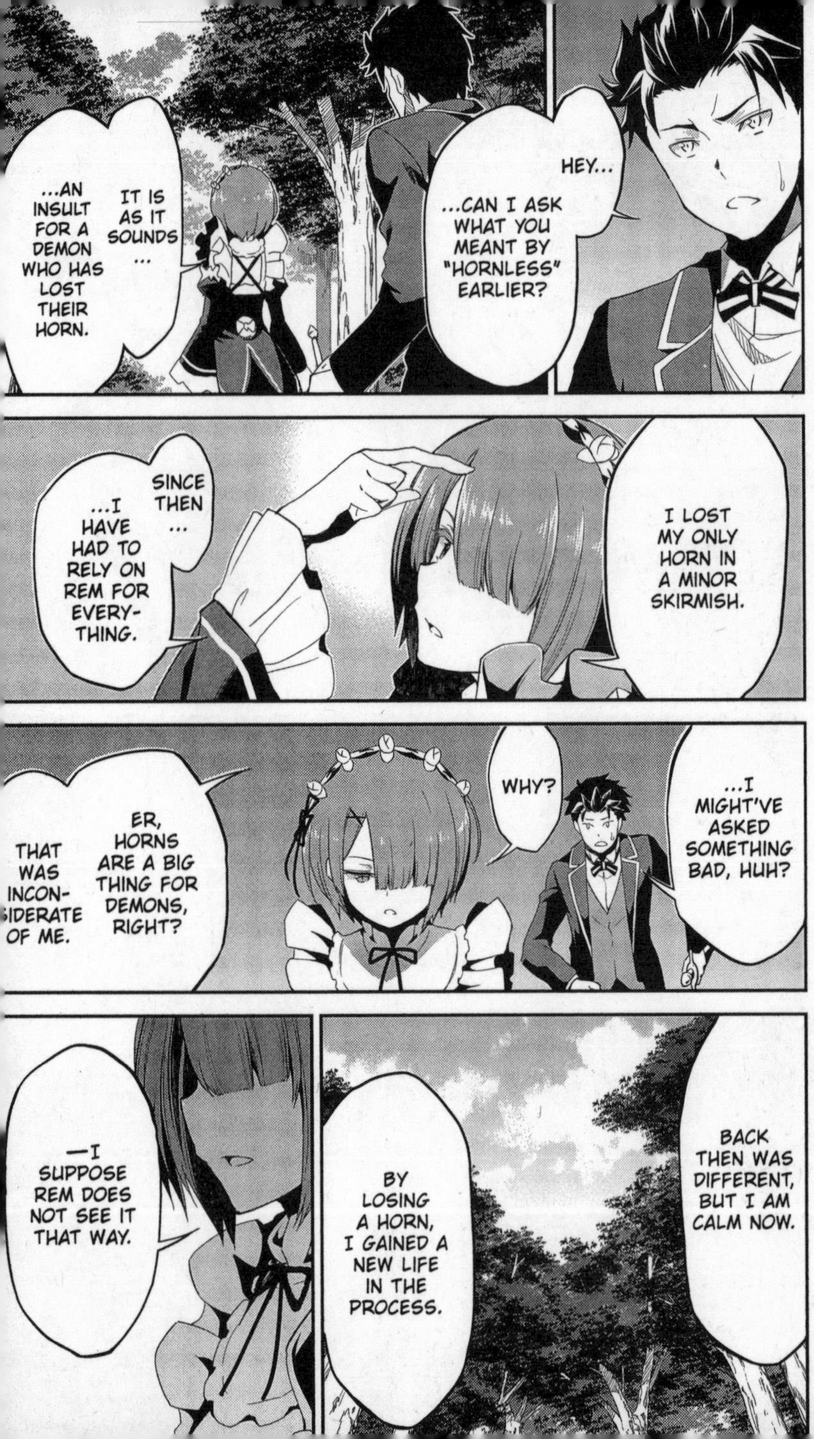
HEY...
...CAN I ASK WHAT YOU MEANT BY "HORNLESS" EARLIER?
IT IS AS IT SOUNDS ...
...AN INSULT FOR A DEMON WHO HAS LOST THEIR HORN.
I LOST MY ONLY HORN IN A MINOR SKIRMISH.
SINCE THEN ...
...I HAVE HAD TO RELY ON REM FOR EVERYTHING.
...I MIGHT'VE ASKED SOMETHING BAD, HUH?
WHY?
ER, HORNS ARE A BIG THING FOR DEMONS, RIGHT?
THAT WAS INCONSIDERATE OF ME.
BACK THEN WAS DIFFERENT, BUT I AM CALM NOW.
BY LOSING A HORN, I GAINED A NEW LIFE IN THE PROCESS.
—I SUPPOSE REM DOES NOT SEE IT THAT WAY.

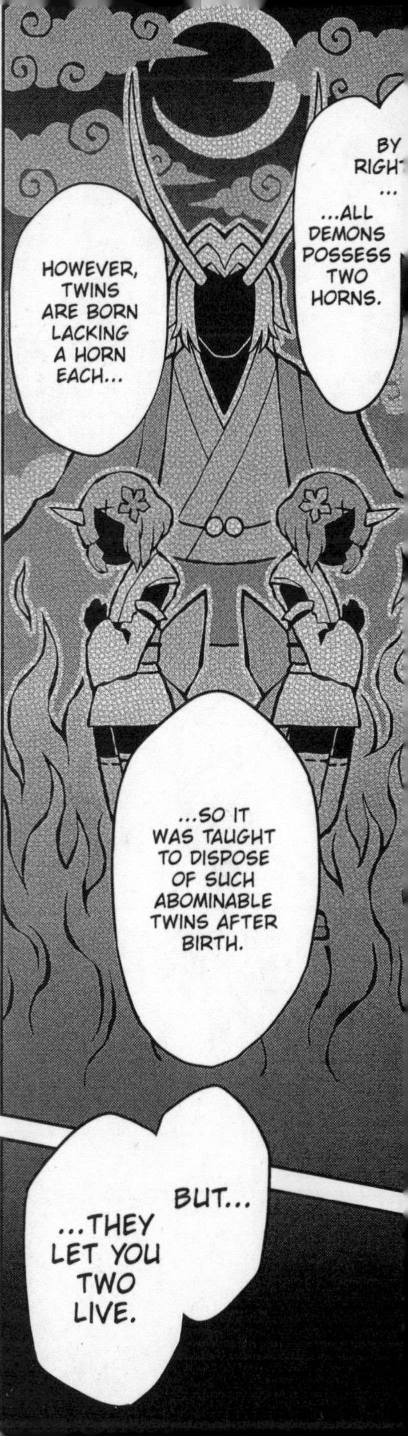
BY RIGHT ...
...ALL DEMONS POSSESS TWO HORNS.
HOWEVER, TWINS ARE BORN LACKING A HORN EACH...
...SO IT WAS TAUGHT TO DISPOSE OF SUCH ABOMINABLE TWINS AFTER BIRTH.
BUT...
...THEY LET YOU TWO LIVE.

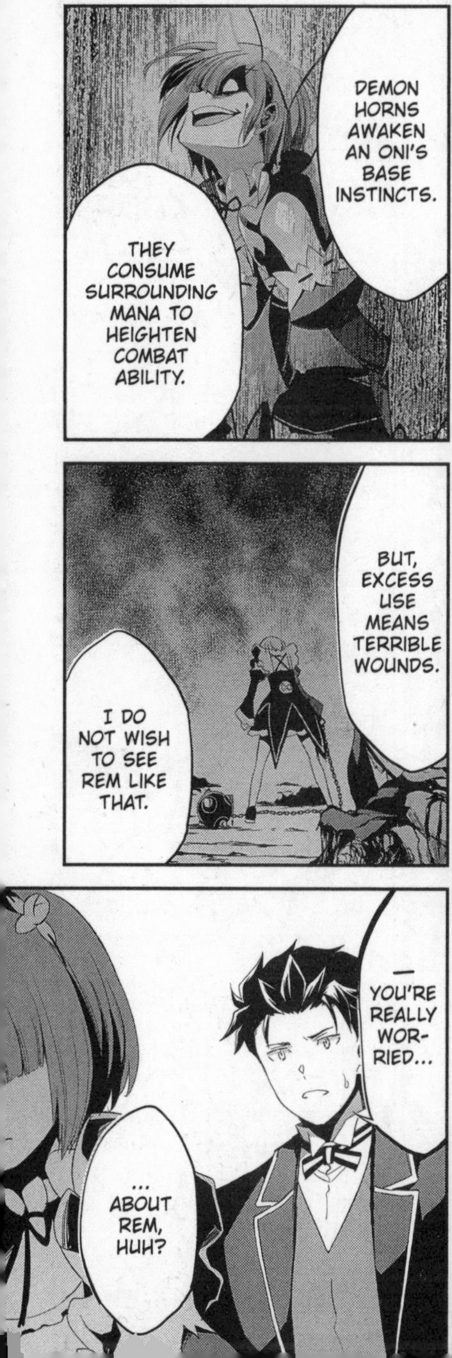
DEMON HORNS AWAKEN AN ONI'S BASE INSTINCTS.
THEY CONSUME SURROUNDING MANA TO HEIGHTEN COMBAT ABILITY.
BUT, EXCESS USE MEANS TERRIBLE WOUNDS.
I DO NOT WISH TO SEE REM LIKE THAT.
—YOU'RE REALLY WOR-RIED...
...ABOUT REM, HUH?

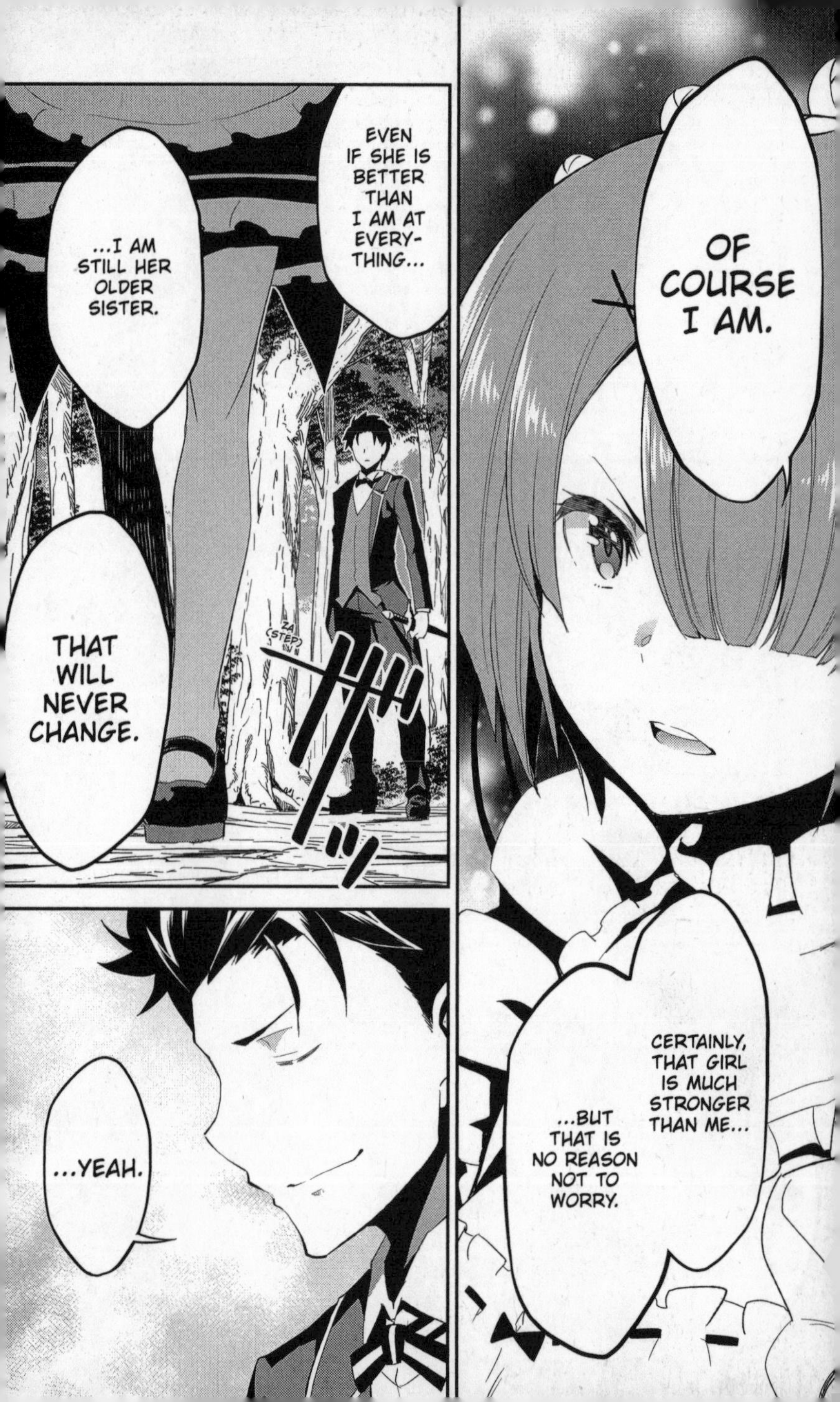
OF COURSE I AM.
CERTAINLY, THAT GIRL IS MUCH STRONGER THAN ME...
...BUT THAT IS NO REASON NOT TO WORRY.
EVEN IF SHE IS BETTER THAN I AM AT EVERY-THING...
...I AM STILL HER OLDER SISTER.
ZA (STEP)
THAT WILL NEVER CHANGE.
...YEAH.

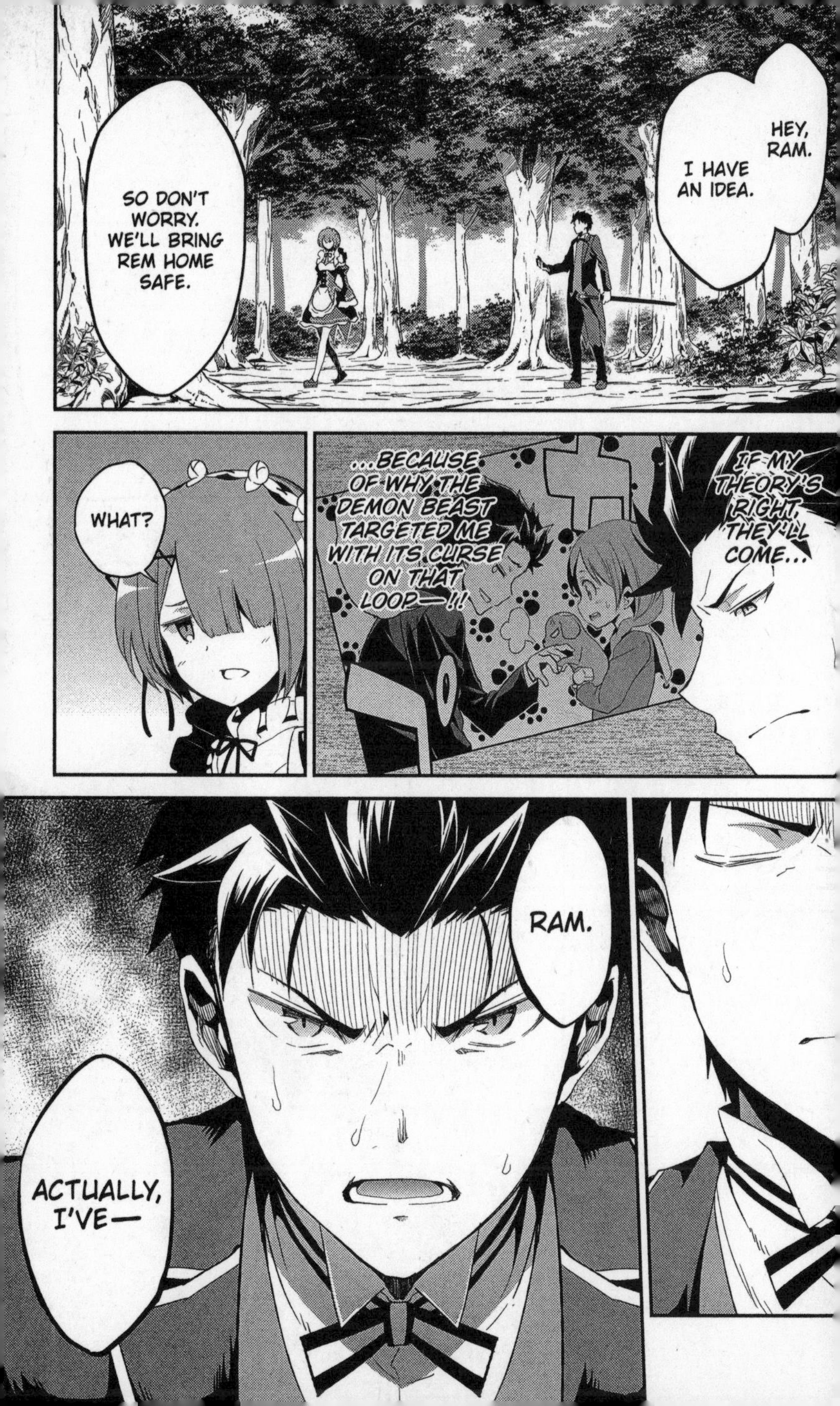
HEY, RAM. I HAVE AN IDEA.
SO DON'T WORRY. WE'LL BRING REM HOME SAFE.
IF MY THEORY'S RIGHT, THEY'LL COME...
...BECAUSE OF WHY THE DEMON BEAST TARGETED ME WITH ITS CURSE ON THAT LOOP—!!
WHAT?
RAM.
ACTUALLY, I'VE—

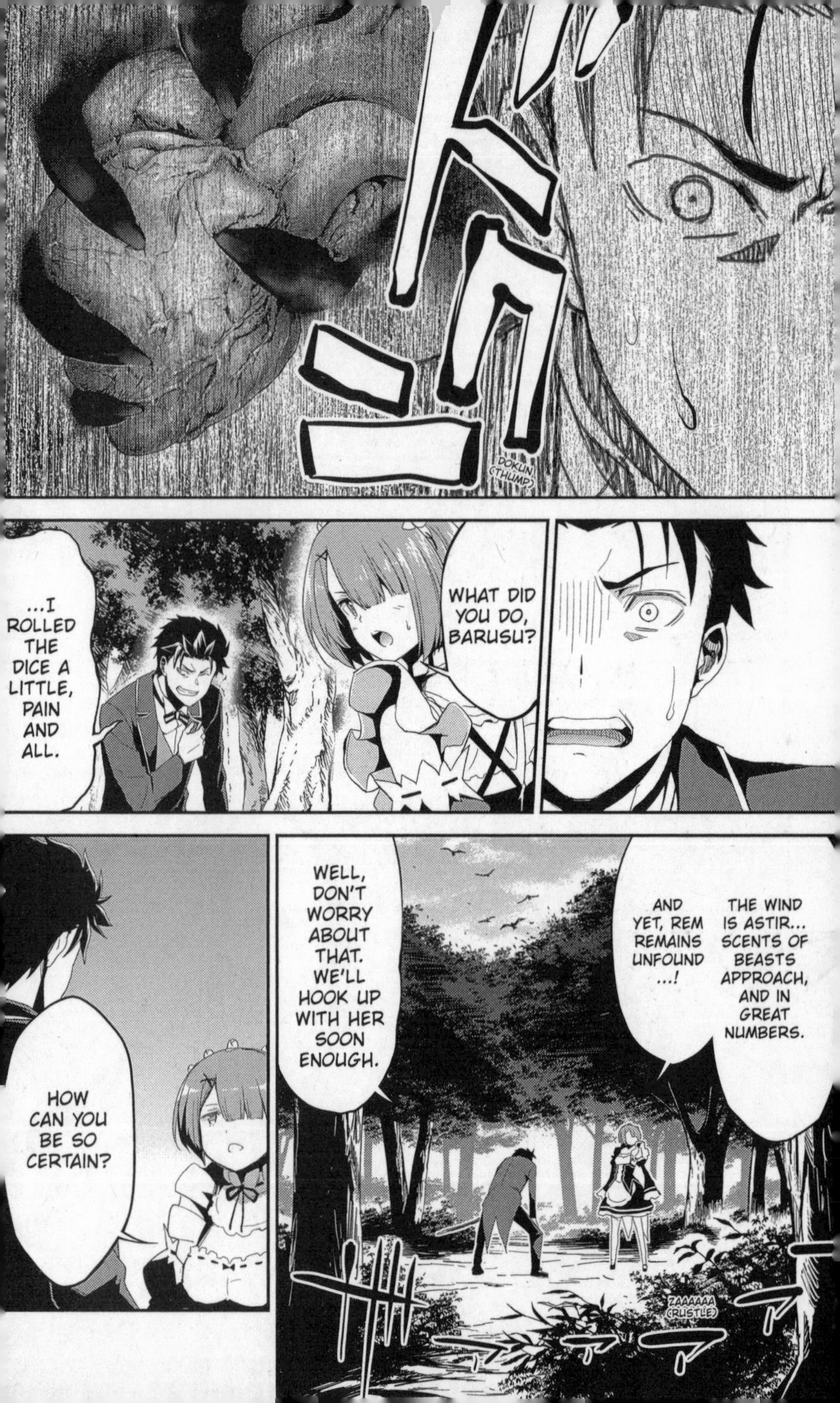
DOKUN (THUMP)
WHAT DID YOU DO, BARUSU?
...I ROLLED THE DICE A LITTLE, PAIN AND ALL.
THE WIND IS ASTIR... SCENTS OF BEASTS APPROACH, AND IN GREAT NUMBERS.
AND YET, REM REMAINS UNFOUND...!
WELL, DON'T WORRY ABOUT THAT. WE'LL HOOK UP WITH HER SOON ENOUGH.
ZAAAAAA (RUSTLE)
HOW CAN YOU BE SO CERTAIN?

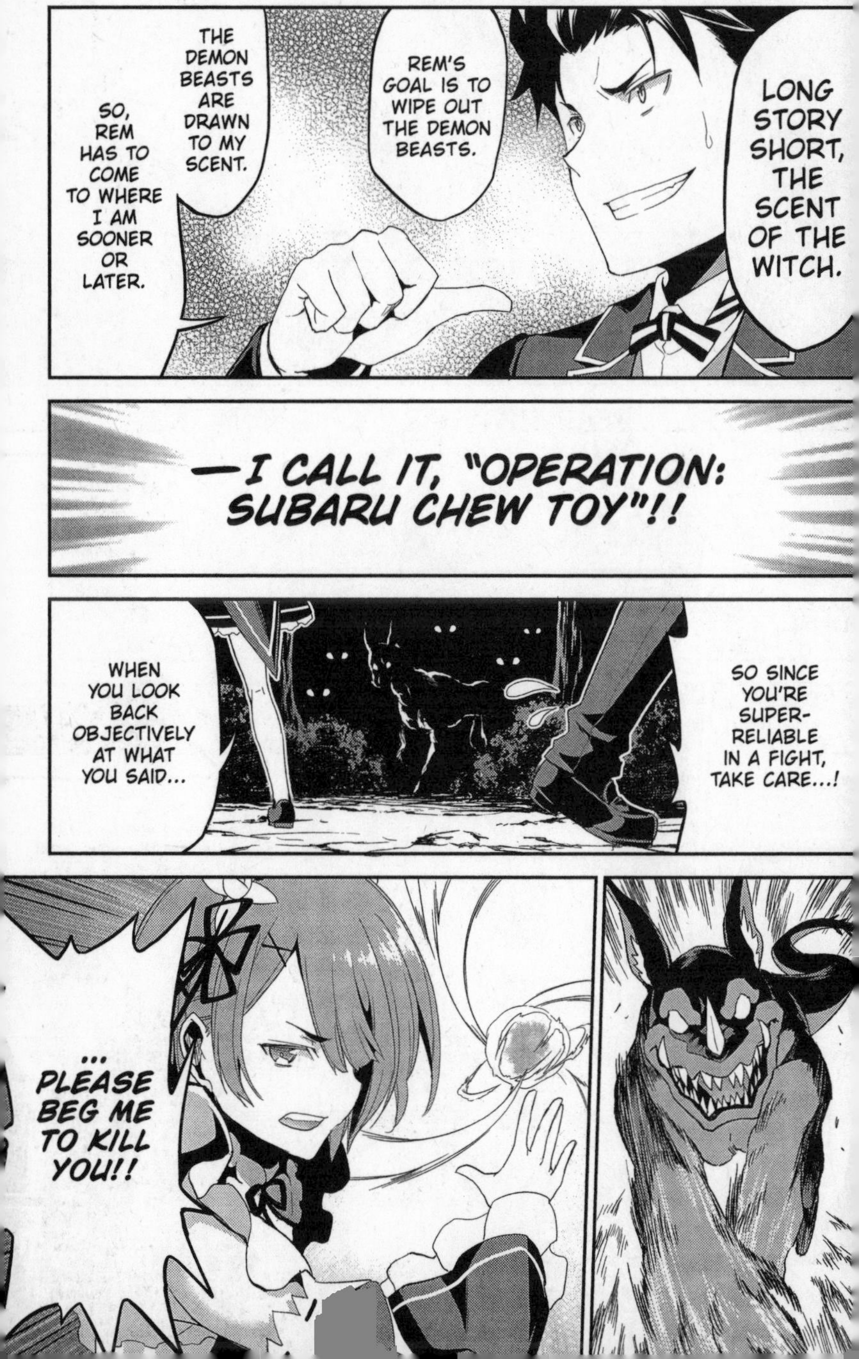
LONG STORY SHORT, THE SCENT OF THE WITCH.
REM'S GOAL IS TO WIPE OUT THE DEMON BEASTS.
THE DEMON BEASTS ARE DRAWN TO MY SCENT.
SO, REM HAS TO COME TO WHERE I AM SOONER OR LATER.
—I CALL IT, "OPERATION: SUBARU CHEW TOY"!!
SO SINCE YOU'RE SUPER-RELIABLE IN A FIGHT, TAKE CARE...!
WHEN YOU LOOK BACK OBJECTIVELY AT WHAT YOU SAID...
...PLEASE BEG ME TO KILL YOU!!

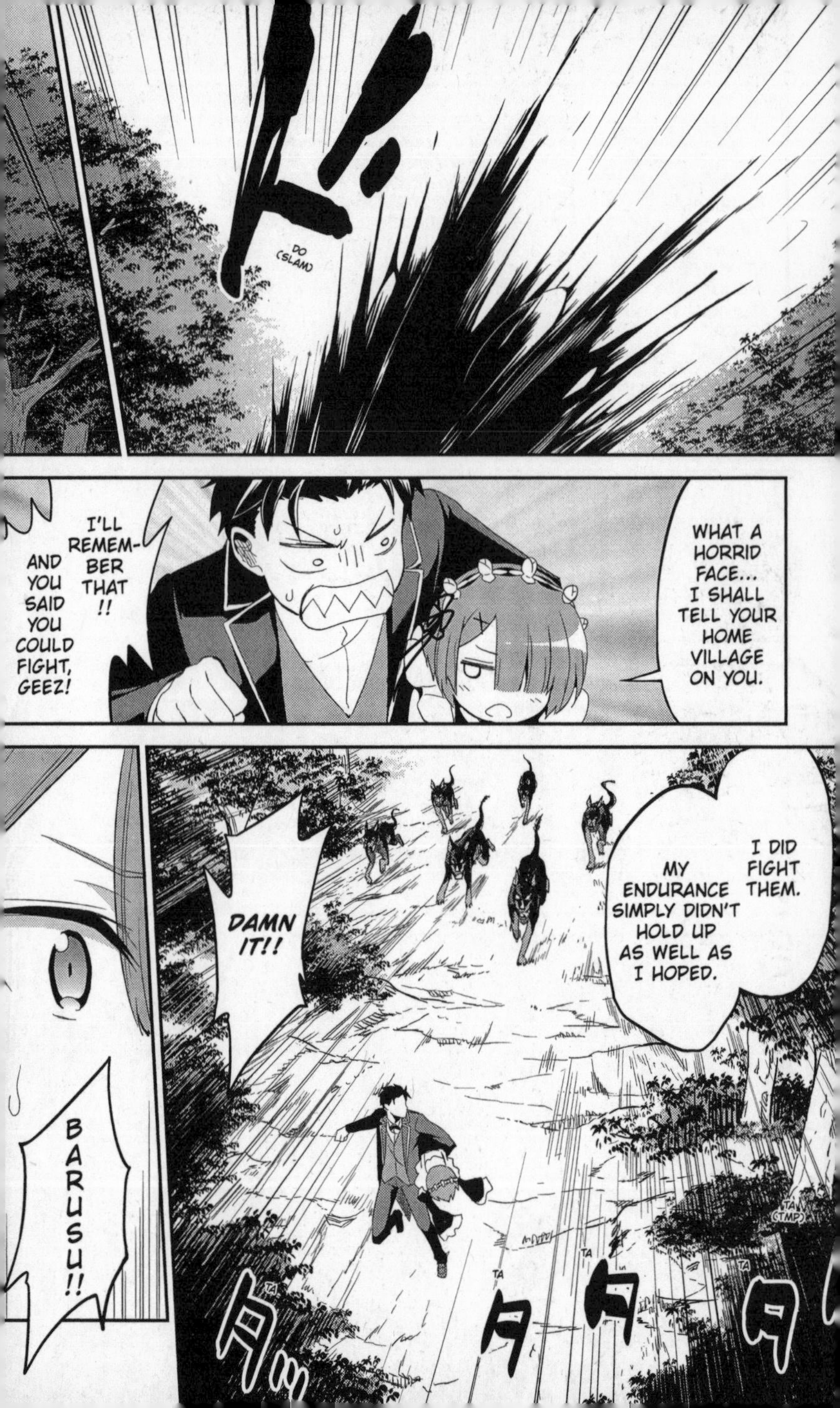
DO (SLAM)
WHAT A HORRID FACE... I SHALL TELL YOUR HOME VILLAGE ON YOU.
I'LL REMEMBER THAT!!
AND YOU SAID YOU COULD FIGHT, GEEZ!
I DID FIGHT THEM.
MY ENDURANCE SIMPLY DIDN'T HOLD UP AS WELL AS I HOPED.
DAMN IT!!
TA (TMP)
TA
TA
TA
BARUSU!!

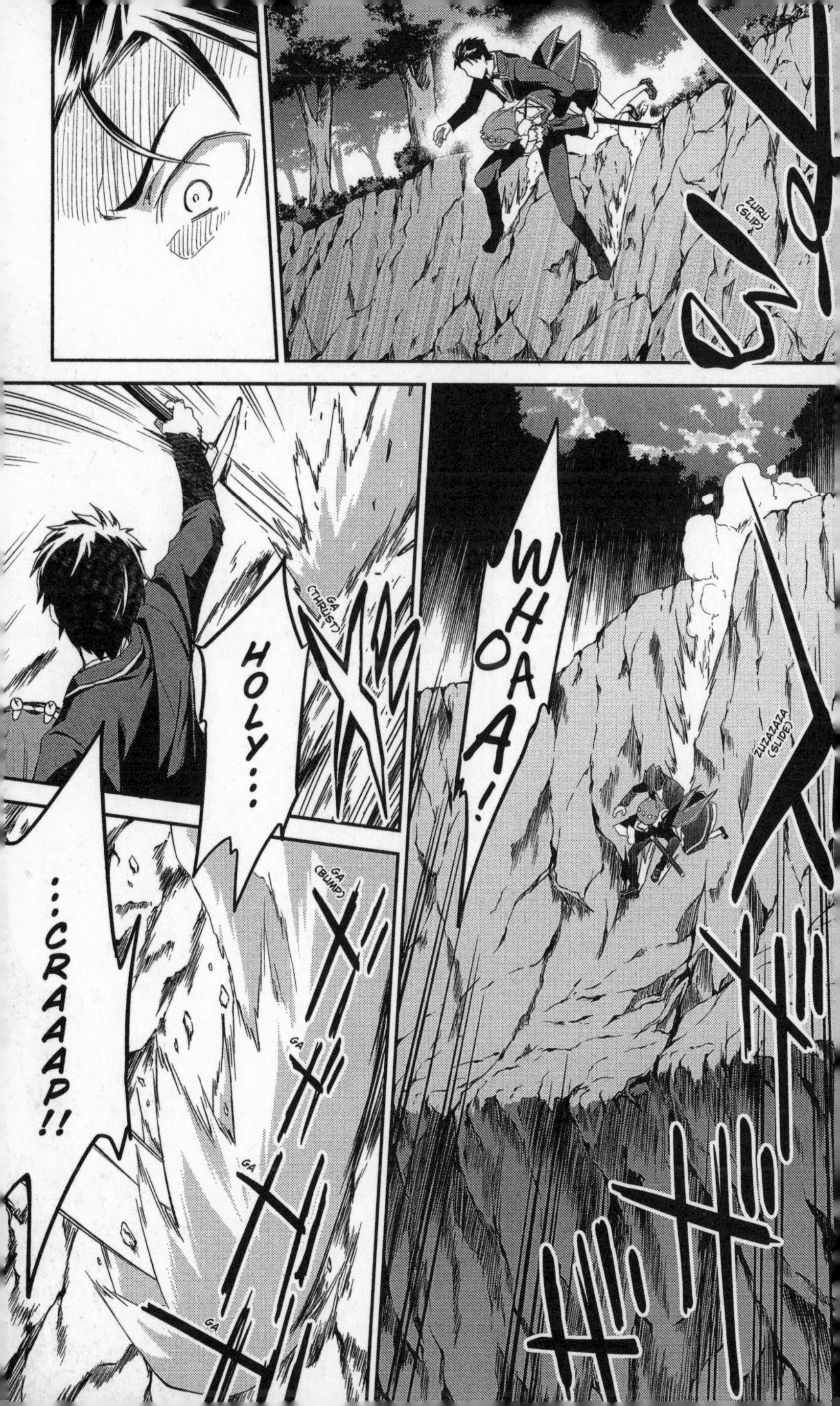
ZURU (SLIP)
WHOA A!
ZUZAZAZA (SLIDE)
HOLY...
GA (THRUST)
...CRAAAAP!!
GA (BUMP)
GA
GA
GA

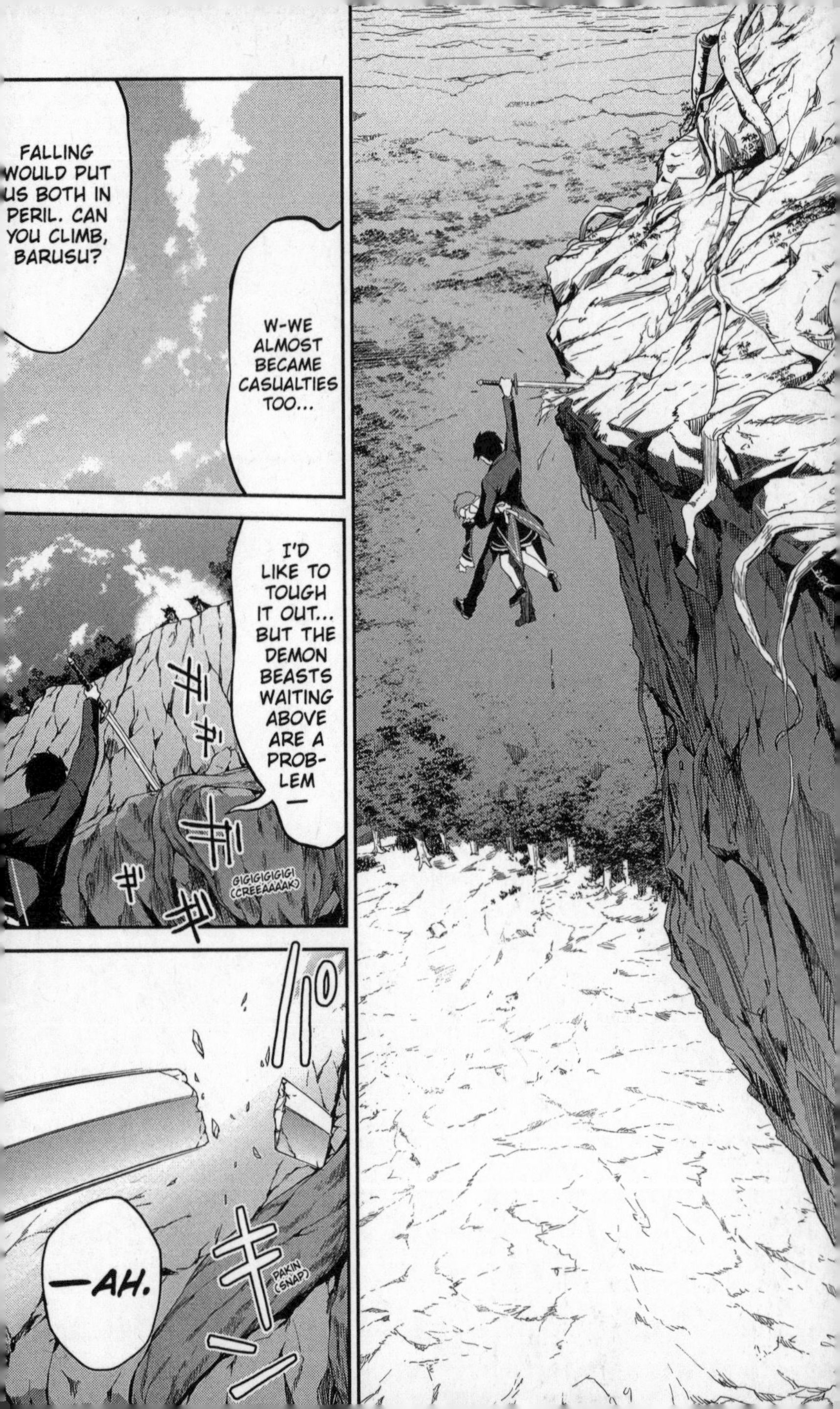

W-WE ALMOST BECAME CASUALTIES TOO...
FALLING WOULD PUT US BOTH IN PERIL. CAN YOU CLIMB, BARUSU?
I'D LIKE TO TOUGH IT OUT... BUT THE DEMON BEASTS WAITING ABOVE ARE A PROB-LEM—
GIGIGIGIGIGI (CREEAAAAK)
PAKIN (SNAP)
—AH.

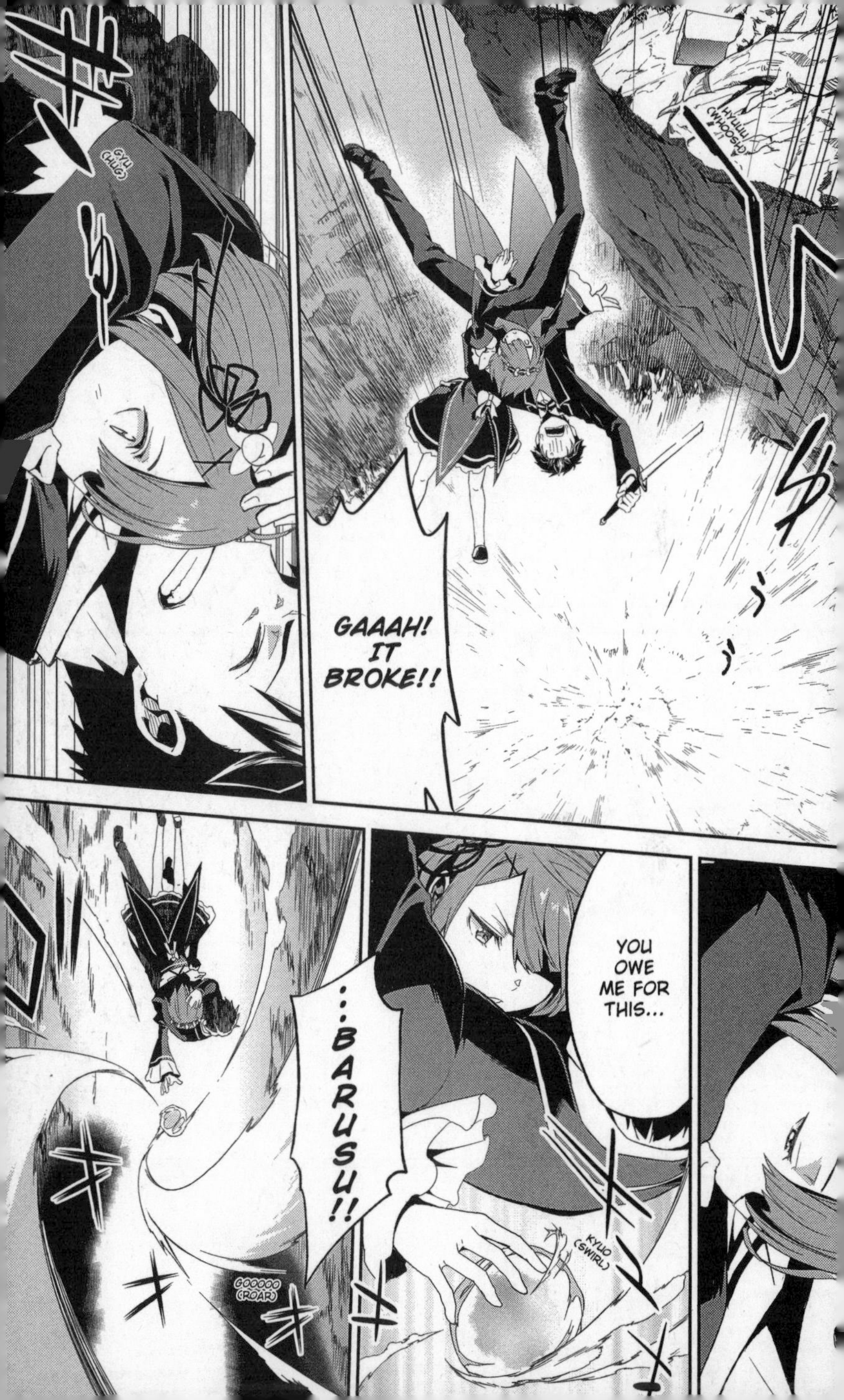
HYUUUN (WHOOSH)
GAAAH! IT BROKE!!
GYU (HUG)
YOU OWE ME FOR THIS...
KYUO (SWIRL)
...BARUSU!!
GOOOOO (ROAR)

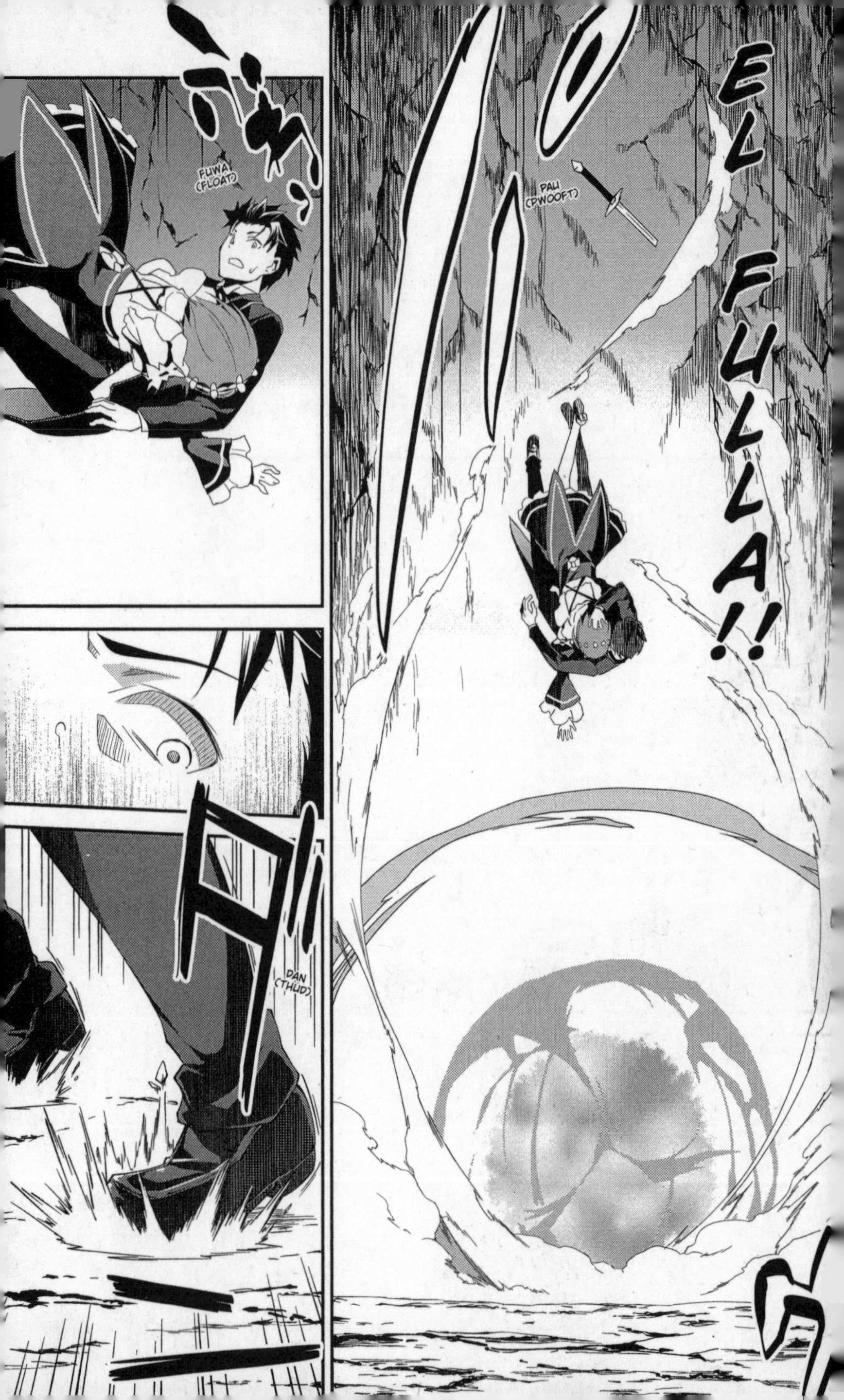
PAU
(PWOOFT)
EL FULLA!!
FUWA
(FLOAT)
DAN
(THUD)

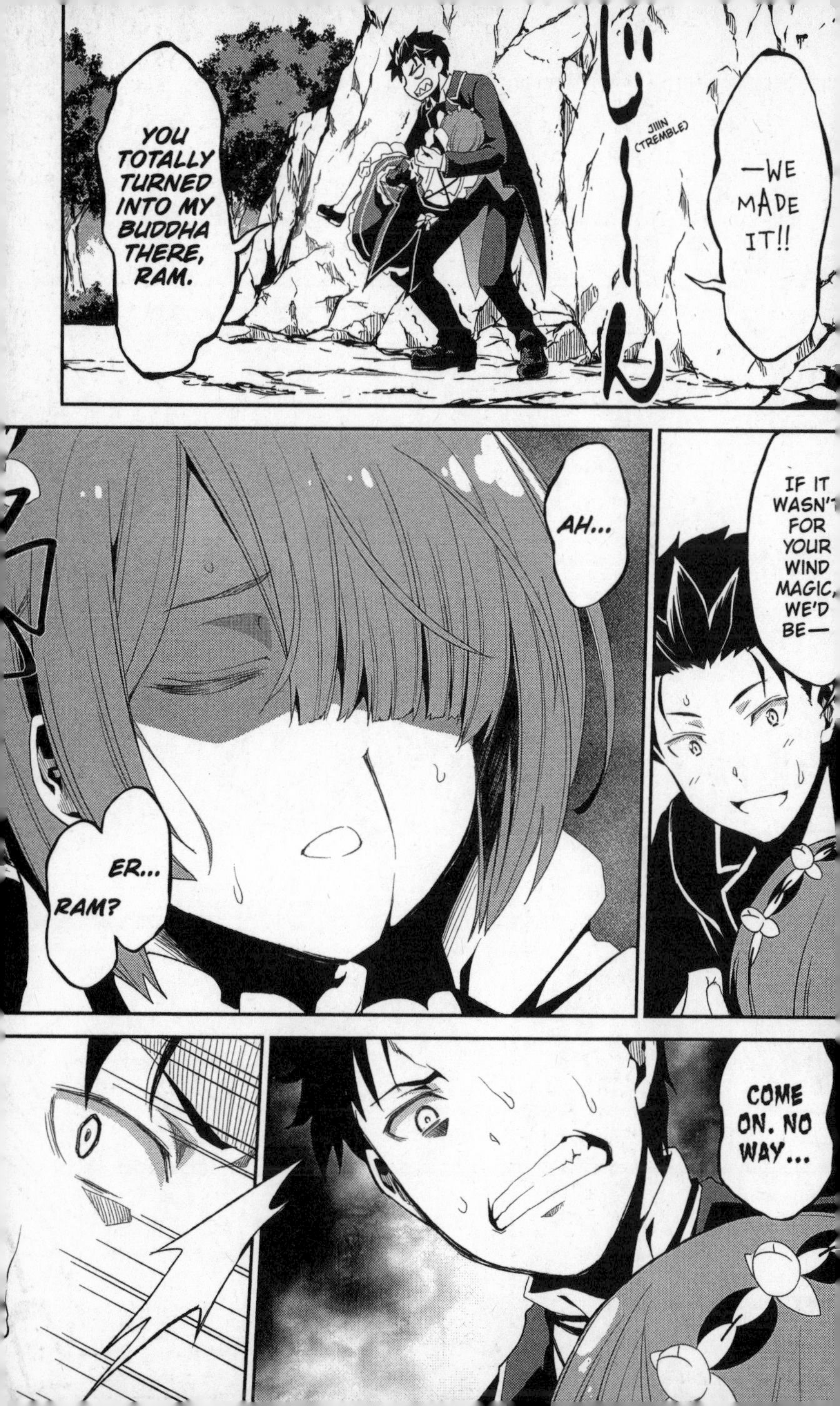
—WE MADE IT!!
JIIIN (TREMBLE)
YOU TOTALLY TURNED INTO MY BUDDHA THERE, RAM.
IF IT WASN'T FOR YOUR WIND MAGIC, WE'D BE—
AH...
ER... RAM?
COME ON. NO WAY...

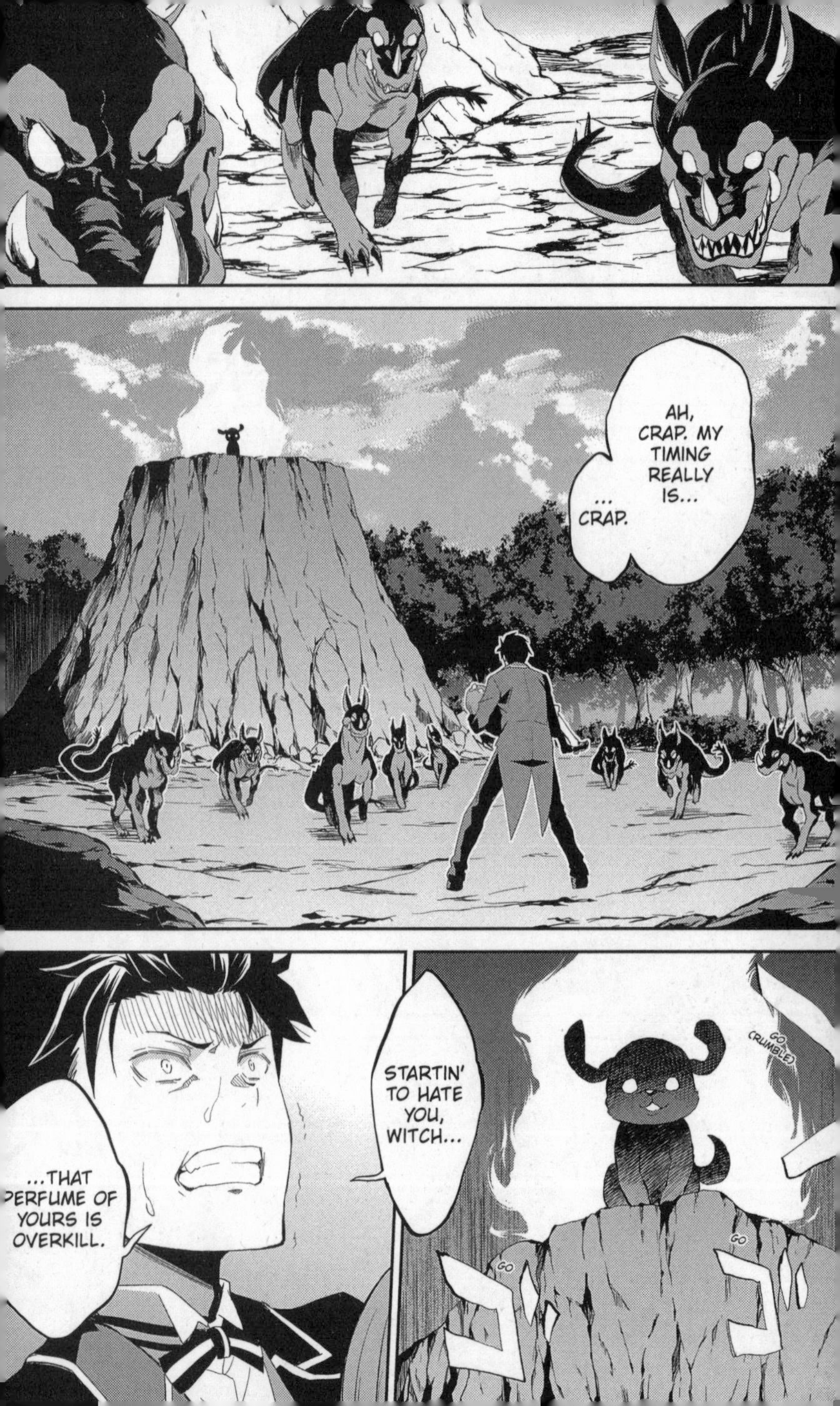
AH, CRAP. MY TIMING REALLY IS...
...CRAP.
GO (CRUMBLE)
GO
GO
STARTIN' TO HATE YOU, WITCH...
...THAT PERFUME OF YOURS IS OVERKILL.

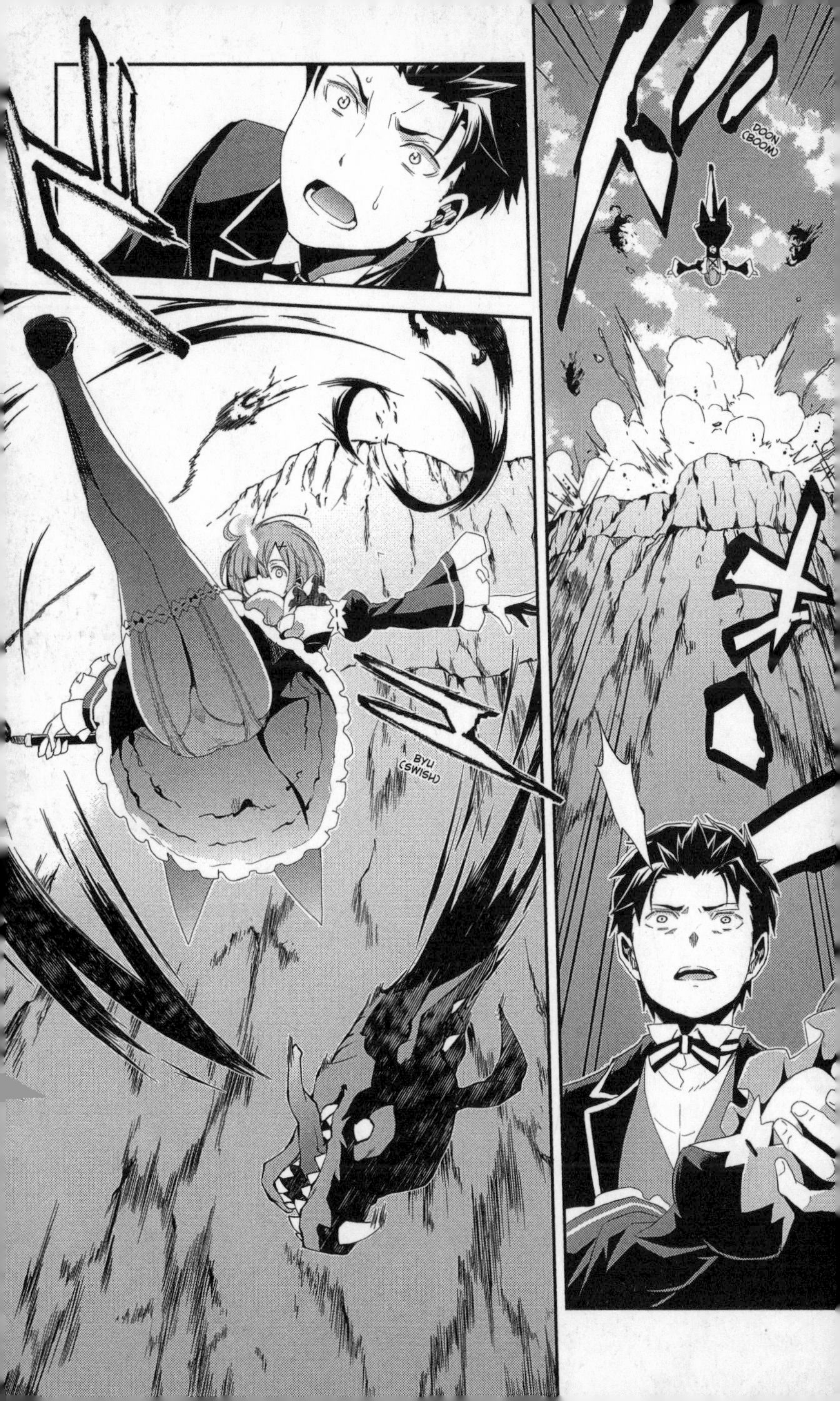
DOON
(BOOM)
BYU
(SWISH)

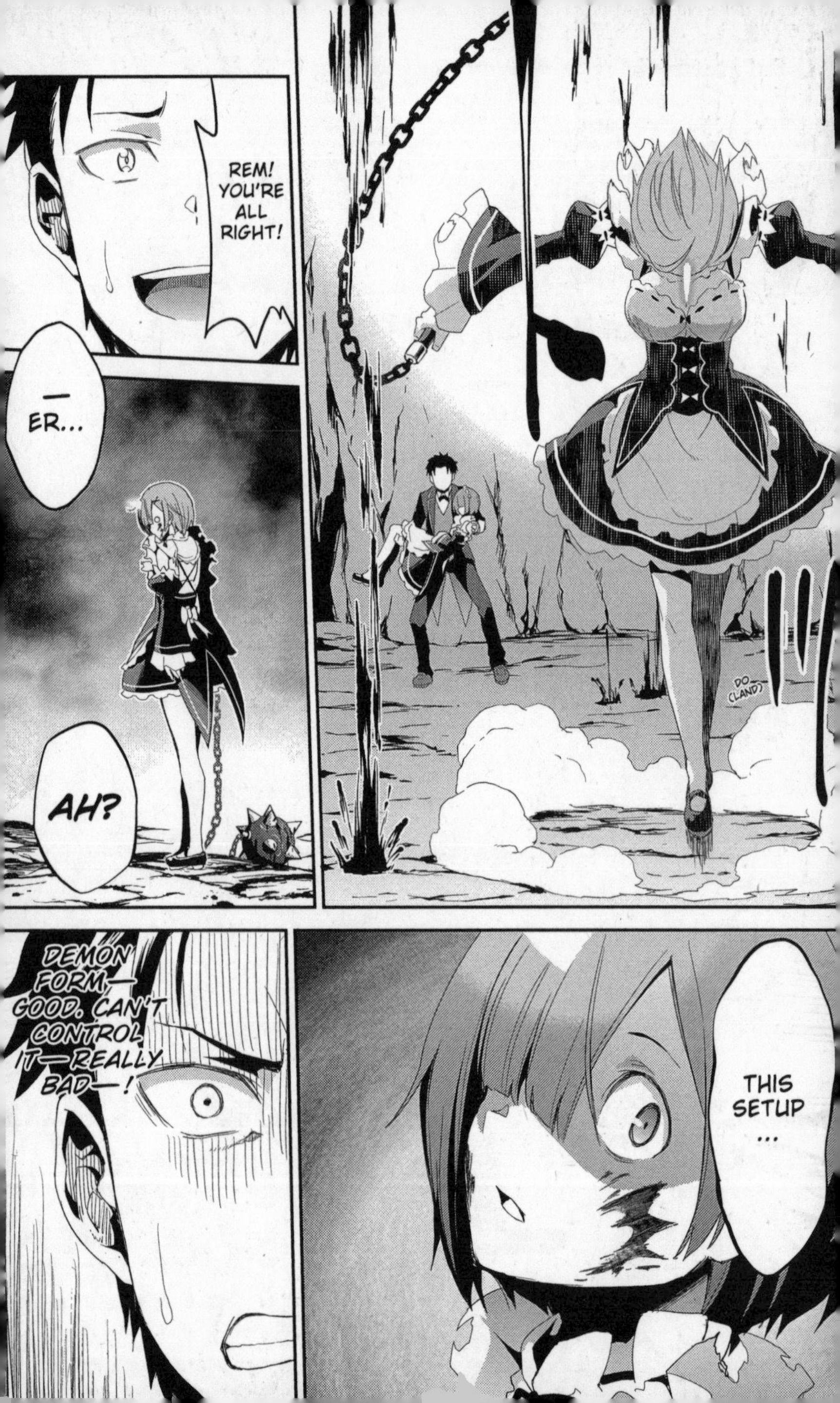

DO (LAND)
REM! YOU'RE ALL RIGHT!
—ER...
AH?
THIS SETUP ...
DEMON FORM—GOOD. CAN'T CONTROL IT—REALLY BAD—!

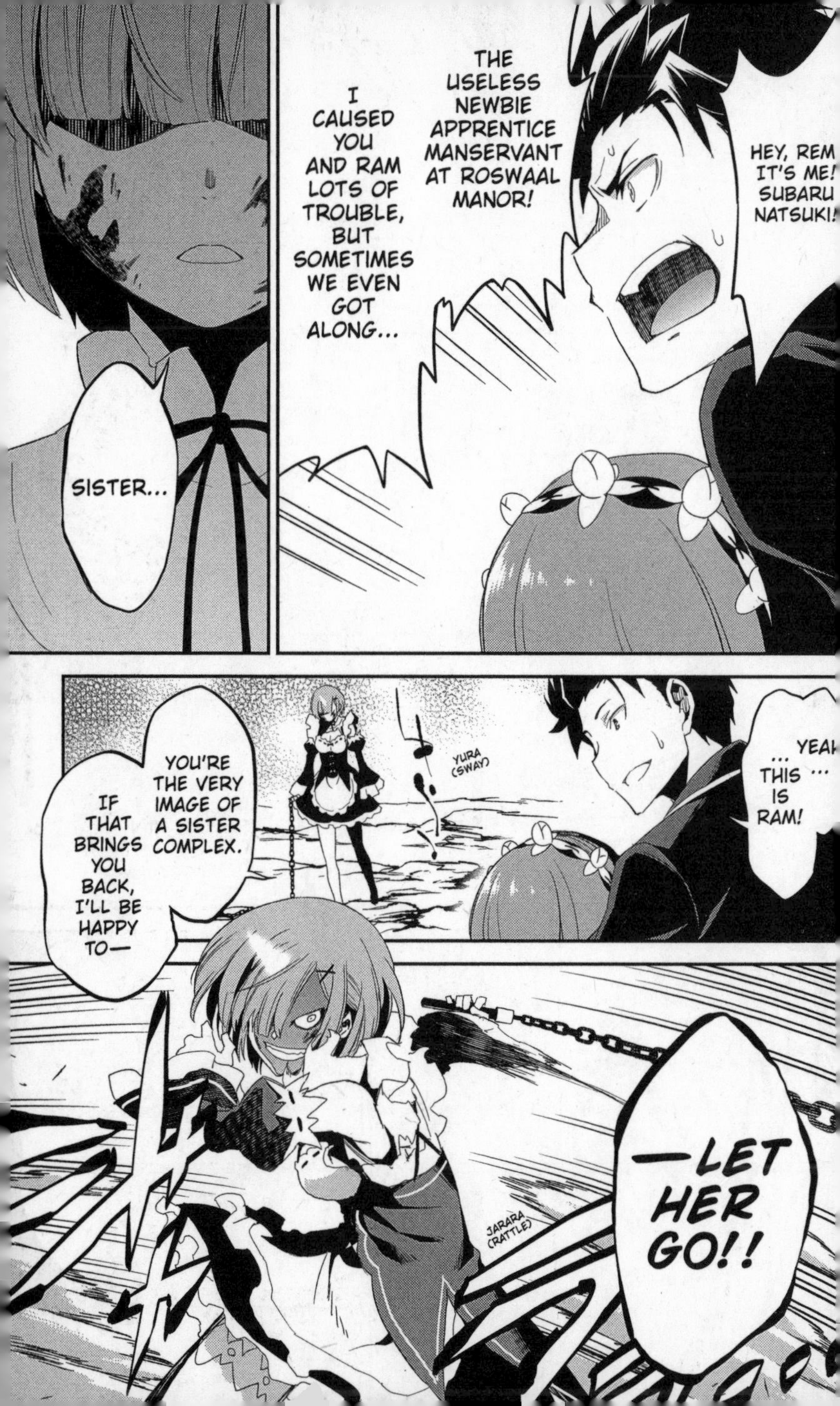
HEY, REM IT'S ME! SUBARU NATSUKI!
THE USELESS NEWBIE APPRENTICE MANSERVANT AT ROSWAAL MANOR!
I CAUSED YOU AND RAM LOTS OF TROUBLE, BUT SOMETIMES WE EVEN GOT ALONG...
SISTER...
YEAH... THIS... IS RAM!
YURA (SWAY)
YOU'RE THE VERY IMAGE OF A SISTER COMPLEX.
IF THAT BRINGS YOU BACK, I'LL BE HAPPY TO—
—LET HER GO!!
JARARA (RATTLE)

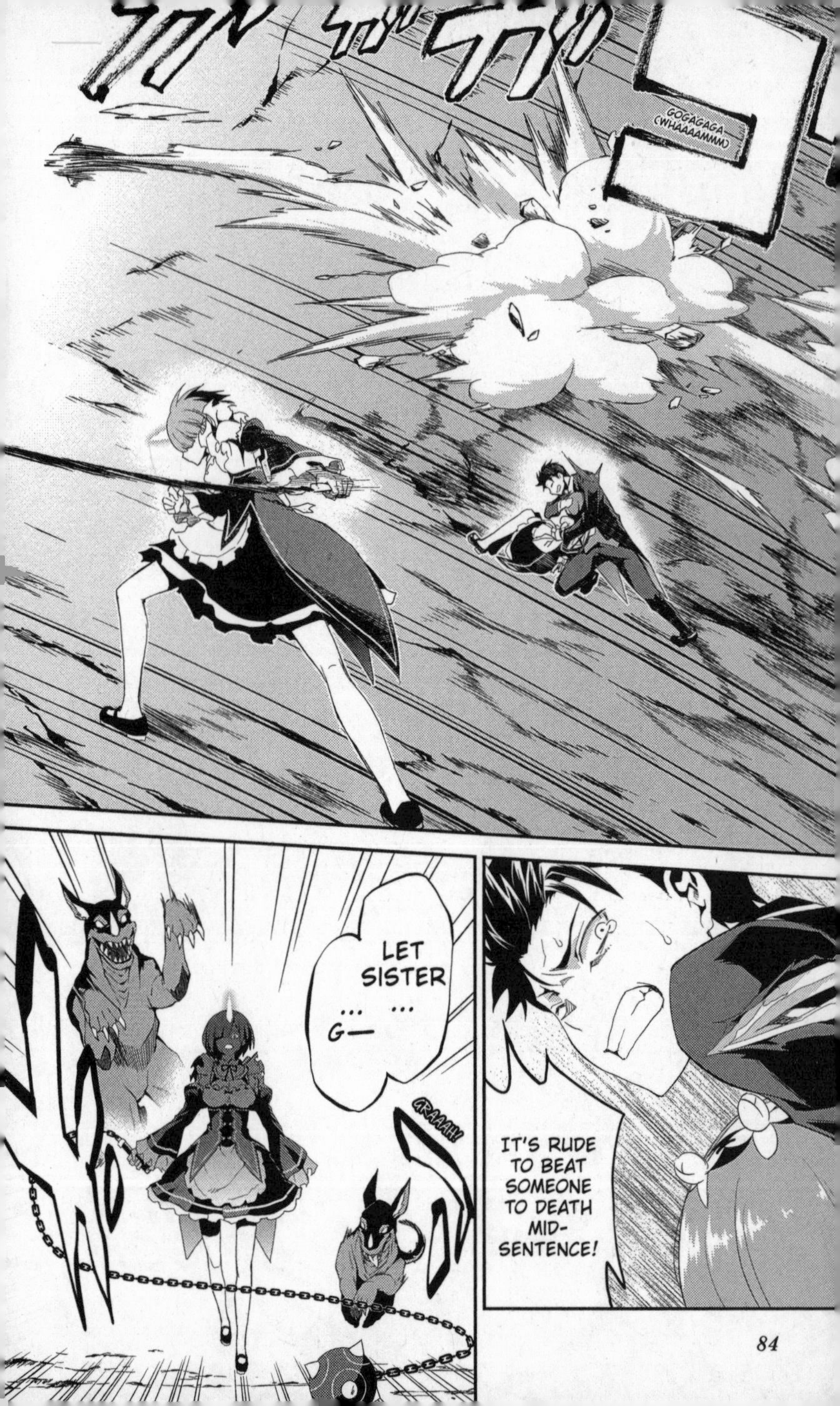
GOGAGAGA (WHAAAAMMM)
IT'S RUDE TO BEAT SOMEONE TO DEATH MID-SENTENCE!
LET SISTER ... ... G—
GRAAAH!

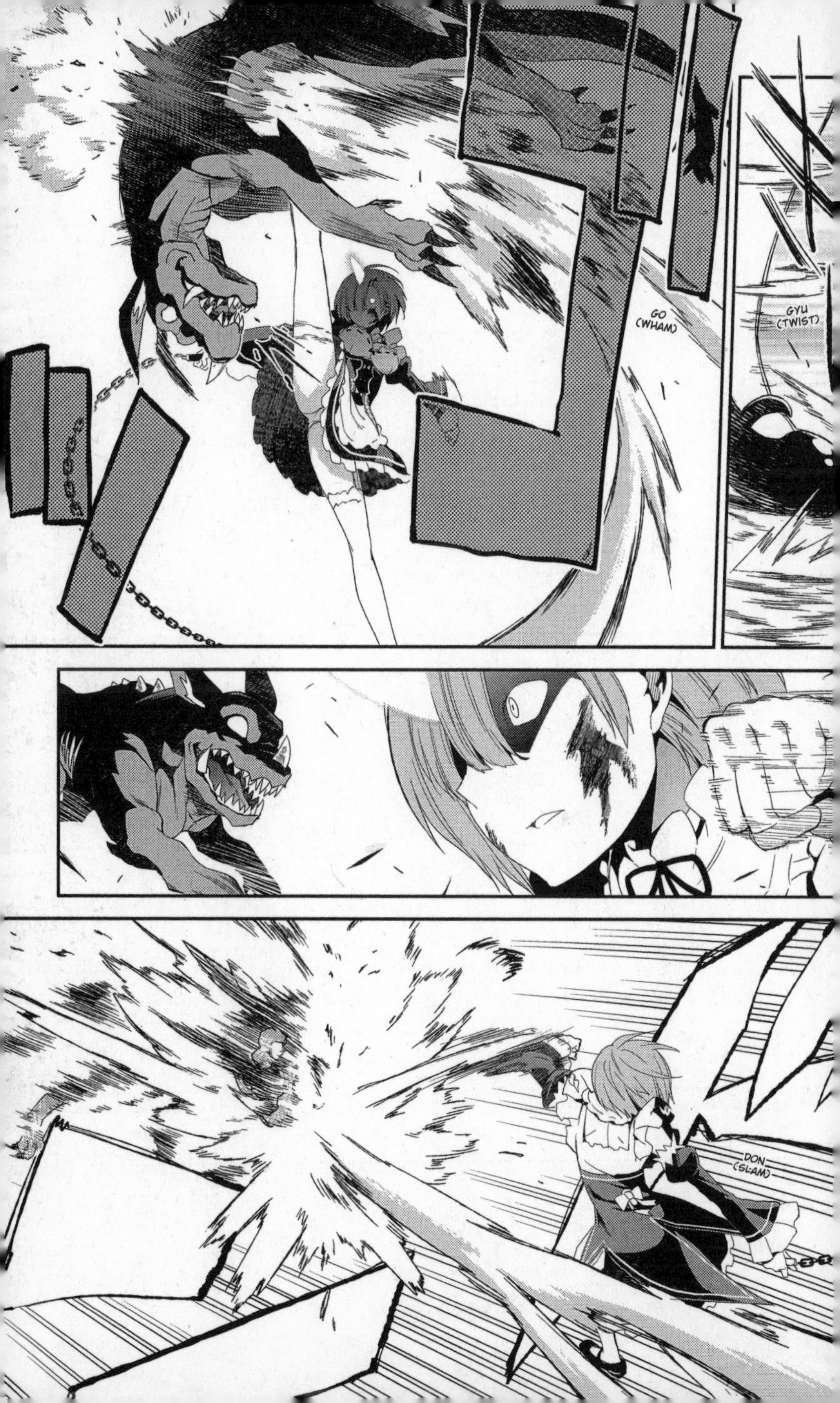
GYU (TWIST)
GO (WHAM)
DON (SLAM)

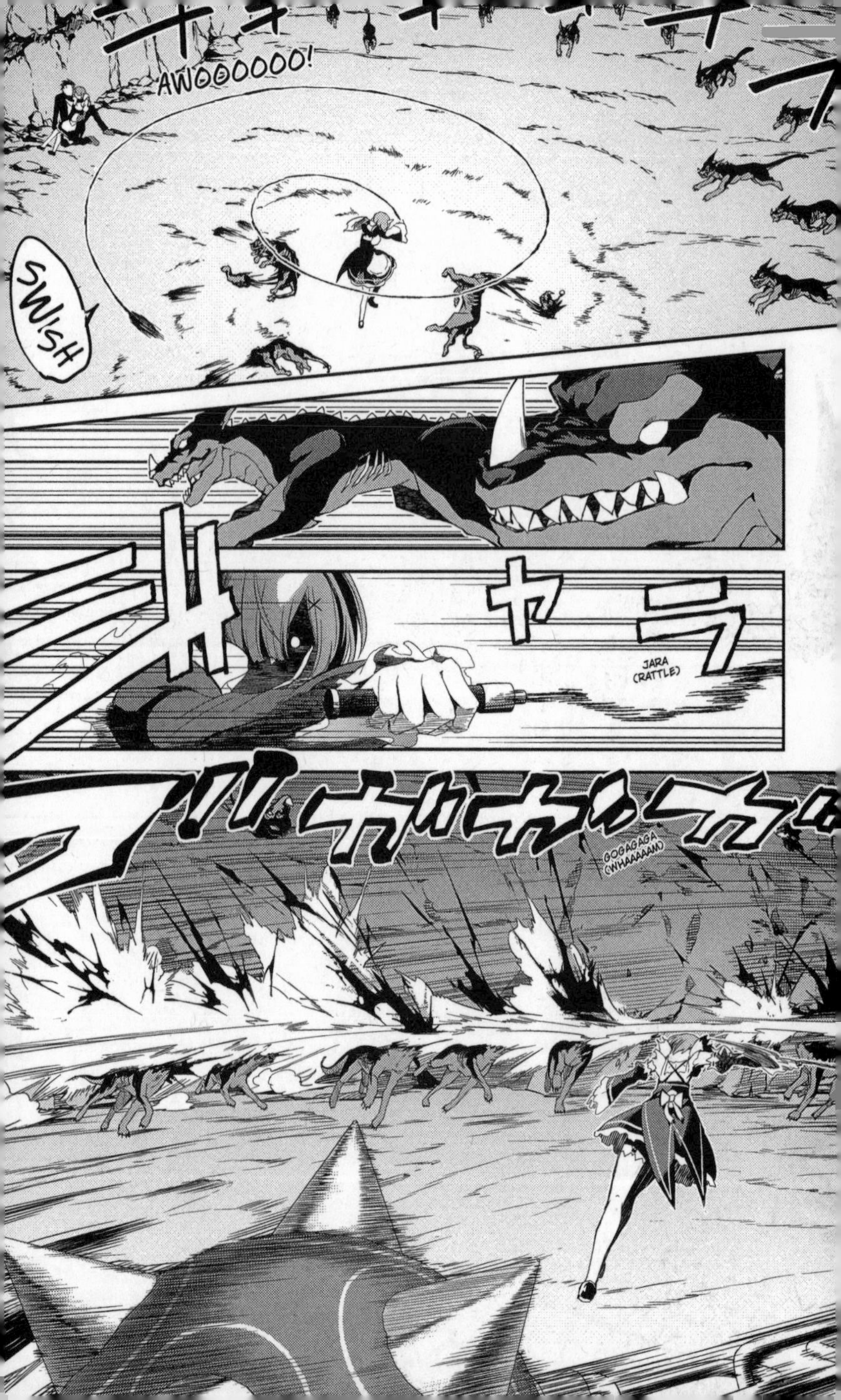
AWOOOOOO!
SWISH
JARA (RATTLE)
GOGAGAGA (WHAAAAAM)

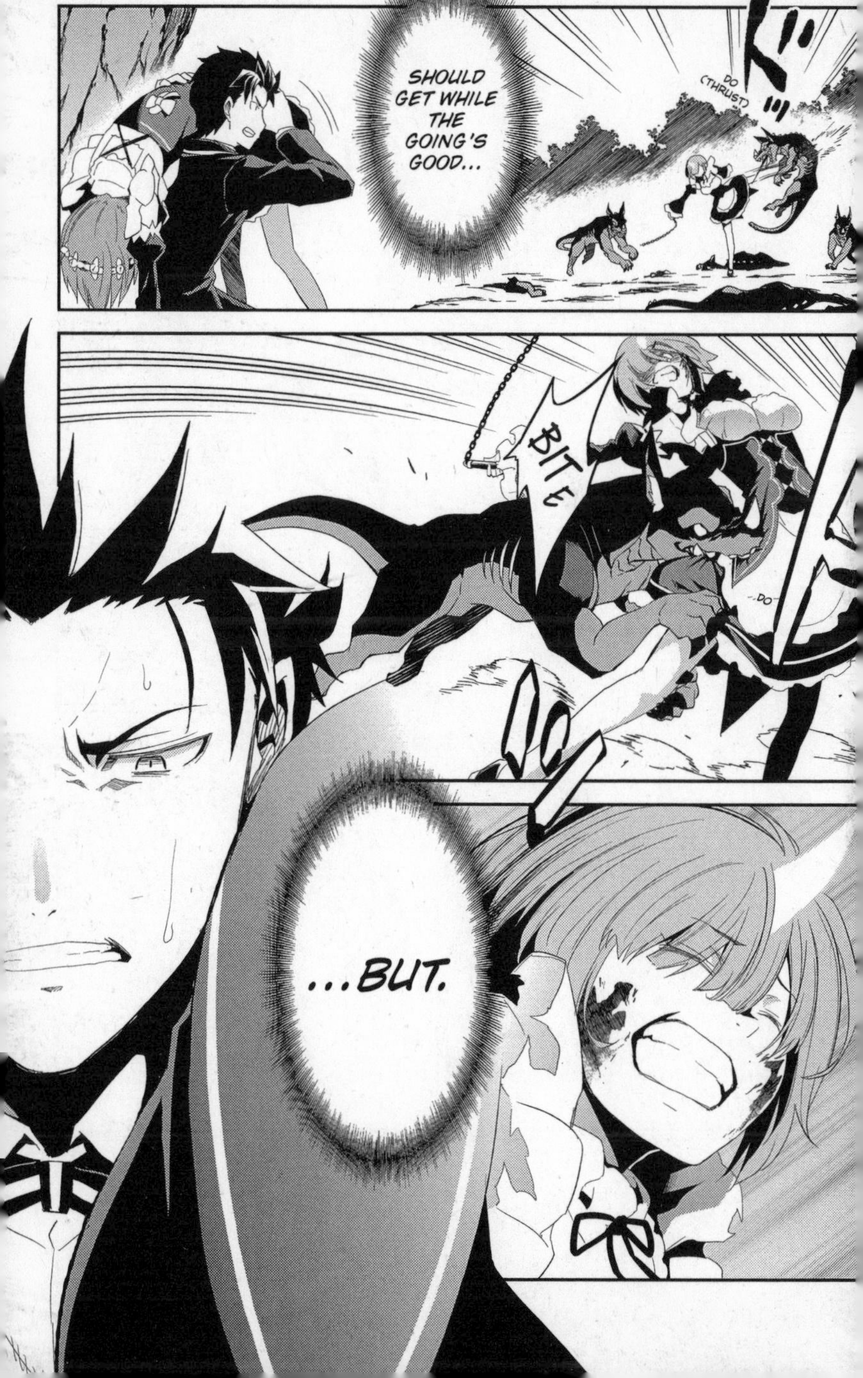

ドッ
DO (THRUST)
SHOULD GET WHILE THE GOING'S GOOD...
BITE
DO
DO
...BUT.

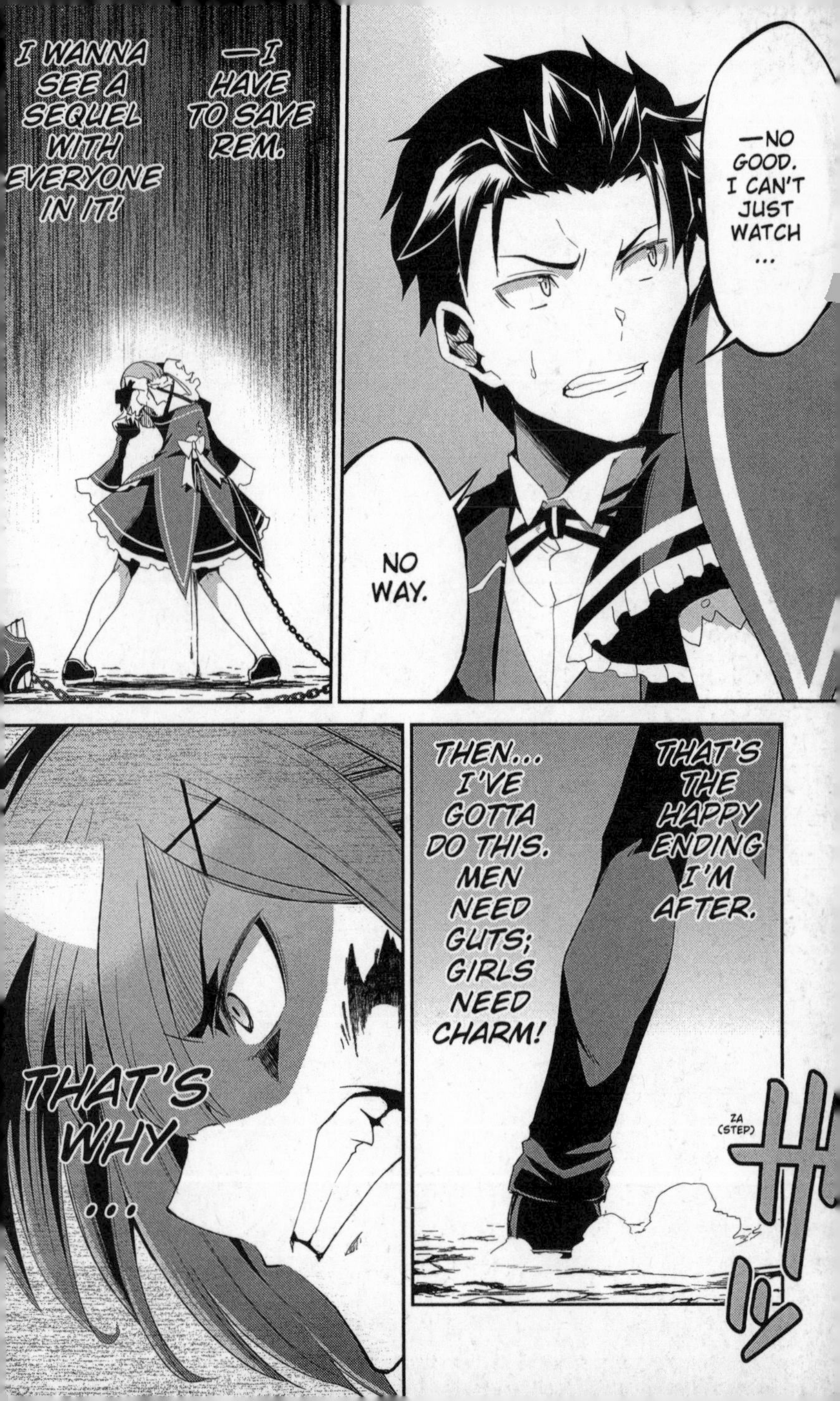
—NO GOOD. I CAN'T JUST WATCH...
NO WAY.
—I HAVE TO SAVE REM.
I WANNA SEE A SEQUEL WITH EVERYONE IN IT!
THAT'S THE HAPPY ENDING I'M AFTER.
THEN... I'VE GOTTA DO THIS. MEN NEED GUTS; GIRLS NEED CHARM!
ZA (STEP)
THAT'S WHY...

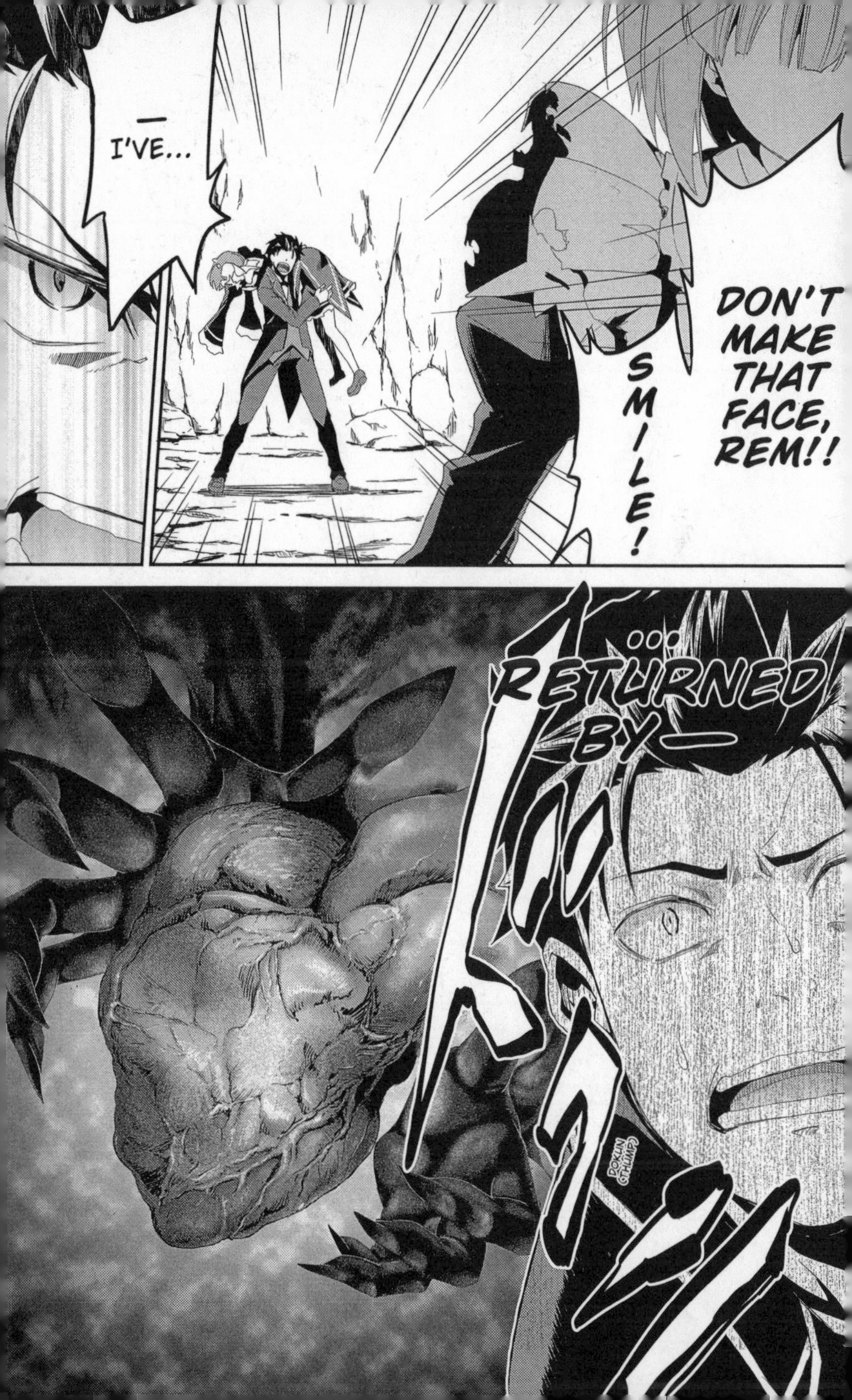
DON'T MAKE THAT FACE, REM!!
SMILE!
—I'VE...
...RETURNED BY—
DOKUN (THUMP)

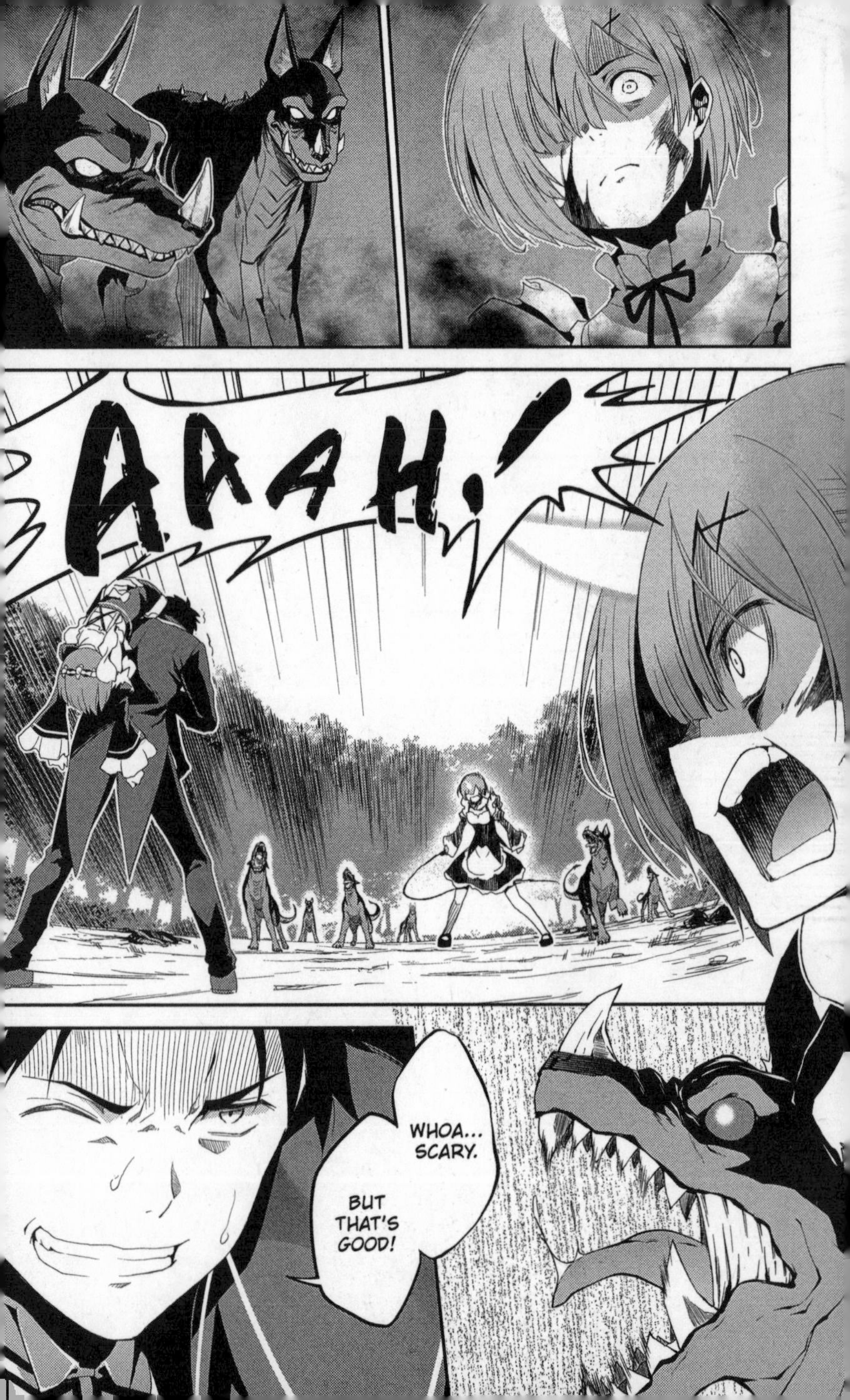
AAAH!
WHOA... SCARY.
BUT THAT'S GOOD!

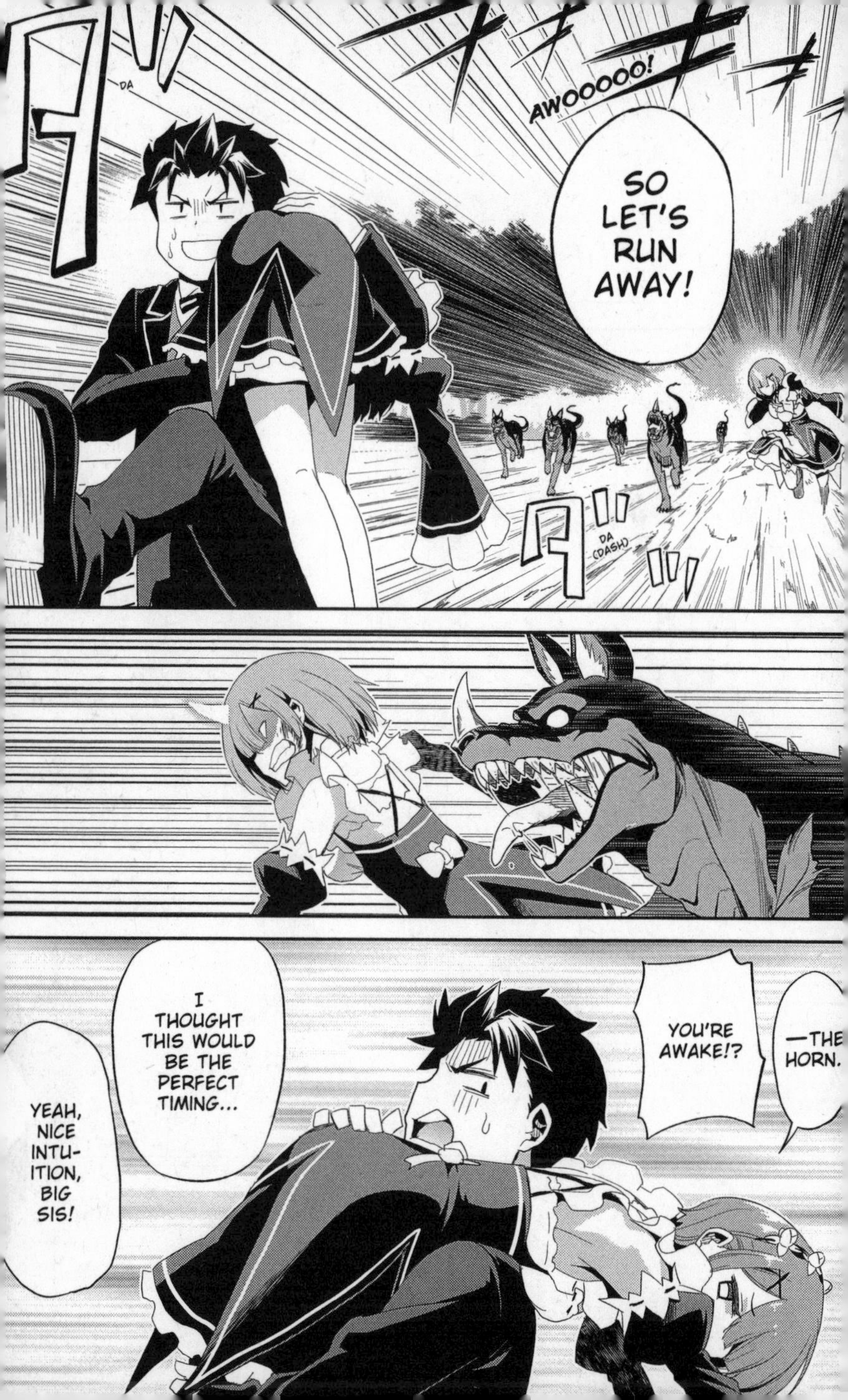
AWOOOOO!
SO LET'S RUN AWAY!
DA
DA (DASH)
—THE HORN.
YOU'RE AWAKE!?
I THOUGHT THIS WOULD BE THE PERFECT TIMING...
YEAH, NICE INTUITION, BIG SIS!

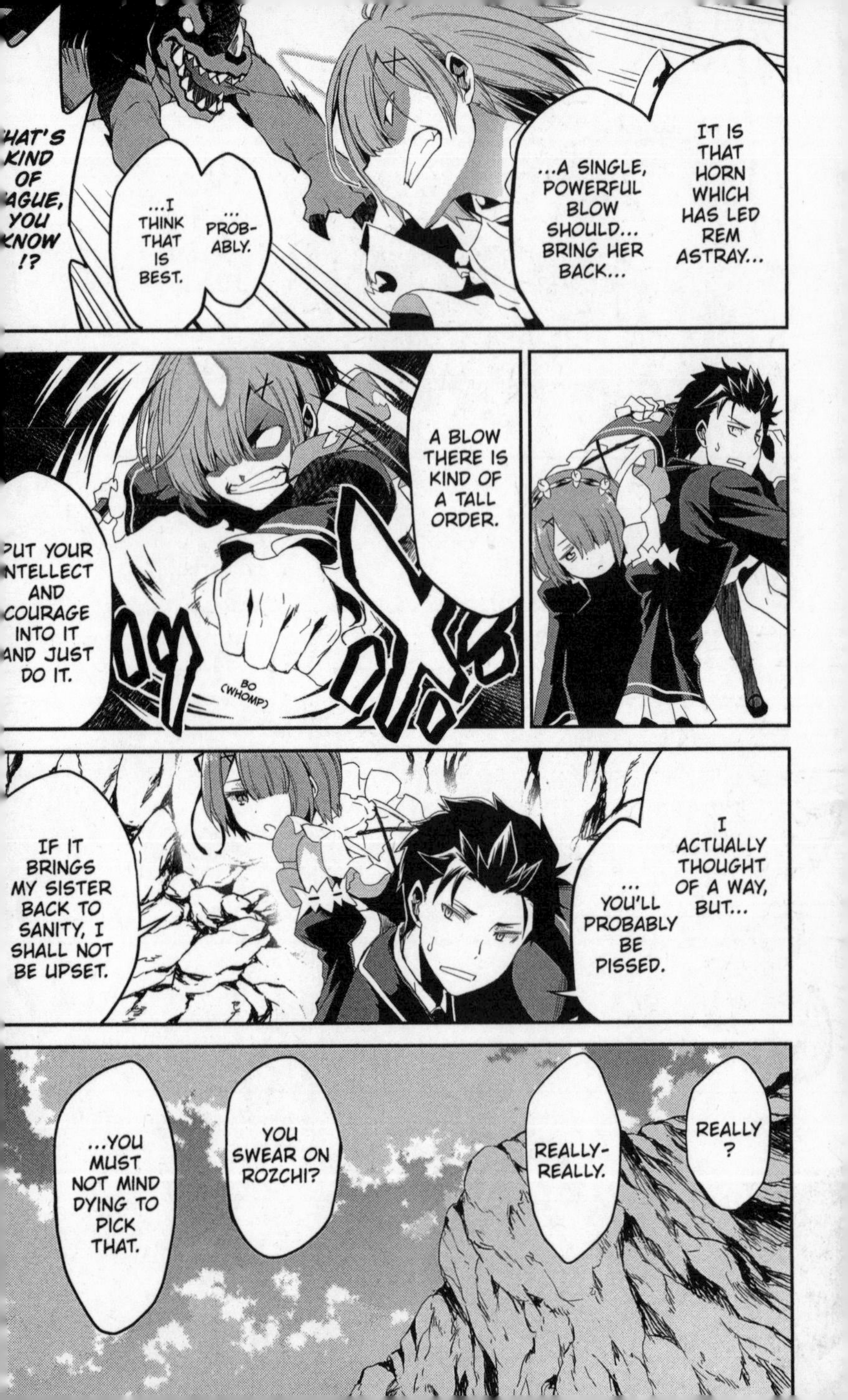
IT IS THAT HORN WHICH HAS LED REM ASTRAY...
...A SINGLE, POWERFUL BLOW SHOULD... BRING HER BACK...
... PROBABLY.
...I THINK THAT IS BEST.
HAT'S KIND OF AGUE, YOU KNOW !?
A BLOW THERE IS KIND OF A TALL ORDER.
UT YOUR NTELLECT AND COURAGE INTO IT AND JUST DO IT.
BO (WHOMP)
I ACTUALLY THOUGHT OF A WAY, BUT...
... YOU'LL PROBABLY BE PISSED.
IF IT BRINGS MY SISTER BACK TO SANITY, I SHALL NOT BE UPSET.
REALLY?
REALLY-REALLY.
YOU SWEAR ON ROZCHI?
...YOU MUST NOT MIND DYING TO PICK THAT.

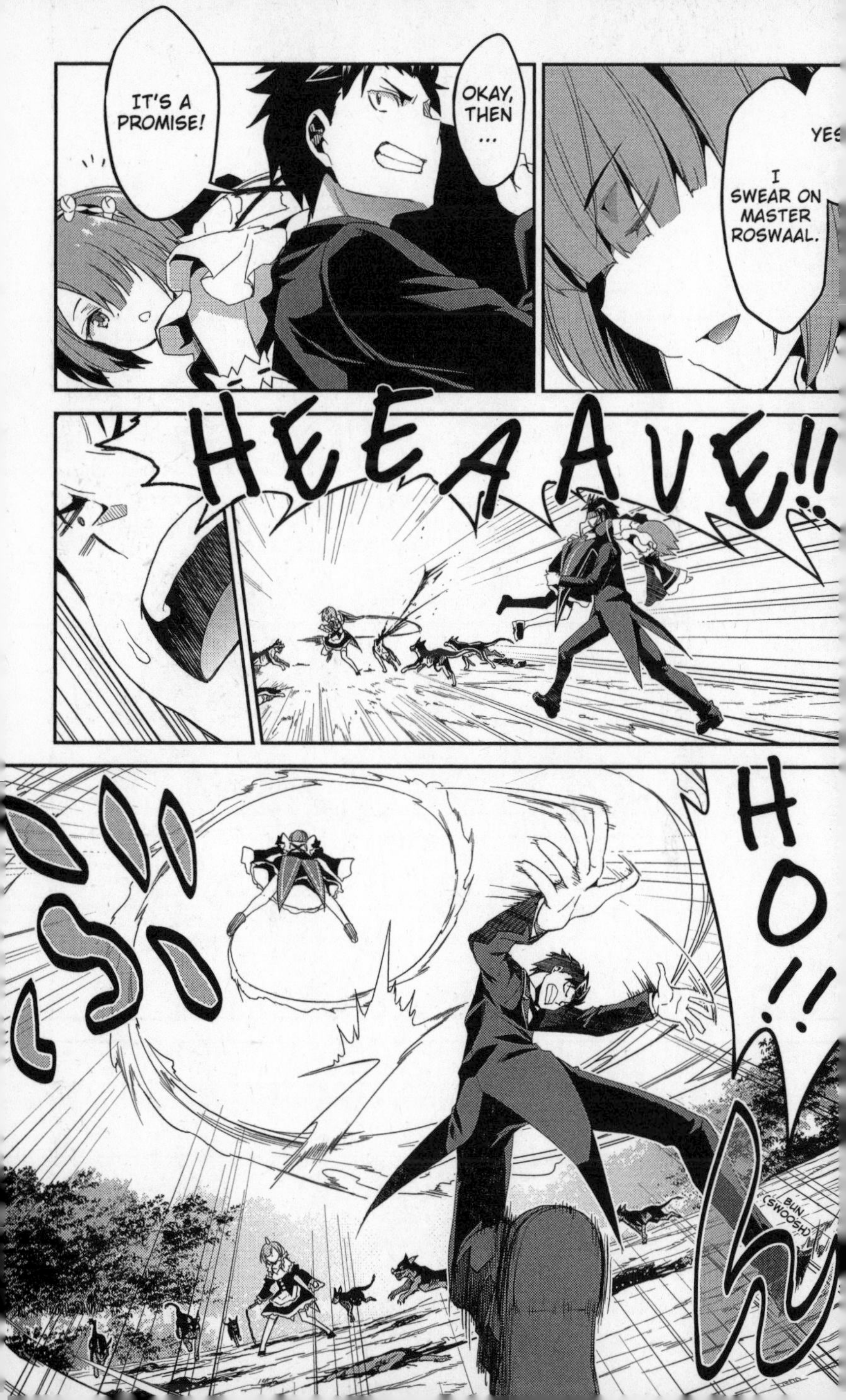
YES
I SWEAR ON MASTER ROSWAAL.
OKAY, THEN ...
IT'S A PROMISE!
HEEAAVE!!
HO!!
BUN (SWOOSH)

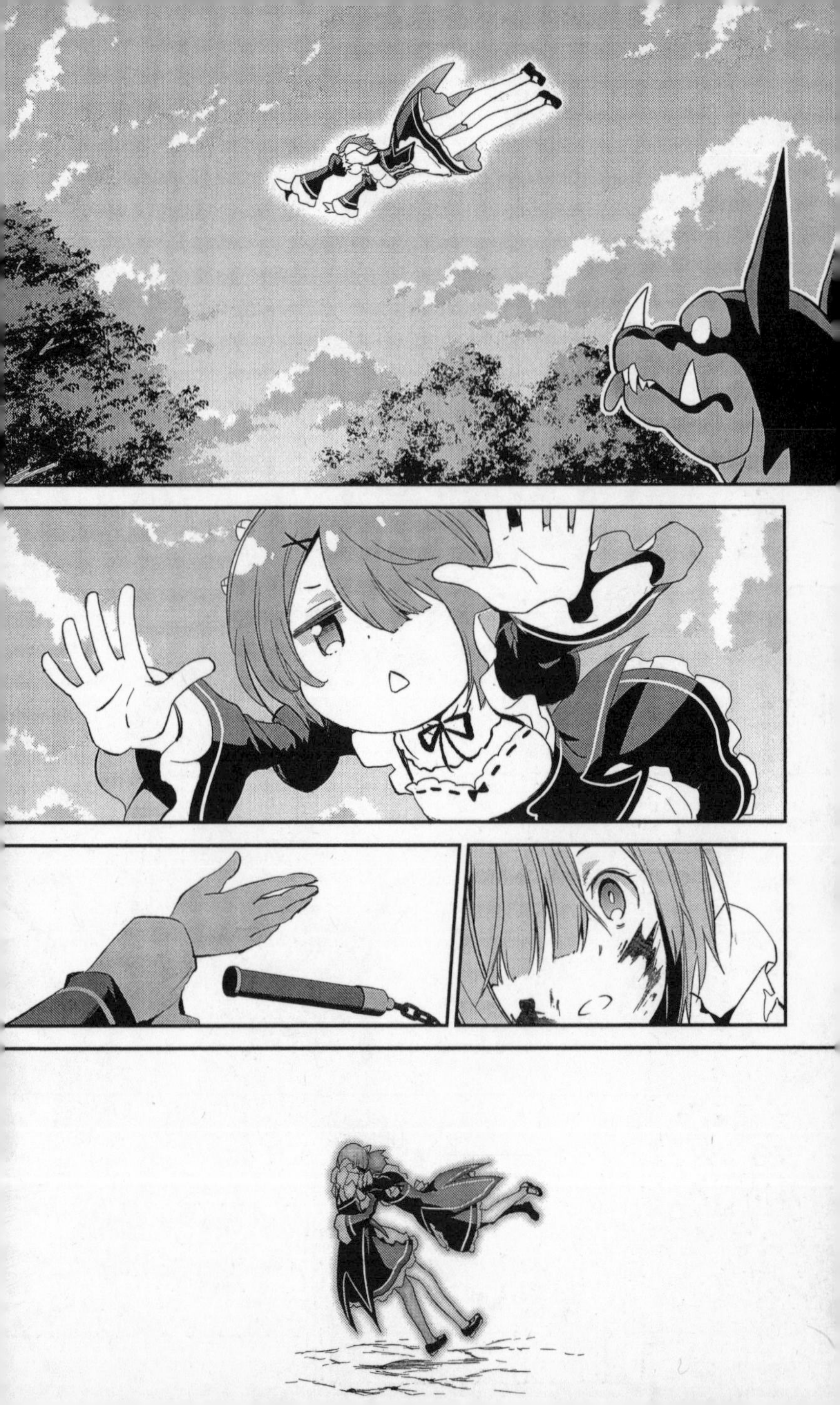

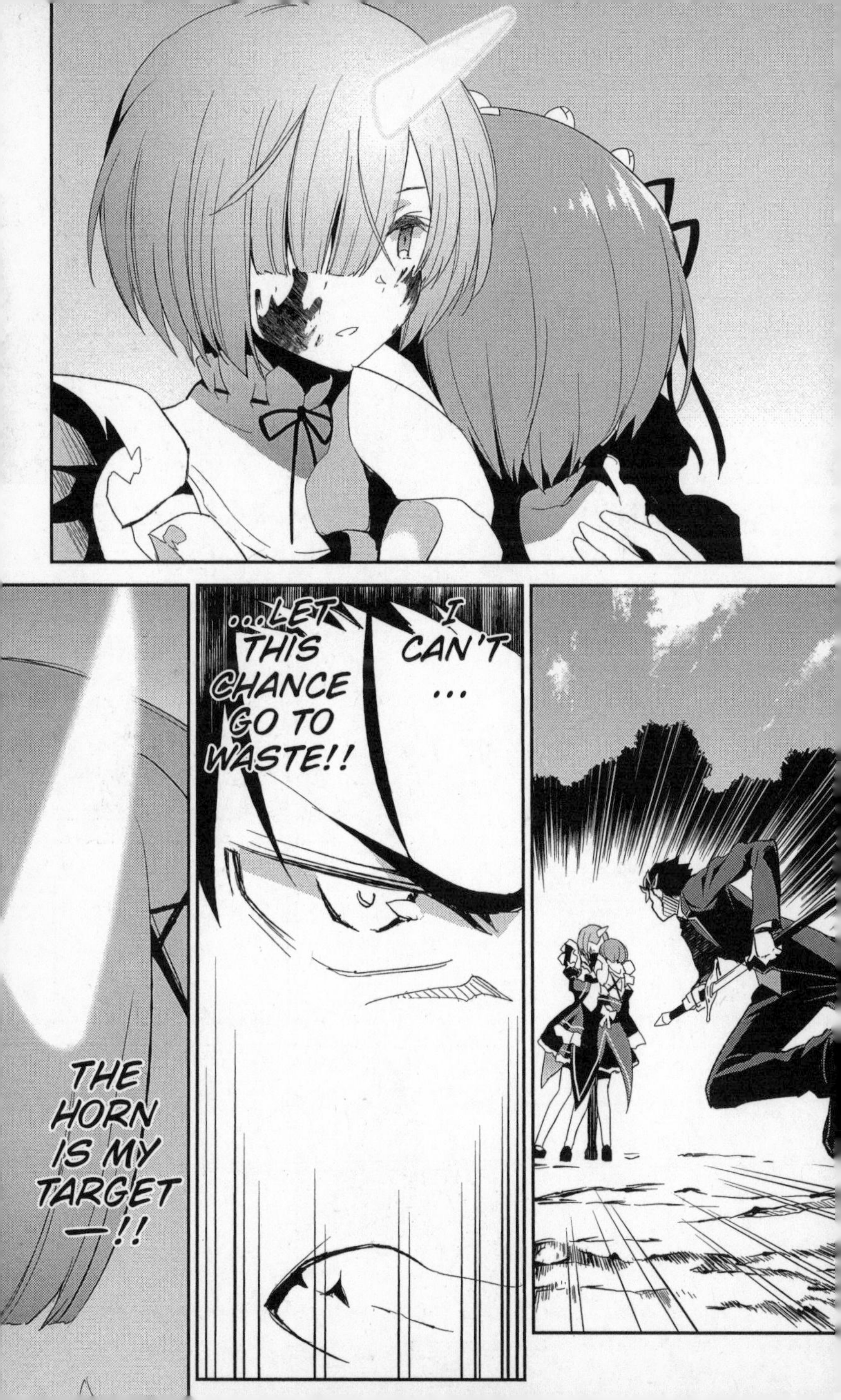
I CAN'T...
...LET THIS CHANCE GO TO WASTE!!
THE HORN IS MY TARGET—!!

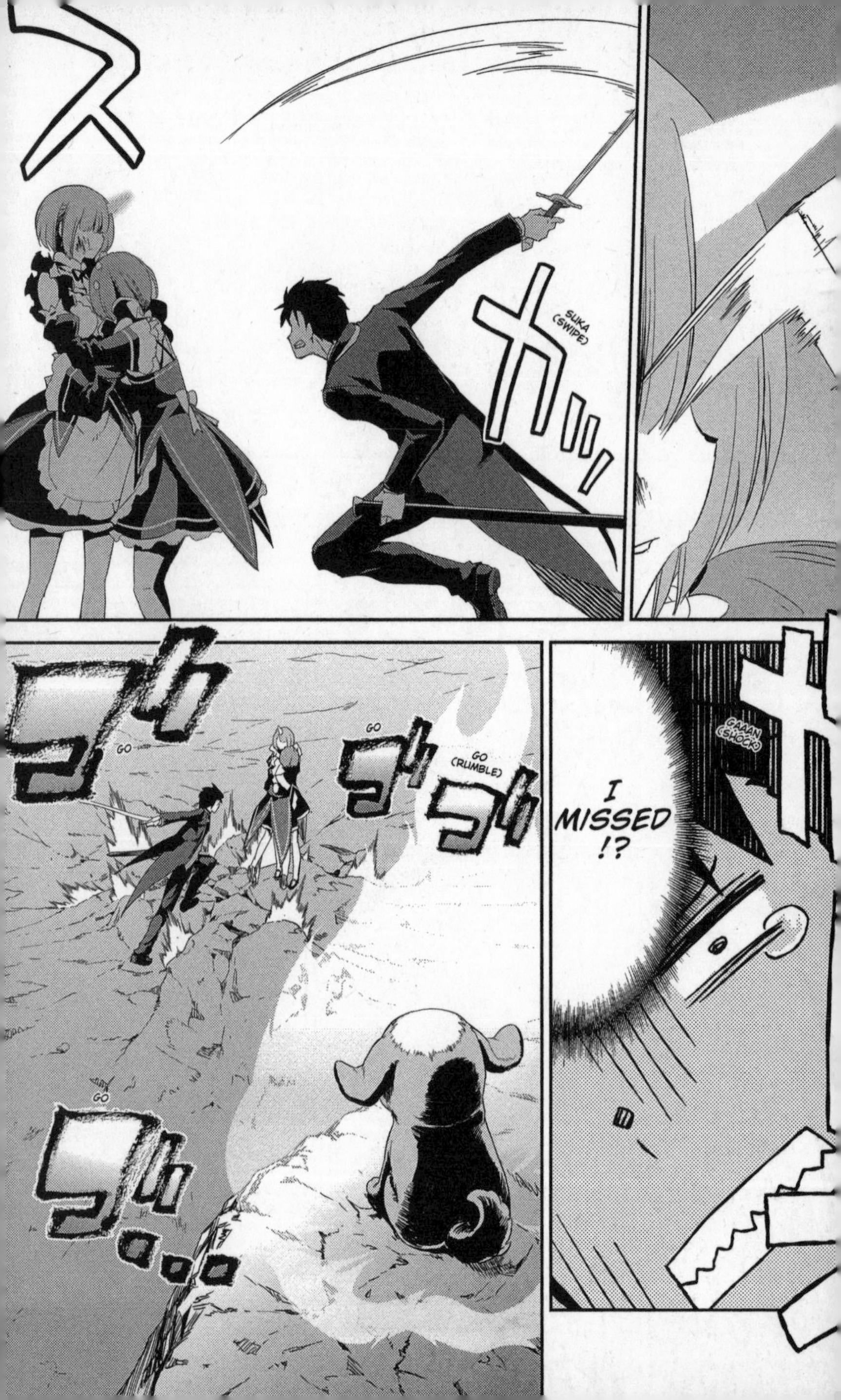
SUKA (SWIPE)
GAAAN (SHOCK)
I MISSED !?
GO
GO (RUMBLE)
GO
GO

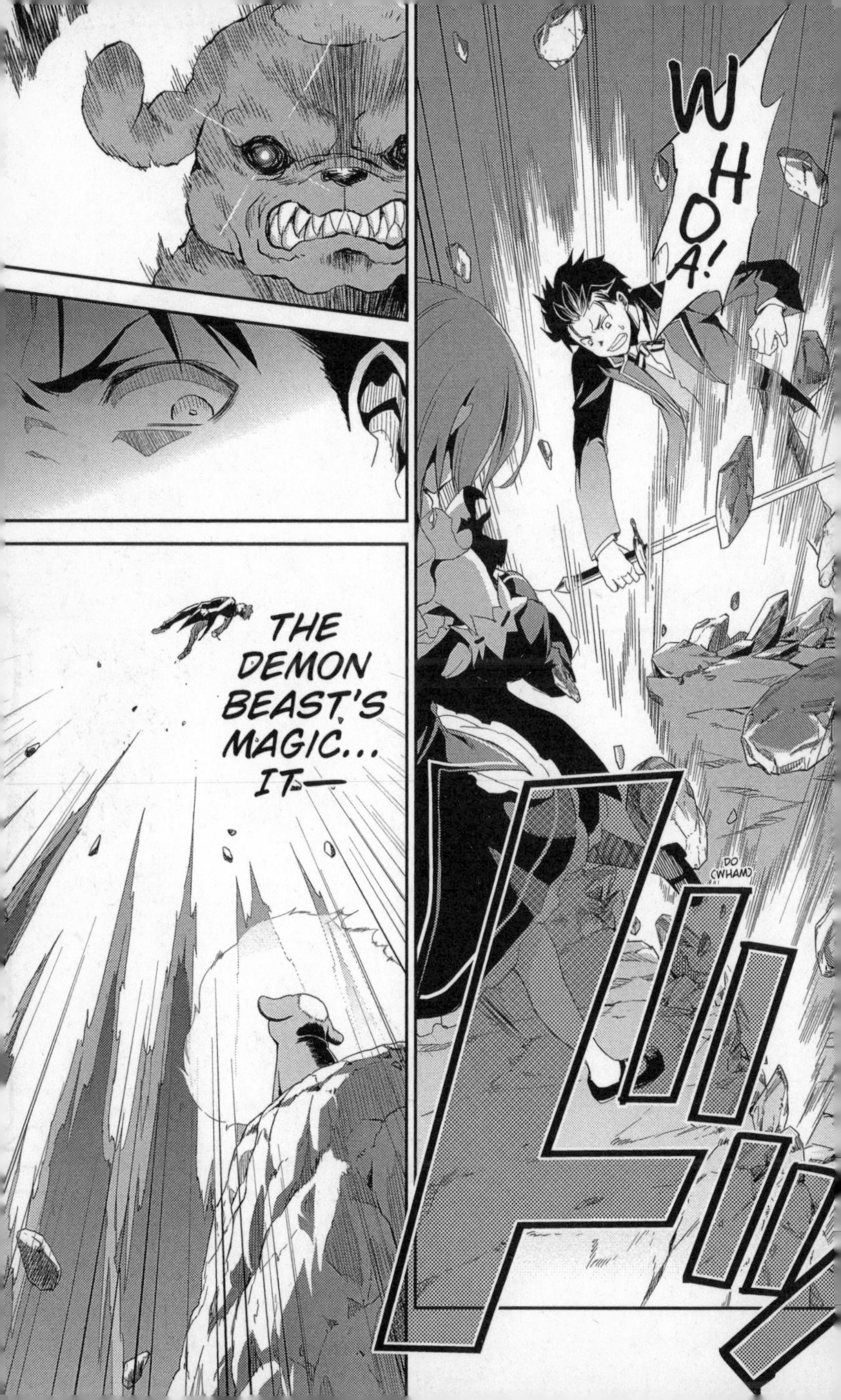
WHOA!
DO
(WHAM)
THE DEMON BEAST'S MAGIC... IT—

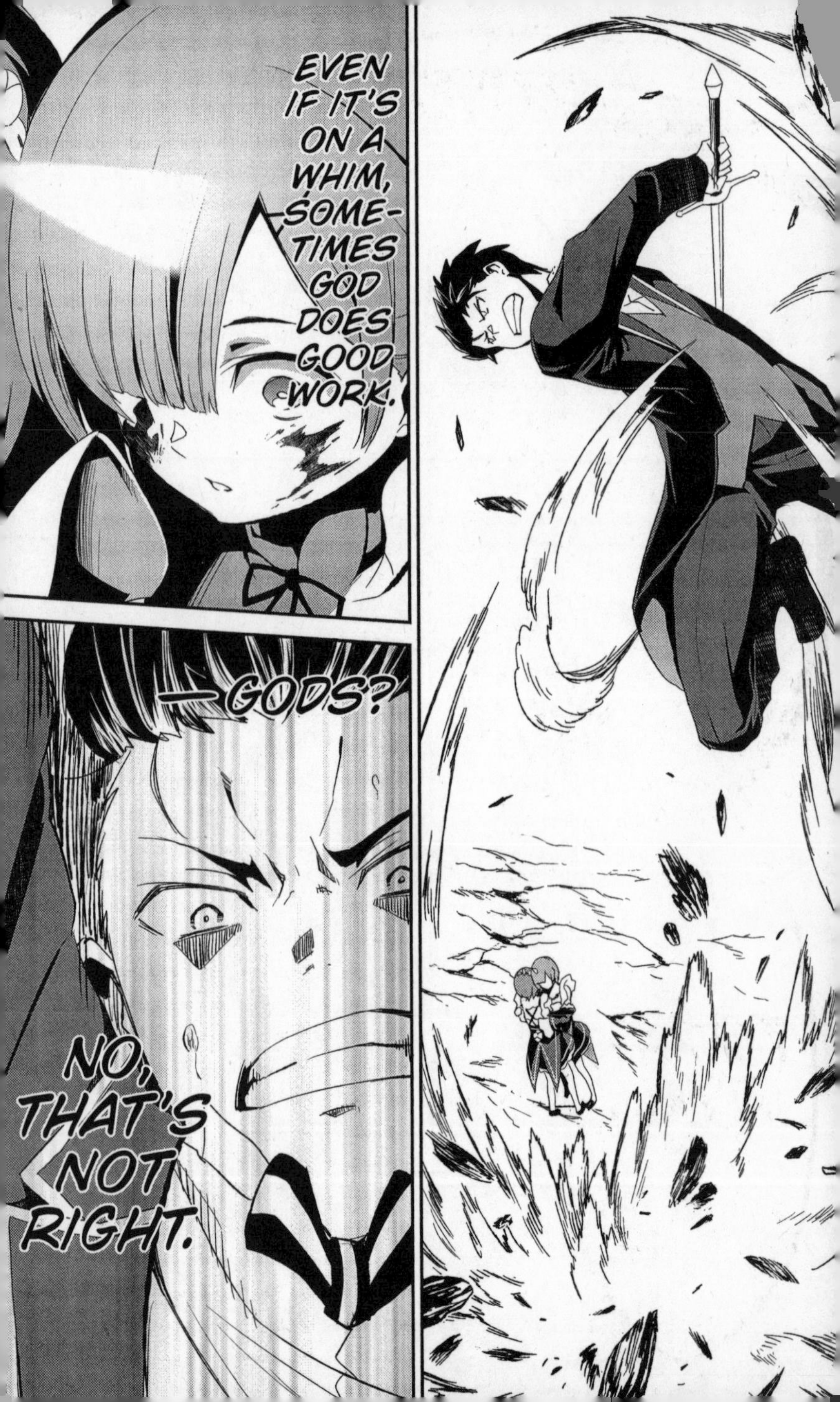
EVEN IF IT'S ON A WHIM, SOMETIMES GOD DOES GOOD WORK.
—GODS?
NO, THAT'S NOT RIGHT.

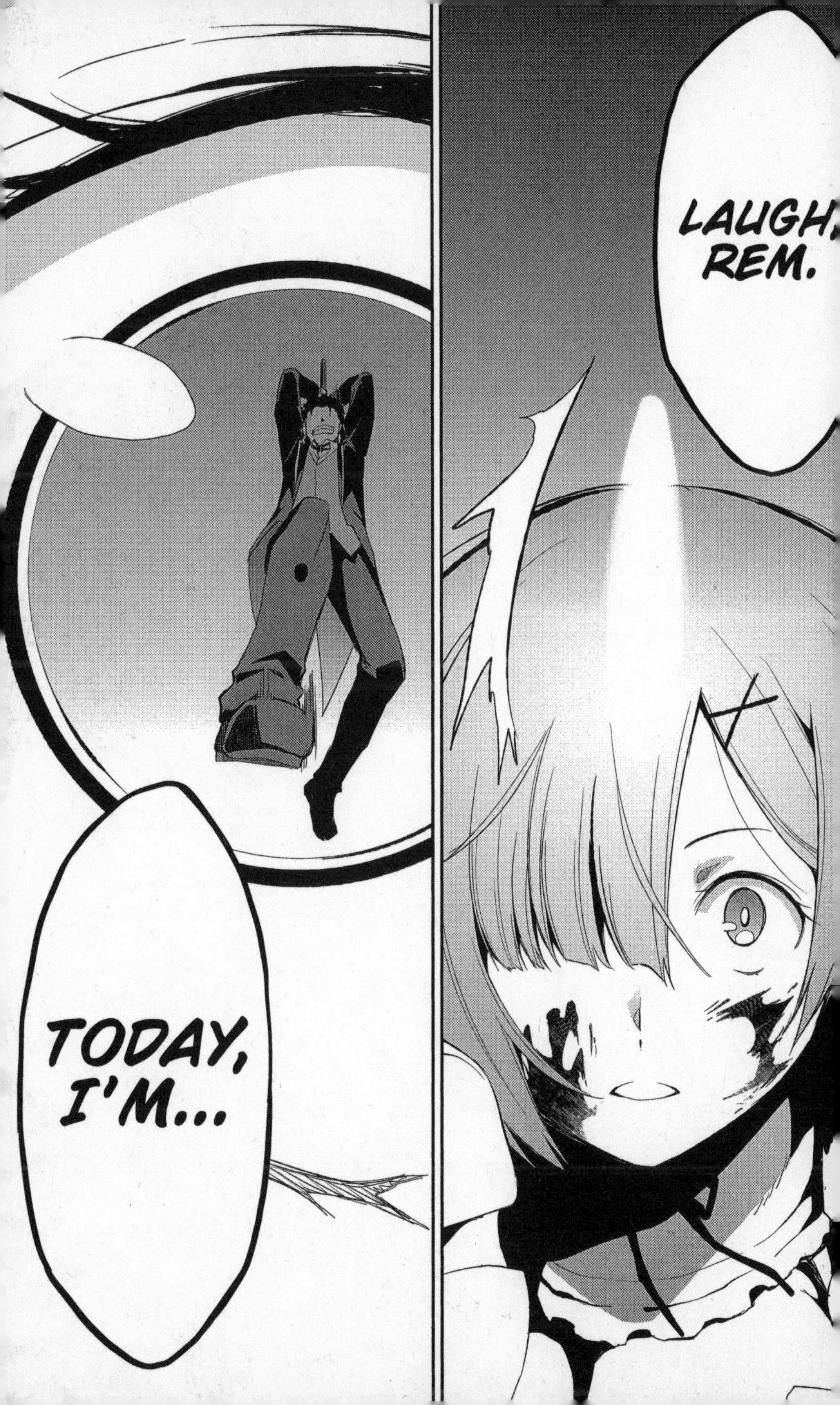
LAUGH, REM.
TODAY, I'M...

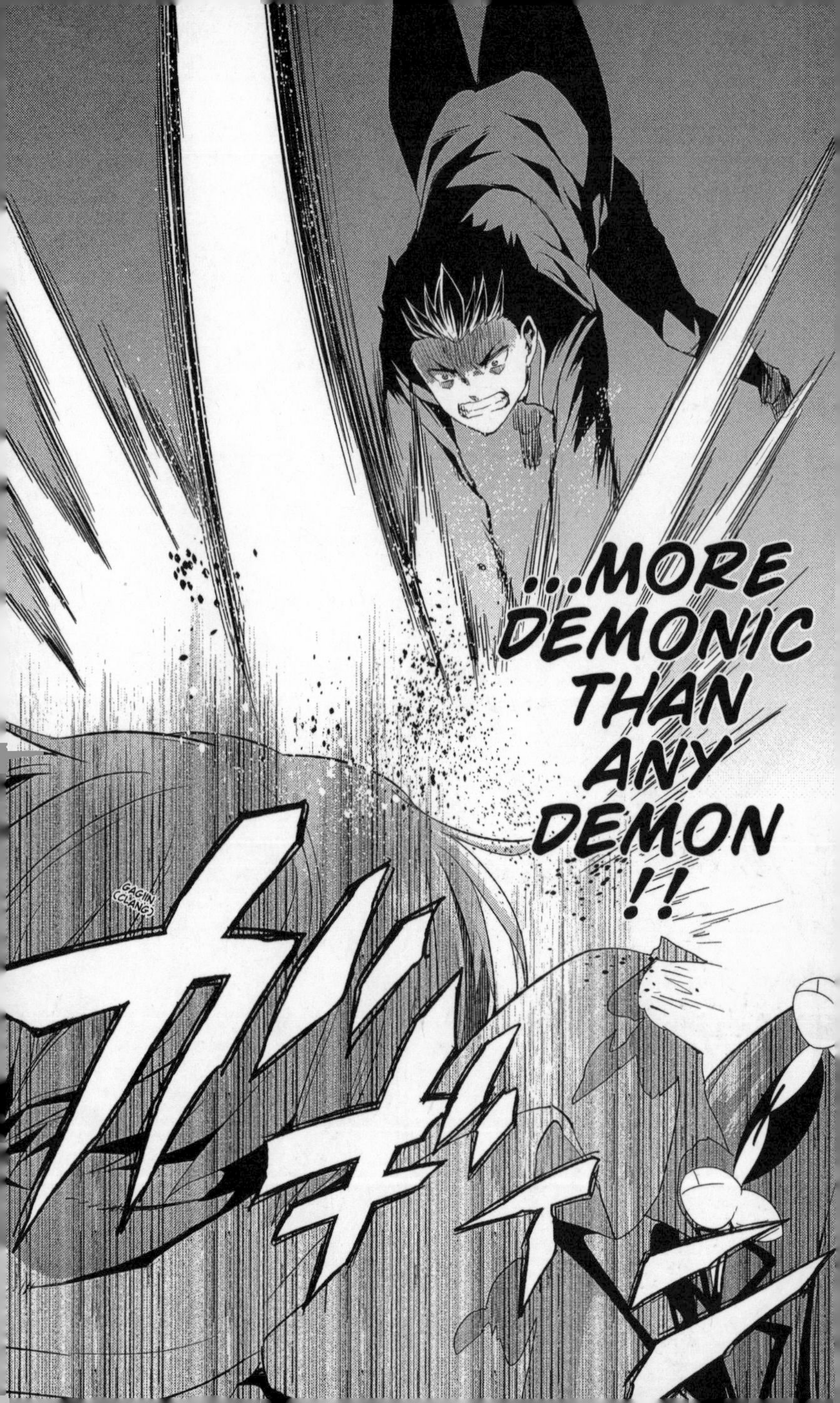
...MORE DEMONIC THAN ANY DEMON !!
GAGIIN (CLANG)

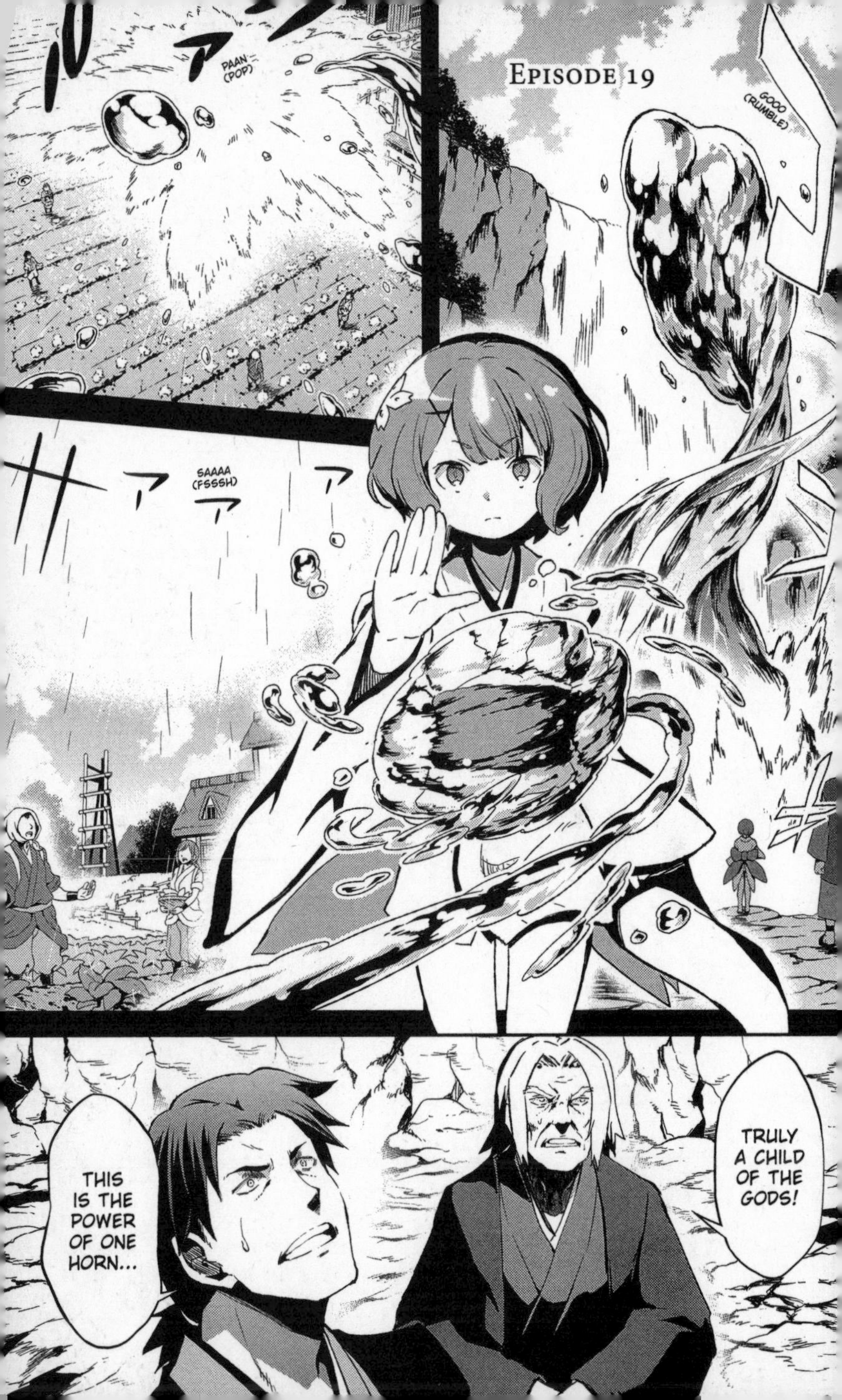

EPISODE 19
GOOO (RUMBLE)
PAAN (POP)
SAAAA (FSSSH)
TRULY A CHILD OF THE GODS!
THIS IS THE POWER OF ONE HORN...

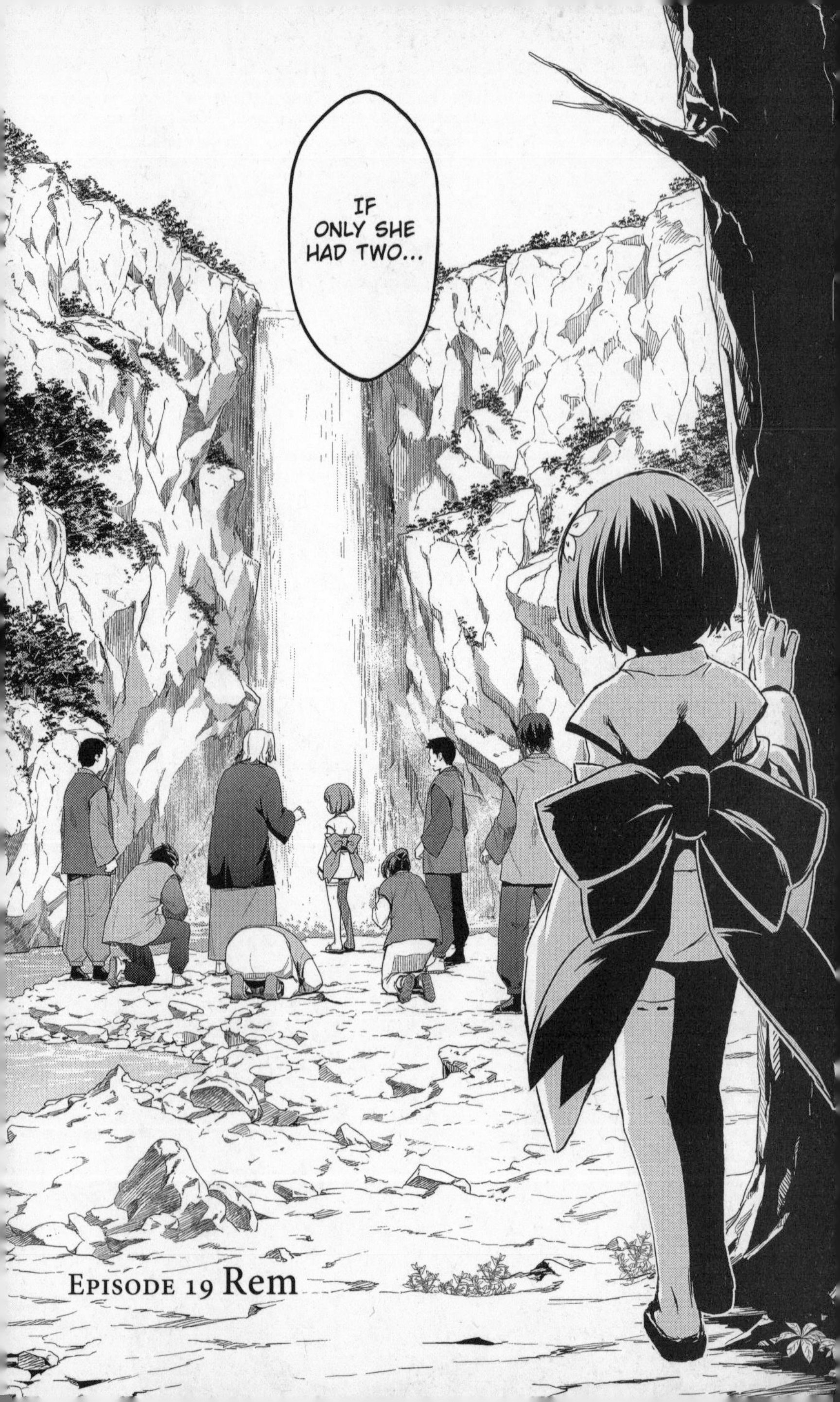
IF ONLY SHE HAD TWO...
Episode 19 Rem

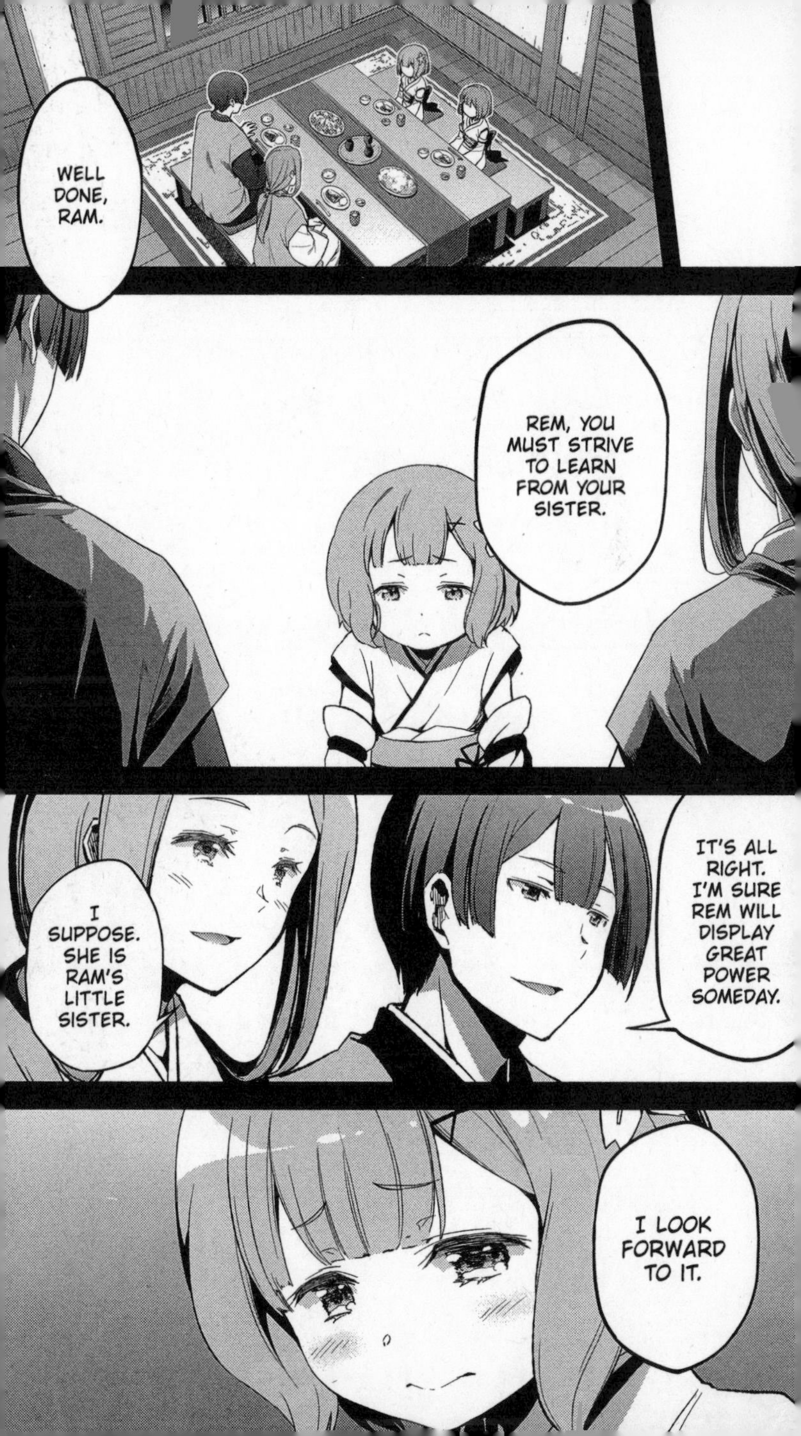
WELL DONE, RAM.
REM, YOU MUST STRIVE TO LEARN FROM YOUR SISTER.
IT'S ALL RIGHT. I'M SURE REM WILL DISPLAY GREAT POWER SOMEDAY.
I SUPPOSE. SHE IS RAM'S LITTLE SISTER.
I LOOK FORWARD TO IT.

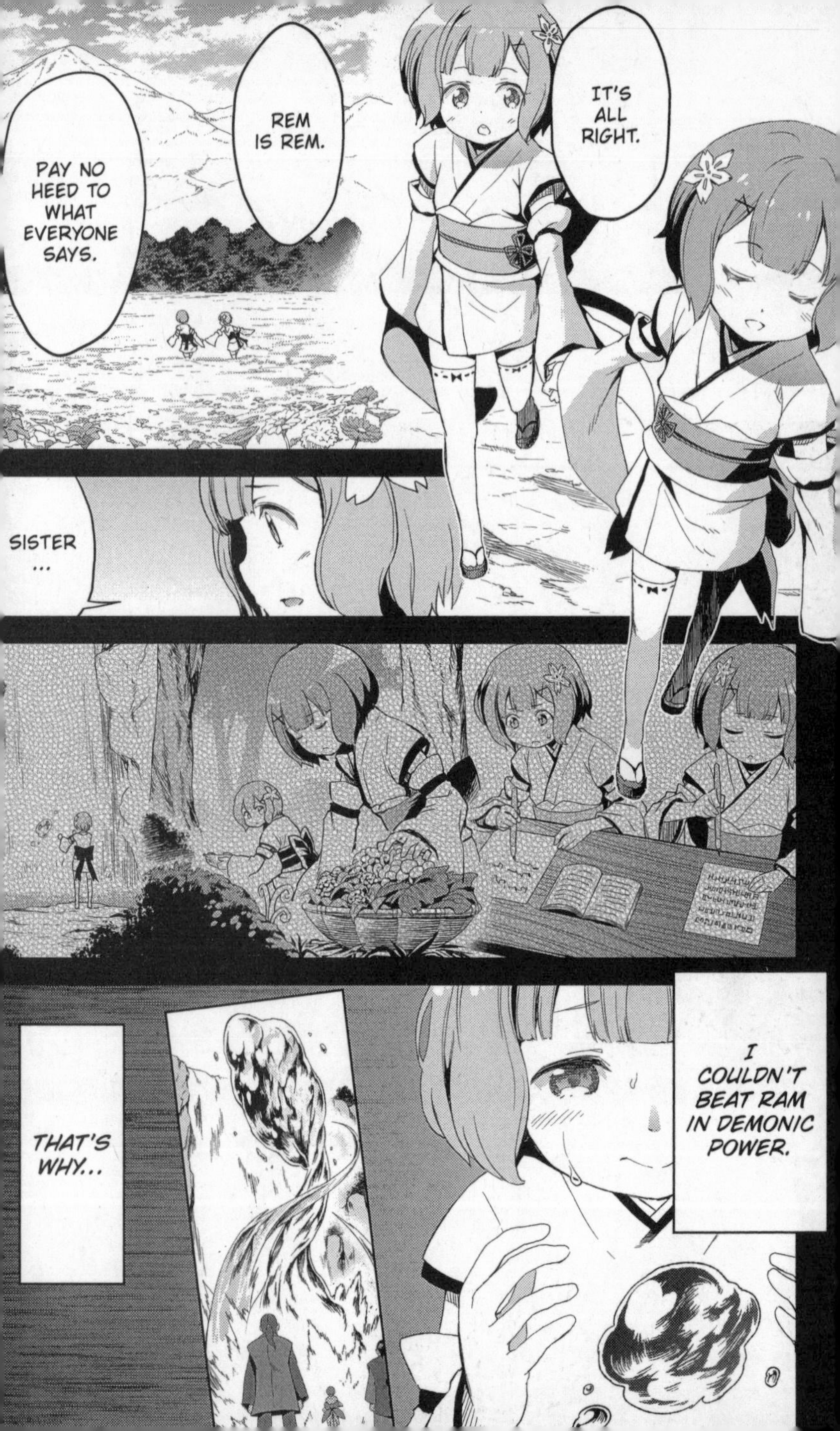
IT'S ALL RIGHT.
REM IS REM.
PAY NO HEED TO WHAT EVERYONE SAYS.
SISTER...
I COULDN'T BEAT RAM IN DEMONIC POWER.
THAT'S WHY...

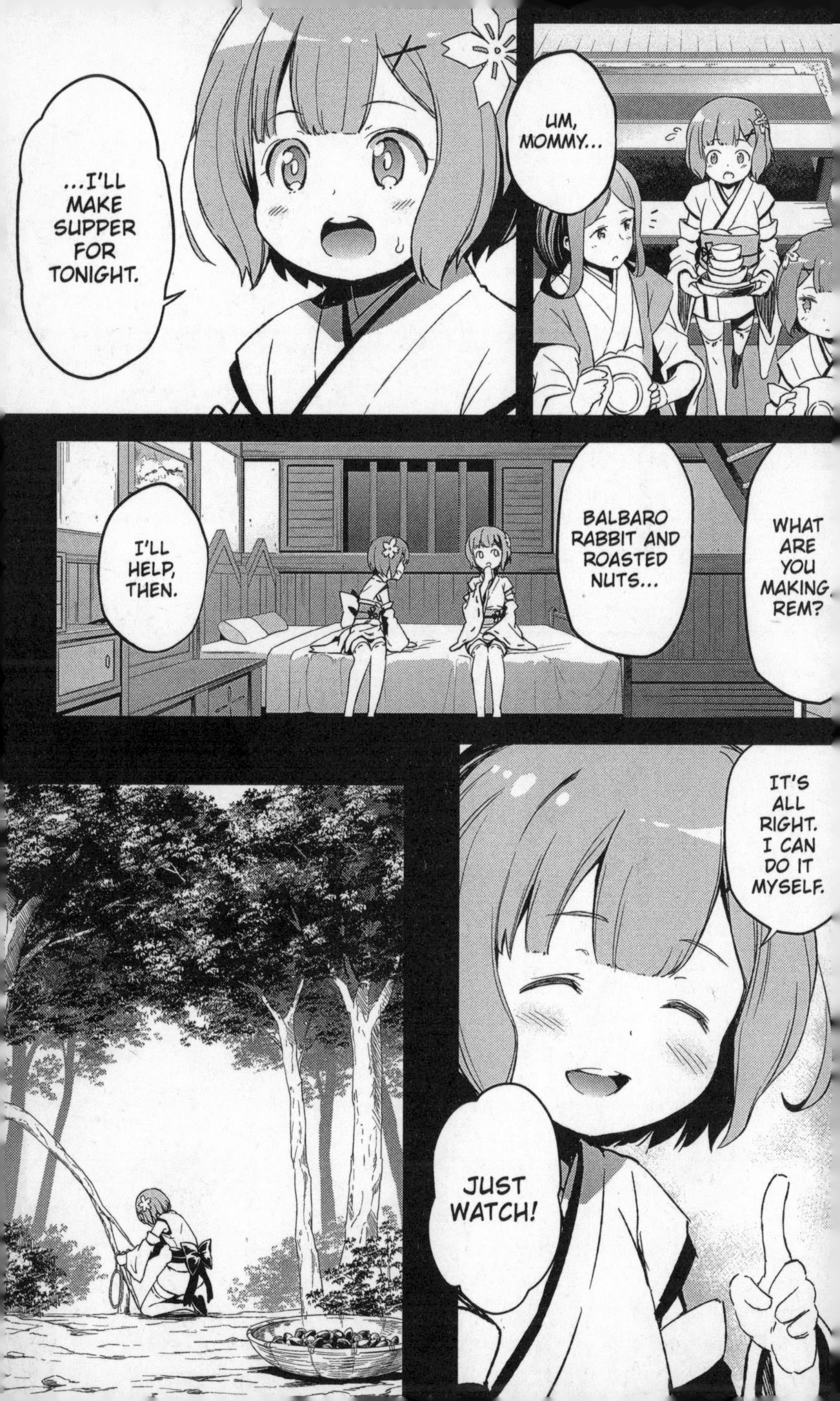
UM, MOMMY...
...I'LL MAKE SUPPER FOR TONIGHT.
WHAT ARE YOU MAKING, REM?
BALBARO RABBIT AND ROASTED NUTS...
I'LL HELP, THEN.
IT'S ALL RIGHT. I CAN DO IT MYSELF.
JUST WATCH!

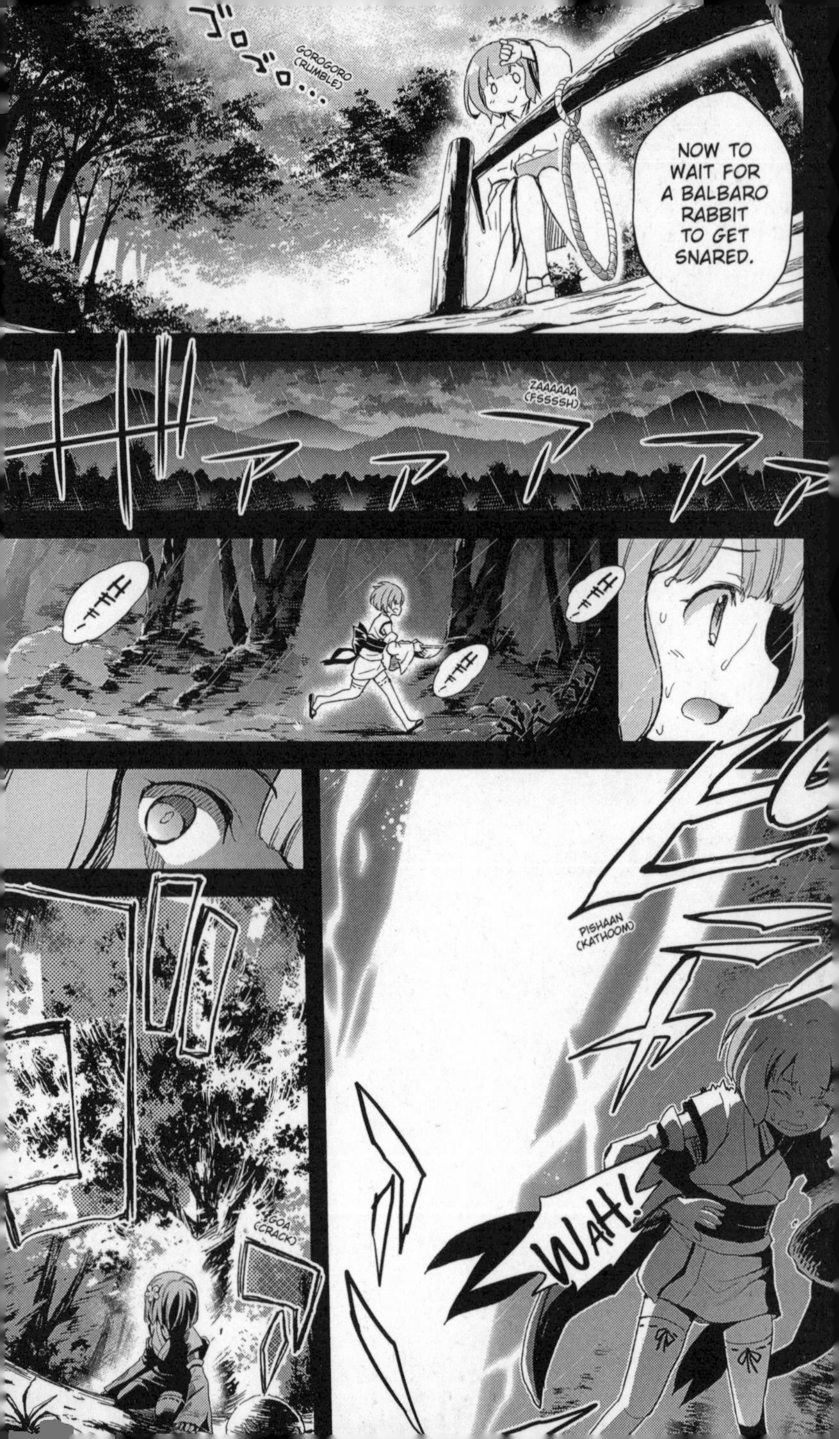
ゴロゴロ・・・
GOROGORO (RUMBLE)
NOW TO WAIT FOR A BALBARO RABBIT TO GET SNARED.
ZAAAAAA (FSSSSH)
PISHAAN (KATHOOM)
WAH!
GOA (CRACK)

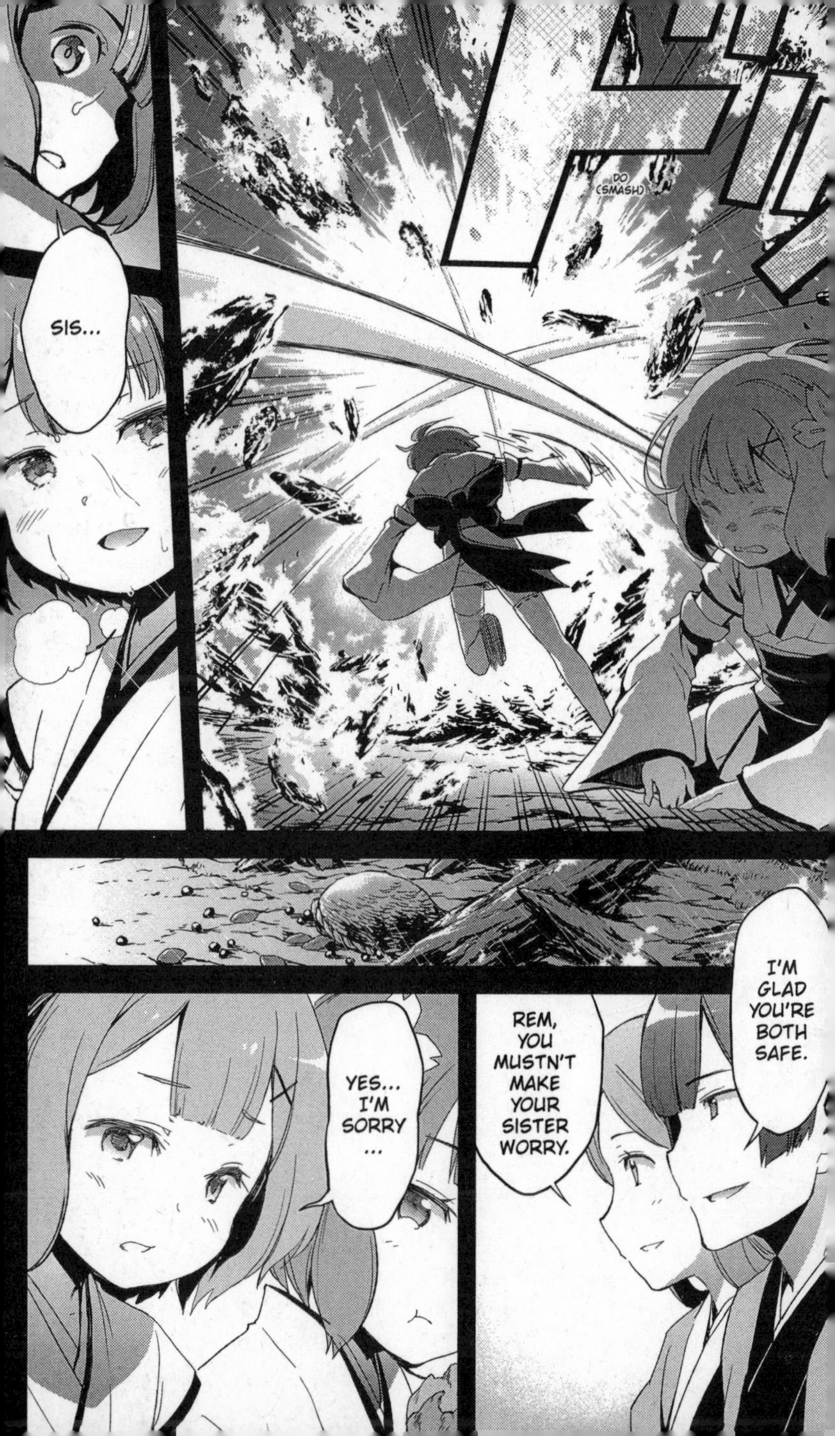
DO (SMASH)
SIS...
I'M GLAD YOU'RE BOTH SAFE.
REM, YOU MUSTN'T MAKE YOUR SISTER WORRY.
YES... I'M SORRY ...

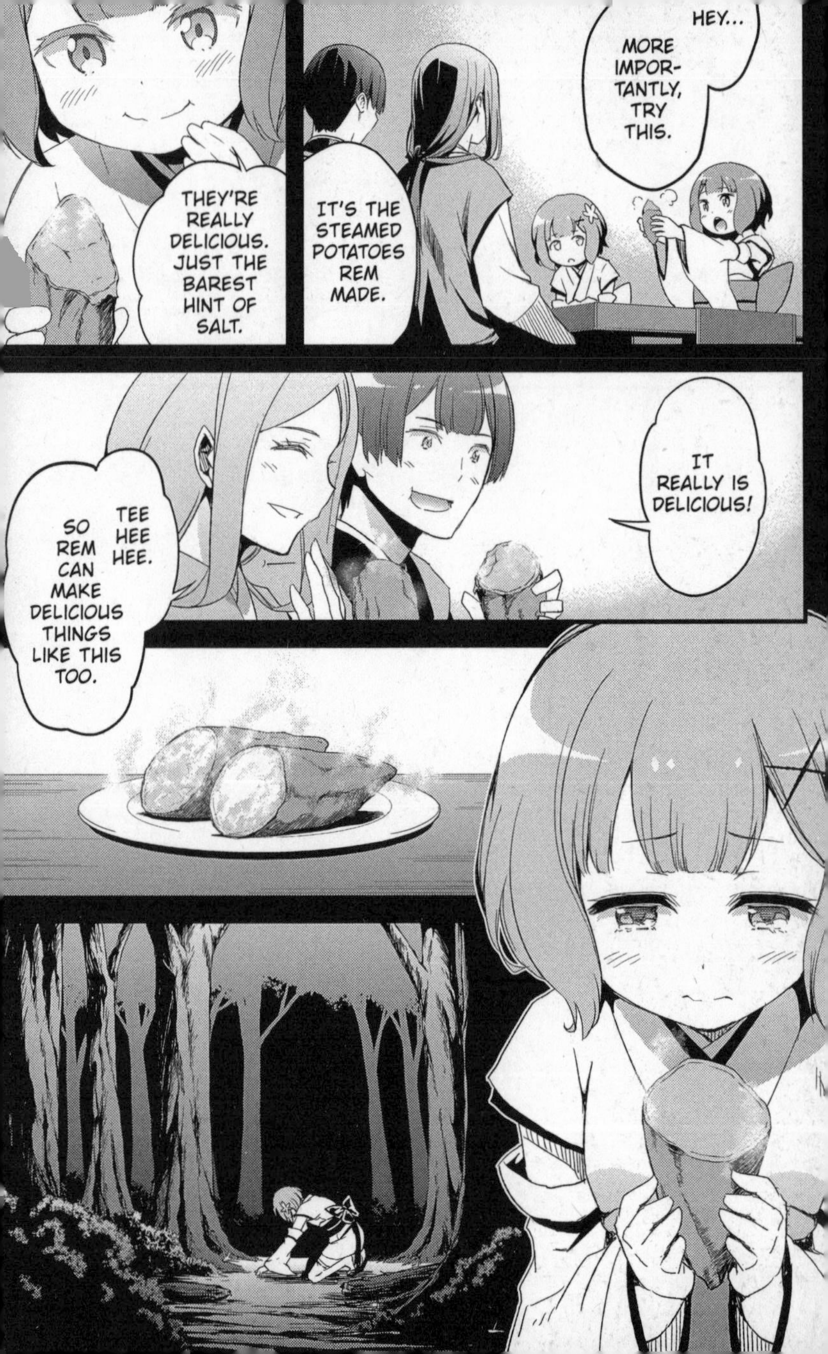
HEY...
MORE IMPORTANTLY, TRY THIS.
IT'S THE STEAMED POTATOES REM MADE.
THEY'RE REALLY DELICIOUS. JUST THE BAREST HINT OF SALT.
IT REALLY IS DELICIOUS!
TEE HEE HEE.
SO REM CAN MAKE DELICIOUS THINGS LIKE THIS TOO.

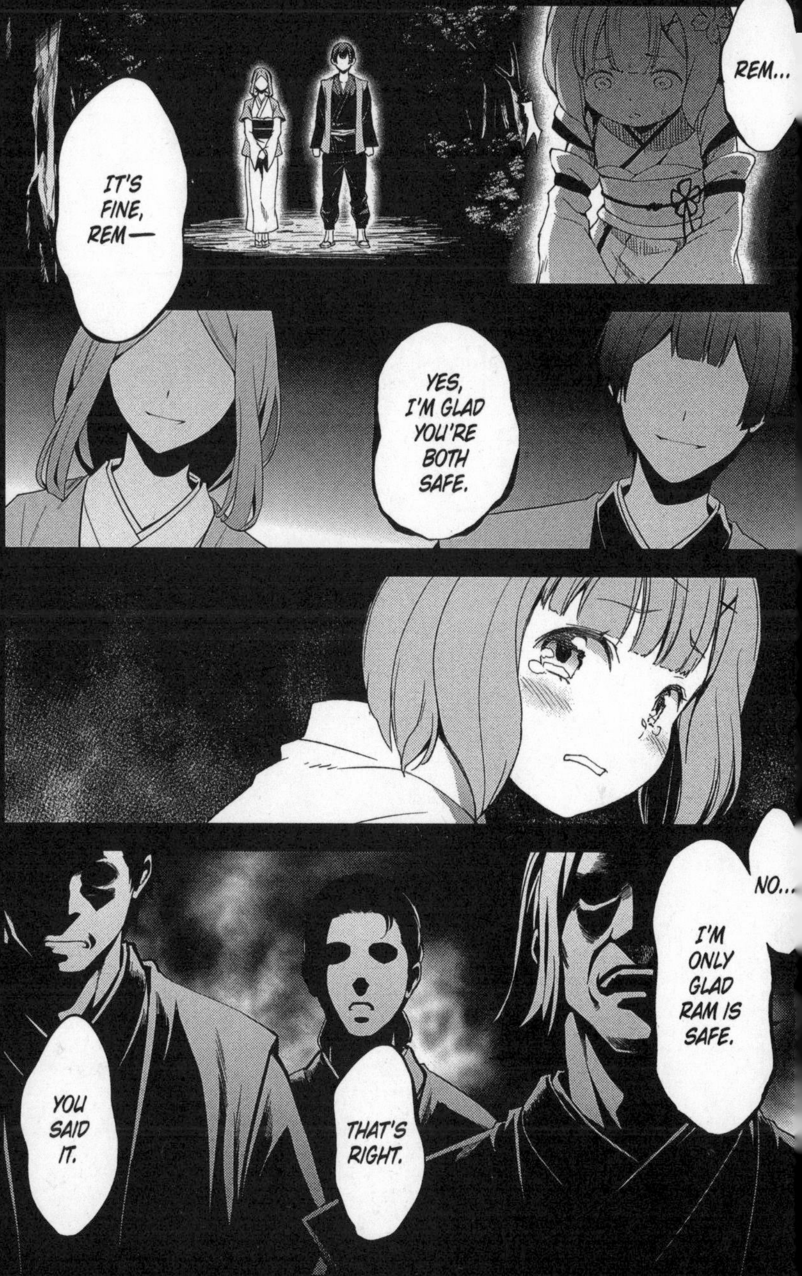
REM...
IT'S FINE, REM—
YES, I'M GLAD YOU'RE BOTH SAFE.
NO...
I'M ONLY GLAD RAM IS SAFE.
THAT'S RIGHT.
YOU SAID IT.

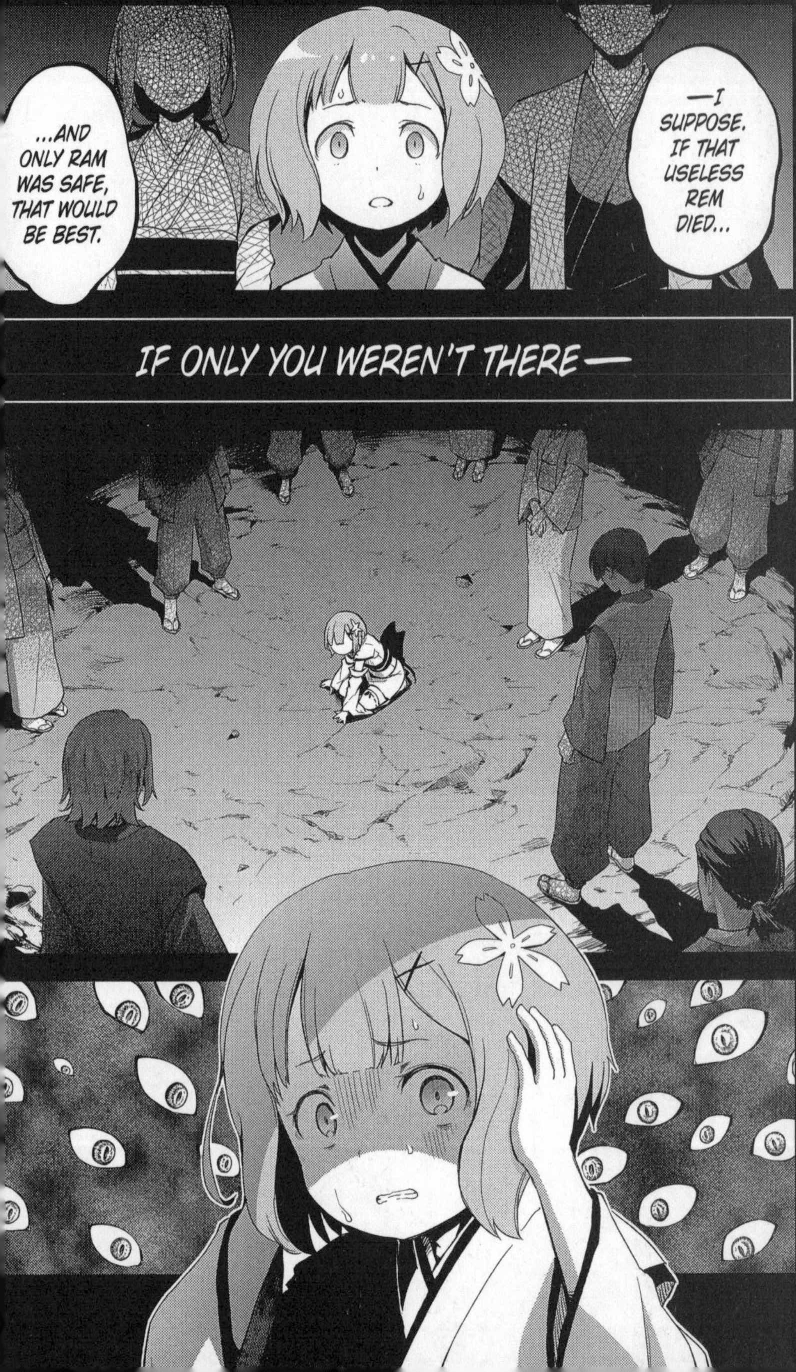
—I SUPPOSE. IF THAT USELESS REM DIED...
...AND ONLY RAM WAS SAFE, THAT WOULD BE BEST.
IF ONLY YOU WEREN'T THERE—

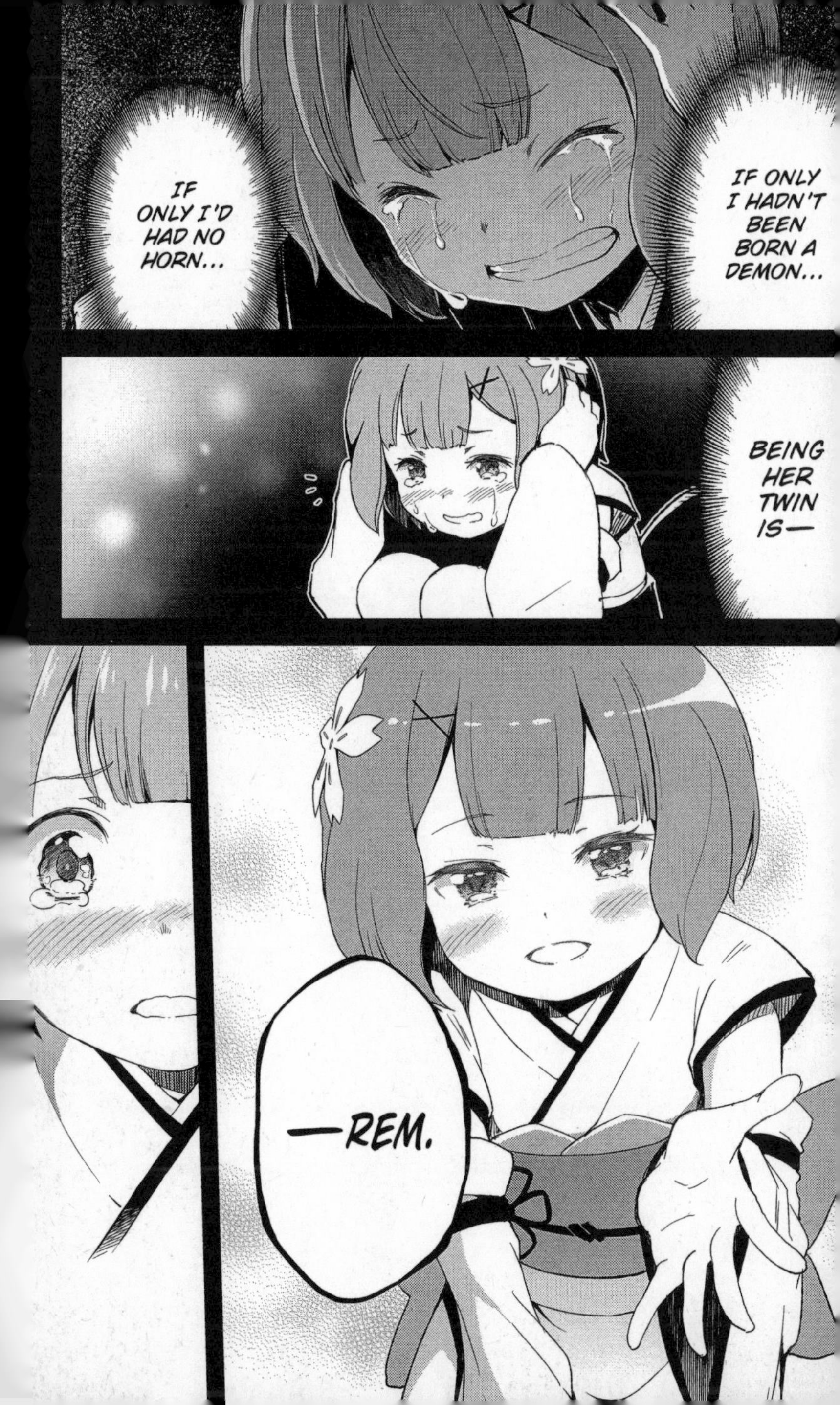
IF ONLY I HADN'T BEEN BORN A DEMON...
IF ONLY I'D HAD NO HORN...
BEING HER TWIN IS—
—REM.

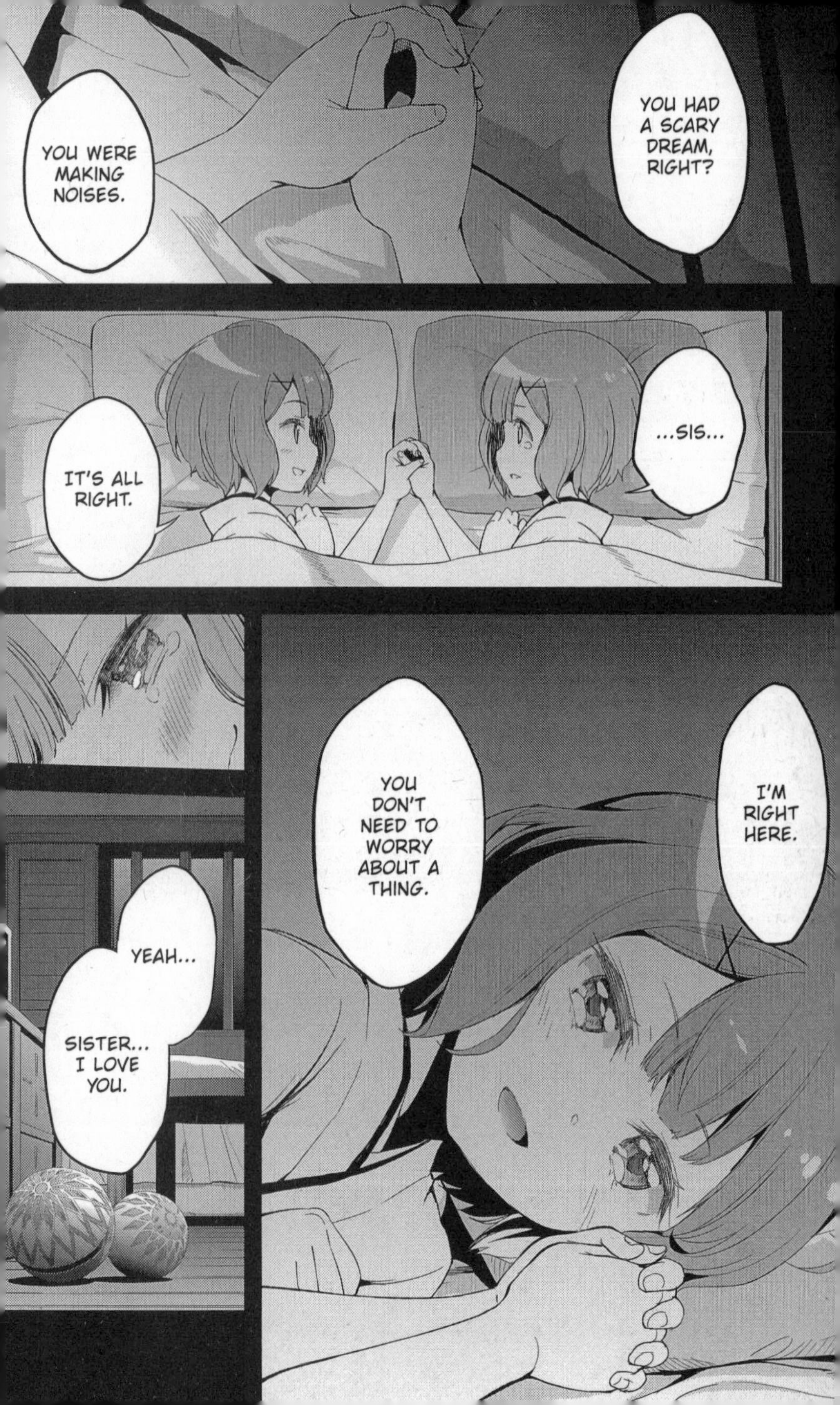
YOU HAD A SCARY DREAM, RIGHT?
YOU WERE MAKING NOISES.
...SIS...
IT'S ALL RIGHT.
I'M RIGHT HERE.
YOU DON'T NEED TO WORRY ABOUT A THING.
YEAH...
SISTER... I LOVE YOU.

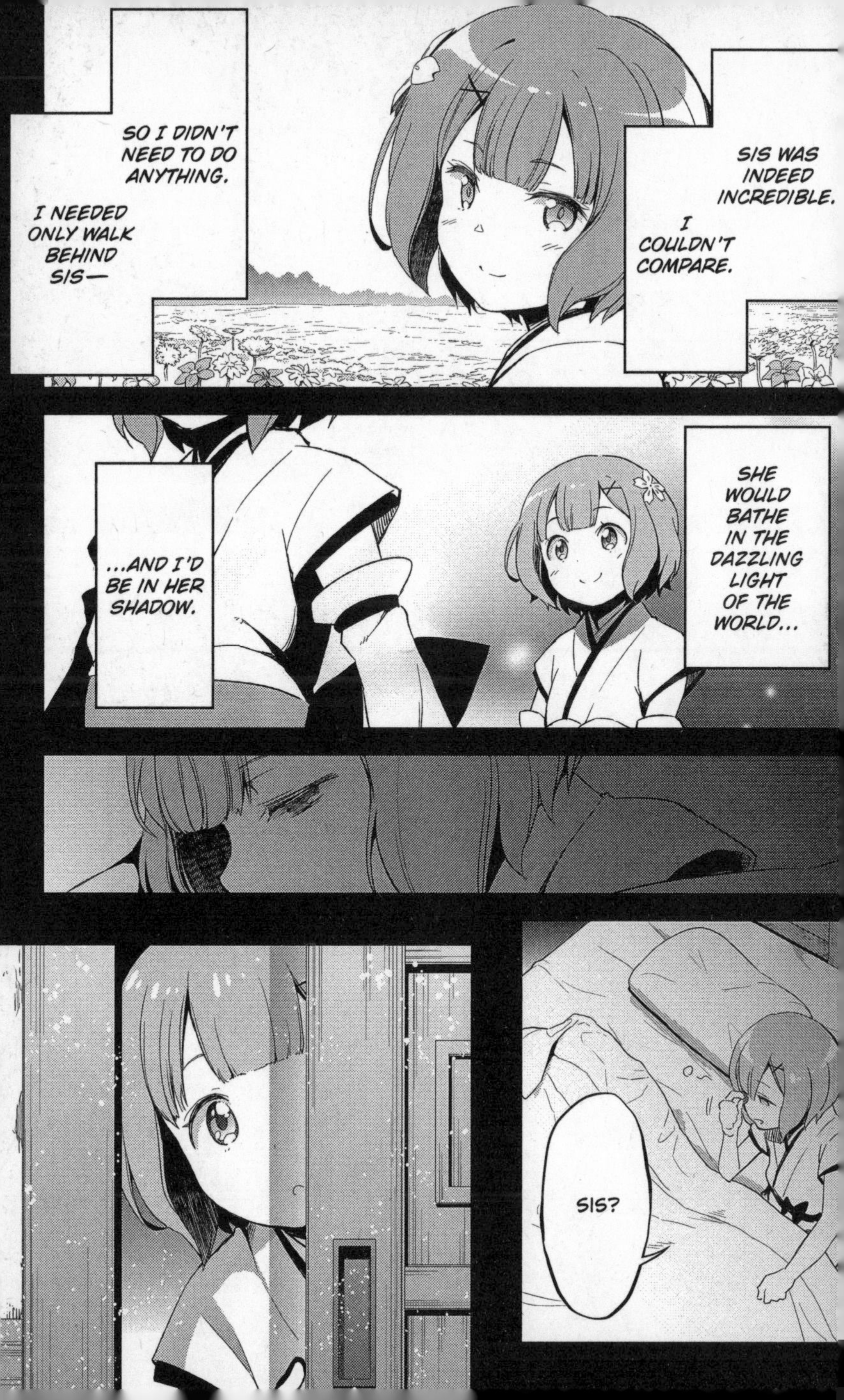
SIS WAS INDEED INCREDIBLE.
I COULDN'T COMPARE.
SO I DIDN'T NEED TO DO ANYTHING.
I NEEDED ONLY WALK BEHIND SIS—
SHE WOULD BATHE IN THE DAZZLING LIGHT OF THE WORLD...
...AND I'D BE IN HER SHADOW.
SIS?

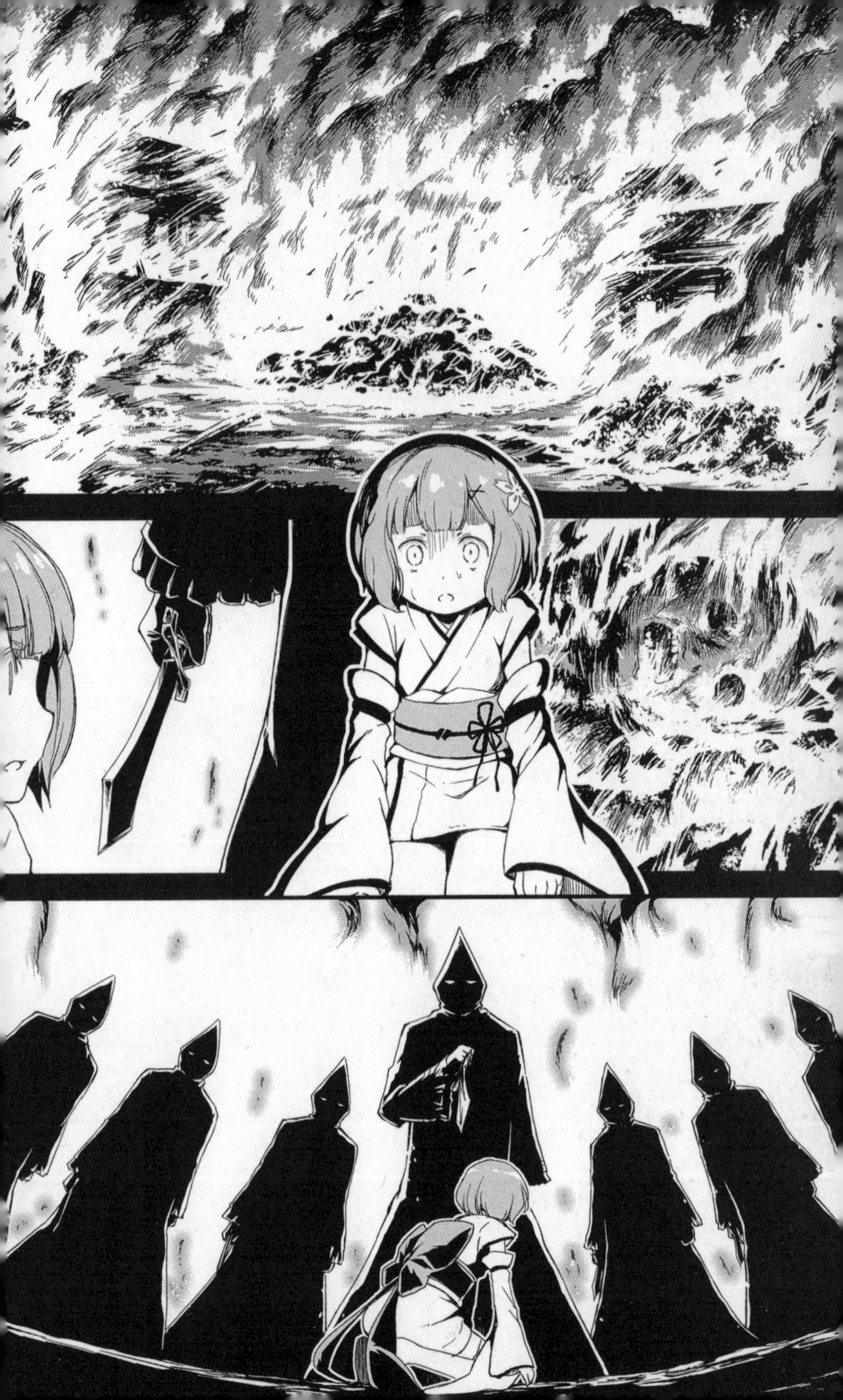

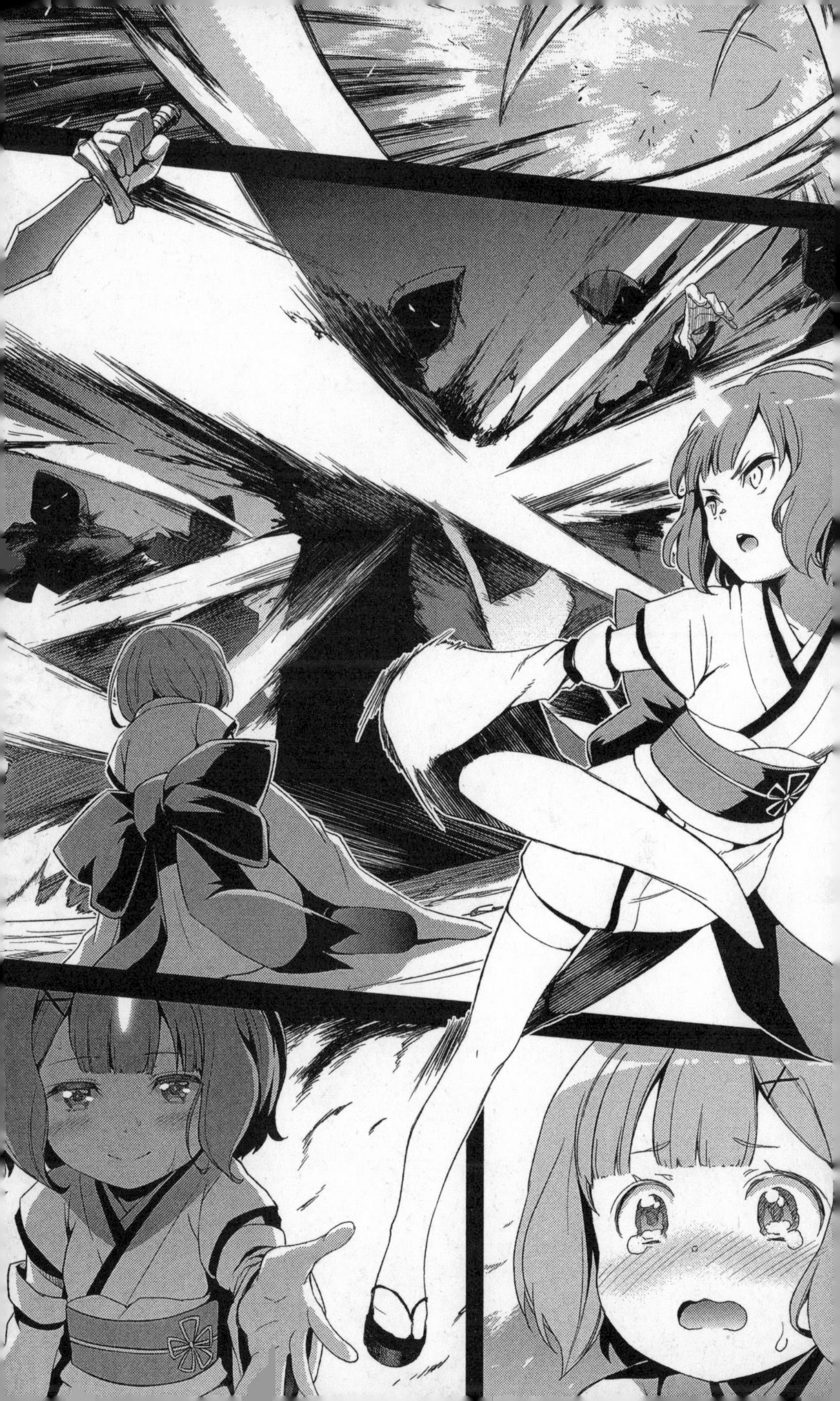

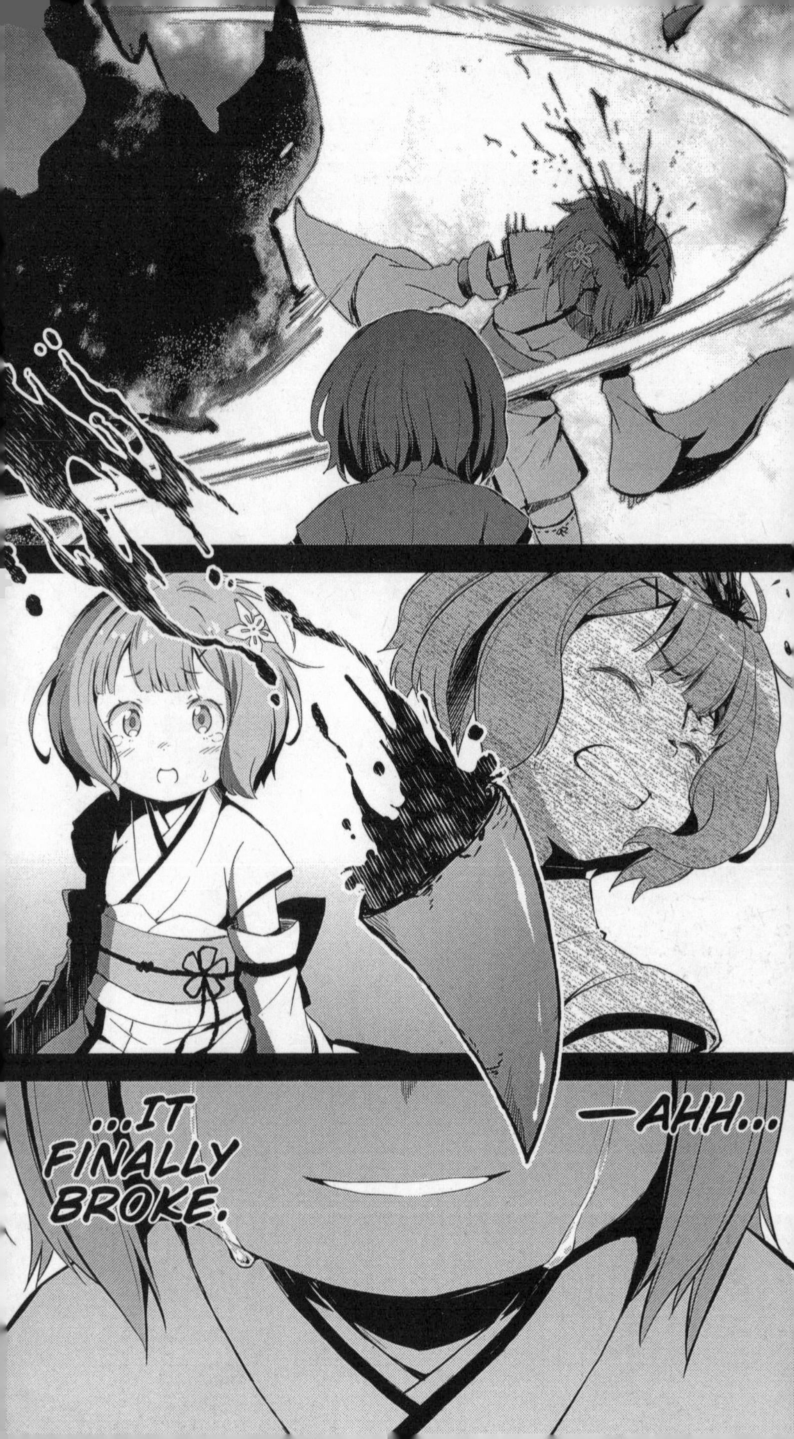
—AHH...
...IT FINALLY BROKE.

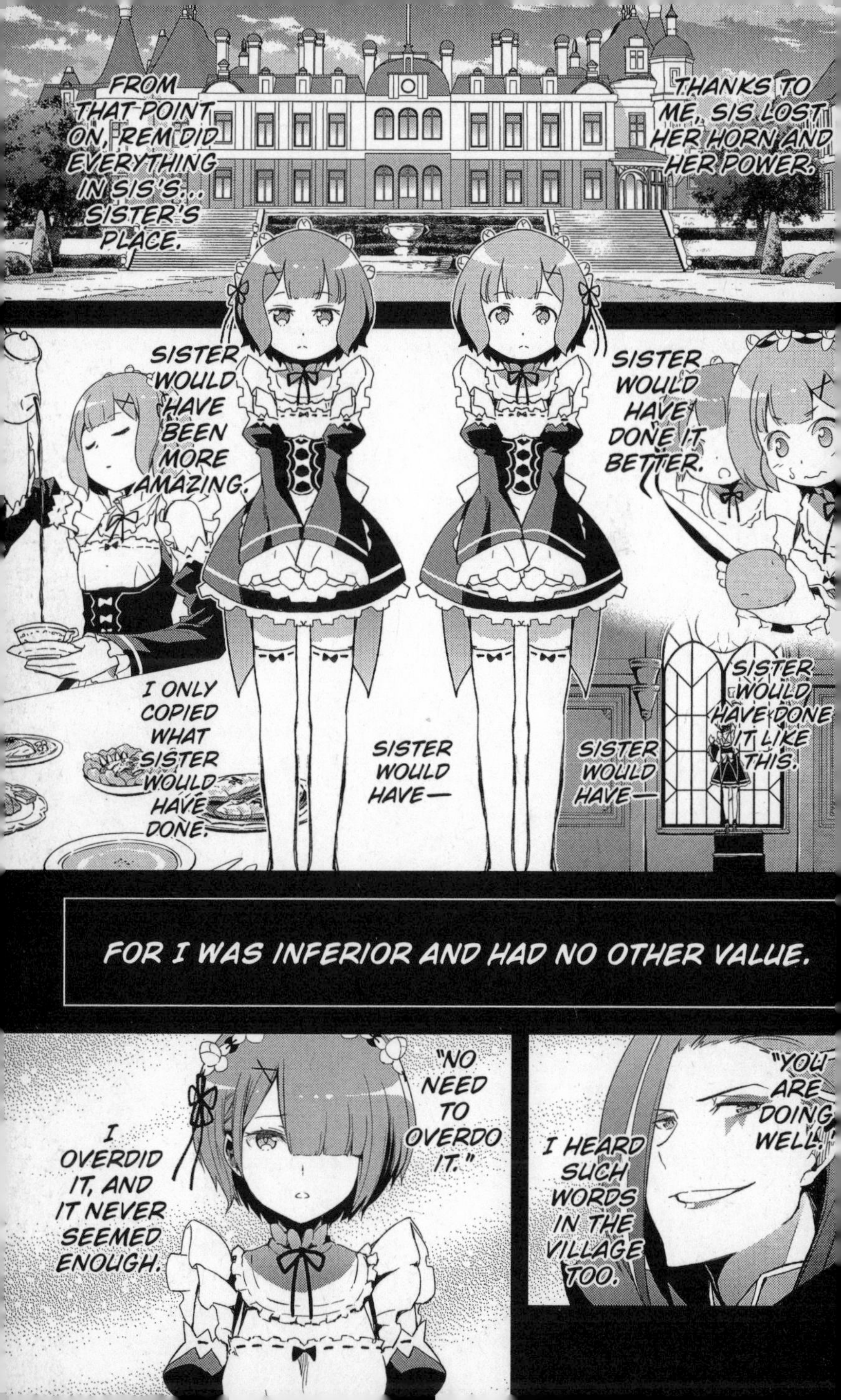
THANKS TO ME, SIS LOST HER HORN AND HER POWER.
FROM THAT POINT ON, REM DID EVERYTHING IN SIS'S... SISTER'S PLACE.
SISTER WOULD HAVE DONE IT BETTER.
SISTER WOULD HAVE BEEN MORE AMAZING.
SISTER WOULD HAVE DONE IT LIKE THIS.
SISTER WOULD HAVE—
SISTER WOULD HAVE—
I ONLY COPIED WHAT SISTER WOULD HAVE DONE.
FOR I WAS INFERIOR AND HAD NO OTHER VALUE.
"YOU ARE DOING WELL."
I HEARD SUCH WORDS IN THE VILLAGE TOO.
"NO NEED TO OVERDO IT."
I OVERDID IT, AND IT NEVER SEEMED ENOUGH.

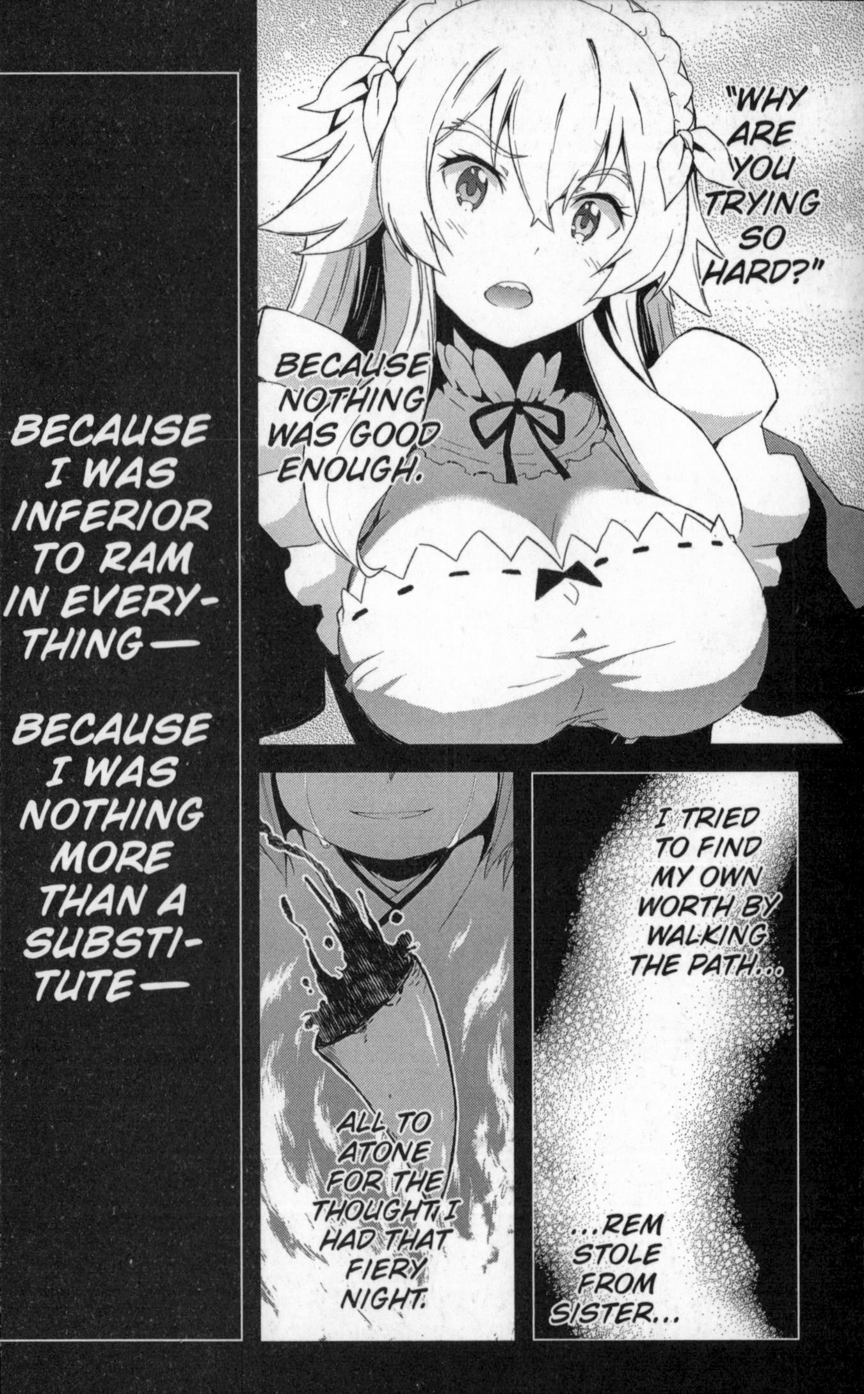
"WHY ARE YOU TRYING SO HARD?"
BECAUSE NOTHING WAS GOOD ENOUGH.
I TRIED TO FIND MY OWN WORTH BY WALKING THE PATH...
...REM STOLE FROM SISTER...
ALL TO ATONE FOR THE THOUGHT I HAD THAT FIERY NIGHT.
BECAUSE I WAS INFERIOR TO RAM IN EVERY-THING—
BECAUSE I WAS NOTHING MORE THAN A SUBSTI-TUTE—

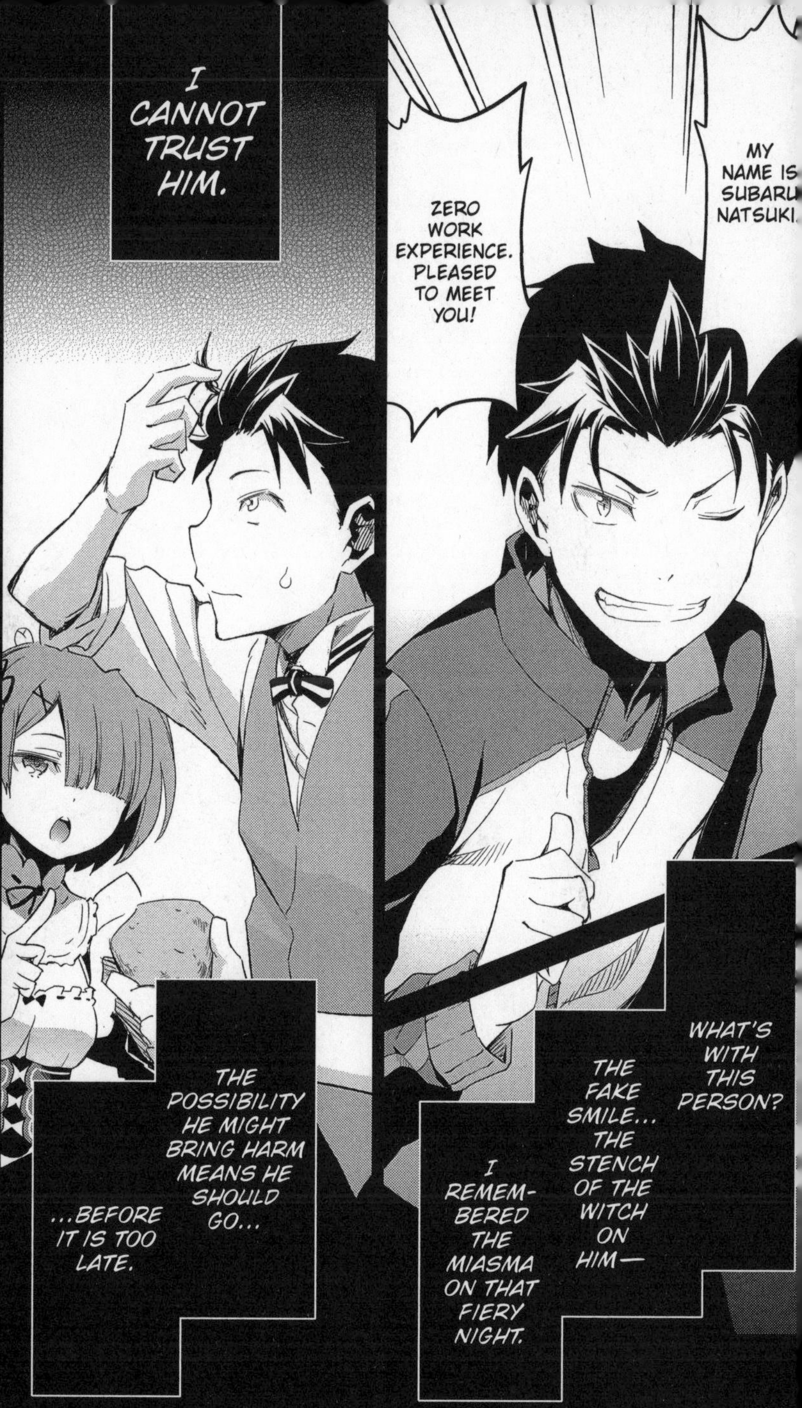
MY NAME IS SUBARU NATSUKI.
ZERO WORK EXPERIENCE. PLEASED TO MEET YOU!
WHAT'S WITH THIS PERSON?
THE FAKE SMILE... THE STENCH OF THE WITCH ON HIM—
I REMEMBERED THE MIASMA ON THAT FIERY NIGHT.
I CANNOT TRUST HIM.
THE POSSIBILITY HE MIGHT BRING HARM MEANS HE SHOULD GO...
...BEFORE IT IS TOO LATE.

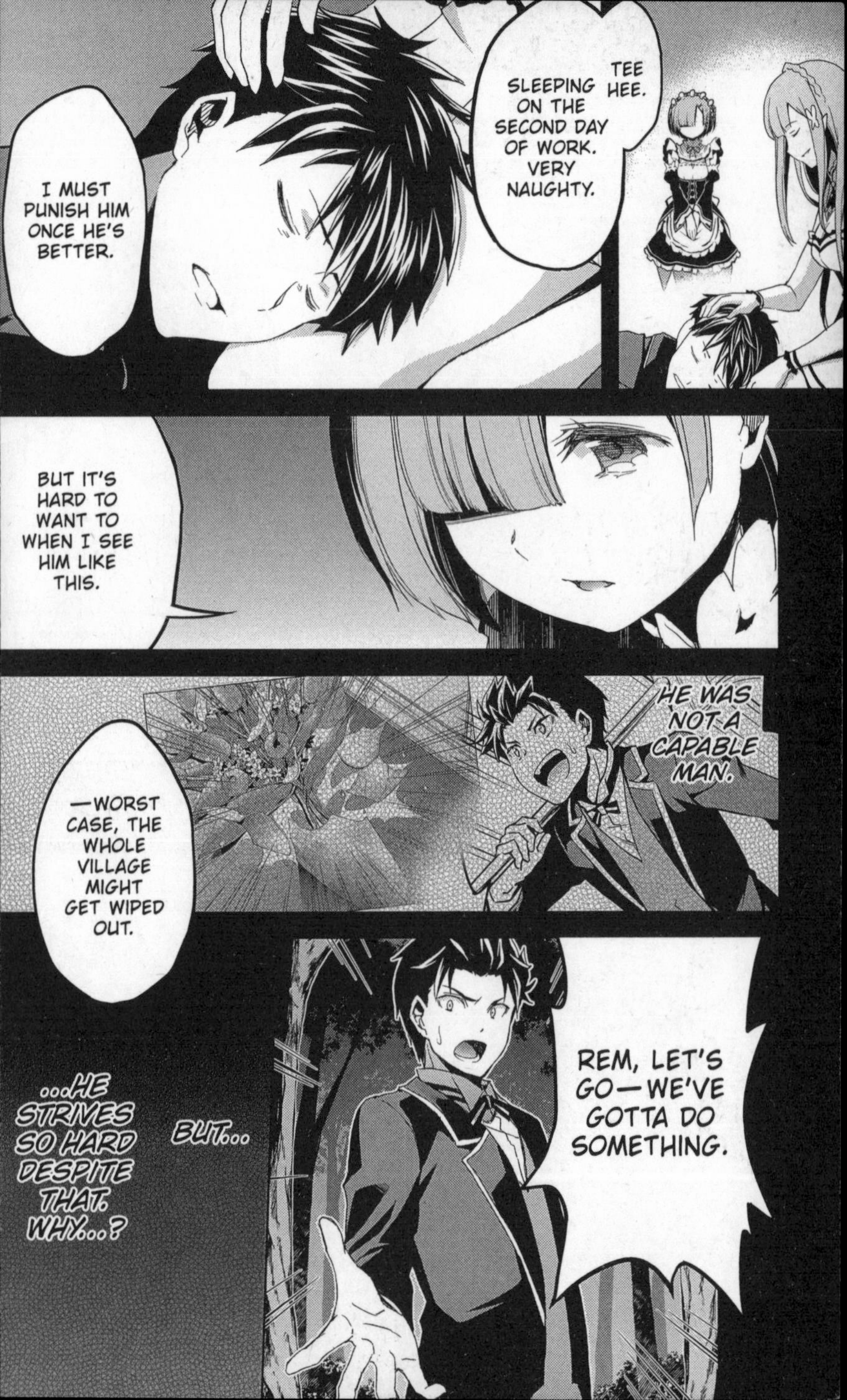
TEE HEE. SLEEPING ON THE SECOND DAY OF WORK. VERY NAUGHTY.
I MUST PUNISH HIM ONCE HE'S BETTER.
BUT IT'S HARD TO WANT TO WHEN I SEE HIM LIKE THIS.
HE WAS NOT A CAPABLE MAN.
—WORST CASE, THE WHOLE VILLAGE MIGHT GET WIPED OUT.
REM, LET'S GO—WE'VE GOTTA DO SOMETHING.
BUT...
...HE STRIVES SO HARD DESPITE THAT. WHY...?

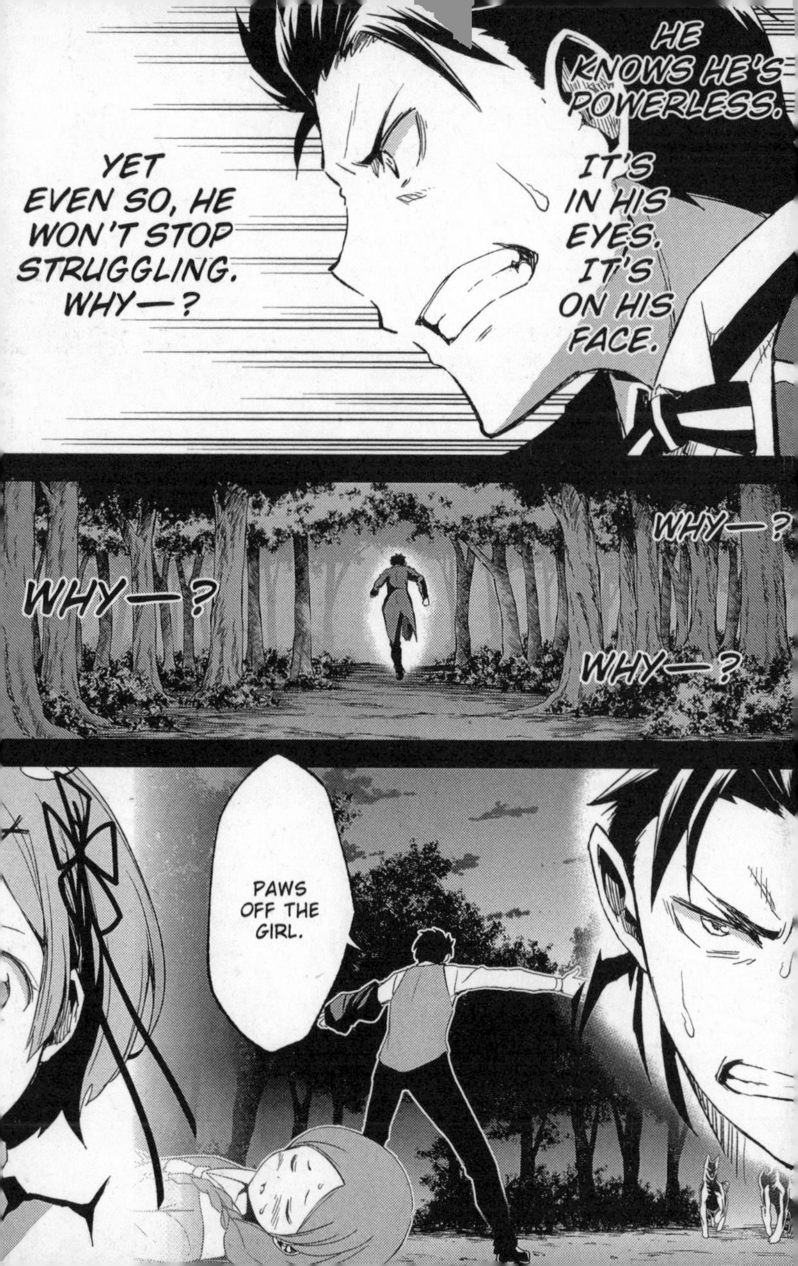
HE KNOWS HE'S POWERLESS.
IT'S IN HIS EYES. IT'S ON HIS FACE.
YET EVEN SO, HE WON'T STOP STRUGGLING. WHY—?
WHY—?
WHY—?
WHY—?
PAWS OFF THE GIRL.

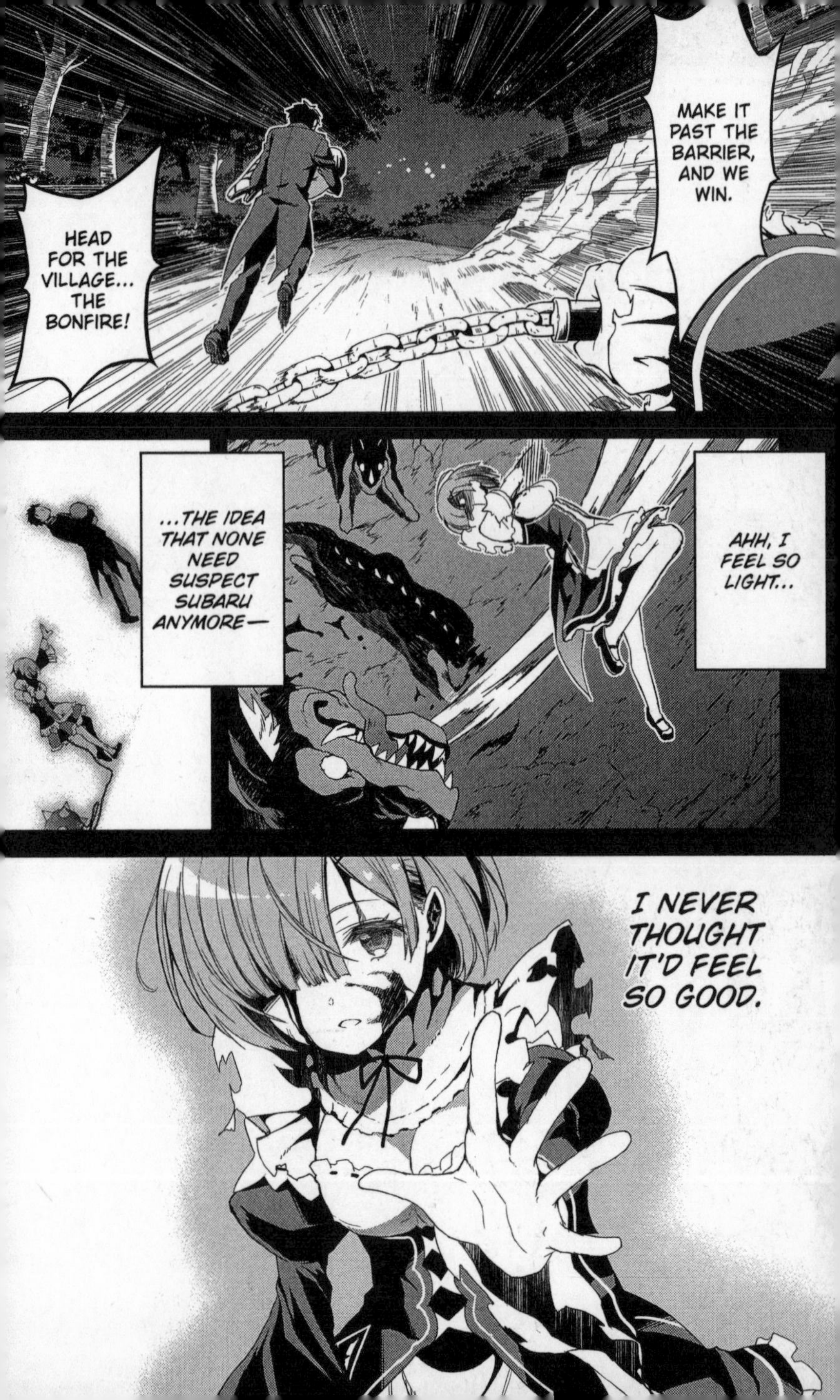
MAKE IT PAST THE BARRIER, AND WE WIN.
HEAD FOR THE VILLAGE... THE BONFIRE!
AHH, I FEEL SO LIGHT...
...THE IDEA THAT NONE NEED SUSPECT SUBARU ANYMORE—
I NEVER THOUGHT IT'D FEEL SO GOOD.

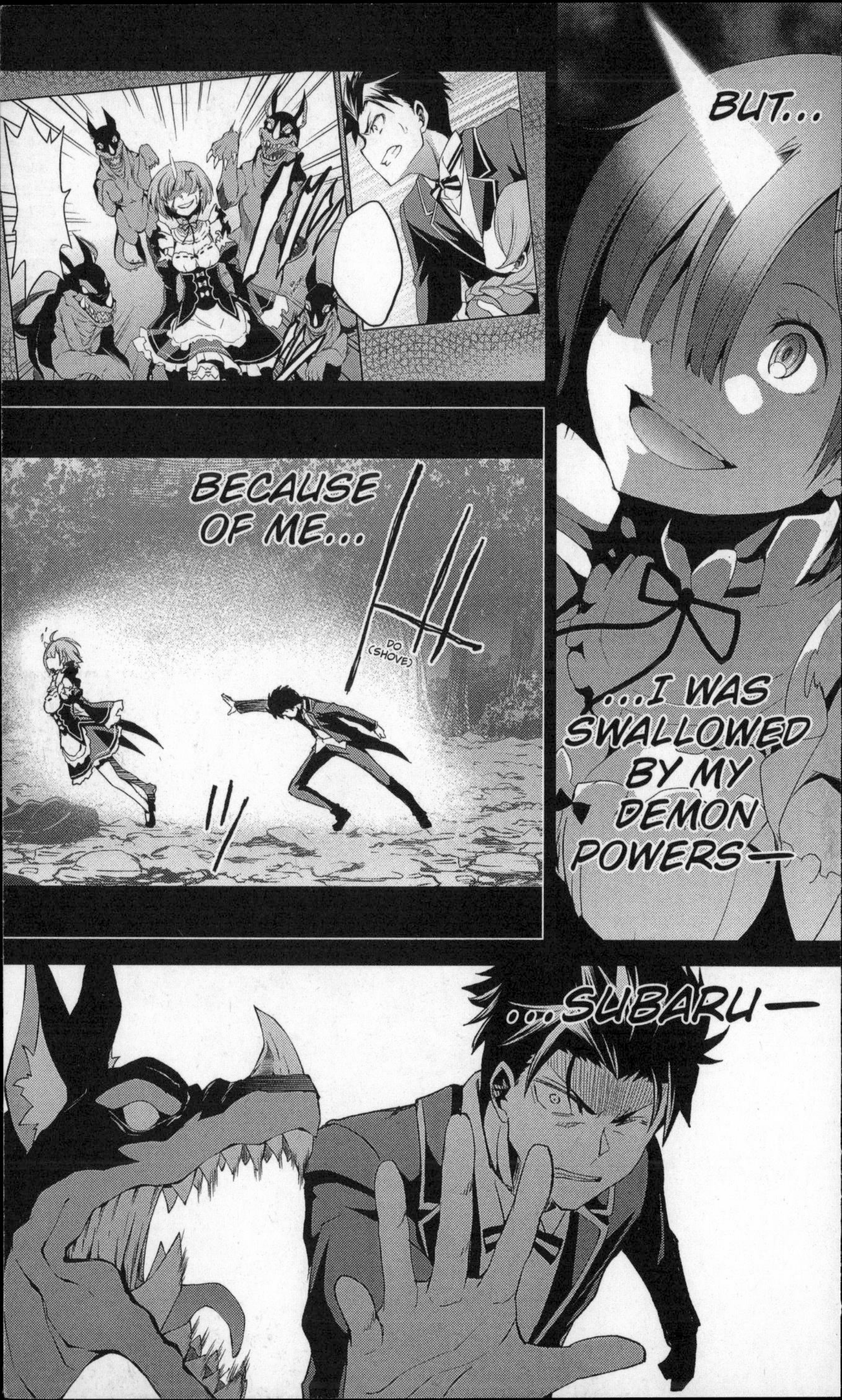
BUT...
...I WAS SWALLOWED BY MY DEMON POWERS—
BECAUSE OF ME...
DO
(SHOVE)
...SUBARU—

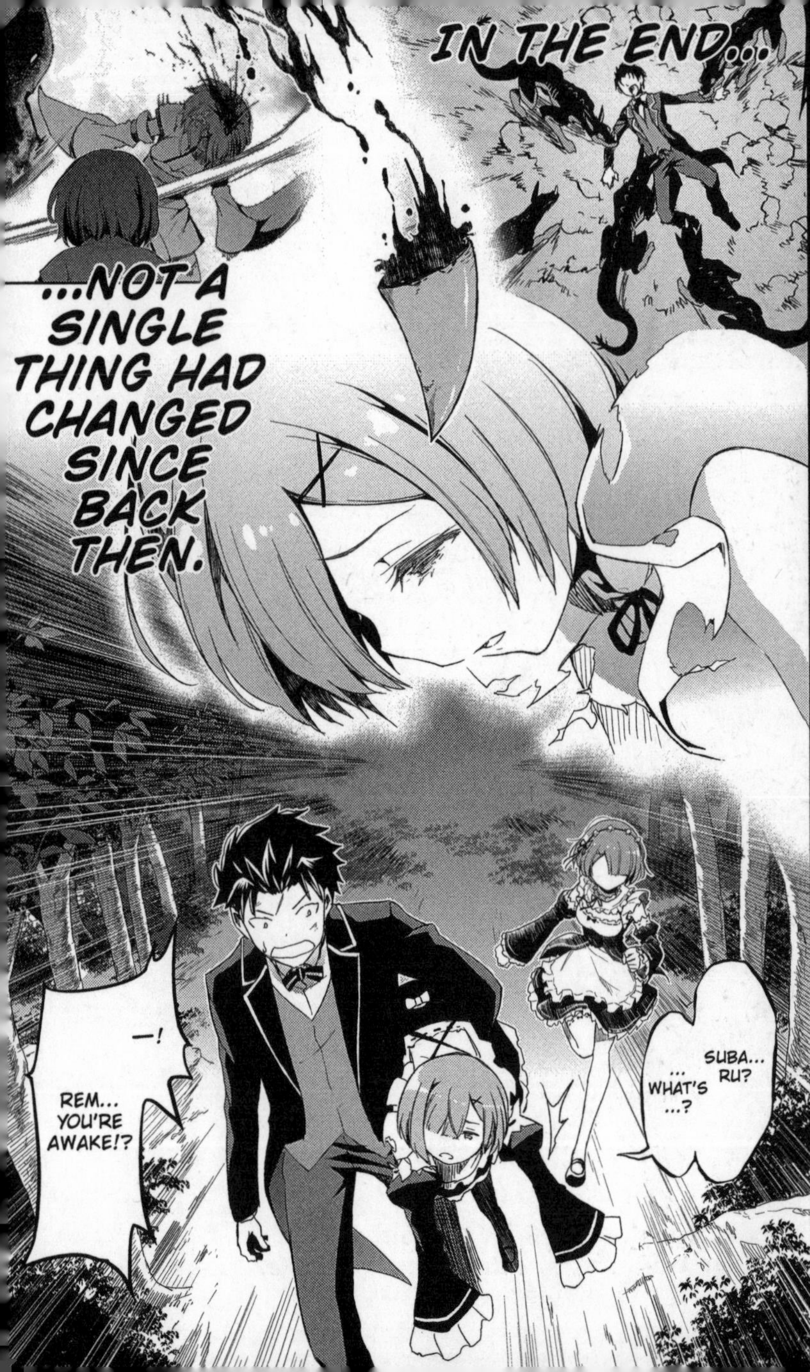
IN THE END...
...NOT A SINGLE THING HAD CHANGED SINCE BACK THEN.
SUBA... RU?
... WHAT'S ...?
—!
REM... YOU'RE AWAKE!?

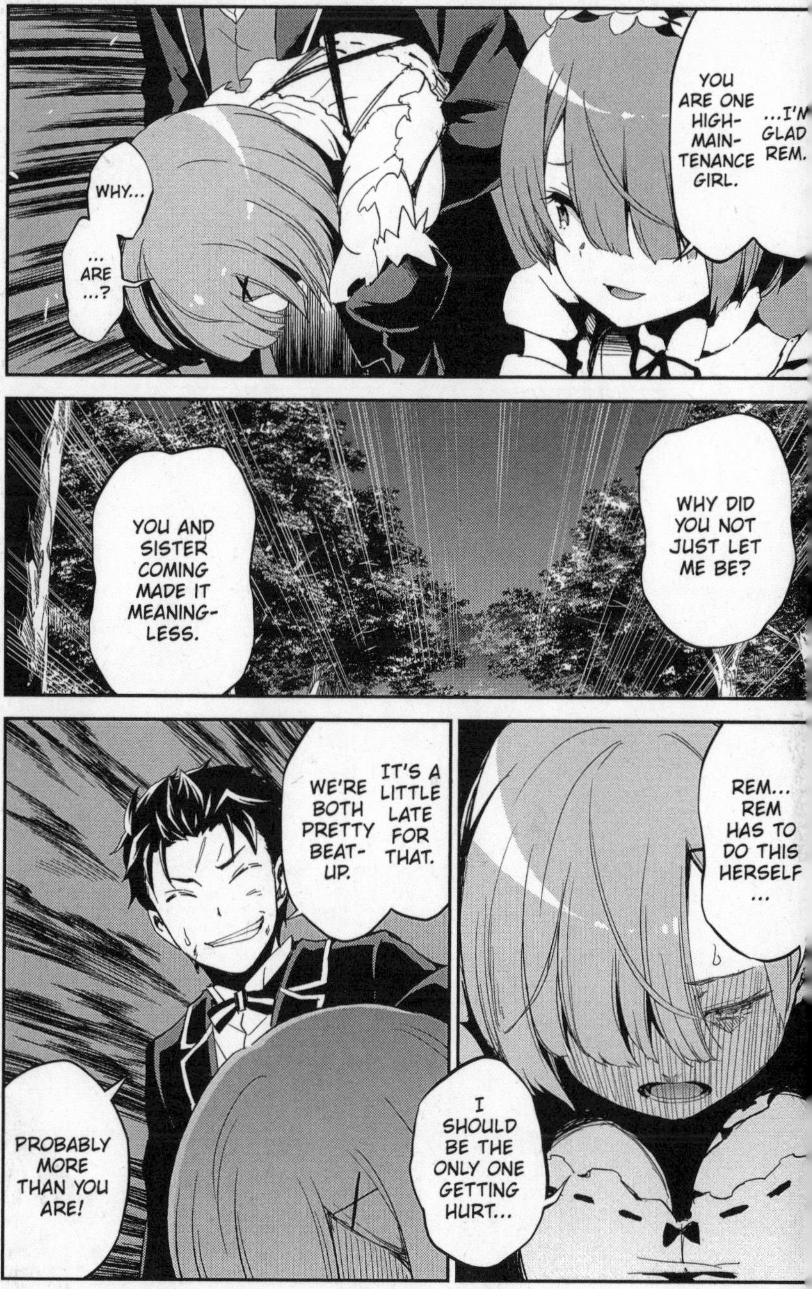
...I'M GLAD REM.
YOU ARE ONE HIGH-MAINTENANCE GIRL.
WHY...
...ARE...?
WHY DID YOU NOT JUST LET ME BE?
YOU AND SISTER COMING MADE IT MEANINGLESS.
REM... REM HAS TO DO THIS HERSELF...
I SHOULD BE THE ONLY ONE GETTING HURT...
IT'S A LITTLE LATE FOR THAT.
WE'RE BOTH PRETTY BEAT-UP.
PROBABLY MORE THAN YOU ARE!

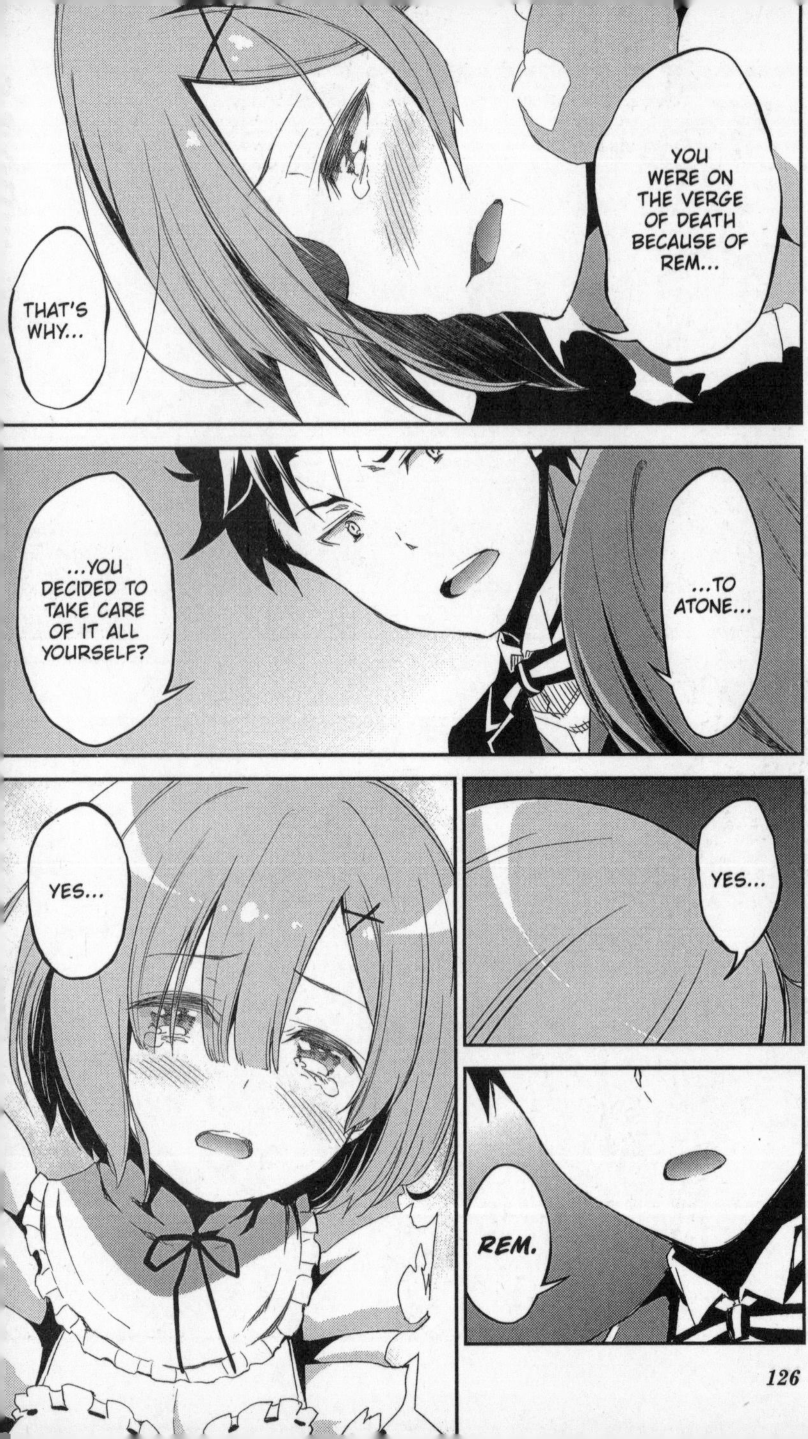

YOU WERE ON THE VERGE OF DEATH BECAUSE OF REM...
THAT'S WHY...
...TO ATONE...
...YOU DECIDED TO TAKE CARE OF IT ALL YOURSELF?
YES...
REM.
YES...

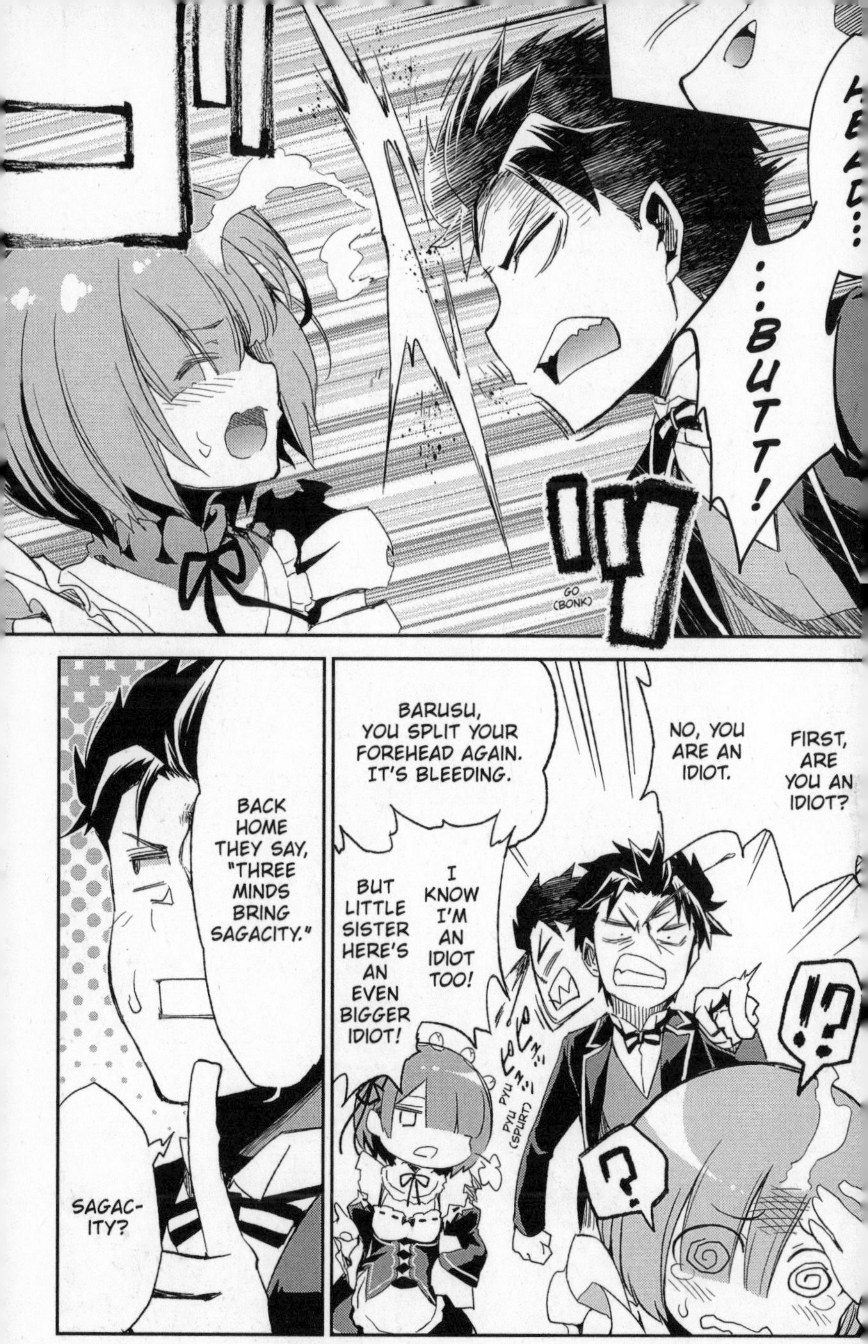
HEAD... ...BUTT!
GO (BONK)
FIRST, ARE YOU AN IDIOT?
NO, YOU ARE AN IDIOT.
BARUSU, YOU SPLIT YOUR FOREHEAD AGAIN. IT'S BLEEDING.
I KNOW I'M AN IDIOT TOO!
BUT LITTLE SISTER HERE'S AN EVEN BIGGER IDIOT!
!?
PYU PYU (SPURT)
?
BACK HOME THEY SAY, "THREE MINDS BRING SAGACITY."
SAGAC-ITY?

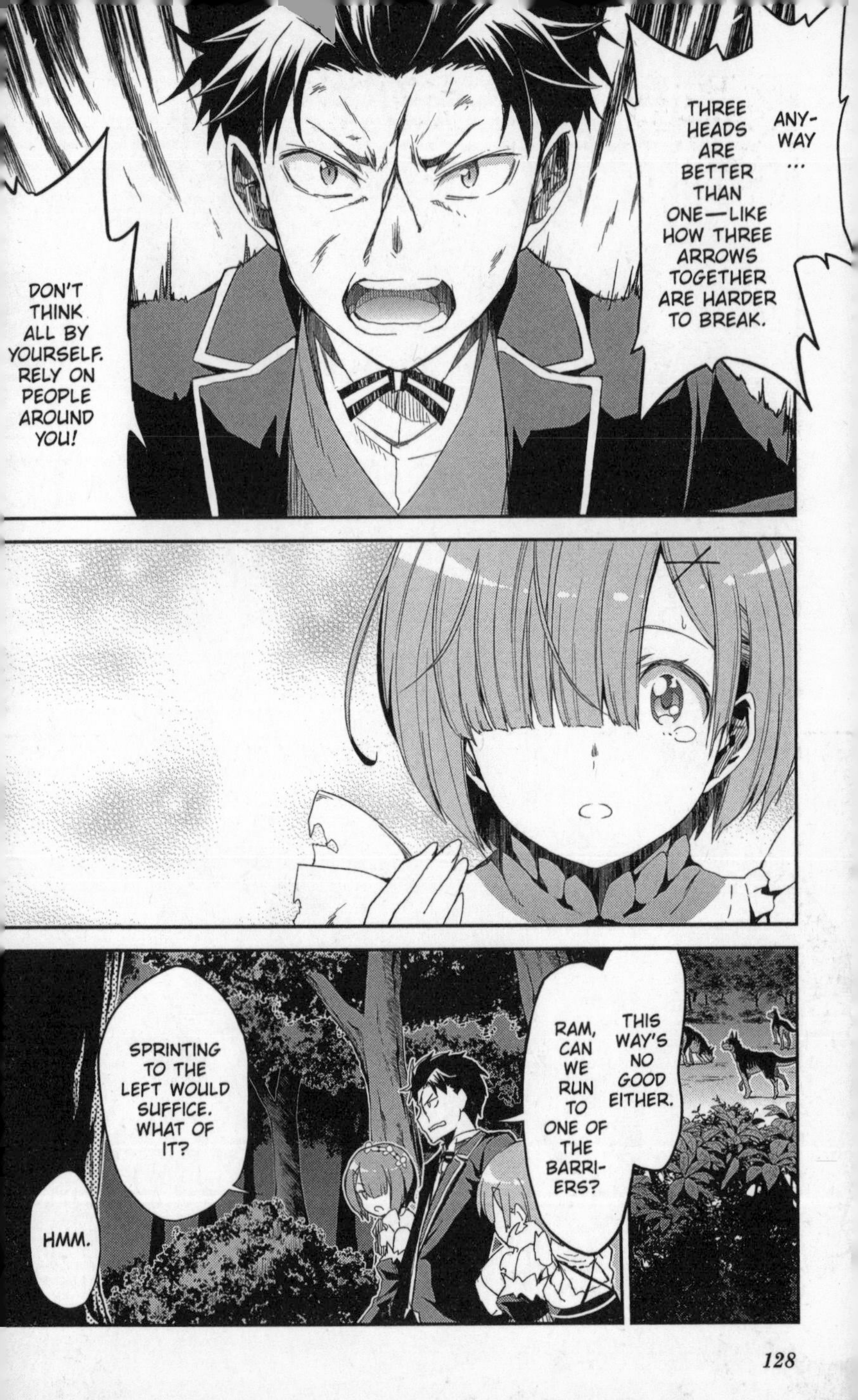
ANYWAY...
THREE HEADS ARE BETTER THAN ONE—LIKE HOW THREE ARROWS TOGETHER ARE HARDER TO BREAK.
DON'T THINK ALL BY YOURSELF. RELY ON PEOPLE AROUND YOU!
THIS WAY'S NO GOOD EITHER.
RAM, CAN WE RUN TO ONE OF THE BARRIERS?
SPRINTING TO THE LEFT WOULD SUFFICE. WHAT OF IT?
HMM.

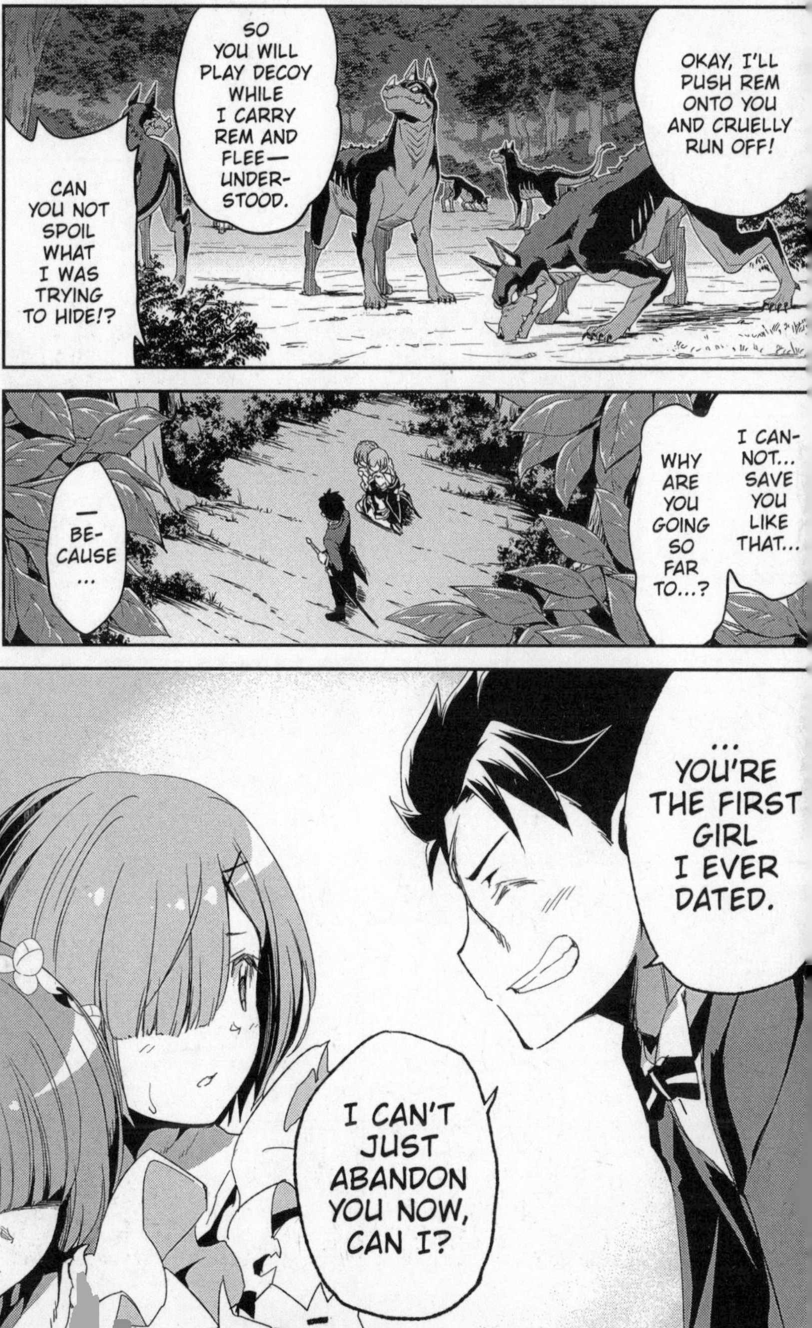
OKAY, I'LL PUSH REM ONTO YOU AND CRUELLY RUN OFF!
SO YOU WILL PLAY DECOY WHILE I CARRY REM AND FLEE—UNDER-STOOD.
CAN YOU NOT SPOIL WHAT I WAS TRYING TO HIDE!?
I CAN-NOT... SAVE YOU LIKE THAT...
WHY ARE YOU GOING SO FAR TO...?
—BE-CAUSE...
...YOU'RE THE FIRST GIRL I EVER DATED.
I CAN'T JUST ABANDON YOU NOW, CAN I?

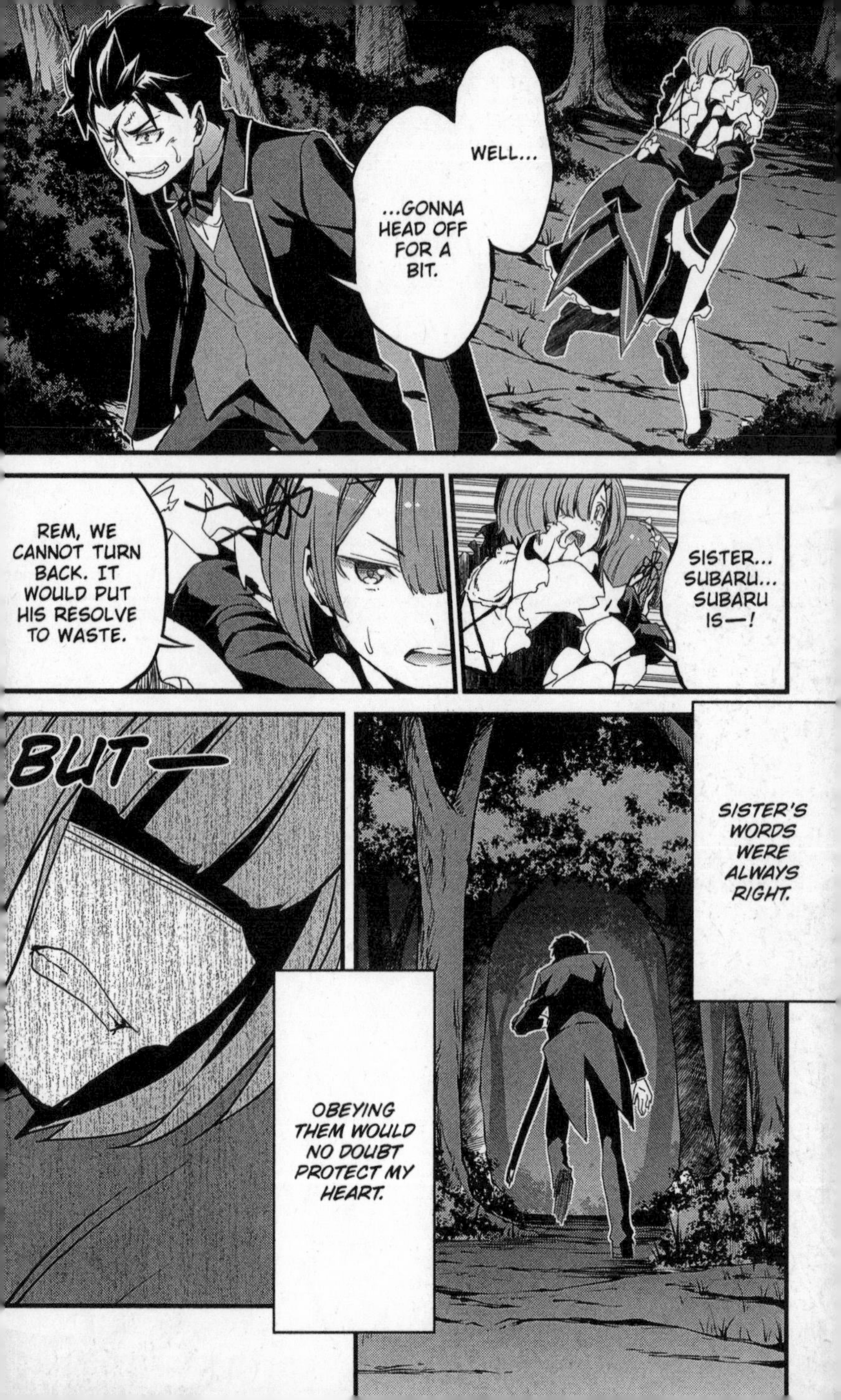
WELL...
...GONNA HEAD OFF FOR A BIT.
SISTER... SUBARU... SUBARU IS—!
REM, WE CANNOT TURN BACK. IT WOULD PUT HIS RESOLVE TO WASTE.
SISTER'S WORDS WERE ALWAYS RIGHT.
OBEYING THEM WOULD NO DOUBT PROTECT MY HEART.
BUT—

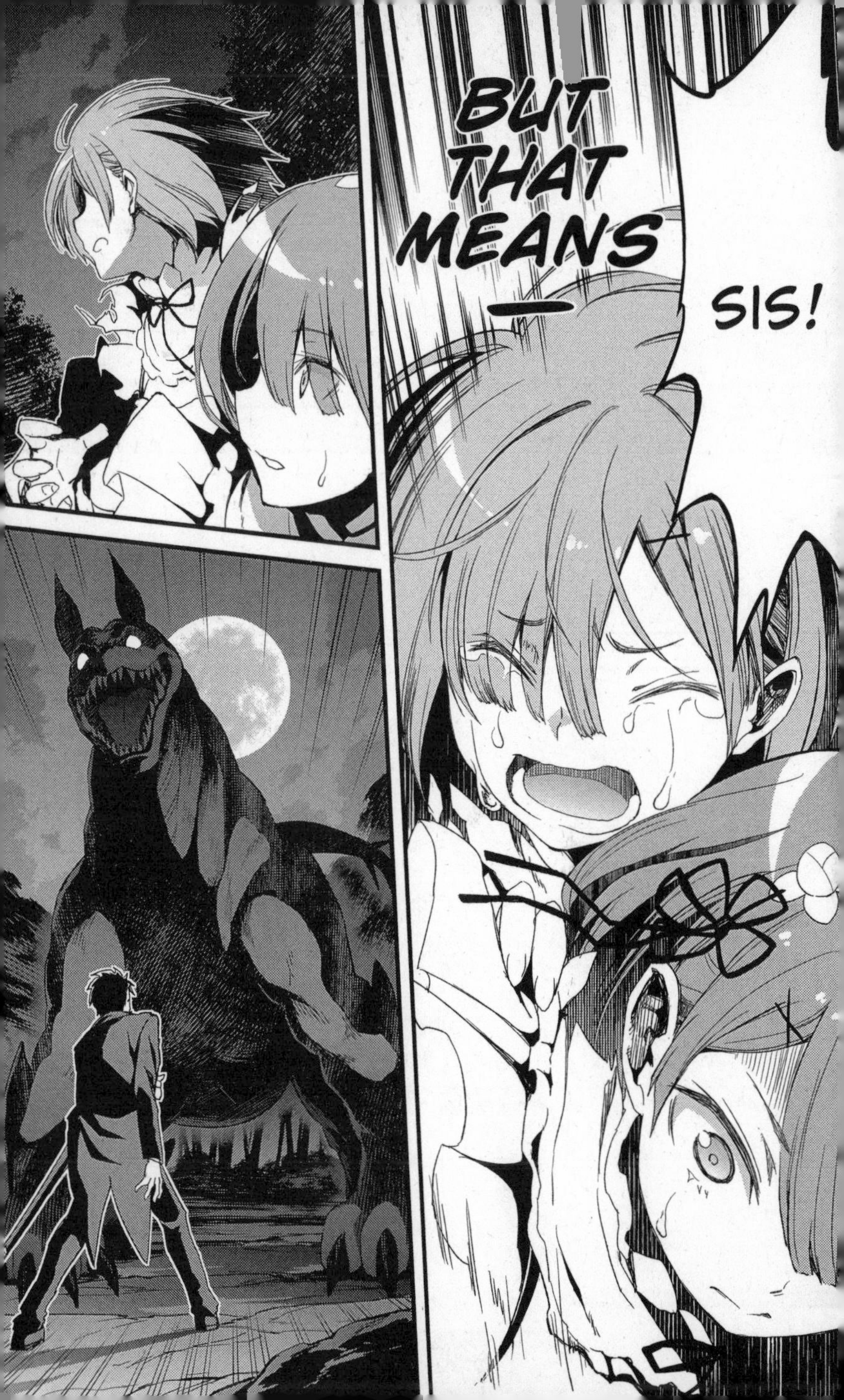
BUT THAT MEANS—
SIS!

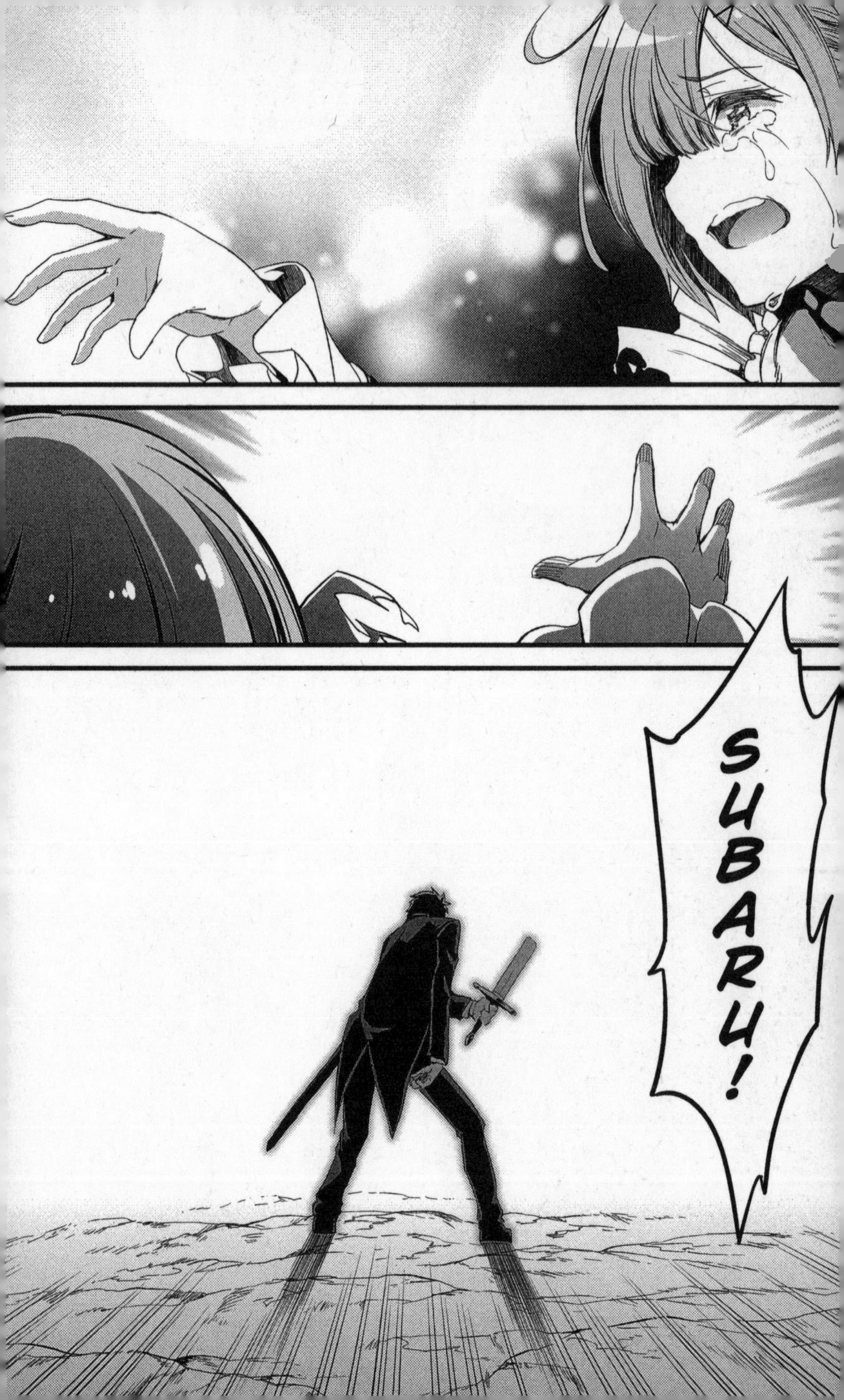
SUBARU!

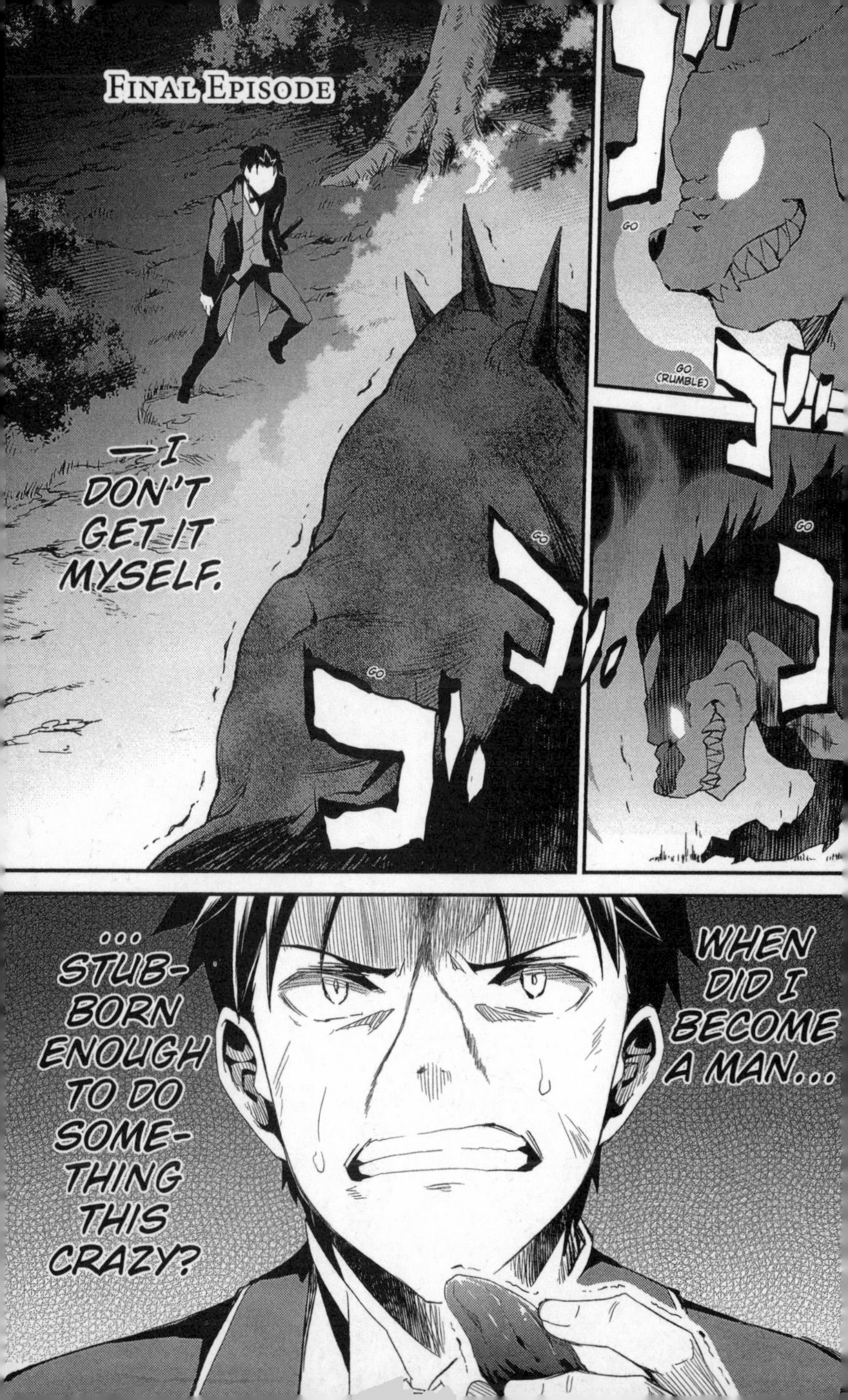
GO
GO (RUMBLE)
GO
FINAL EPISODE
—I DON'T GET IT MYSELF.
GO
GO
WHEN DID I BECOME A MAN...
...STUBBORN ENOUGH TO DO SOMETHING THIS CRAZY?

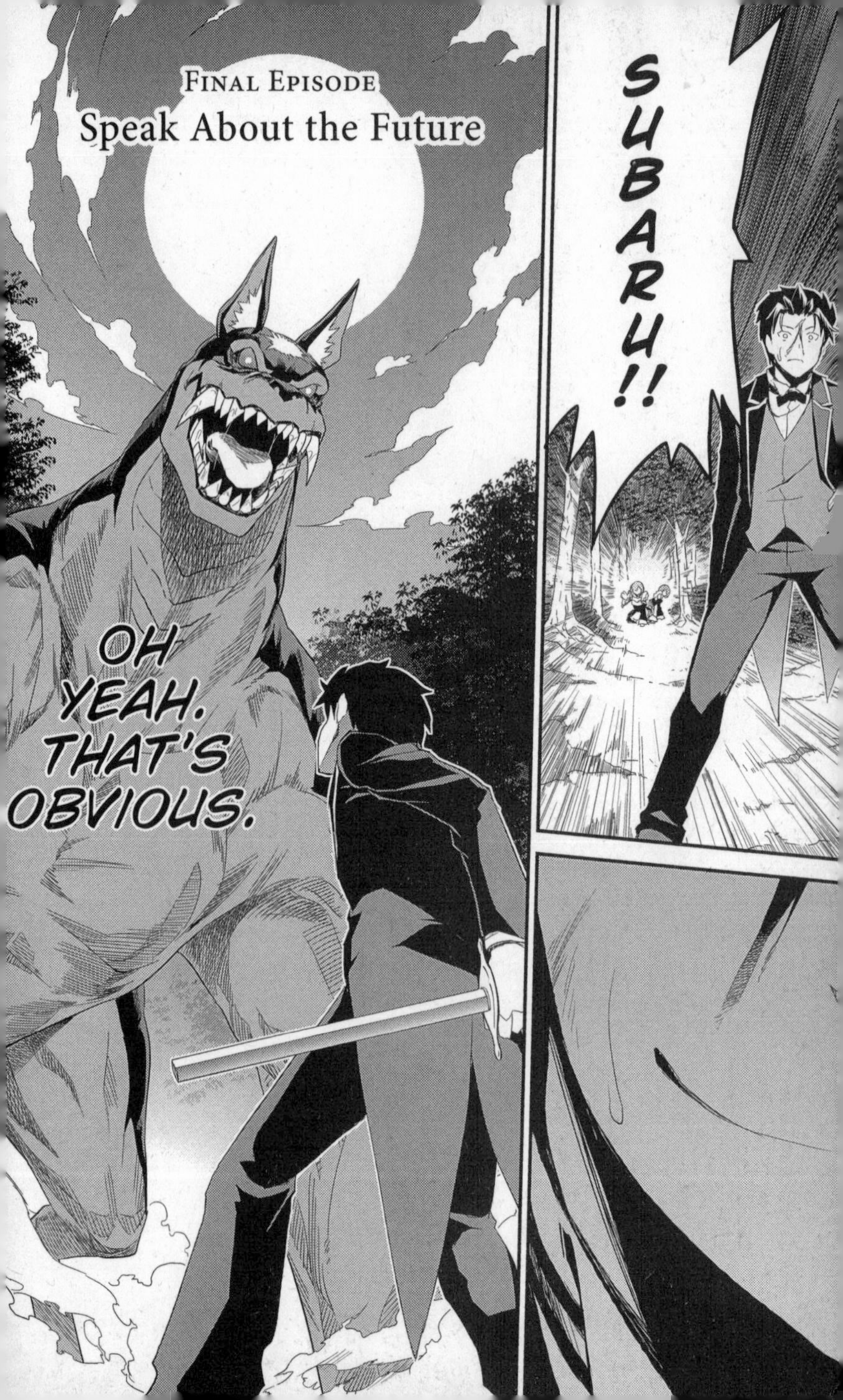
SUBARU!!
FINAL EPISODE
Speak About the Future
OH YEAH. THAT'S OBVIOUS.

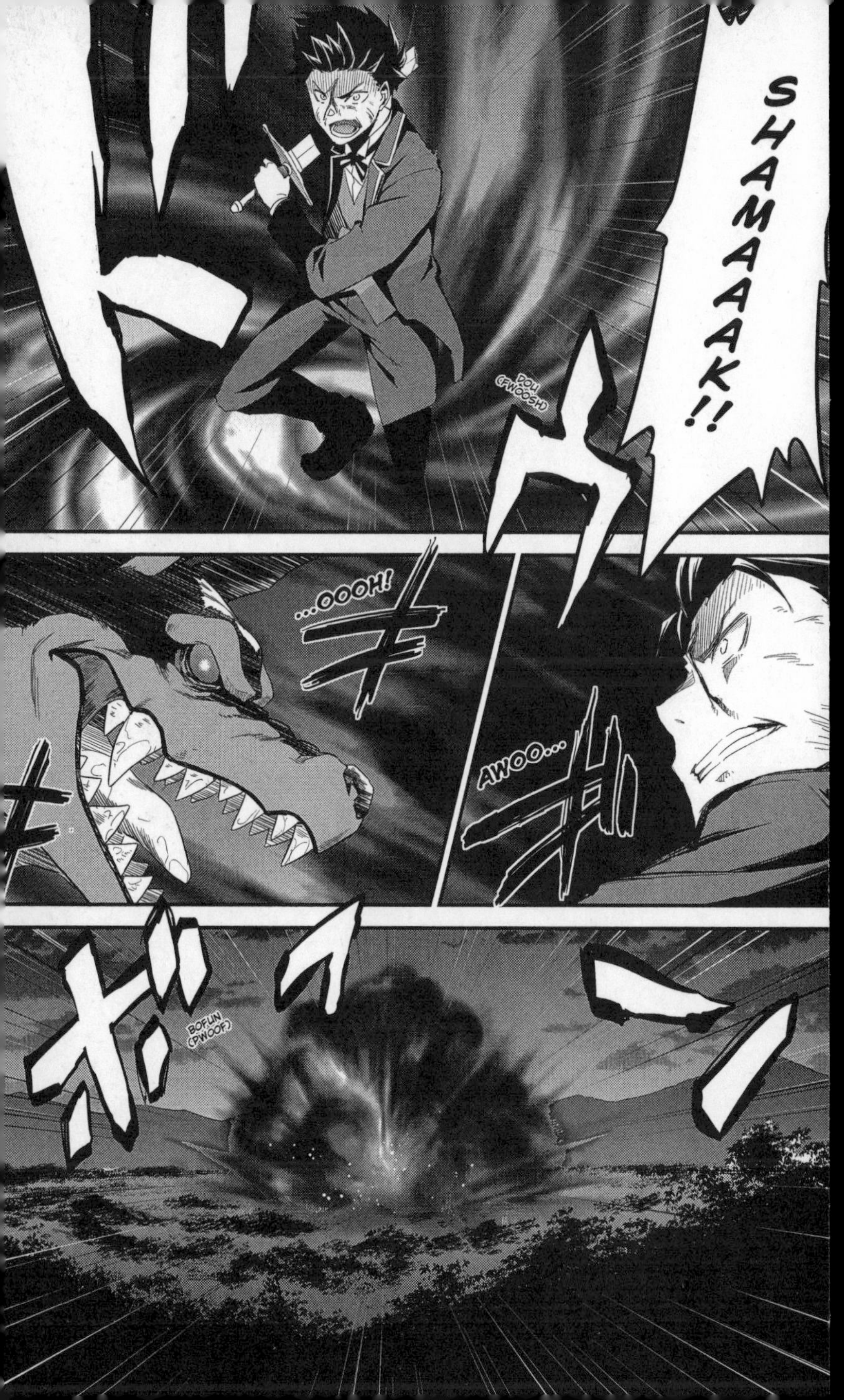
SHAMAAAAK!!
DOU (FWOOSH)
AWOO...
...OOOH!
BOFUN (PWOOF)

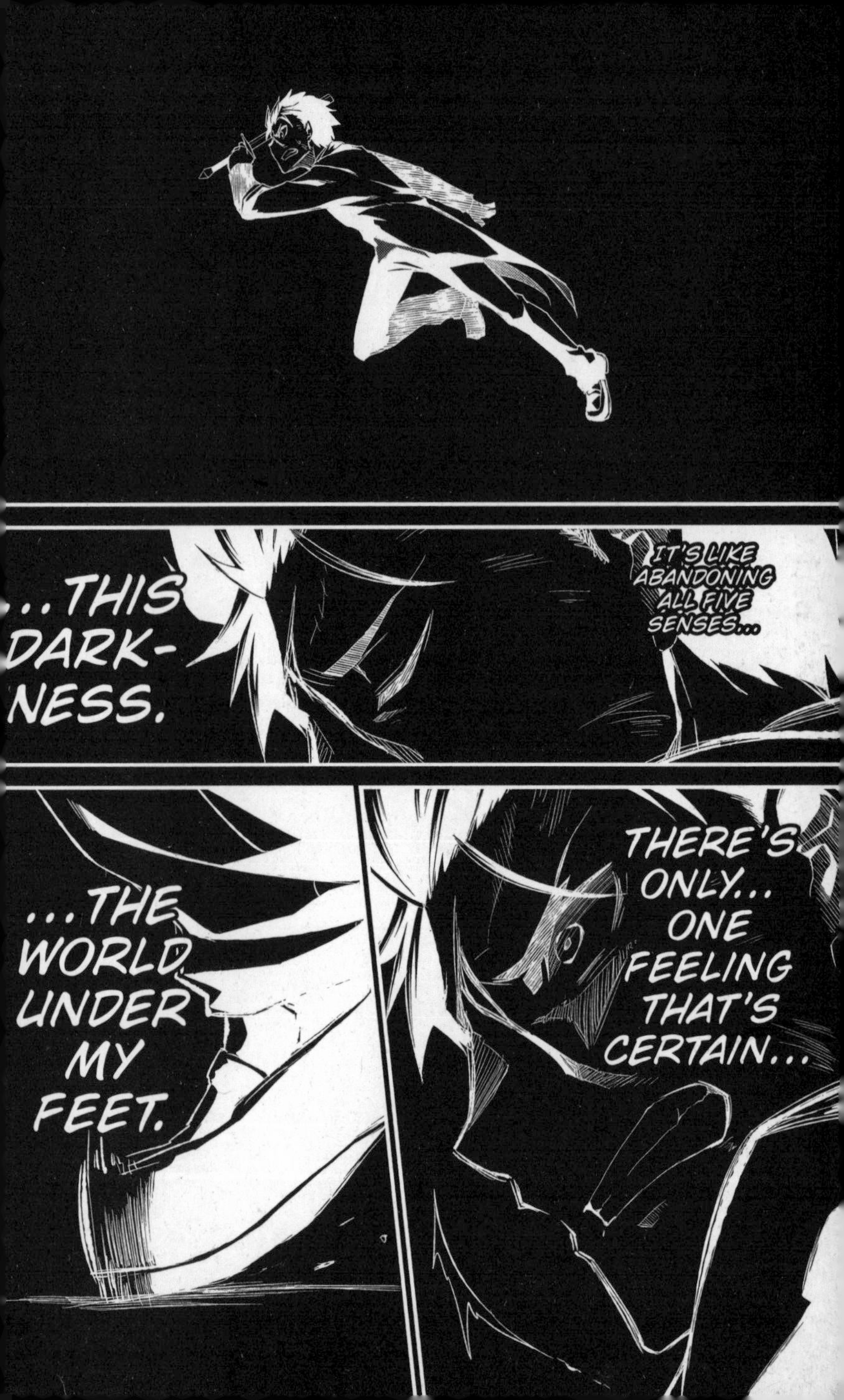
IT'S LIKE ABANDONING ALL FIVE SENSES...
...THIS DARKNESS.
THERE'S ONLY... ONE FEELING THAT'S CERTAIN...
...THE WORLD UNDER MY FEET.

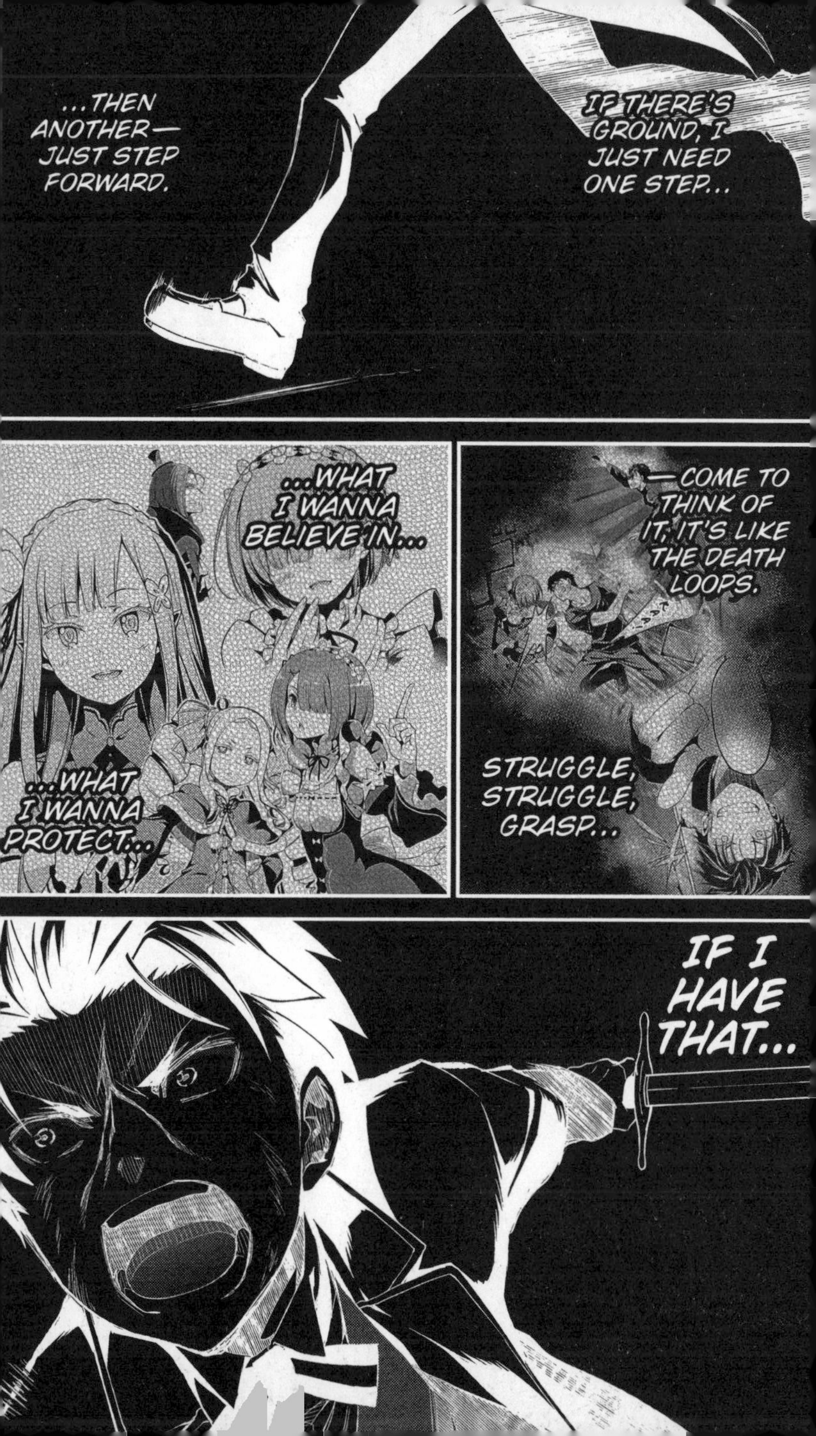
IF THERE'S GROUND, I JUST NEED ONE STEP...
...THEN ANOTHER—JUST STEP FORWARD.
—COME TO THINK OF IT, IT'S LIKE THE DEATH LOOPS.
STRUGGLE, STRUGGLE, GRASP...
...WHAT I WANNA BELIEVE IN...
...WHAT I WANNA PROTECT...
IF I HAVE THAT...

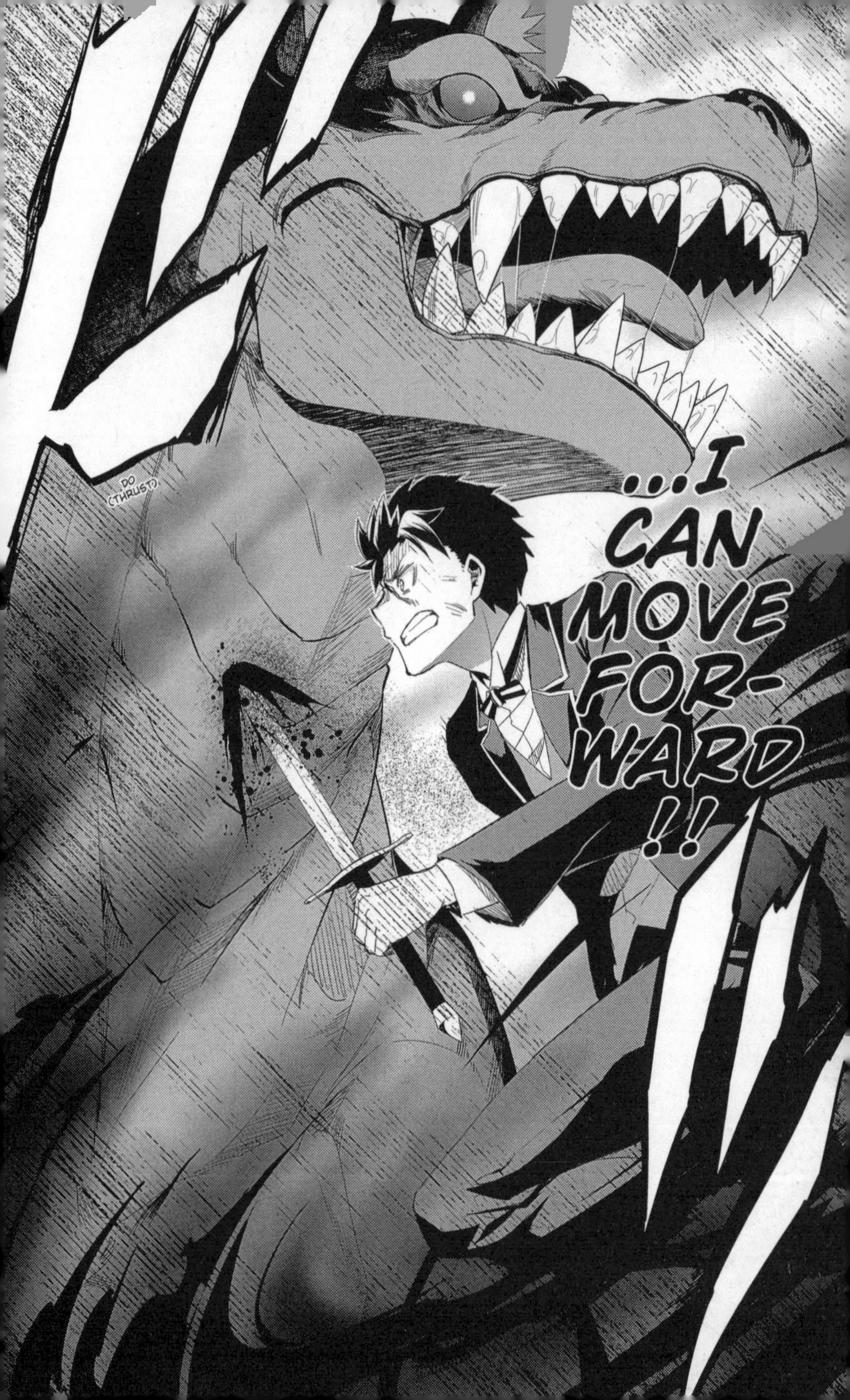

...I CAN MOVE FOR-WARD!!
DO (THRUST)

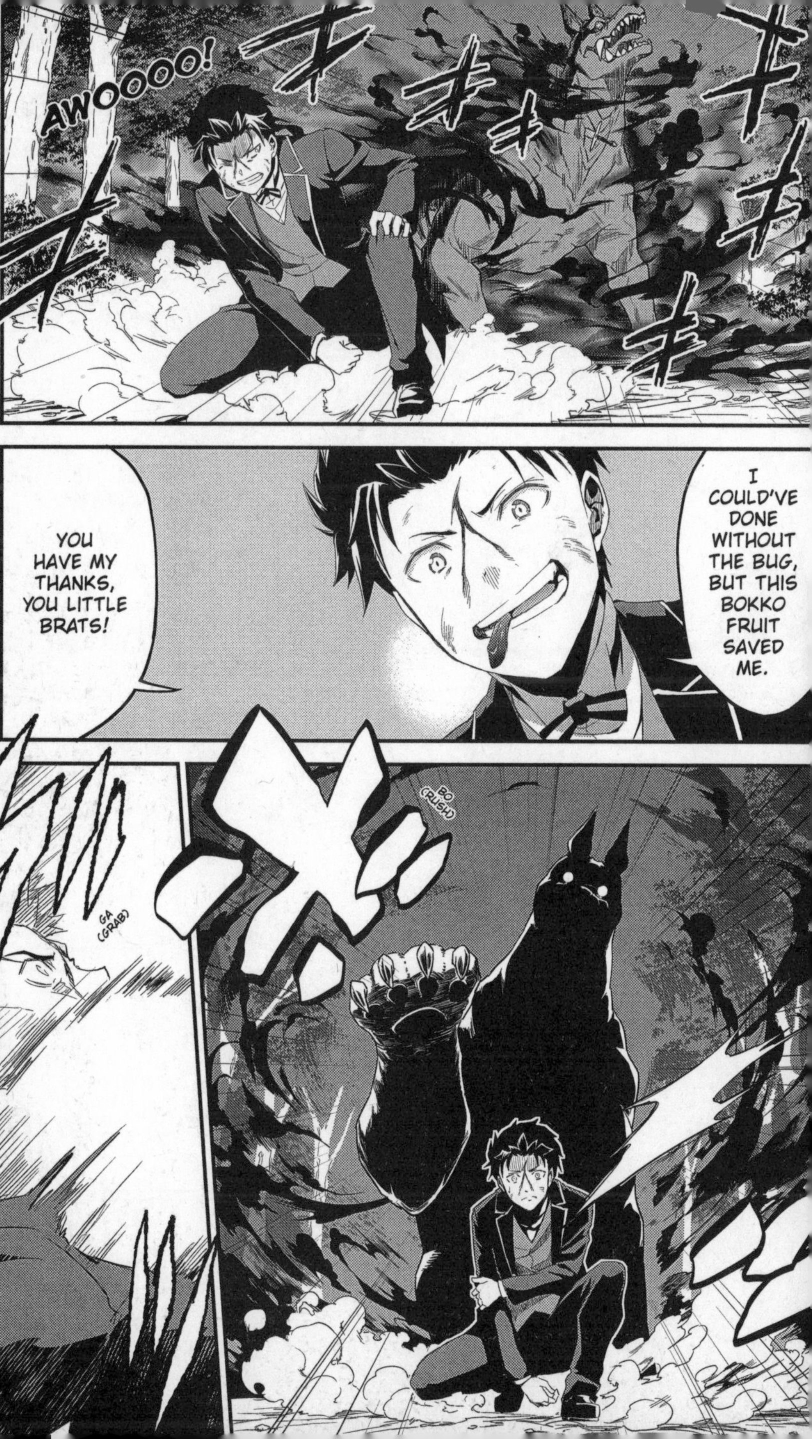
AWOOOO!
I COULD'VE DONE WITHOUT THE BUG, BUT THIS BOKKO FRUIT SAVED ME.
YOU HAVE MY THANKS, YOU LITTLE BRATS!
BO (RUSH)
GA (GRAB)

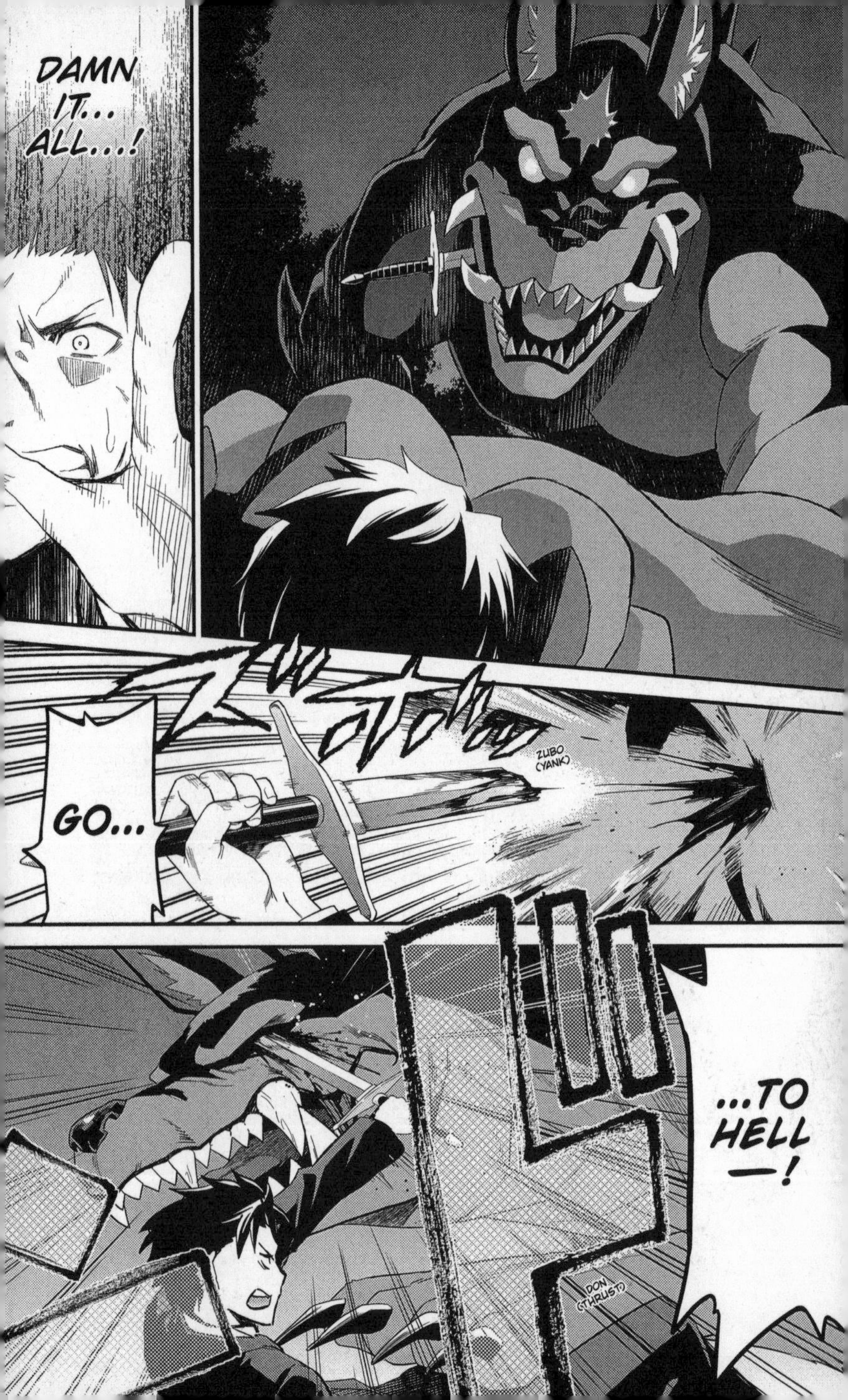
DAMN IT... ALL...!
ZUBO (YANK)
GO...
...TO HELL—!
DON (THRUST)

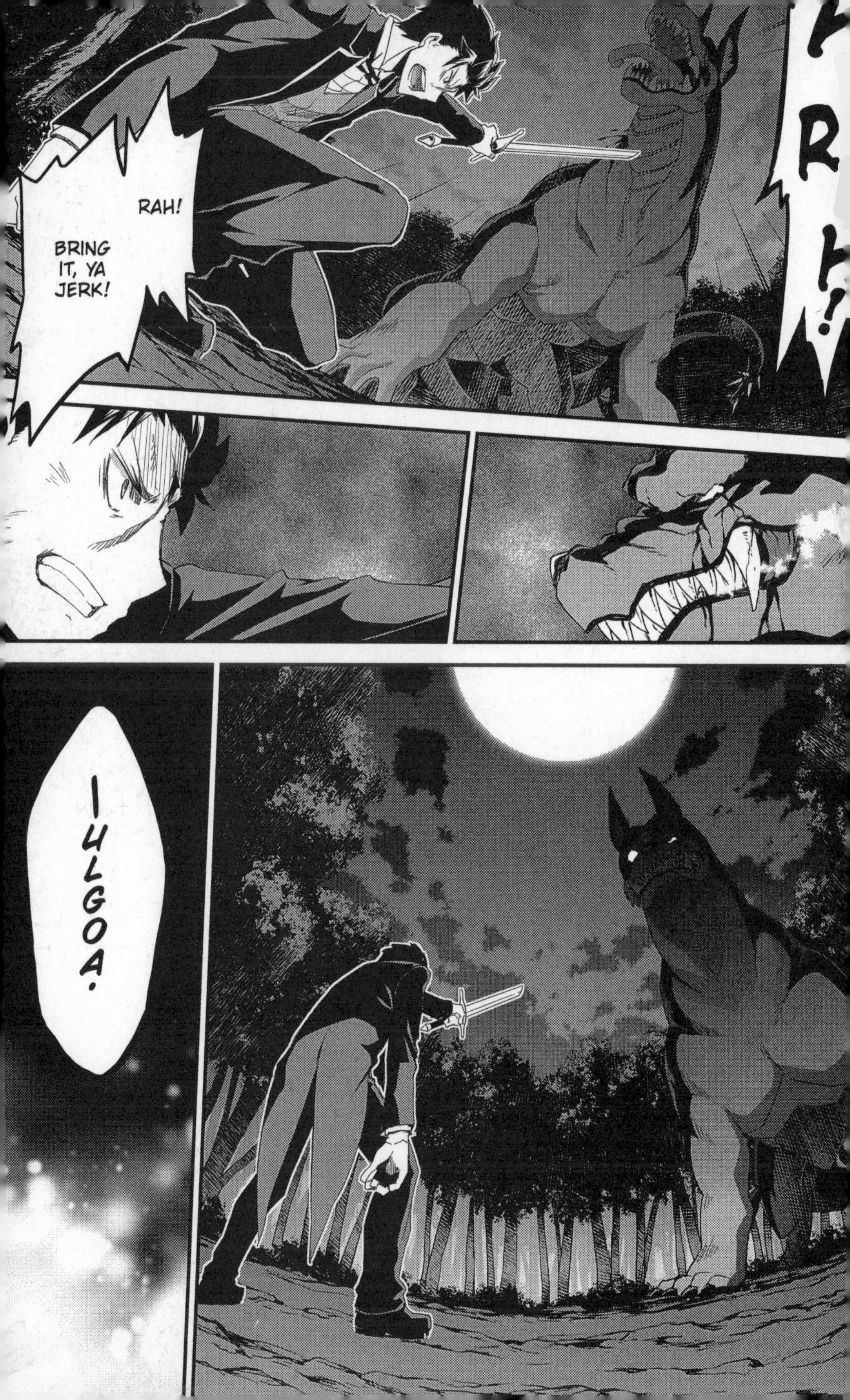
RAH!
BRING IT, YA JERK!
—ULGOA.

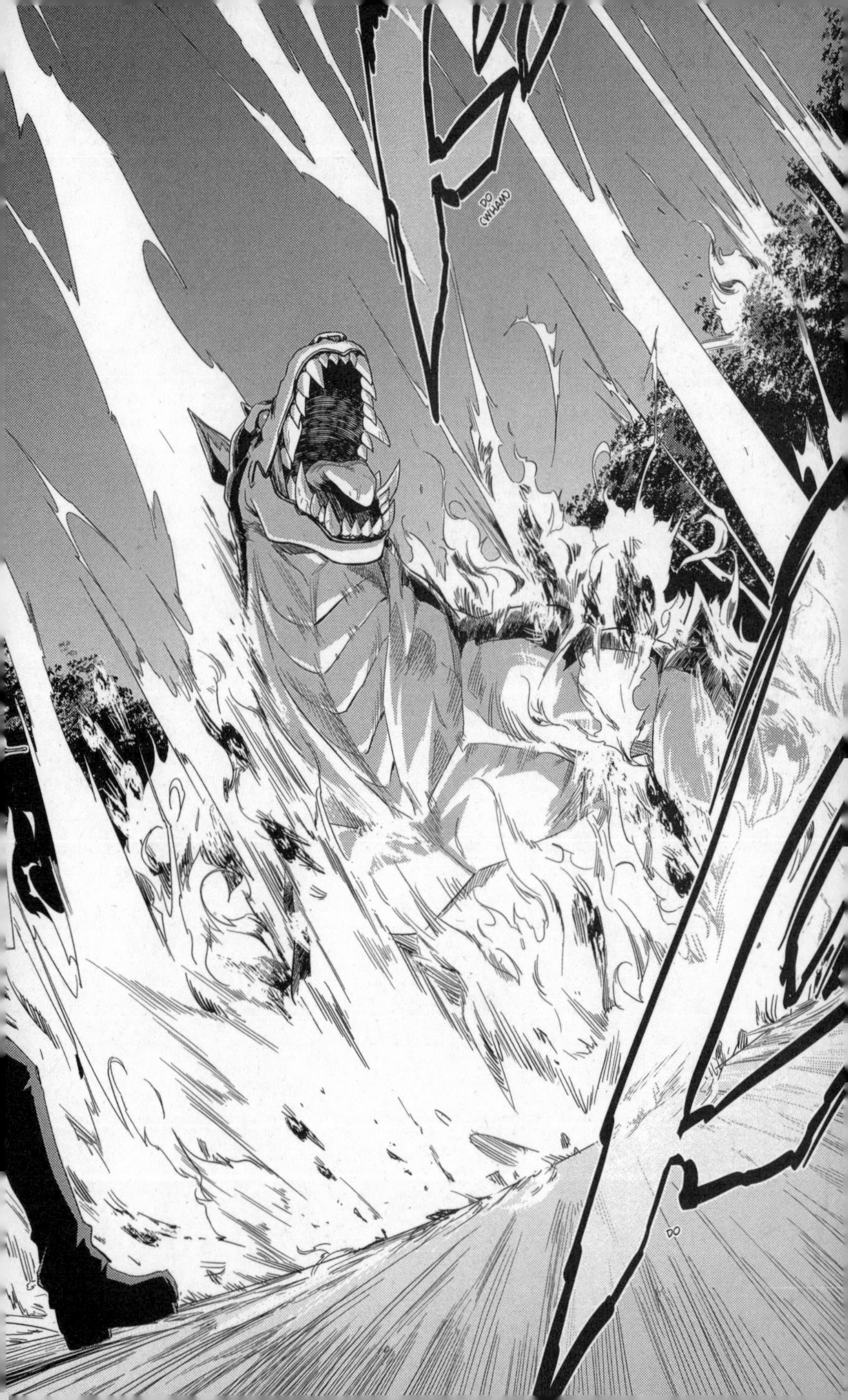
DO (WHAM)
DO

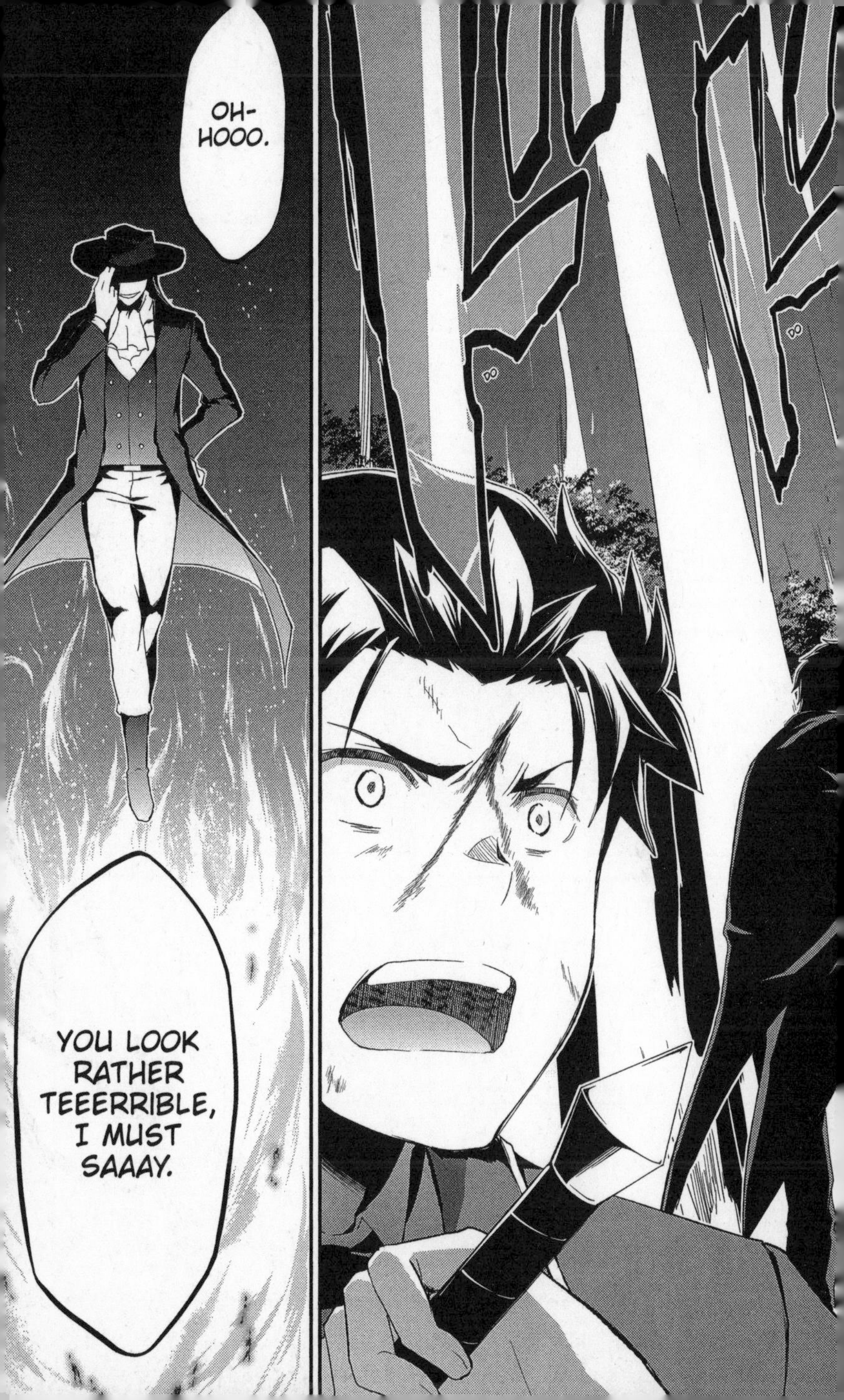
DO
DO
OH-HOOO.
YOU LOOK RATHER TEEERRIBLE, I MUST SAAAY.

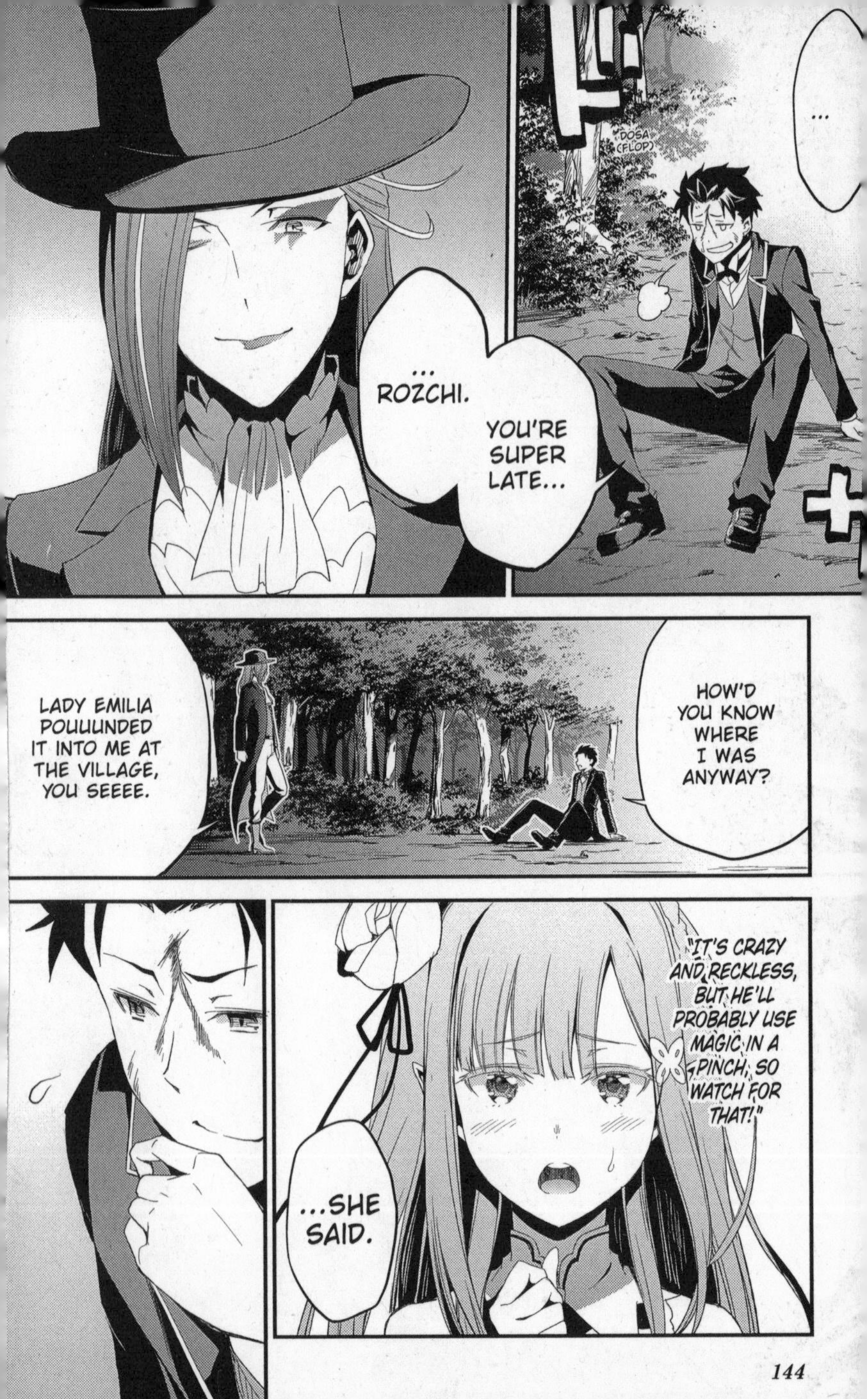
...
DOSA (FLOP)
... ROZCHI.
YOU'RE SUPER LATE...
HOW'D YOU KNOW WHERE I WAS ANYWAY?
LADY EMILIA POUUUNDED IT INTO ME AT THE VILLAGE, YOU SEEEE.
"IT'S CRAZY AND RECKLESS, BUT HE'LL PROBABLY USE MAGIC IN A PINCH, SO WATCH FOR THAT!"
...SHE SAID.

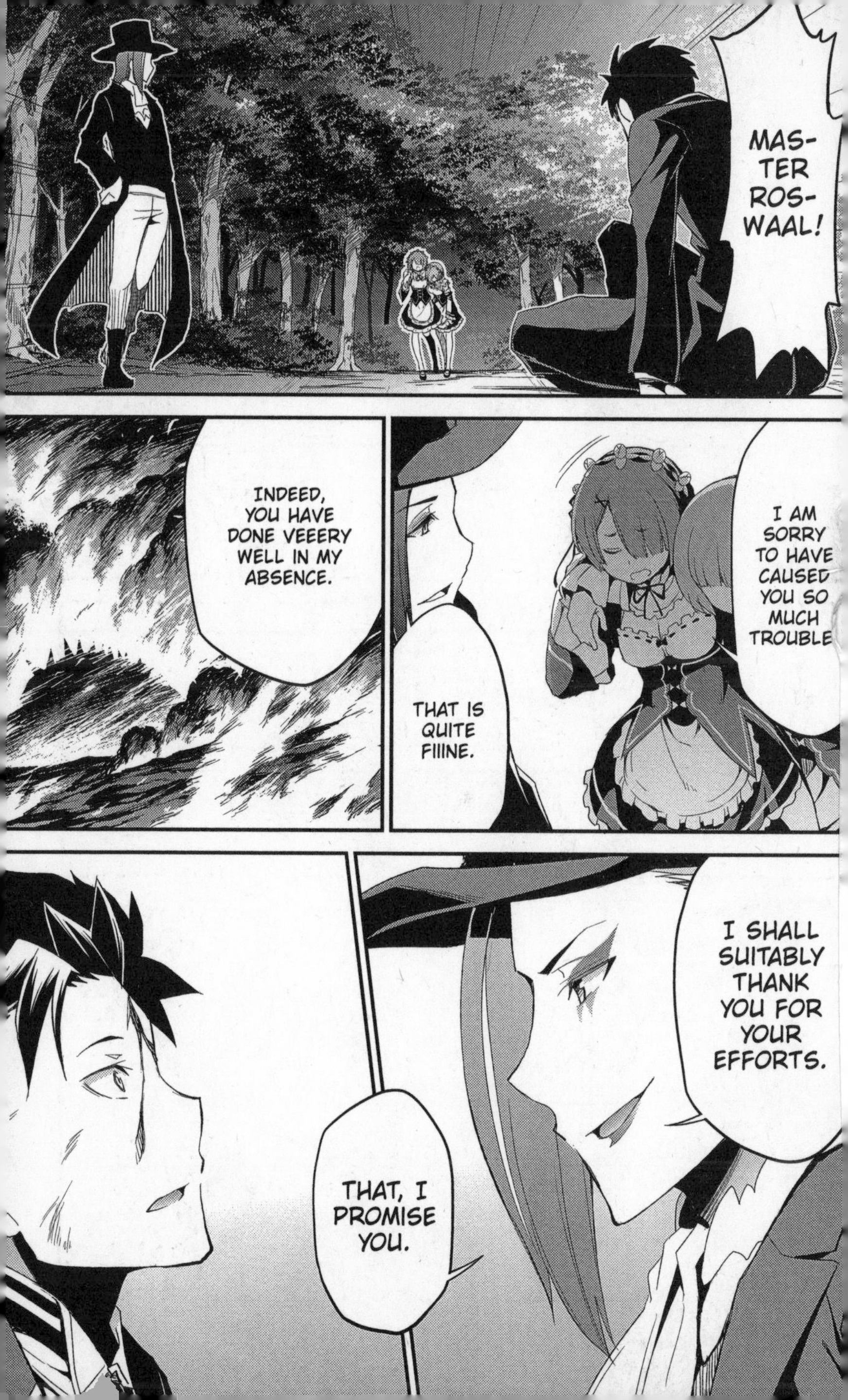
MASTER ROSWAAL!
I AM SORRY TO HAVE CAUSED YOU SO MUCH TROUBLE
THAT IS QUITE FIIINE.
INDEED, YOU HAVE DONE VEEERY WELL IN MY ABSENCE.
I SHALL SUITABLY THANK YOU FOR YOUR EFFORTS.
THAT, I PROMISE YOU.

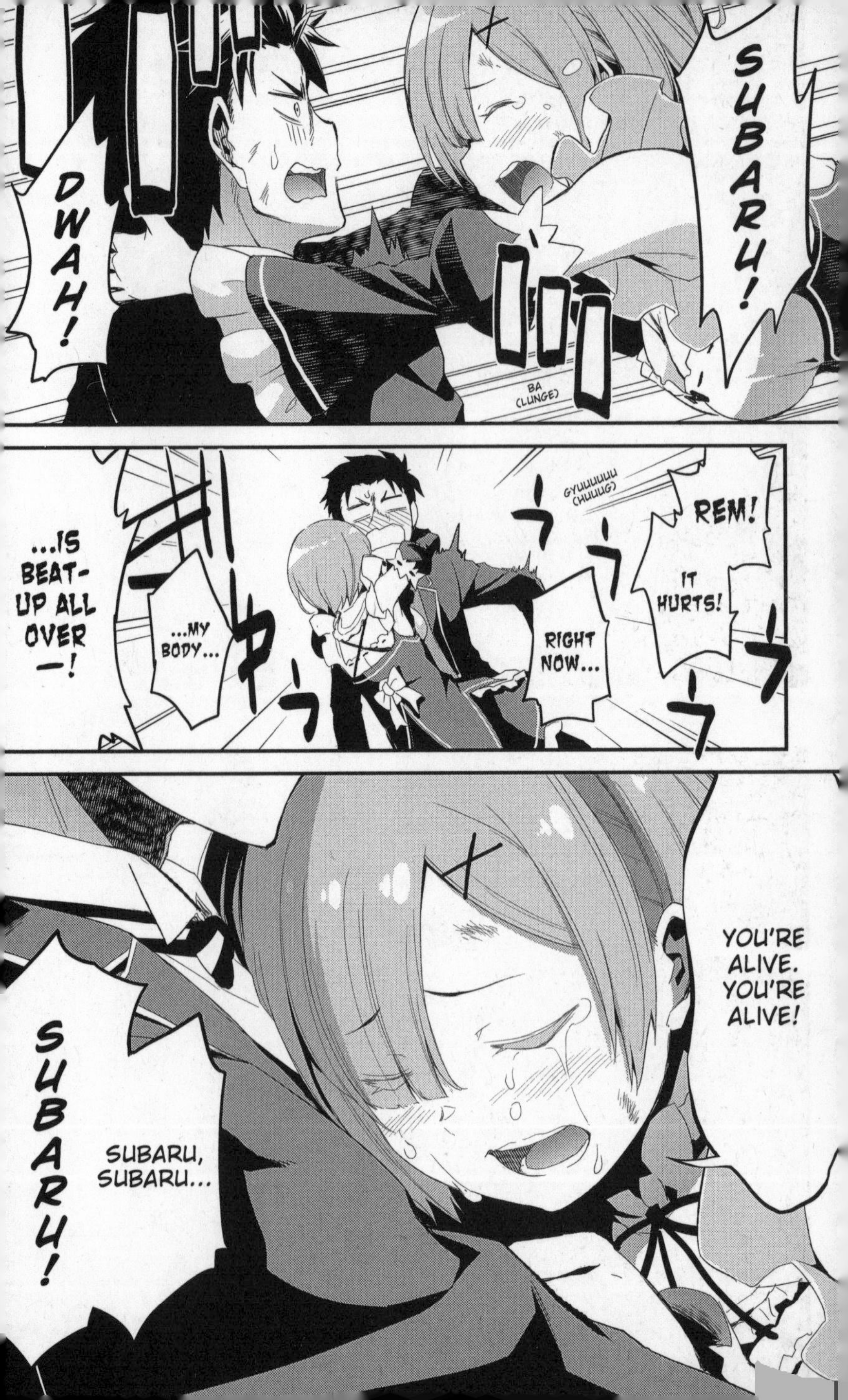
SUBARU!
BA (LUNGE)
DWAH!
REM!
IT HURTS!
GYUUUUUUU (HUUUG)
RIGHT NOW...
...MY BODY...
...IS BEAT-UP ALL OVER—!
YOU'RE ALIVE. YOU'RE ALIVE!
SUBARU, SUBARU...
SUBARU!

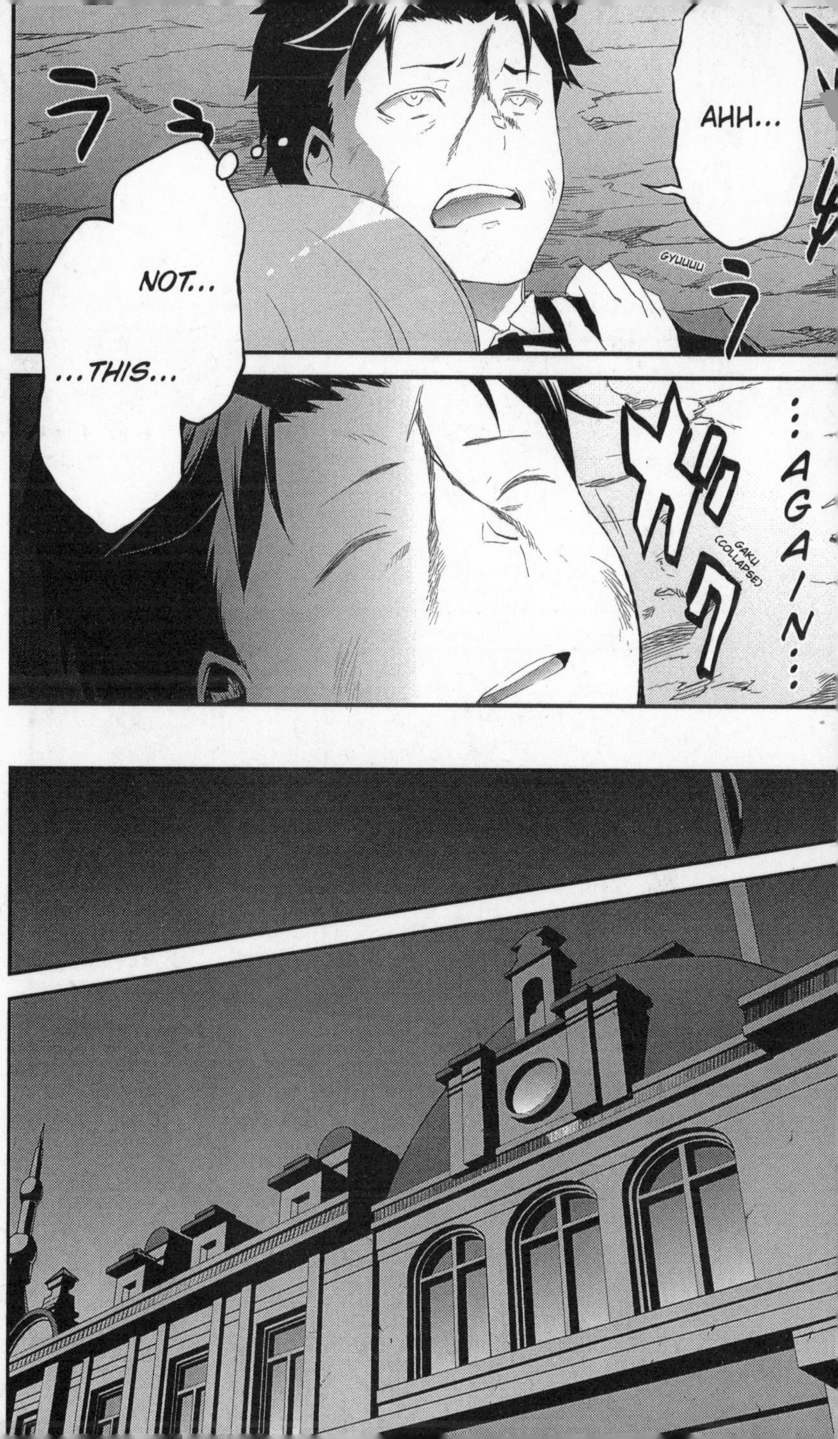
AHH...
GYUUUU
NOT...
...THIS...
...AGAIN...
GAKU (COLLAPSE)

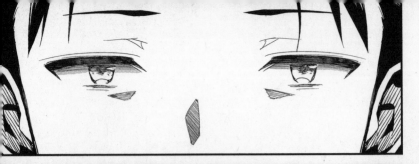

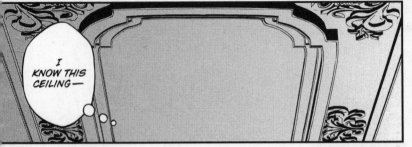

I KNOW THIS CEILING—

—ARE YOU... AWAKE?

148

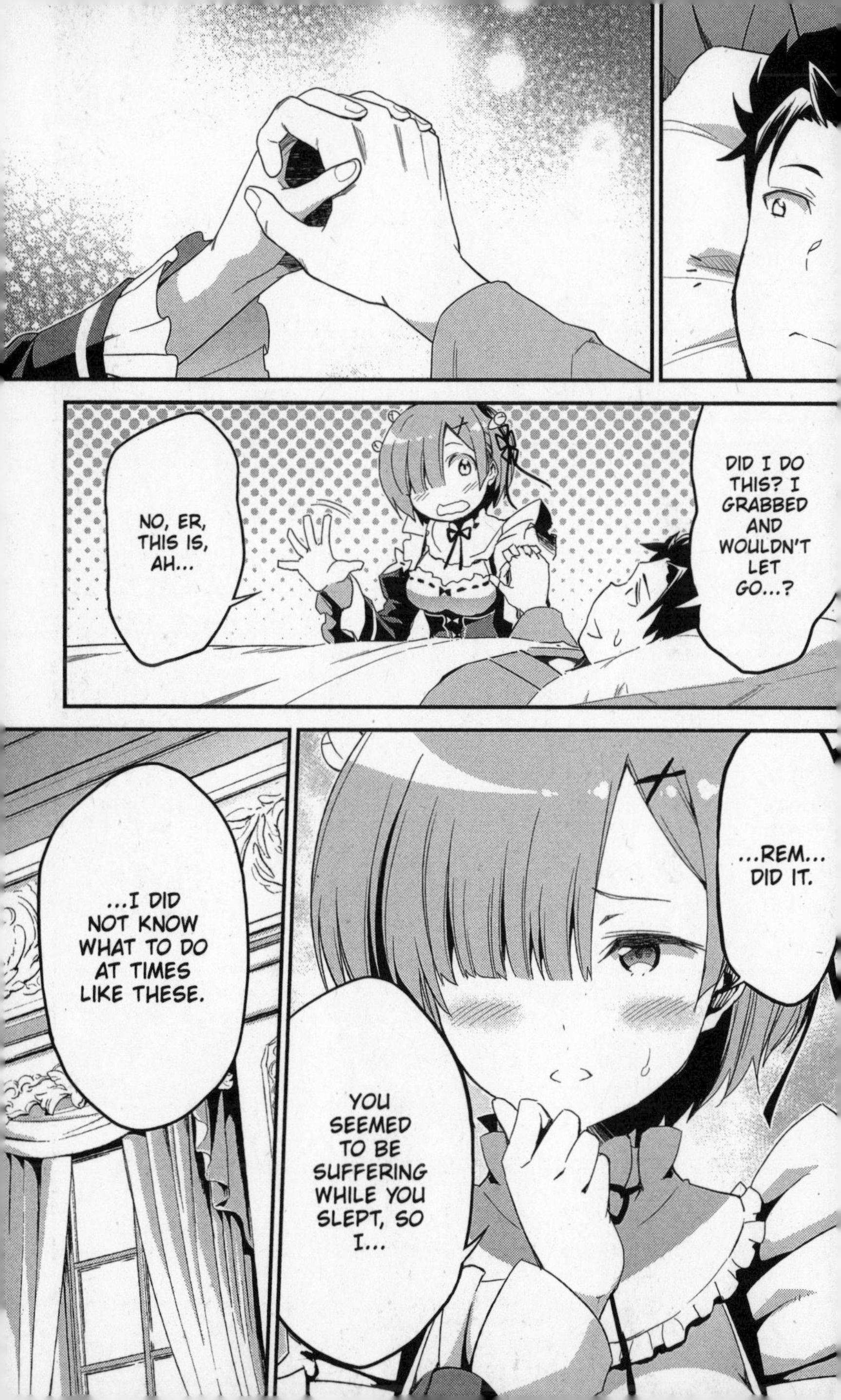
DID I DO THIS? I GRABBED AND WOULDN'T LET GO...?
NO, ER, THIS IS, AH...
...REM... DID IT.
YOU SEEMED TO BE SUFFERING WHILE YOU SLEPT, SO I...
...I DID NOT KNOW WHAT TO DO AT TIMES LIKE THESE.

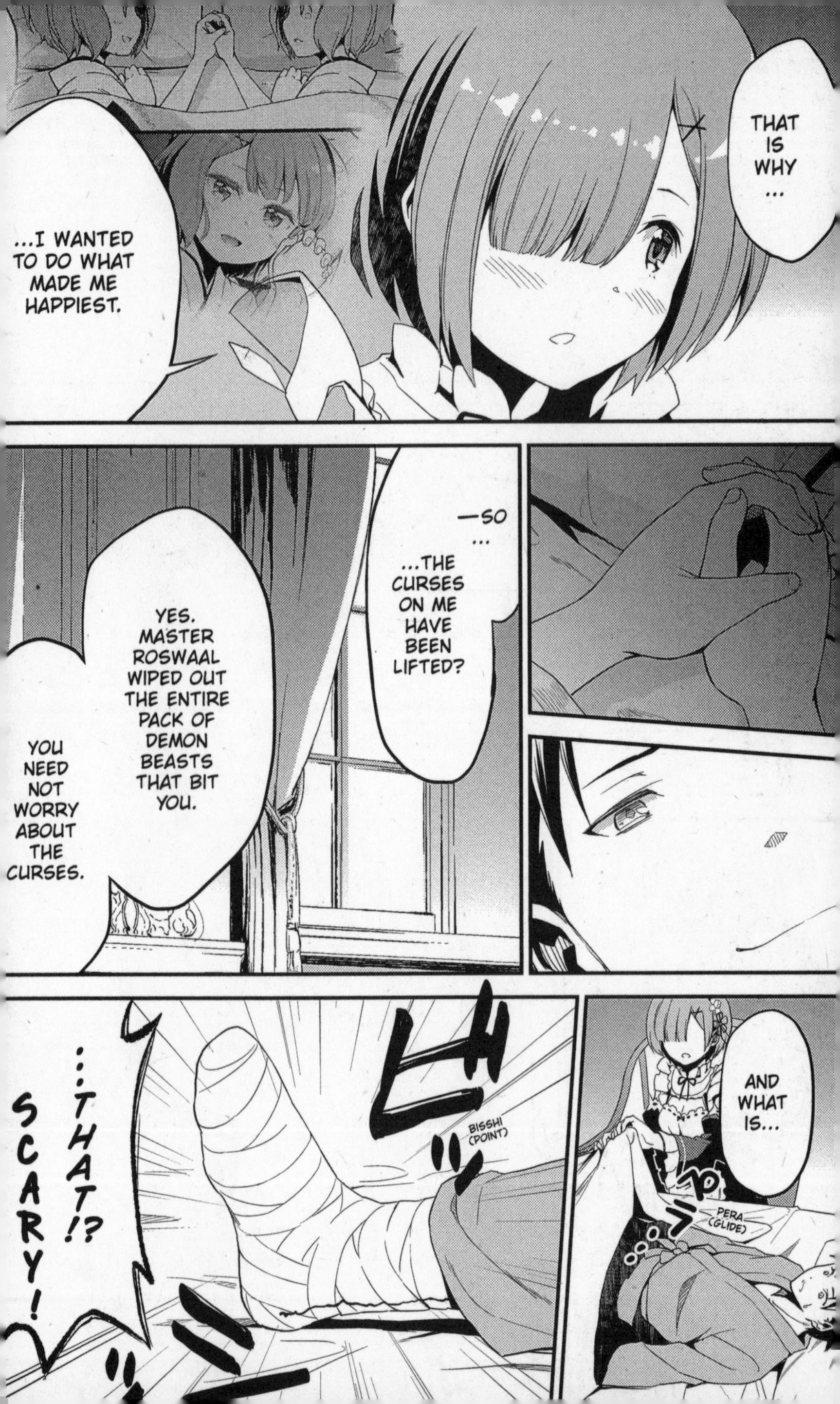
THAT IS WHY...
...I WANTED TO DO WHAT MADE ME HAPPIEST.
—SO... ...THE CURSES ON ME HAVE BEEN LIFTED?
YES. MASTER ROSWAAL WIPED OUT THE ENTIRE PACK OF DEMON BEASTS THAT BIT YOU.
YOU NEED NOT WORRY ABOUT THE CURSES.
AND WHAT IS...
PERA (GLIDE)
...THAT!?
BISSHI (POINT)
SCARY!

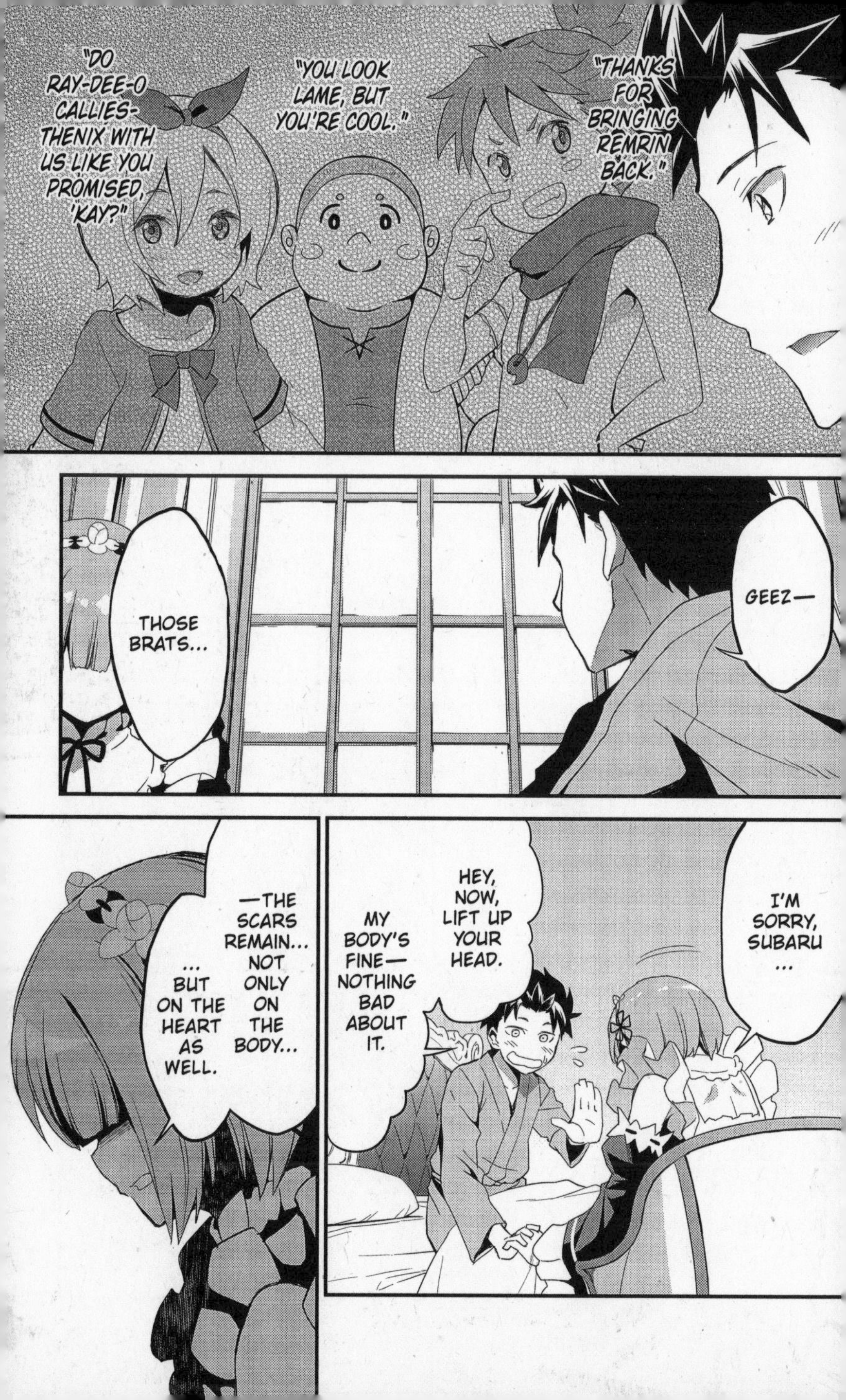
"THANKS FOR BRINGING REMRIN BACK."
"YOU LOOK LAME, BUT YOU'RE COOL."
"DO RAY-DEE-O CALLIES-THENIX WITH US LIKE YOU PROMISED, 'KAY?"
GEEZ—
THOSE BRATS...
I'M SORRY, SUBARU ...
HEY, NOW, LIFT UP YOUR HEAD.
MY BODY'S FINE—NOTHING BAD ABOUT IT.
—THE SCARS REMAIN... NOT ONLY ON THE BODY...
... BUT ON THE HEART AS WELL.

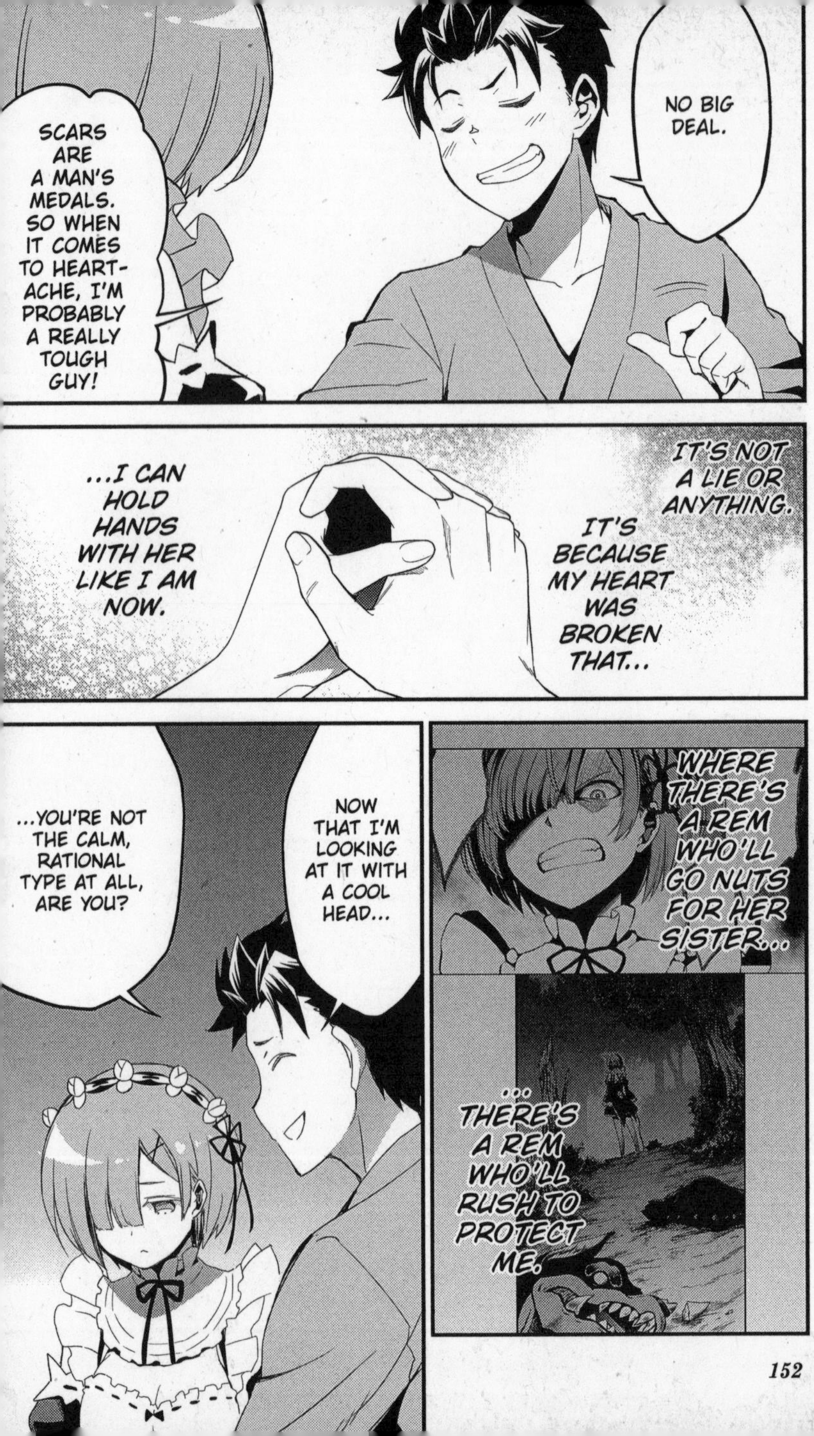
NO BIG DEAL.
SCARS ARE A MAN'S MEDALS. SO WHEN IT COMES TO HEART-ACHE, I'M PROBABLY A REALLY TOUGH GUY!
IT'S NOT A LIE OR ANYTHING.
IT'S BECAUSE MY HEART WAS BROKEN THAT...
...I CAN HOLD HANDS WITH HER LIKE I AM NOW.
WHERE THERE'S A REM WHO'LL GO NUTS FOR HER SISTER...
...THERE'S A REM WHO'LL RUSH TO PROTECT ME.
NOW THAT I'M LOOKING AT IT WITH A COOL HEAD...
...YOU'RE NOT THE CALM, RATIONAL TYPE AT ALL, ARE YOU?

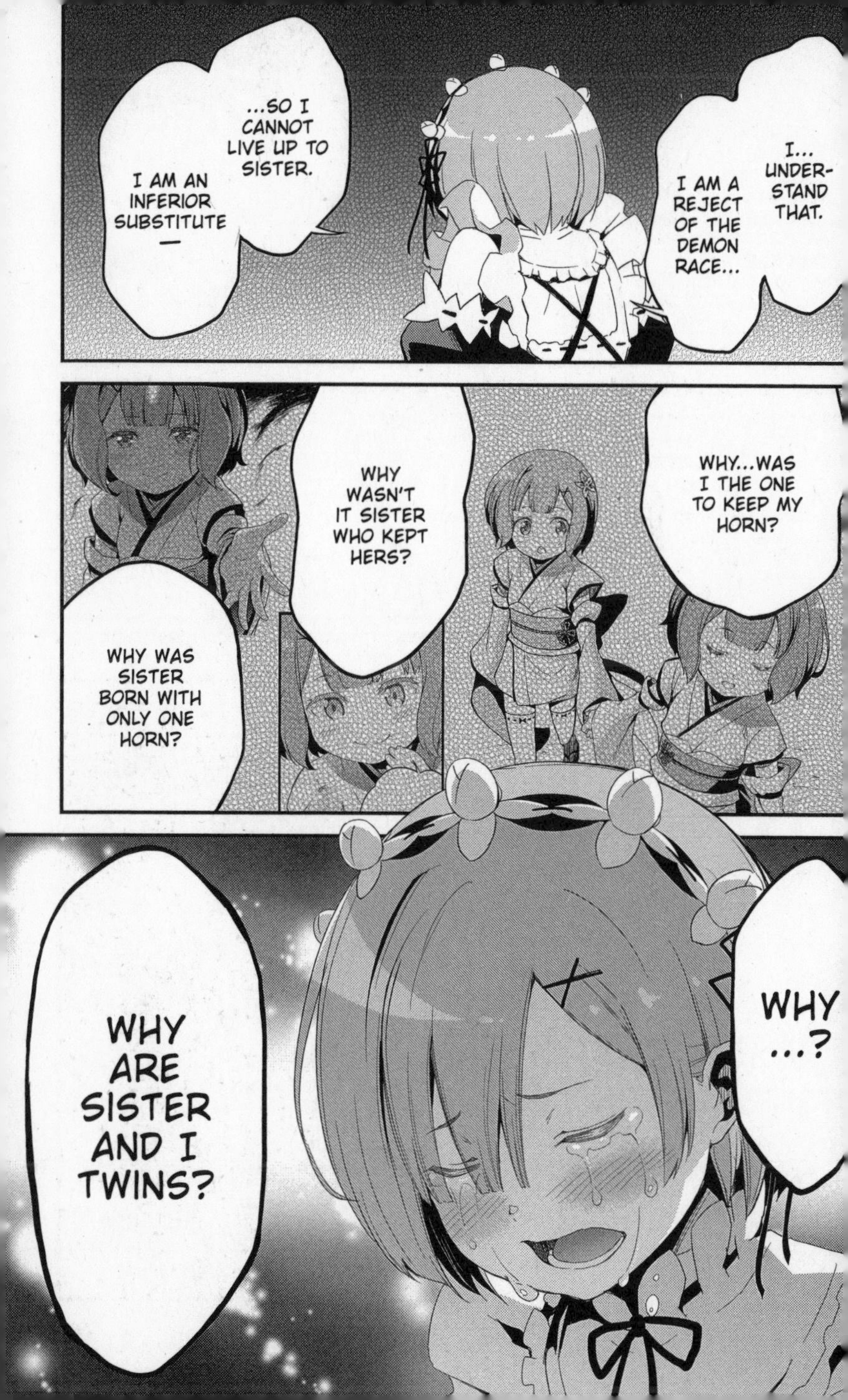
I... UNDERSTAND THAT.
I AM A REJECT OF THE DEMON RACE...
I AM AN INFERIOR SUBSTITUTE—
...SO I CANNOT LIVE UP TO SISTER.
WHY...WAS I THE ONE TO KEEP MY HORN?
WHY WASN'T IT SISTER WHO KEPT HERS?
WHY WAS SISTER BORN WITH ONLY ONE HORN?
WHY...?
WHY ARE SISTER AND I TWINS?

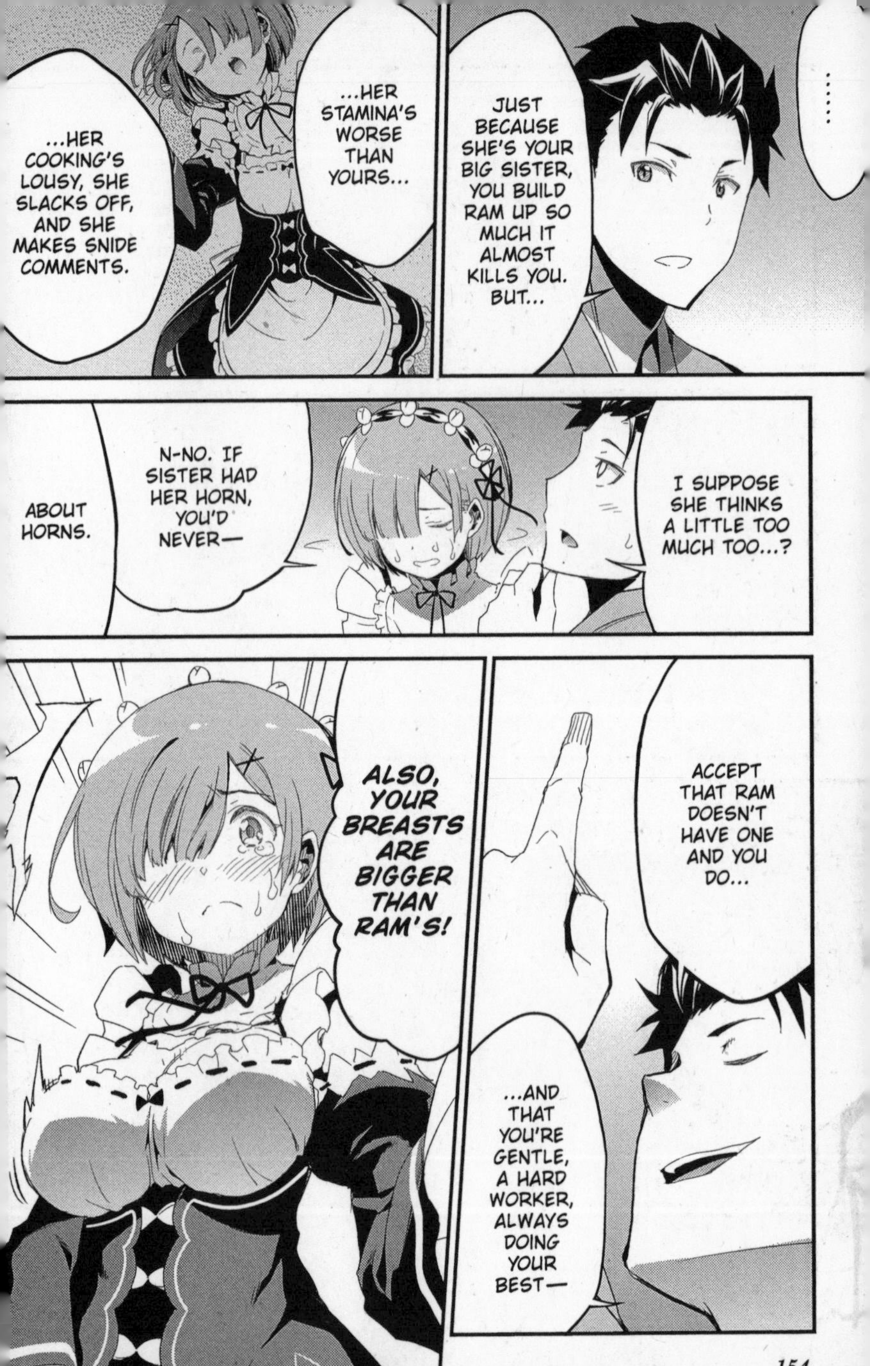
......
JUST BECAUSE SHE'S YOUR BIG SISTER, YOU BUILD RAM UP SO MUCH IT ALMOST KILLS YOU. BUT...
...HER STAMINA'S WORSE THAN YOURS...
...HER COOKING'S LOUSY, SHE SLACKS OFF, AND SHE MAKES SNIDE COMMENTS.
I SUPPOSE SHE THINKS A LITTLE TOO MUCH TOO...?
N-NO. IF SISTER HAD HER HORN, YOU'D NEVER—
ABOUT HORNS.
ACCEPT THAT RAM DOESN'T HAVE ONE AND YOU DO...
...AND THAT YOU'RE GENTLE, A HARD WORKER, ALWAYS DOING YOUR BEST—
ALSO, YOUR BREASTS ARE BIGGER THAN RAM'S!

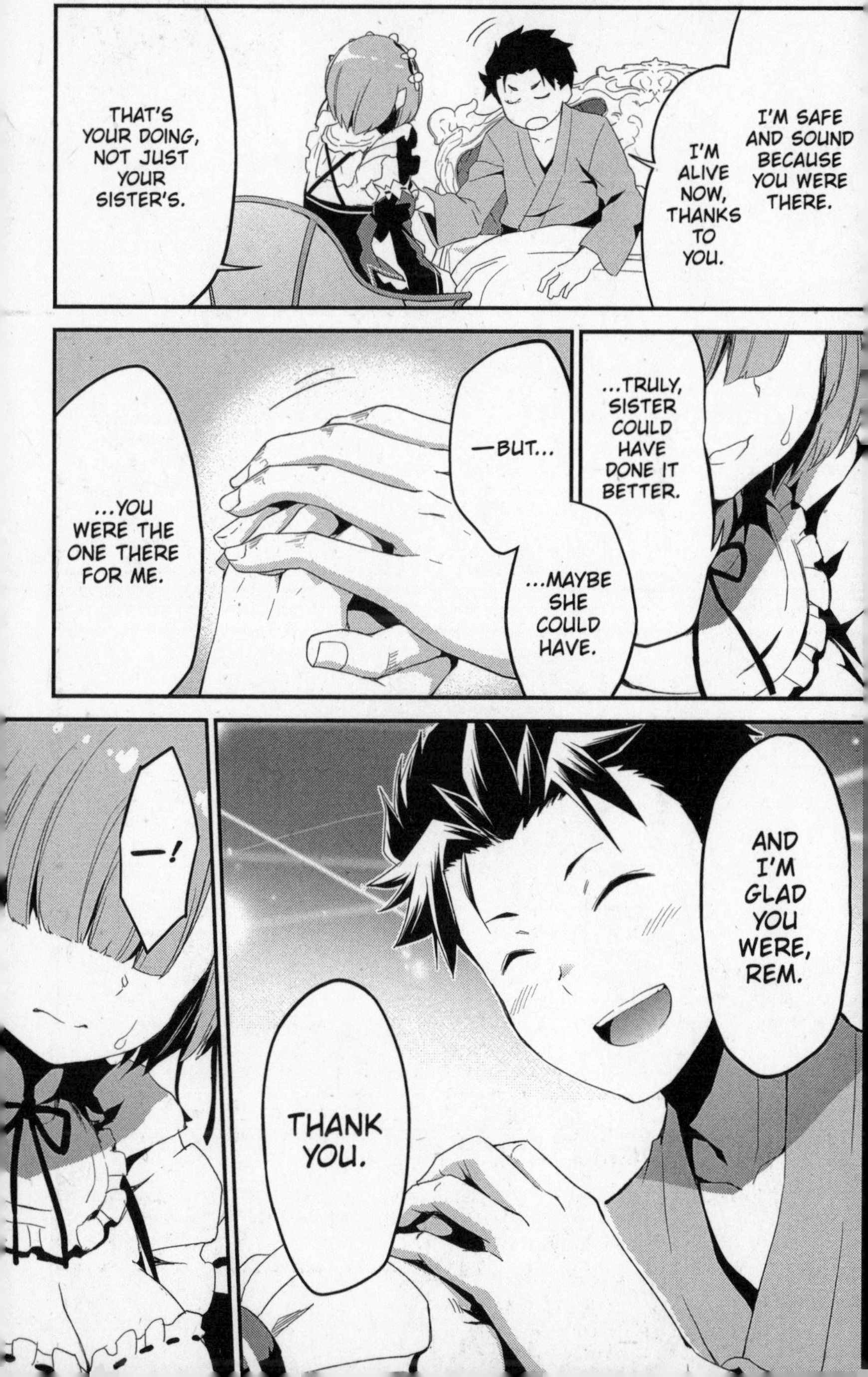
I'M SAFE AND SOUND BECAUSE YOU WERE THERE.
I'M ALIVE NOW, THANKS TO YOU.
THAT'S YOUR DOING, NOT JUST YOUR SISTER'S.
...TRULY, SISTER COULD HAVE DONE IT BETTER.
—BUT...
...MAYBE SHE COULD HAVE.
...YOU WERE THE ONE THERE FOR ME.
AND I'M GLAD YOU WERE, REM.
THANK YOU.
—!

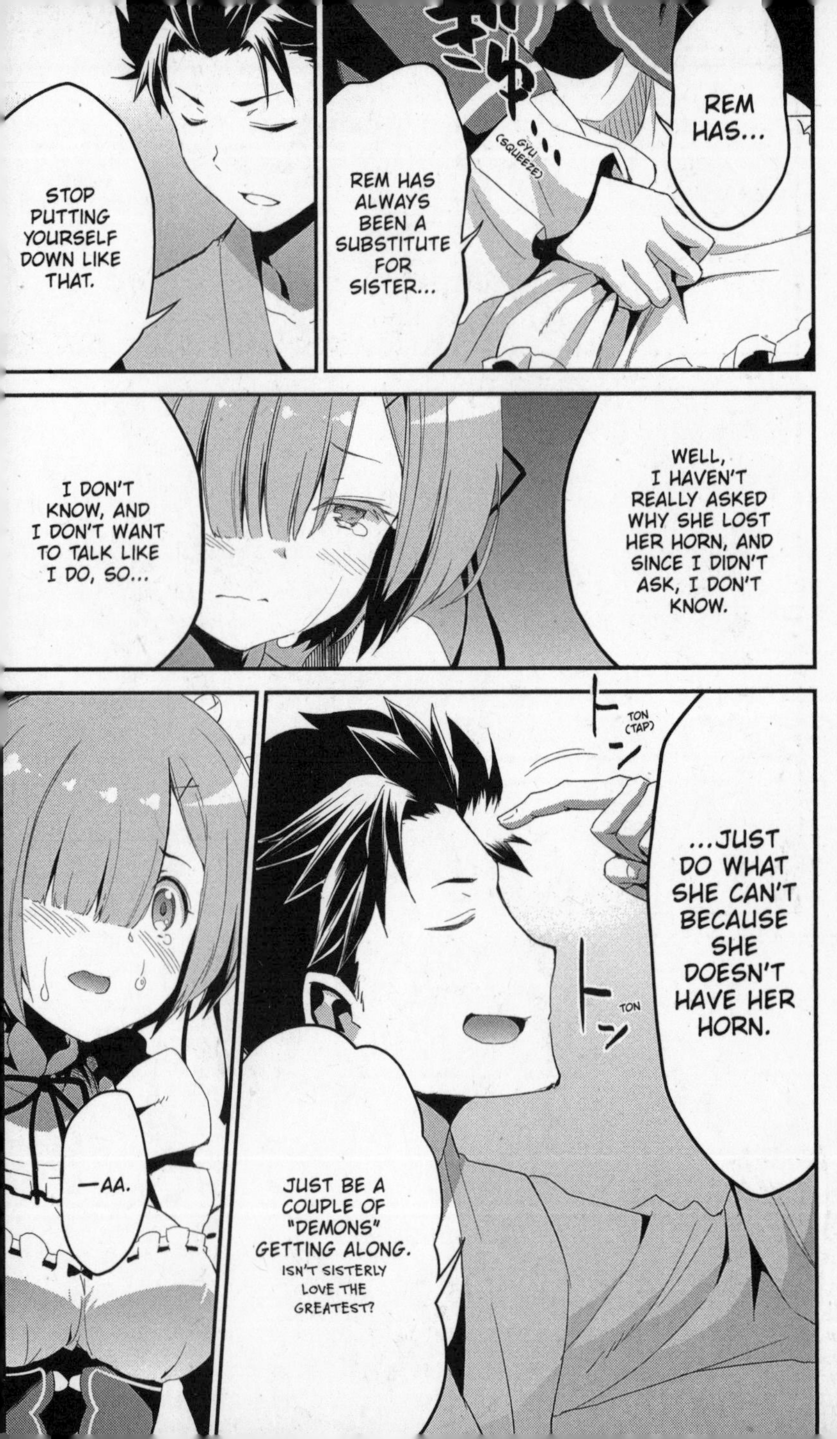
REM HAS...
GYU (SQUEEZE)
REM HAS ALWAYS BEEN A SUBSTITUTE FOR SISTER...
STOP PUTTING YOURSELF DOWN LIKE THAT.
WELL, I HAVEN'T REALLY ASKED WHY SHE LOST HER HORN, AND SINCE I DIDN'T ASK, I DON'T KNOW.
I DON'T KNOW, AND I DON'T WANT TO TALK LIKE I DO, SO...
TON (TAP)
...JUST DO WHAT SHE CAN'T BECAUSE SHE DOESN'T HAVE HER HORN.
TON
JUST BE A COUPLE OF "DEMONS" GETTING ALONG.
ISN'T SISTERLY LOVE THE GREATEST?
—AA.

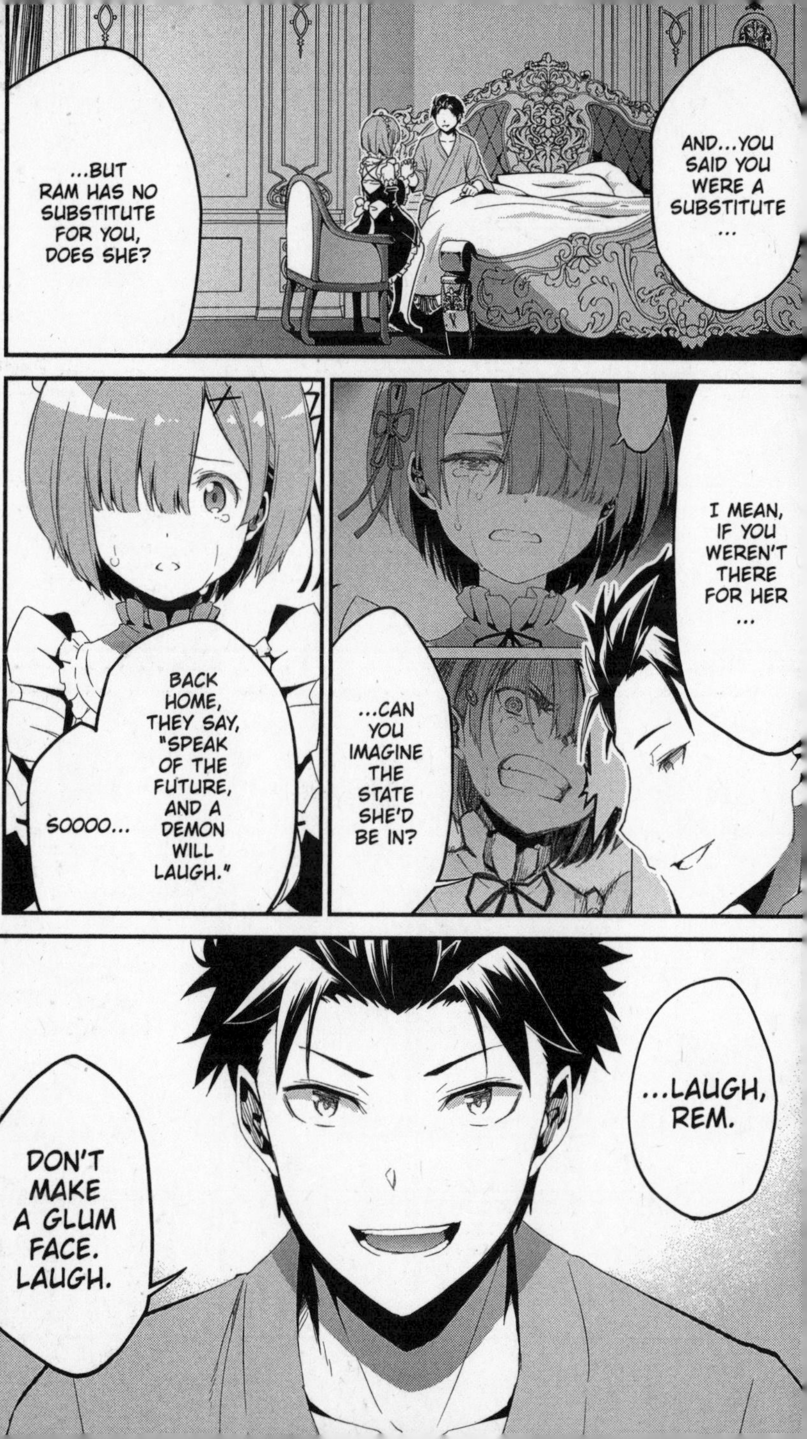
AND...YOU SAID YOU WERE A SUBSTITUTE...
...BUT RAM HAS NO SUBSTITUTE FOR YOU, DOES SHE?
I MEAN, IF YOU WEREN'T THERE FOR HER...
...CAN YOU IMAGINE THE STATE SHE'D BE IN?
BACK HOME, THEY SAY, "SPEAK OF THE FUTURE, AND A DEMON WILL LAUGH."
SOOOO...
...LAUGH, REM.
DON'T MAKE A GLUM FACE. LAUGH.

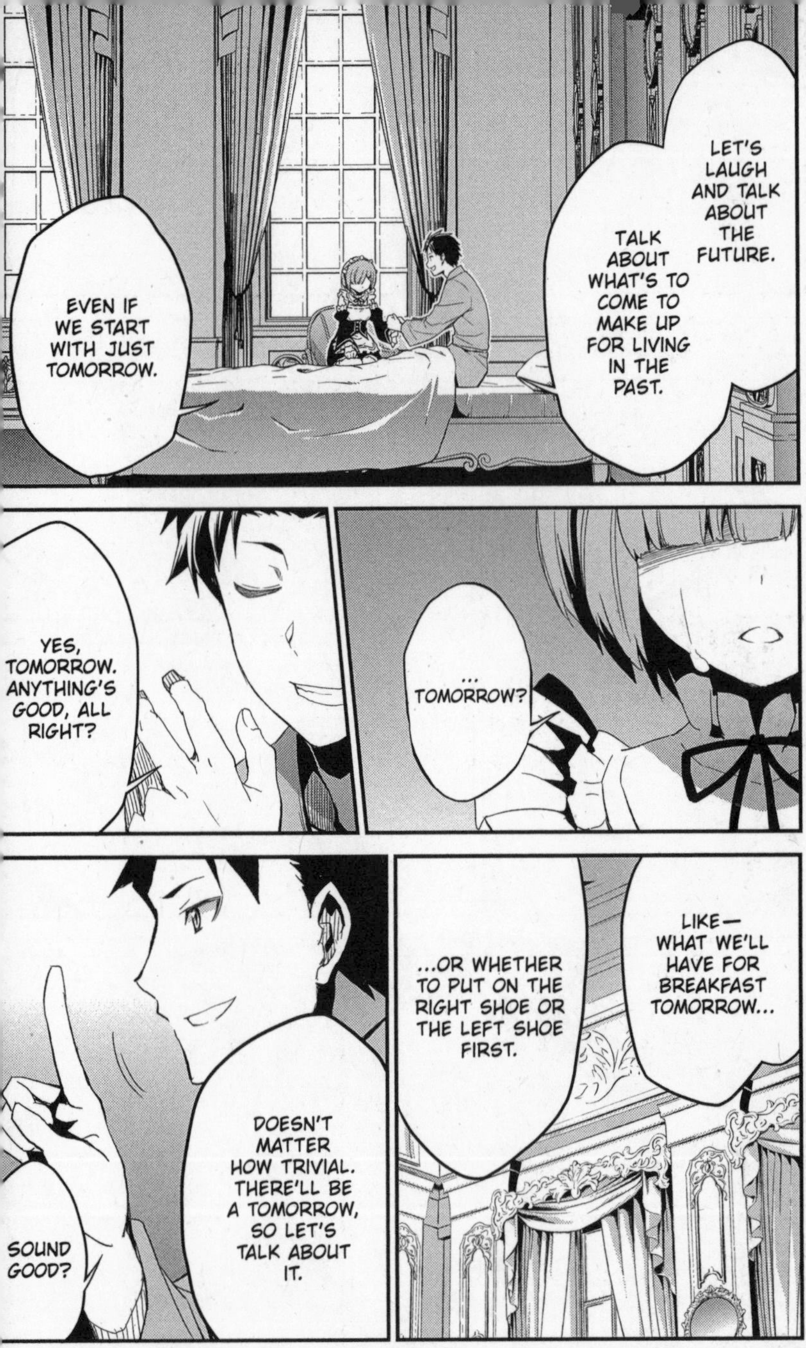
LET'S LAUGH AND TALK ABOUT THE FUTURE.
TALK ABOUT WHAT'S TO COME TO MAKE UP FOR LIVING IN THE PAST.
EVEN IF WE START WITH JUST TOMORROW.
... TOMORROW?
YES, TOMORROW. ANYTHING'S GOOD, ALL RIGHT?
LIKE— WHAT WE'LL HAVE FOR BREAKFAST TOMORROW...
...OR WHETHER TO PUT ON THE RIGHT SHOE OR THE LEFT SHOE FIRST.
DOESN'T MATTER HOW TRIVIAL. THERE'LL BE A TOMORROW, SO LET'S TALK ABOUT IT.
SOUND GOOD?

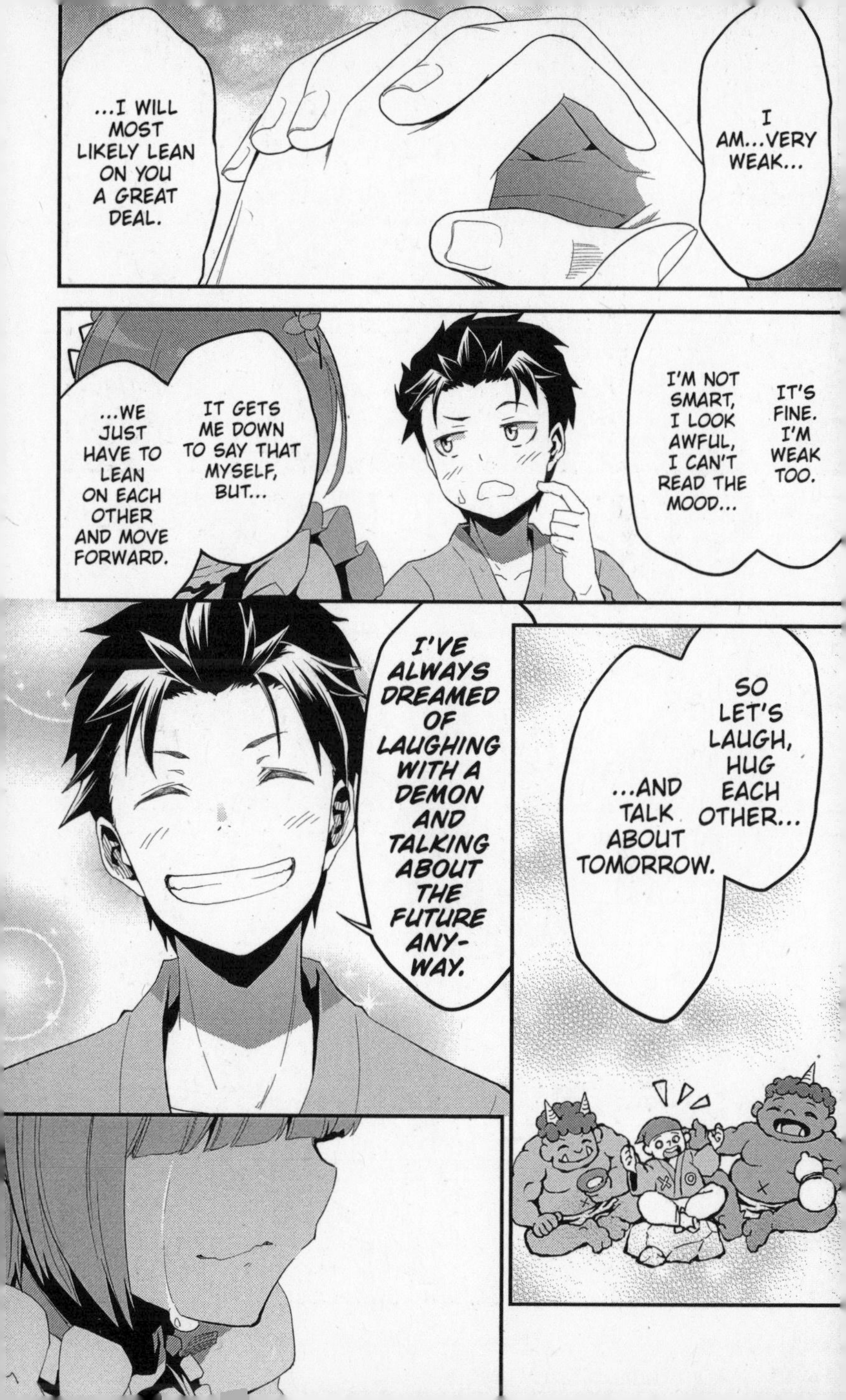
I AM...VERY WEAK...
...I WILL MOST LIKELY LEAN ON YOU A GREAT DEAL.
IT'S FINE. I'M WEAK TOO.
I'M NOT SMART, I LOOK AWFUL, I CAN'T READ THE MOOD...
IT GETS ME DOWN TO SAY THAT MYSELF, BUT...
...WE JUST HAVE TO LEAN ON EACH OTHER AND MOVE FORWARD.
SO LET'S LAUGH, HUG EACH OTHER...
...AND TALK ABOUT TOMORROW.
I'VE ALWAYS DREAMED OF LAUGHING WITH A DEMON AND TALKING ABOUT THE FUTURE ANY-WAY.

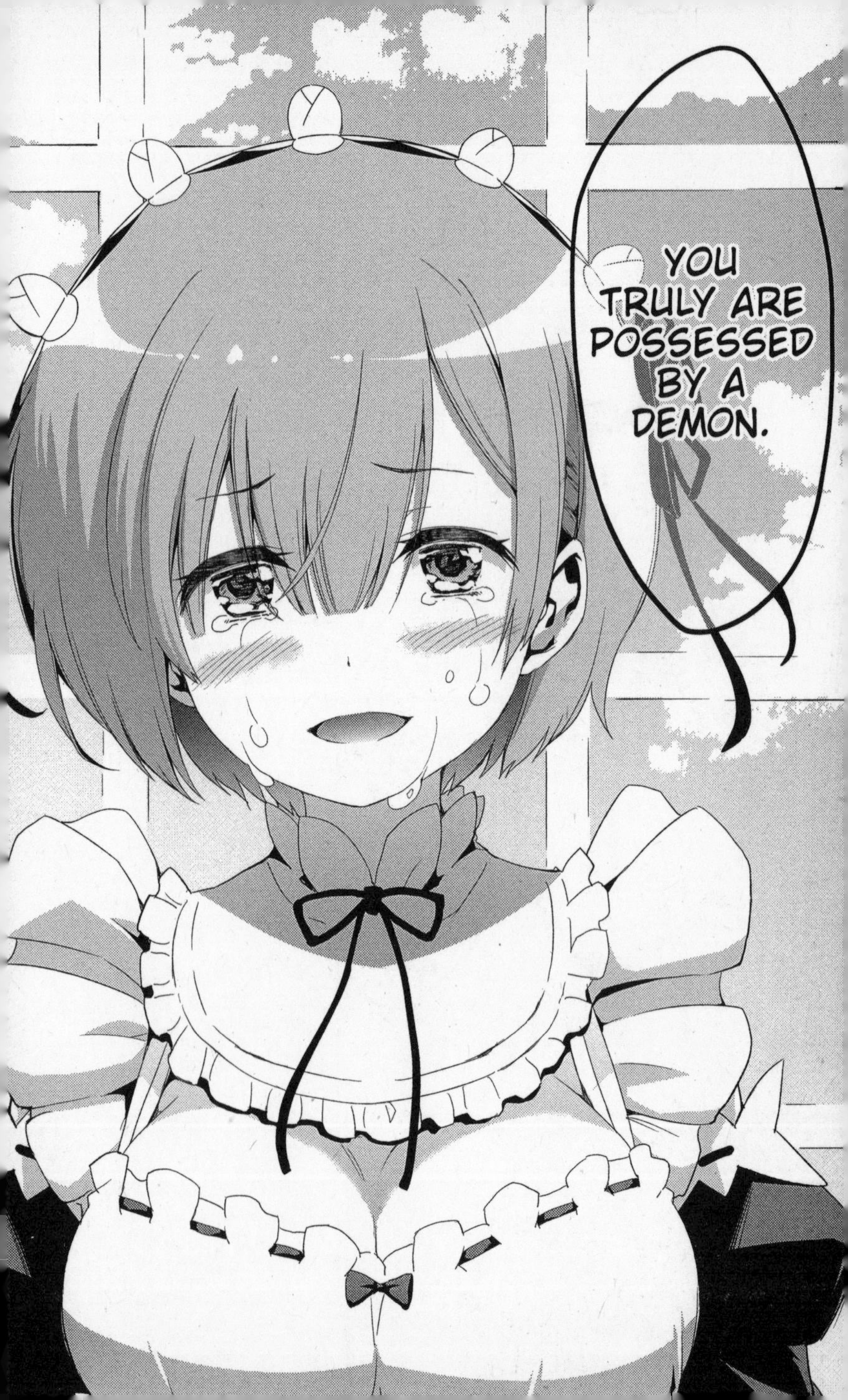
YOU TRULY ARE POSSESSED BY A DEMON.

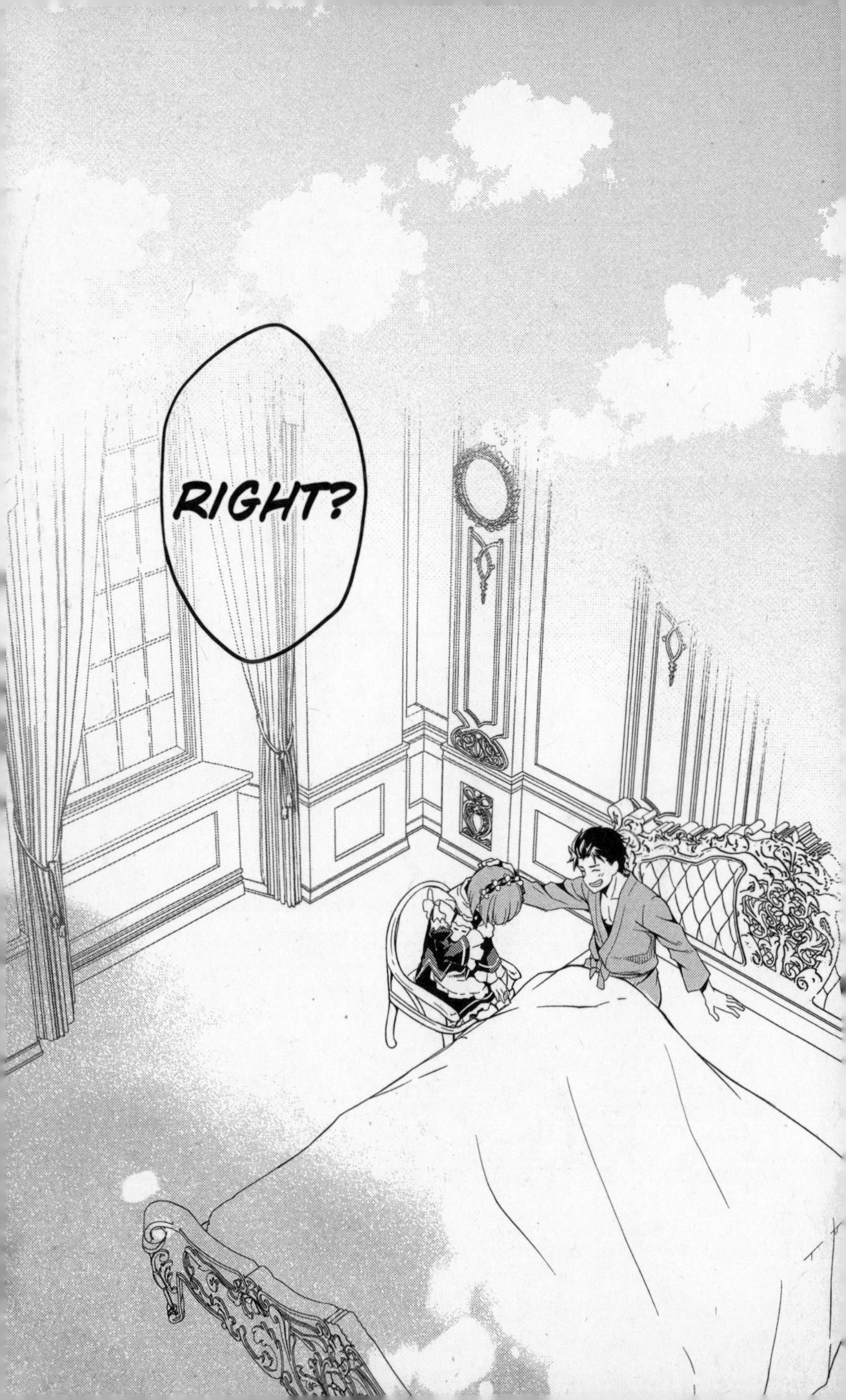
RIGHT?

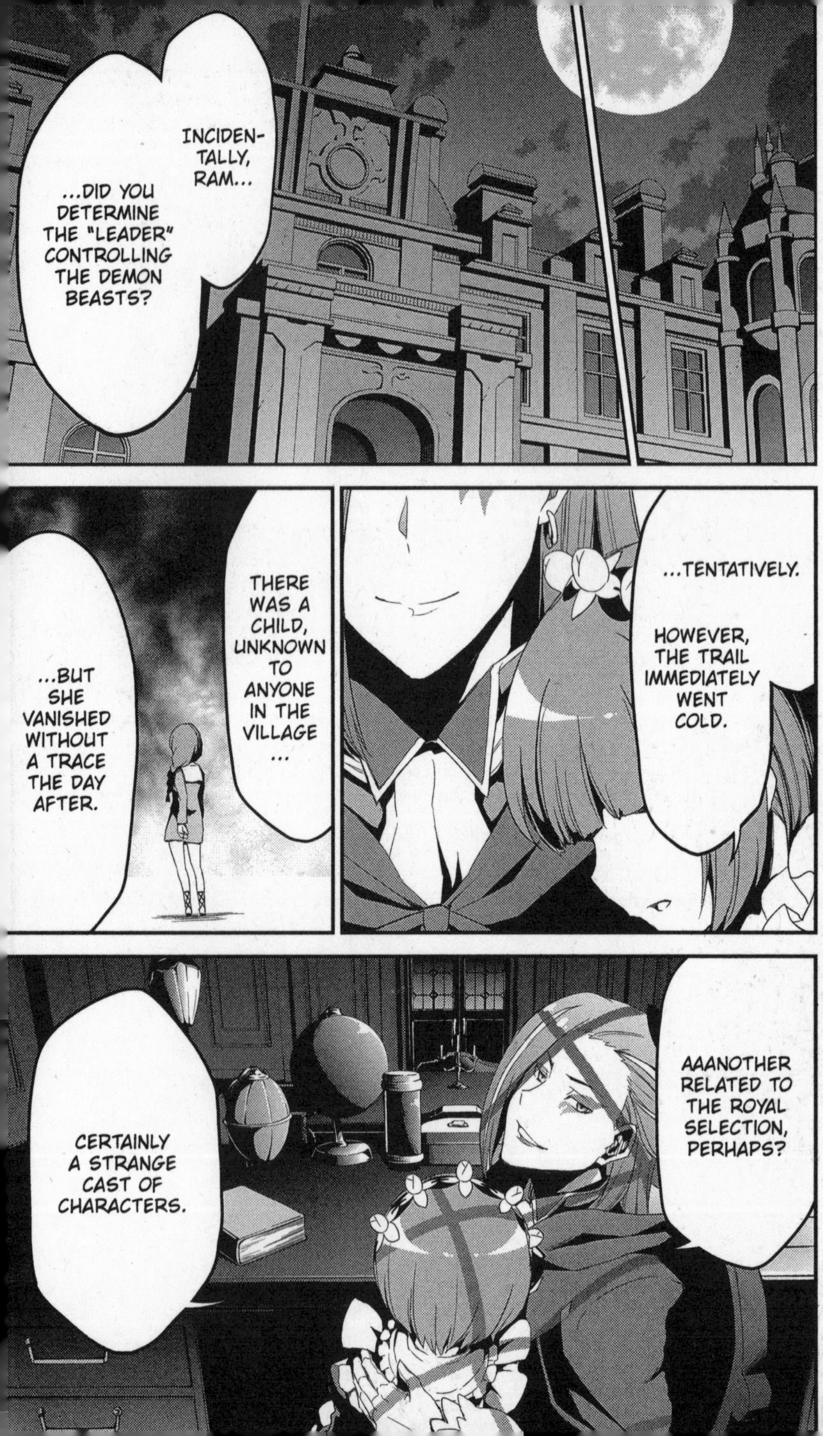
INCIDEN-TALLY, RAM...
...DID YOU DETERMINE THE "LEADER" CONTROLLING THE DEMON BEASTS?
...TENTATIVELY.
HOWEVER, THE TRAIL IMMEDIATELY WENT COLD.
THERE WAS A CHILD, UNKNOWN TO ANYONE IN THE VILLAGE...
...BUT SHE VANISHED WITHOUT A TRACE THE DAY AFTER.
AAANOTHER RELATED TO THE ROYAL SELECTION, PERHAPS?
CERTAINLY A STRANGE CAST OF CHARACTERS.

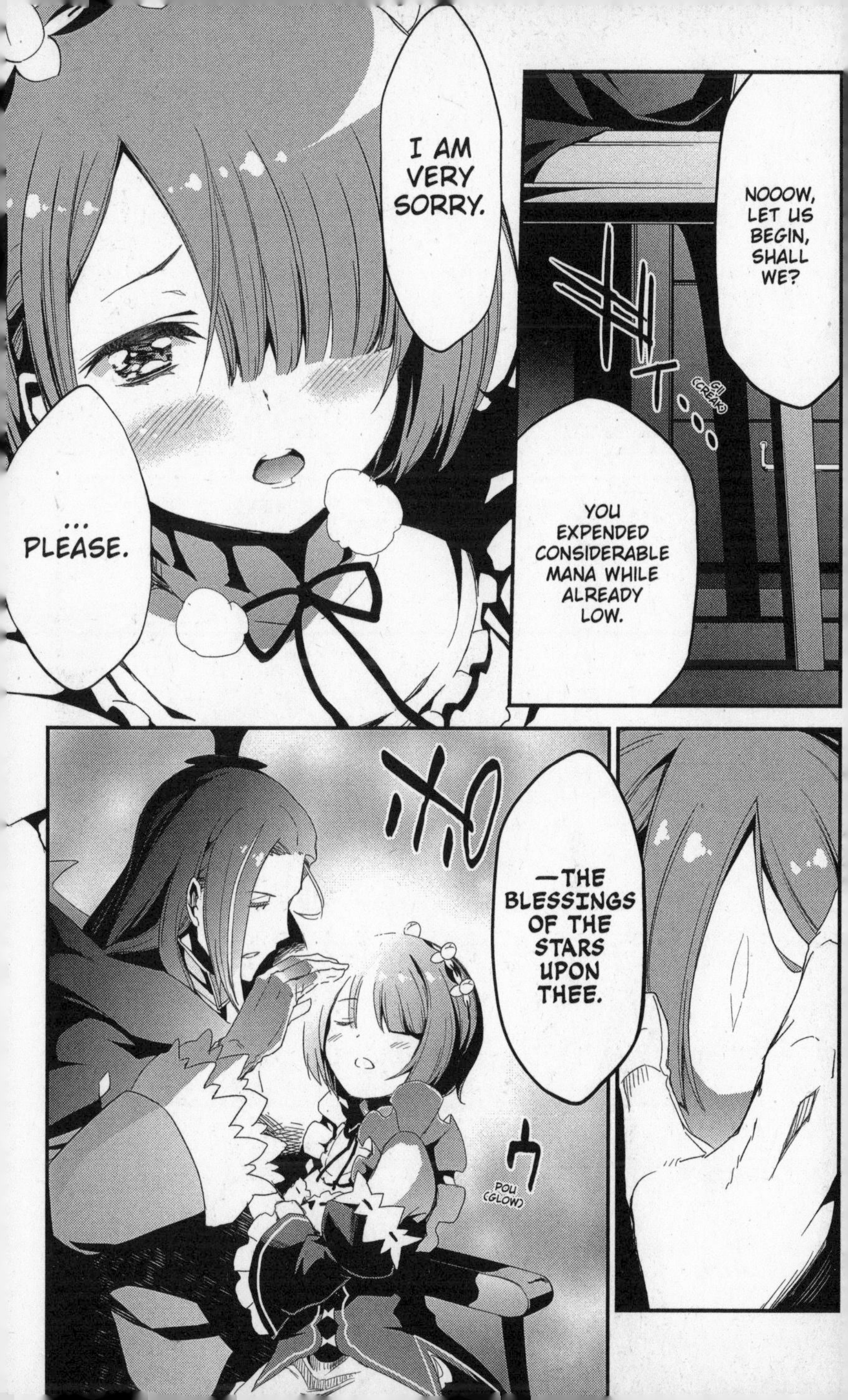
NOOOW, LET US BEGIN, SHALL WE?
GI (CREAK)
YOU EXPENDED CONSIDERABLE MANA WHILE ALREADY LOW.
I AM VERY SORRY.
...PLEASE.
—THE BLESSINGS OF THE STARS UPON THEE.
POU (GLOW)

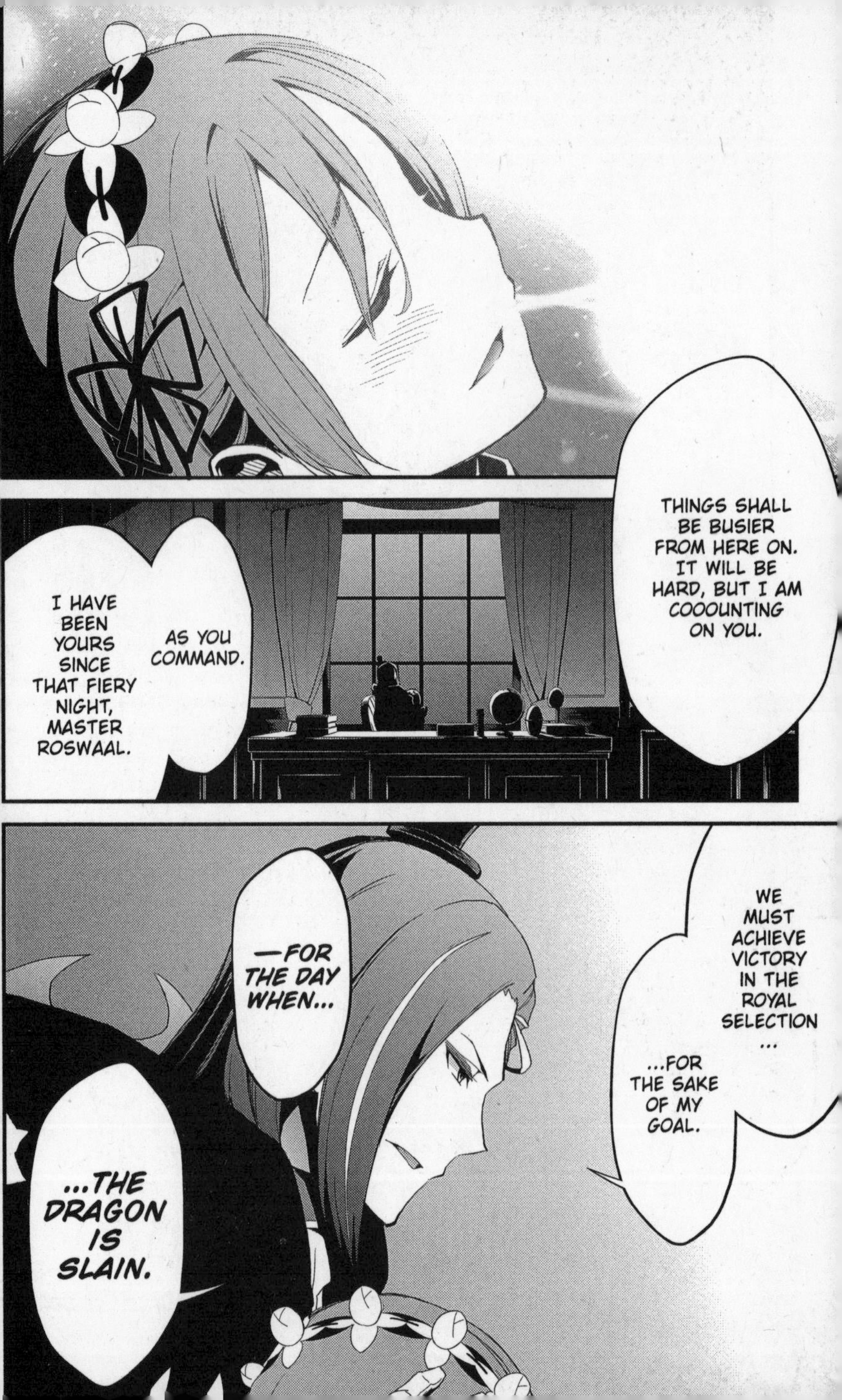
THINGS SHALL BE BUSIER FROM HERE ON. IT WILL BE HARD, BUT I AM COOOUNTING ON YOU.
AS YOU COMMAND.
I HAVE BEEN YOURS SINCE THAT FIERY NIGHT, MASTER ROSWAAL.
WE MUST ACHIEVE VICTORY IN THE ROYAL SELECTION...
...FOR THE SAKE OF MY GOAL.
—FOR THE DAY WHEN...
...THE DRAGON IS SLAIN.

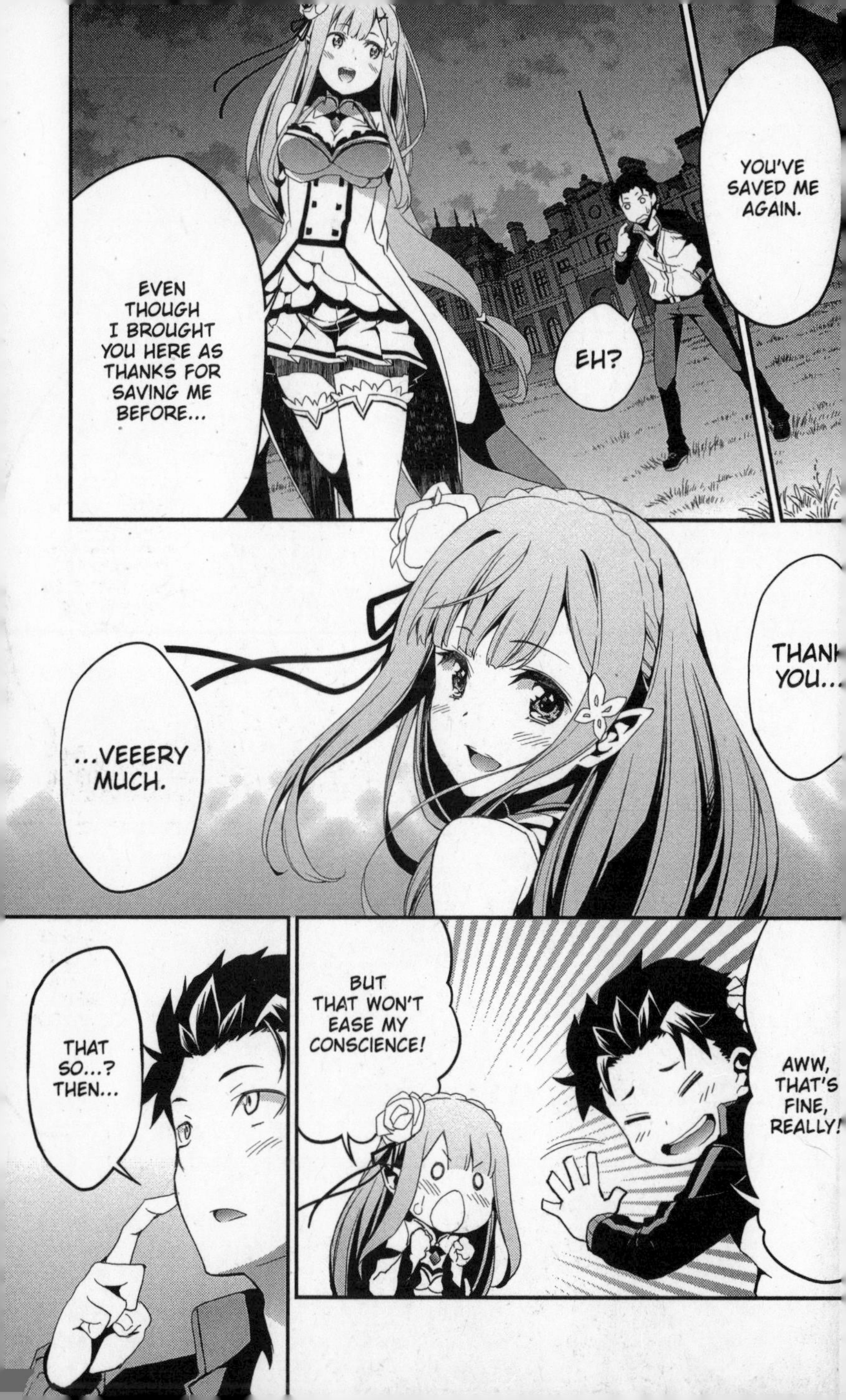
YOU'VE SAVED ME AGAIN.
EH?
EVEN THOUGH I BROUGHT YOU HERE AS THANKS FOR SAVING ME BEFORE...
THANK YOU...
...VEEERY MUCH.
AWW, THAT'S FINE, REALLY!
BUT THAT WON'T EASE MY CONSCIENCE!
THAT SO...? THEN...

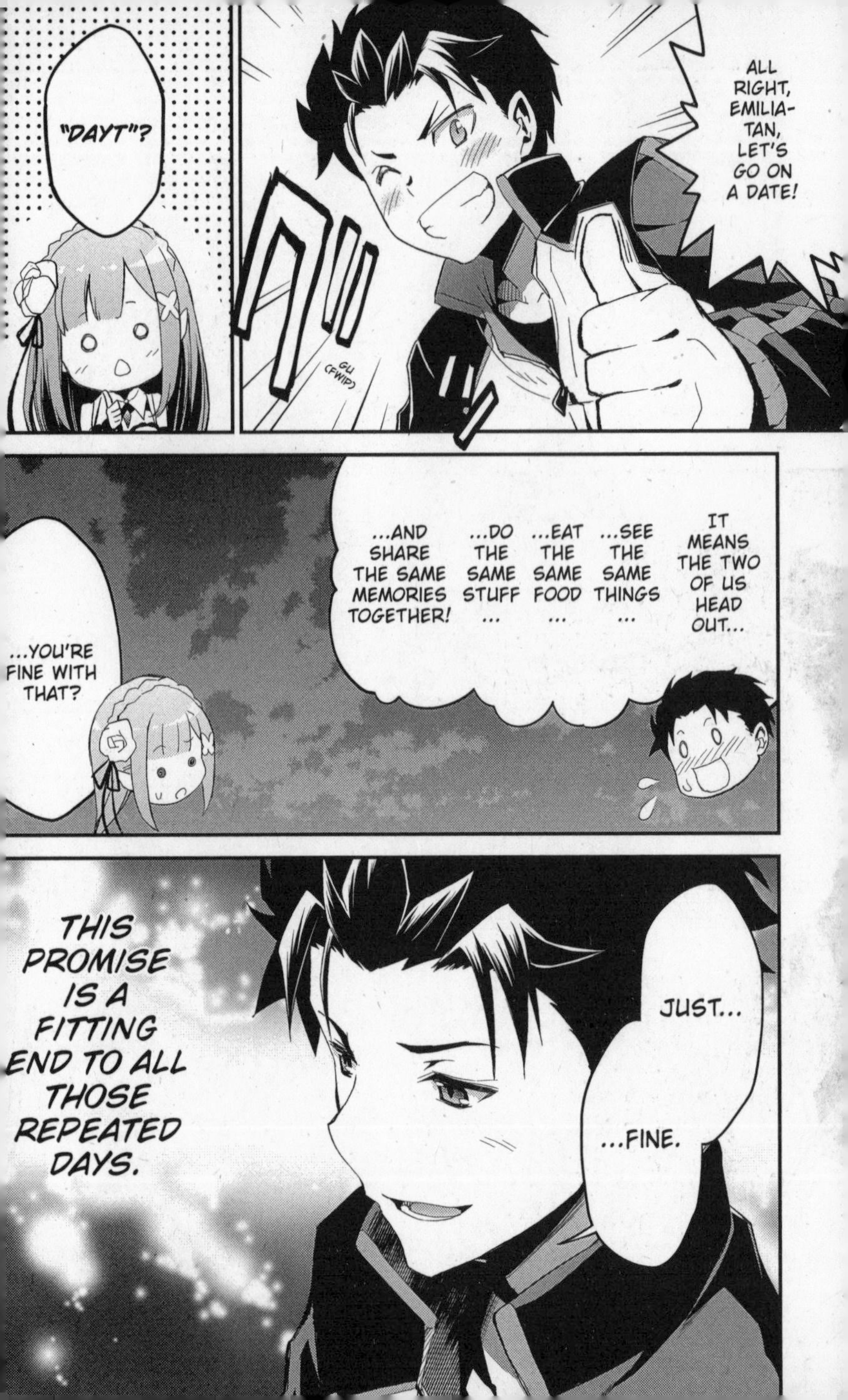
ALL RIGHT, EMILIA-TAN, LET'S GO ON A DATE!
GU (FWIP)
"DAYT"?
IT MEANS THE TWO OF US HEAD OUT...
...SEE THE SAME THINGS...
...EAT THE SAME FOOD...
...DO THE SAME STUFF...
...AND SHARE THE SAME MEMORIES TOGETHER!
...YOU'RE FINE WITH THAT?
JUST...
...FINE.
THIS PROMISE IS A FITTING END TO ALL THOSE REPEATED DAYS.

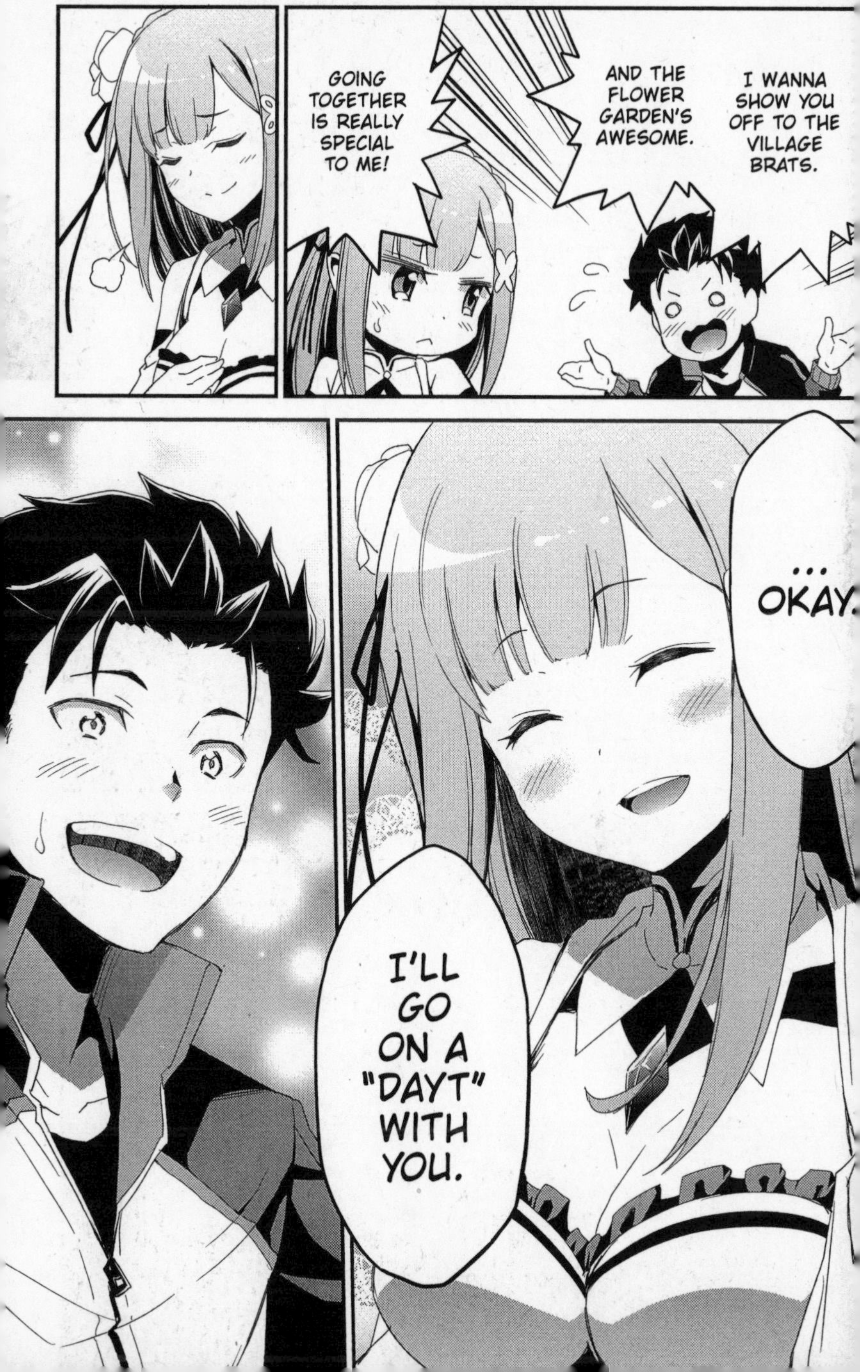
I WANNA SHOW YOU OFF TO THE VILLAGE BRATS.
AND THE FLOWER GARDEN'S AWESOME.
GOING TOGETHER IS REALLY SPECIAL TO ME!
...OKAY.
I'LL GO ON A "DAYT" WITH YOU.

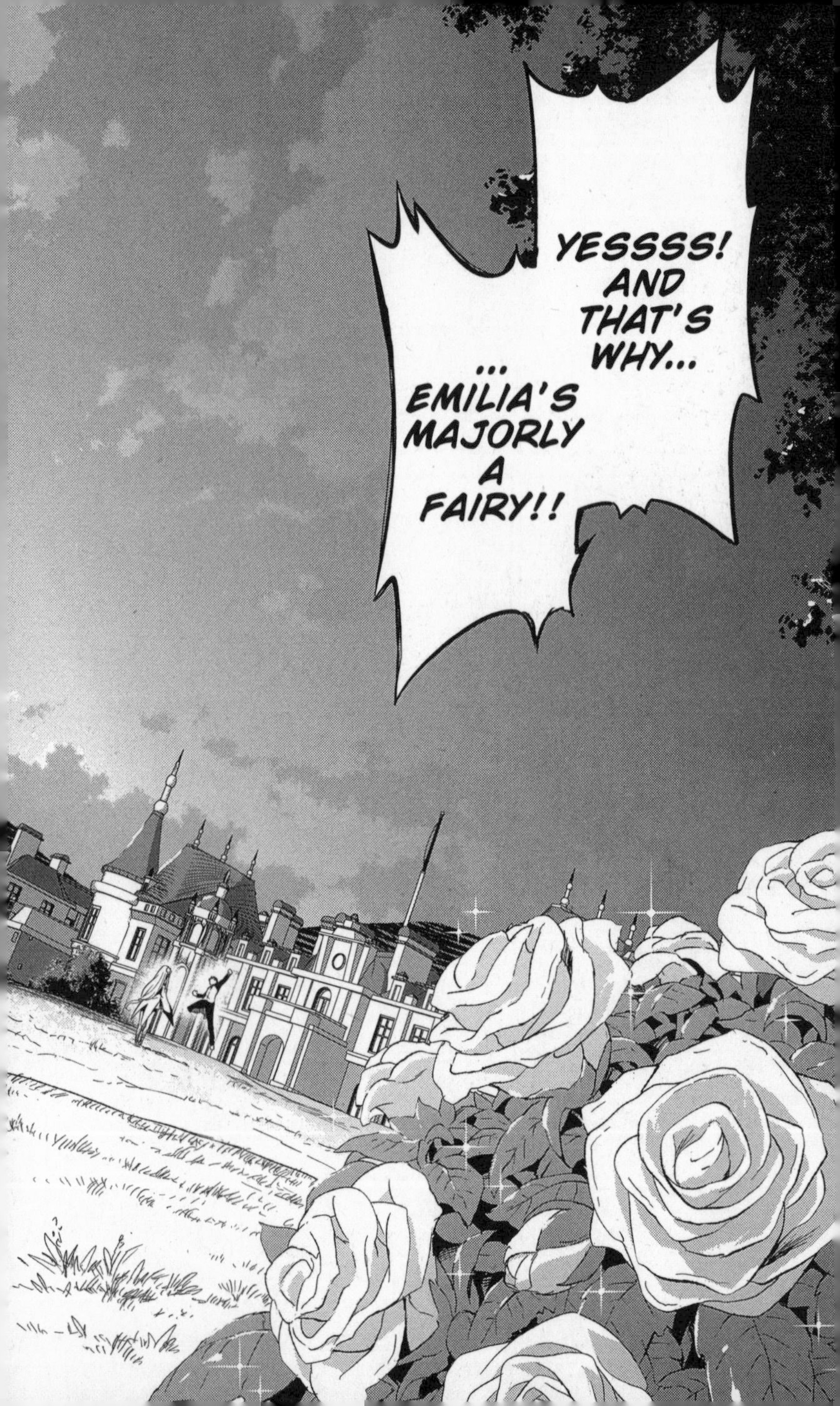
YESSSS! AND THAT'S WHY... ...EMILIA'S MAJORLY A FAIRY!!

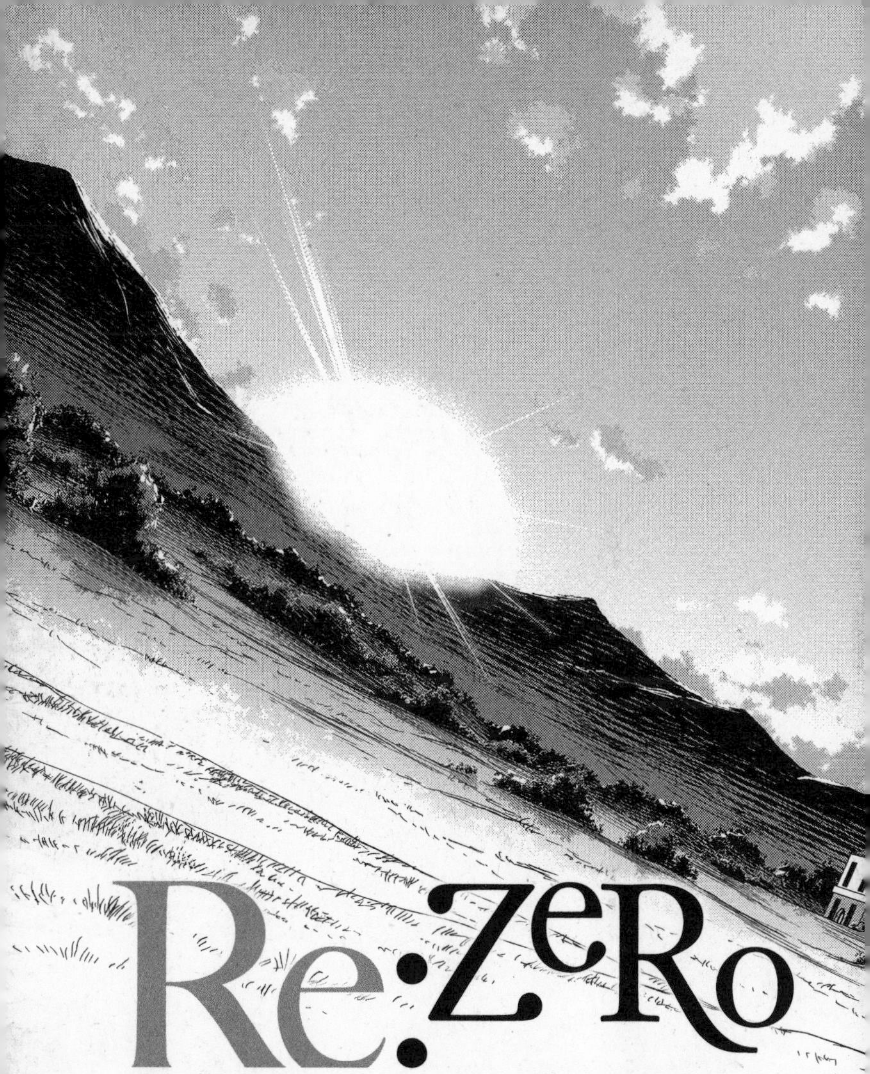
Re:ZeRo

-Starting Life in Another World-

Chapter 2: A Week at the Mansion

FIN

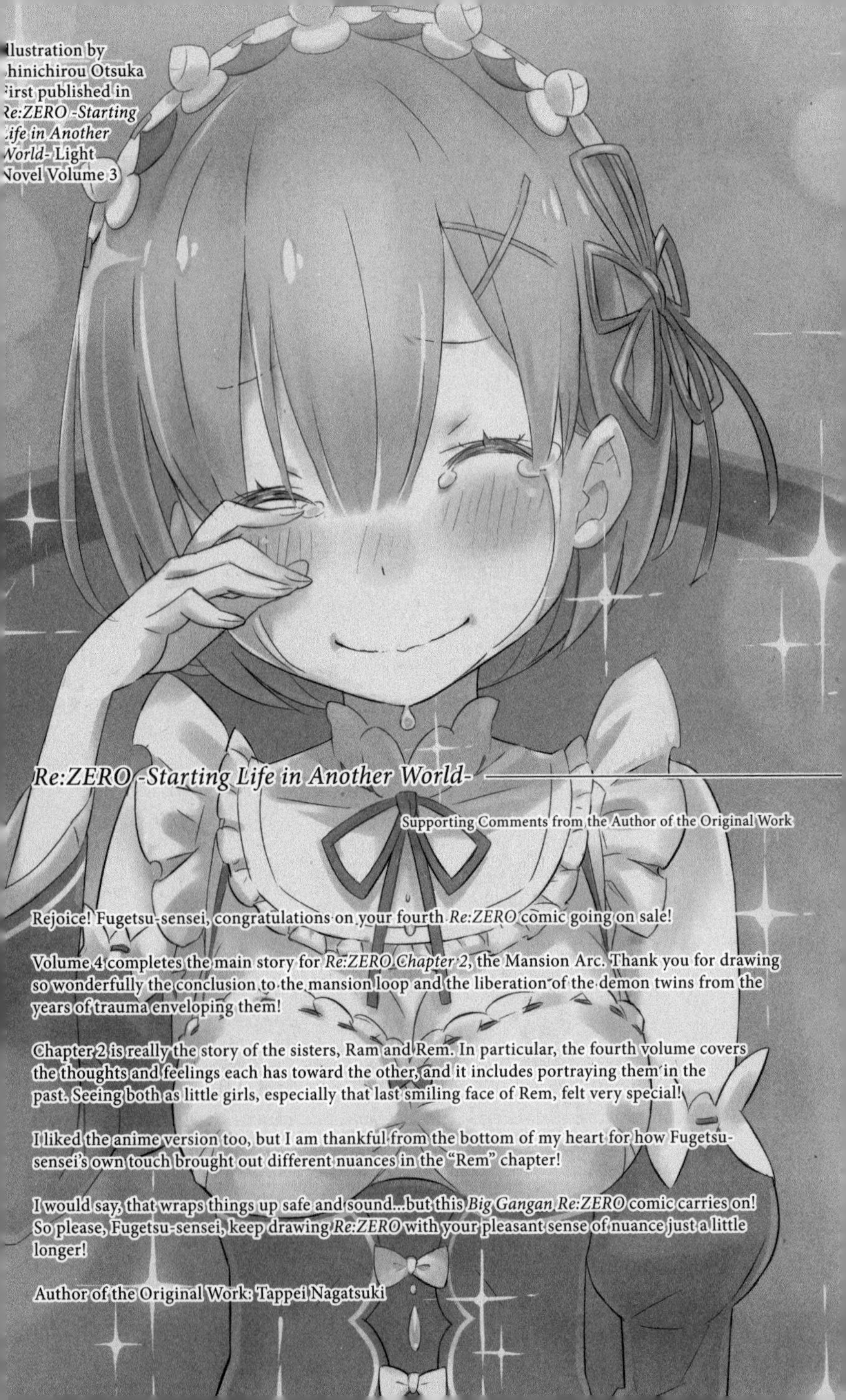

Illustration by Shinichirou Otsuka First published in *Re:ZERO -Starting Life in Another World-* Light Novel Volume 3

Re:ZERO -Starting Life in Another World-

Supporting Comments from the Author of the Original Work

Rejoice! Fugetsu-sensei, congratulations on your fourth *Re:ZERO* comic going on sale!

Volume 4 completes the main story for *Re:ZERO Chapter 2*, the Mansion Arc. Thank you for drawing so wonderfully the conclusion to the mansion loop and the liberation of the demon twins from the years of trauma enveloping them!

Chapter 2 is really the story of the sisters, Ram and Rem. In particular, the fourth volume covers the thoughts and feelings each has toward the other, and it includes portraying them in the past. Seeing both as little girls, especially that last smiling face of Rem, felt very special!

I liked the anime version too, but I am thankful from the bottom of my heart for how Fugetsu-sensei's own touch brought out different nuances in the "Rem" chapter!

I would say, that wraps things up safe and sound...but this *Big Gangan Re:ZERO* comic carries on! So please, Fugetsu-sensei, keep drawing *Re:ZERO* with your pleasant sense of nuance just a little longer!

Author of the Original Work: Tappei Nagatsuki

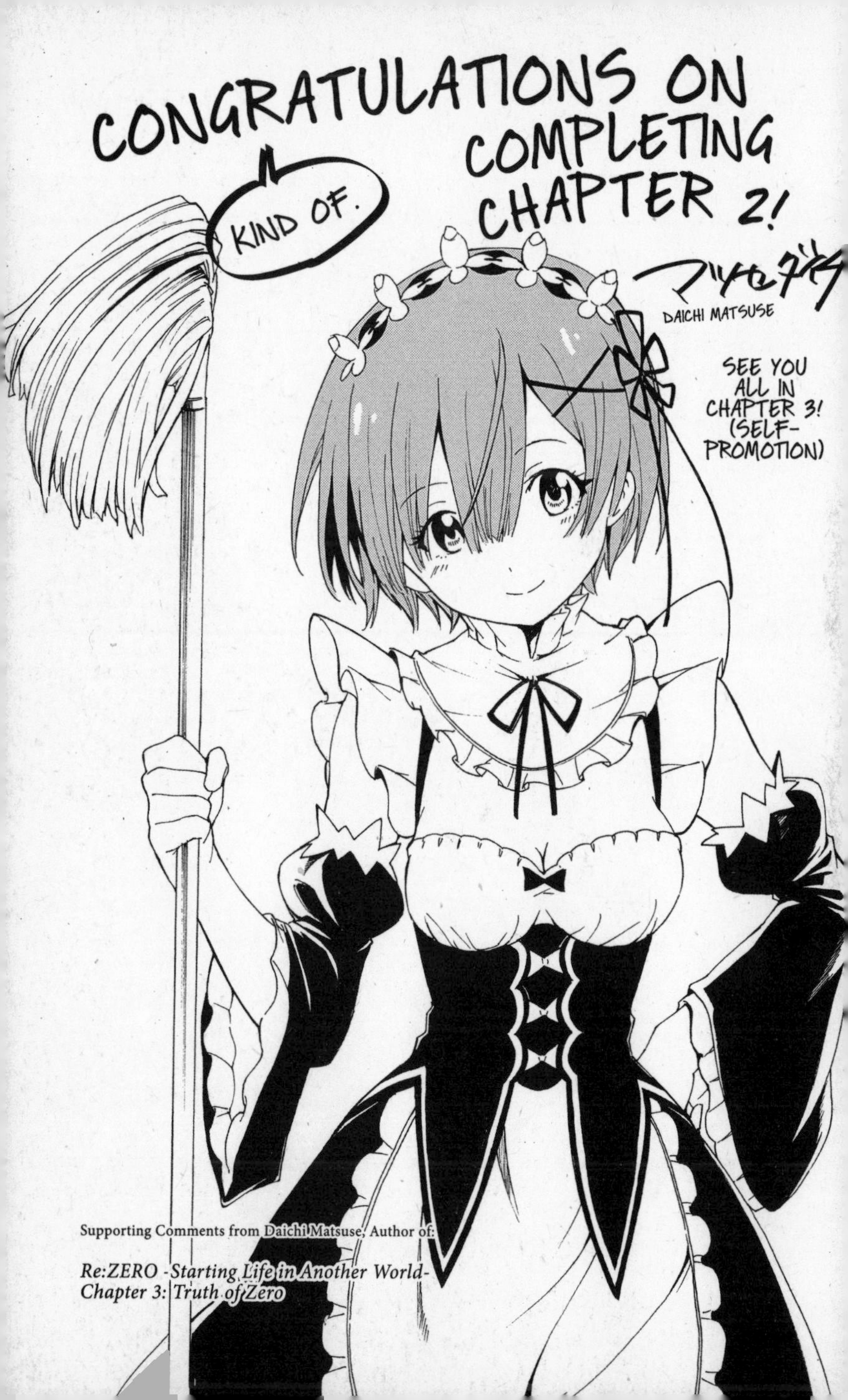
CONGRATULATIONS ON COMPLETING CHAPTER 2!
KIND OF.
DAICHI MATSUSE
SEE YOU ALL IN CHAPTER 3! (SELF-PROMOTION)

Supporting Comments from Daichi Matsuse, Author of:

Re:ZERO -Starting Life in Another World- Chapter 3: Truth of Zero

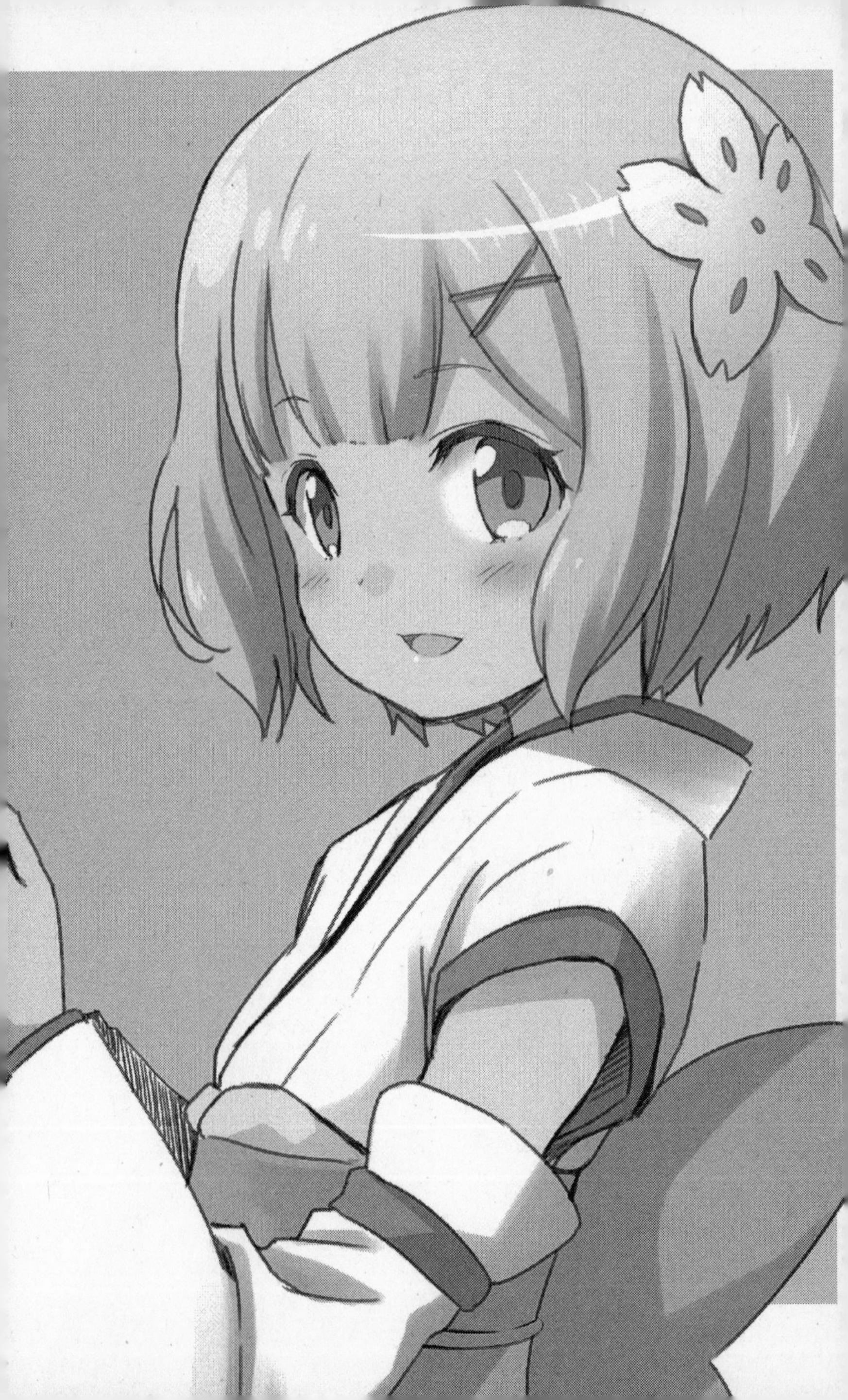

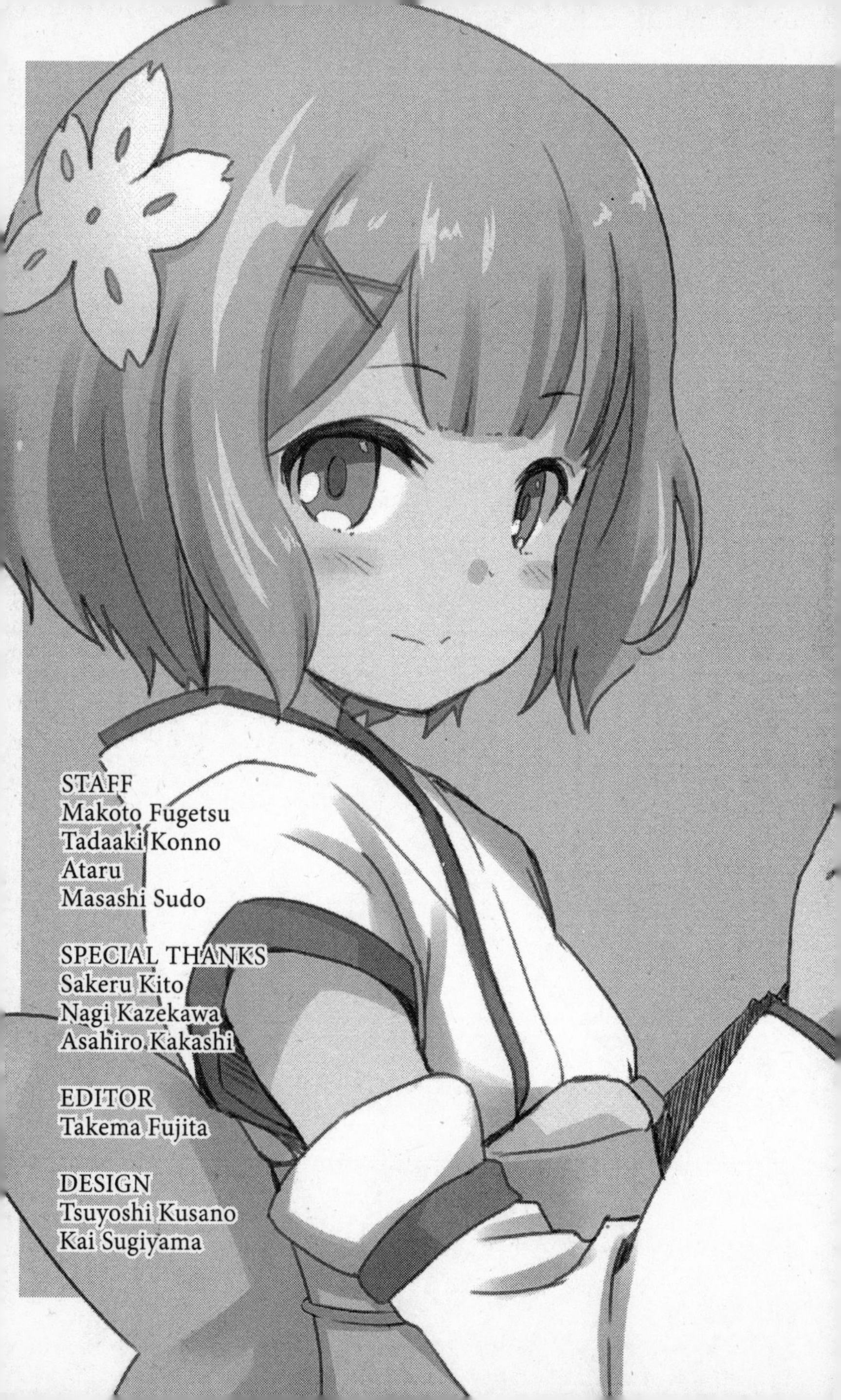

STAFF
Makoto Fugetsu
Tadaaki Konno
Ataru
Masashi Sudo

SPECIAL THANKS
Sakeru Kito
Nagi Kazekawa
Asahiro Kakashi

EDITOR
Takema Fujita

DESIGN
Tsuyoshi Kusano
Kai Sugiyama

Re:ZeRo

-Starting Life in Another World-

Special Story

The Roswaal Manor Girls' Meet (Hot Bath Edition)

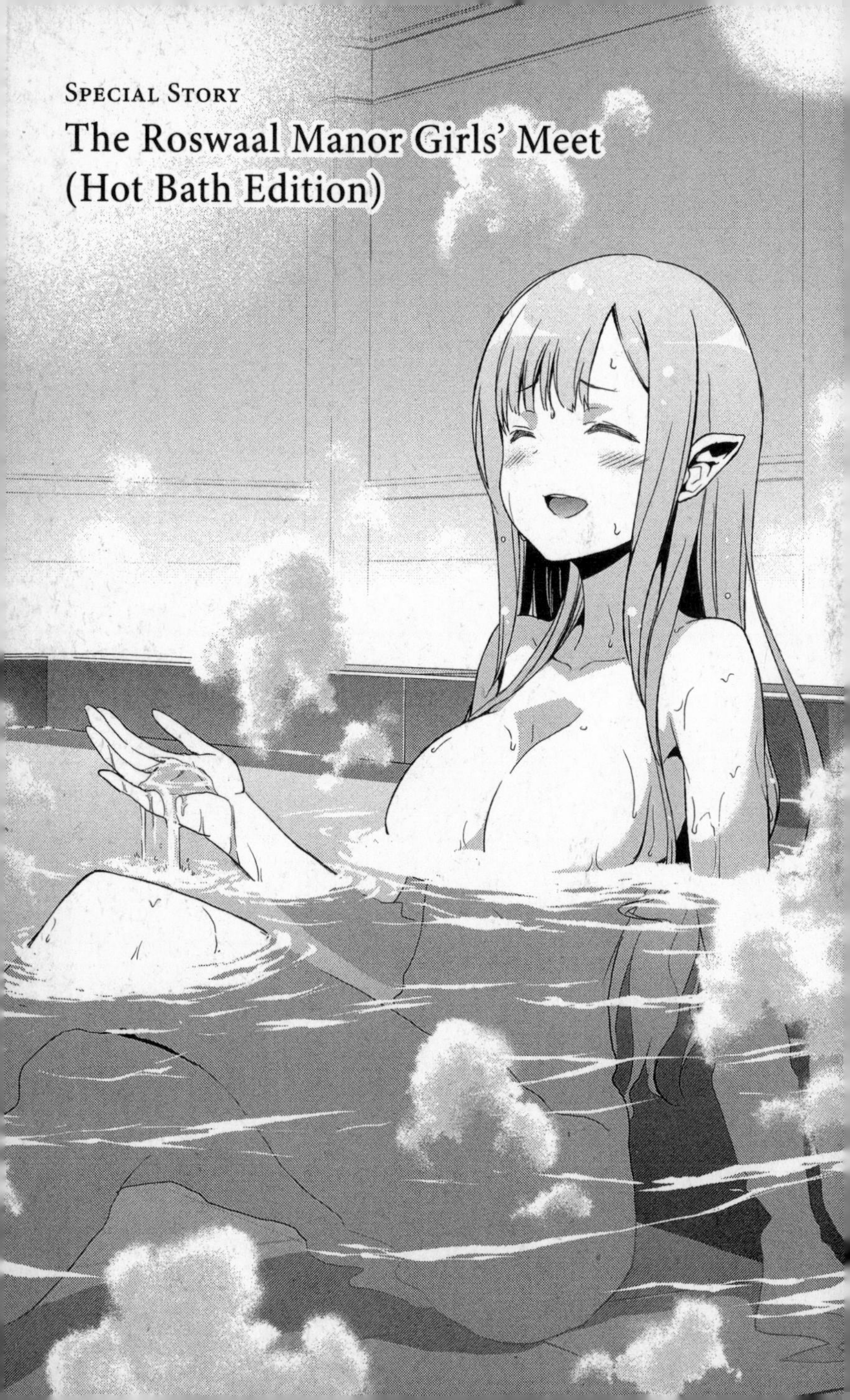

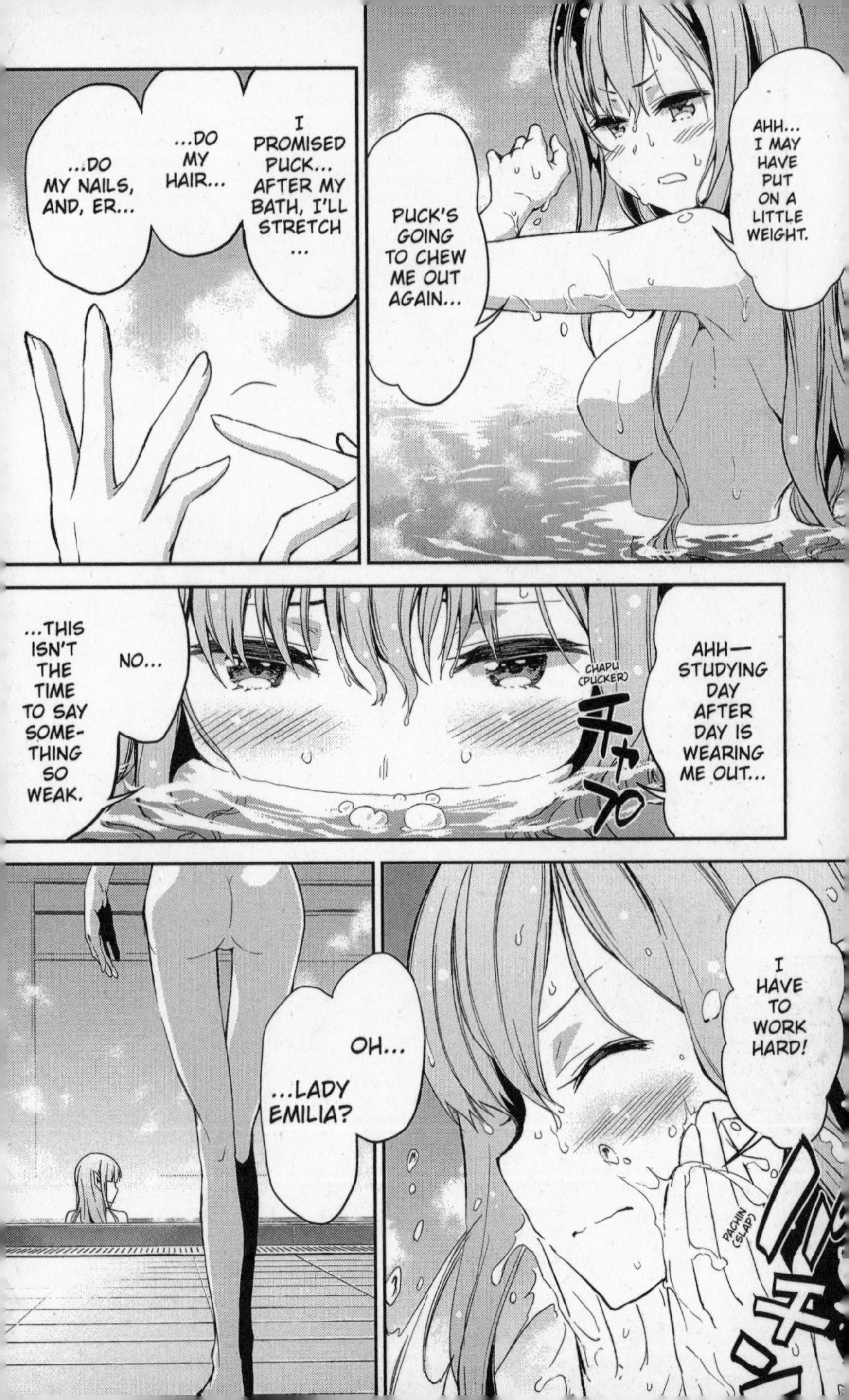
AHH... I MAY HAVE PUT ON A LITTLE WEIGHT.
PUCK'S GOING TO CHEW ME OUT AGAIN...
I PROMISED PUCK... AFTER MY BATH, I'LL STRETCH ...
...DO MY HAIR...
...DO MY NAILS, AND, ER...
AHH— STUDYING DAY AFTER DAY IS WEARING ME OUT...
CHAPU (PUCKER)
NO...
...THIS ISN'T THE TIME TO SAY SOME-THING SO WEAK.
I HAVE TO WORK HARD!
PACHIN (SLAP)
OH...
...LADY EMILIA?

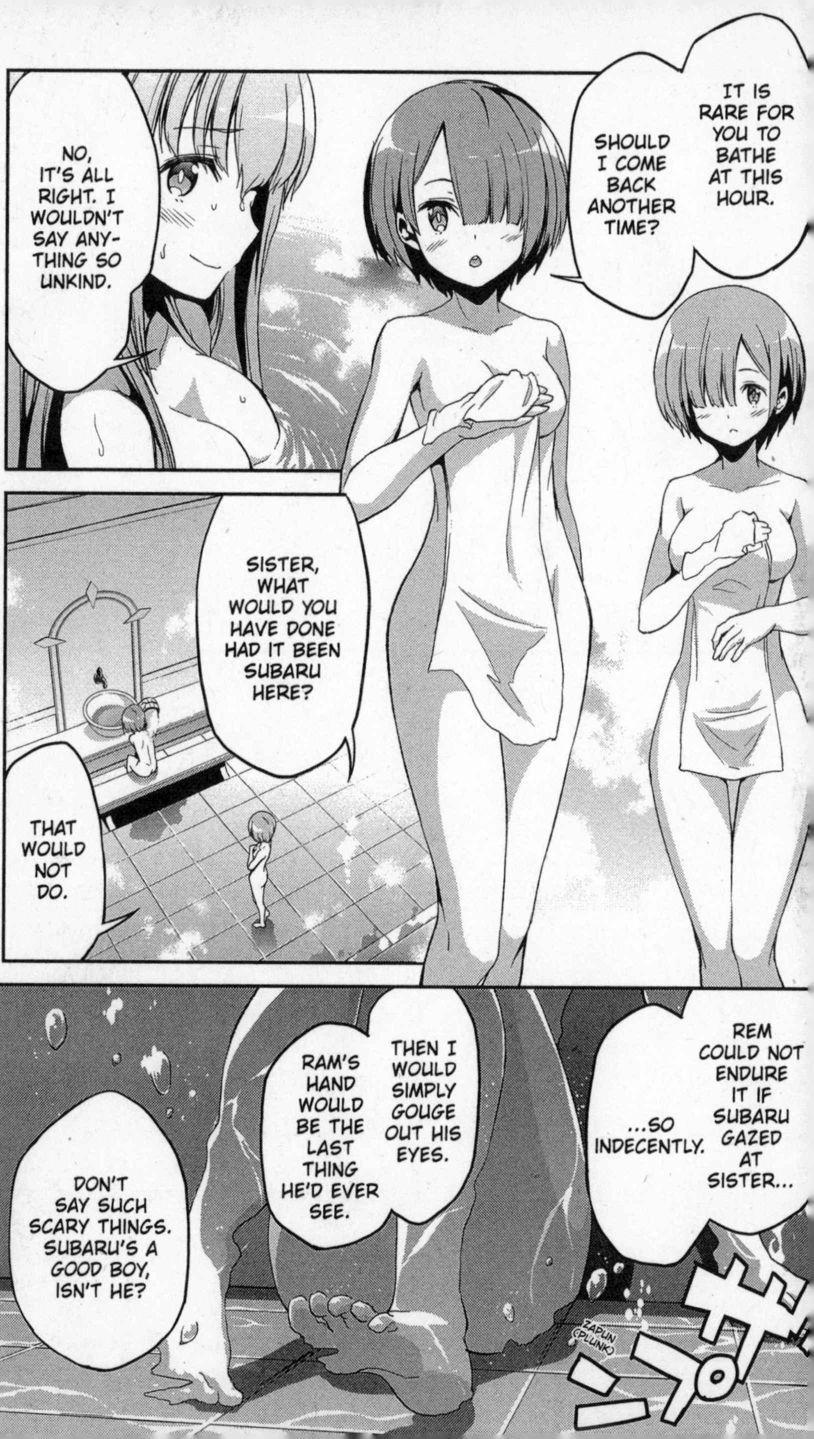
IT IS RARE FOR YOU TO BATHE AT THIS HOUR.
SHOULD I COME BACK ANOTHER TIME?
NO, IT'S ALL RIGHT. I WOULDN'T SAY ANY-THING SO UNKIND.
SISTER, WHAT WOULD YOU HAVE DONE HAD IT BEEN SUBARU HERE?
THAT WOULD NOT DO.
REM COULD NOT ENDURE IT IF SUBARU GAZED AT SISTER...
...SO INDECENTLY.
THEN I WOULD SIMPLY GOUGE OUT HIS EYES.
RAM'S HAND WOULD BE THE LAST THING HE'D EVER SEE.
DON'T SAY SUCH SCARY THINGS. SUBARU'S A GOOD BOY, ISN'T HE?
ZAPUN (PLUNK)

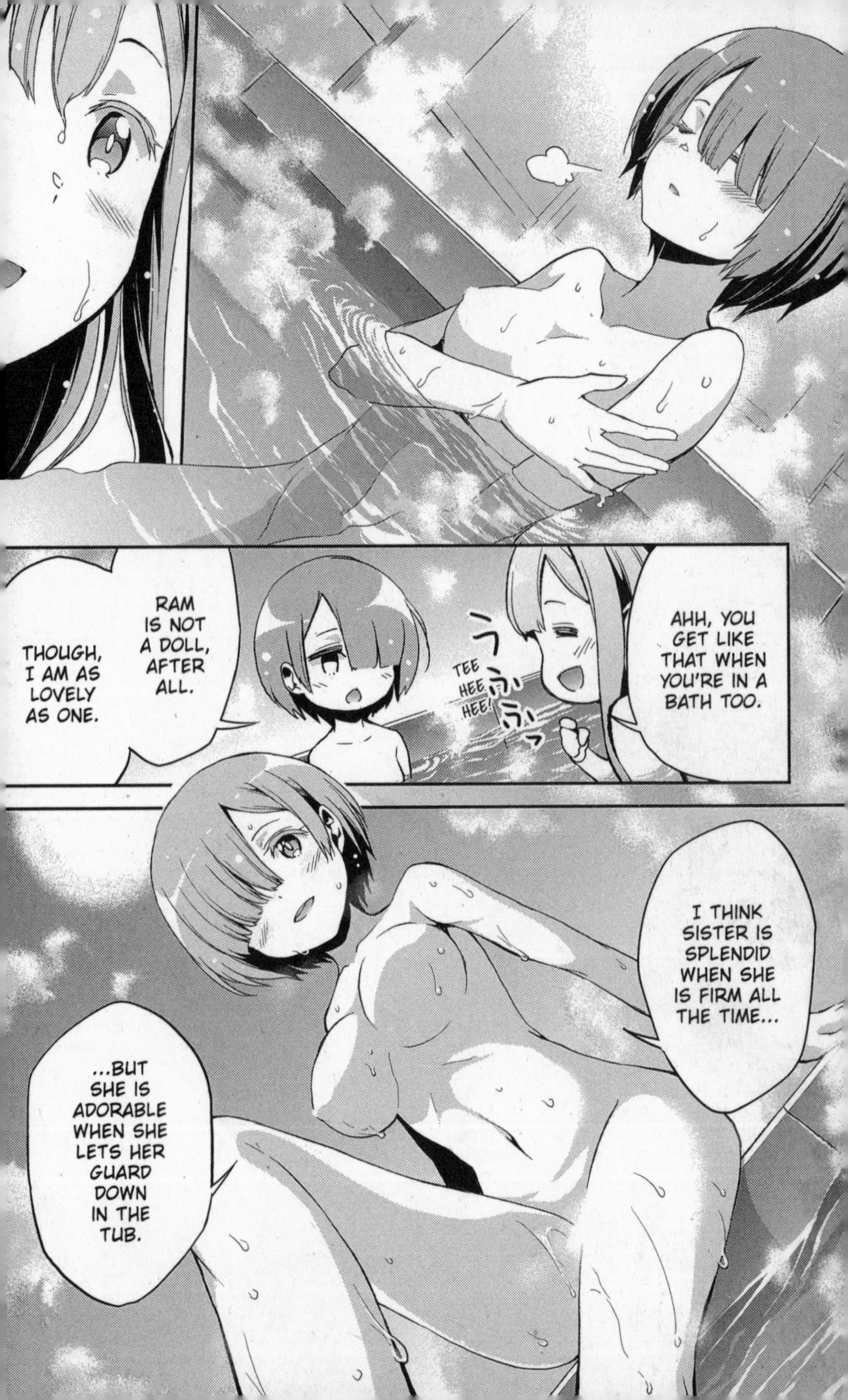
AHH, YOU GET LIKE THAT WHEN YOU'RE IN A BATH TOO.
うふふっ
TEE HEE HEE!
RAM IS NOT A DOLL, AFTER ALL.
THOUGH, I AM AS LOVELY AS ONE.
I THINK SISTER IS SPLENDID WHEN SHE IS FIRM ALL THE TIME...
...BUT SHE IS ADORABLE WHEN SHE LETS HER GUARD DOWN IN THE TUB.

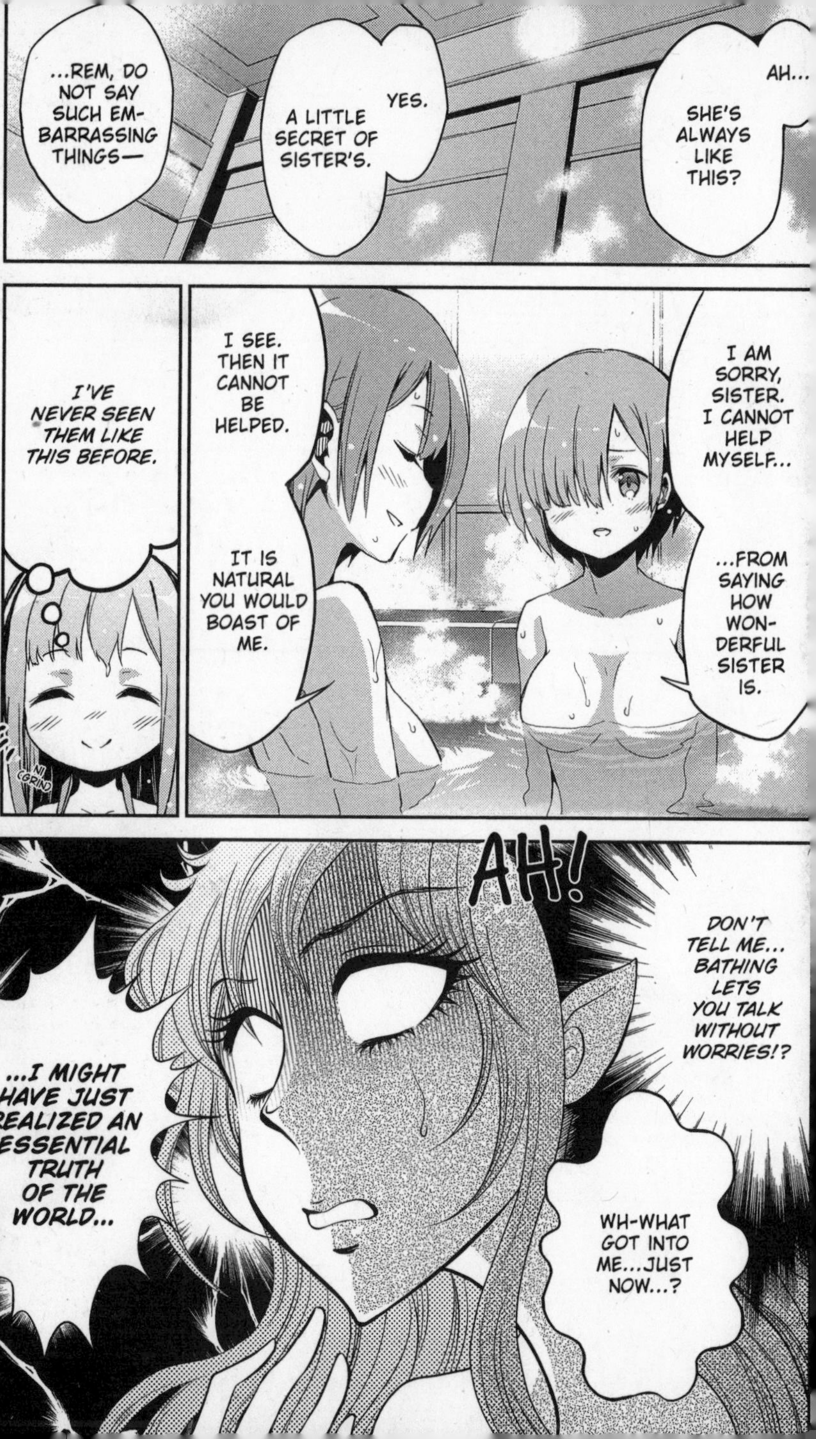
AH... SHE'S ALWAYS LIKE THIS?
YES. A LITTLE SECRET OF SISTER'S.
...REM, DO NOT SAY SUCH EM-BARRASSING THINGS—
I AM SORRY, SISTER. I CANNOT HELP MYSELF...
...FROM SAYING HOW WON-DERFUL SISTER IS.
I SEE. THEN IT CANNOT BE HELPED.
IT IS NATURAL YOU WOULD BOAST OF ME.
I'VE NEVER SEEN THEM LIKE THIS BEFORE.
AH!
DON'T TELL ME... BATHING LETS YOU TALK WITHOUT WORRIES!?
WH-WHAT GOT INTO ME...JUST NOW...?
...I MIGHT HAVE JUST REALIZED AN ESSENTIAL TRUTH OF THE WORLD...

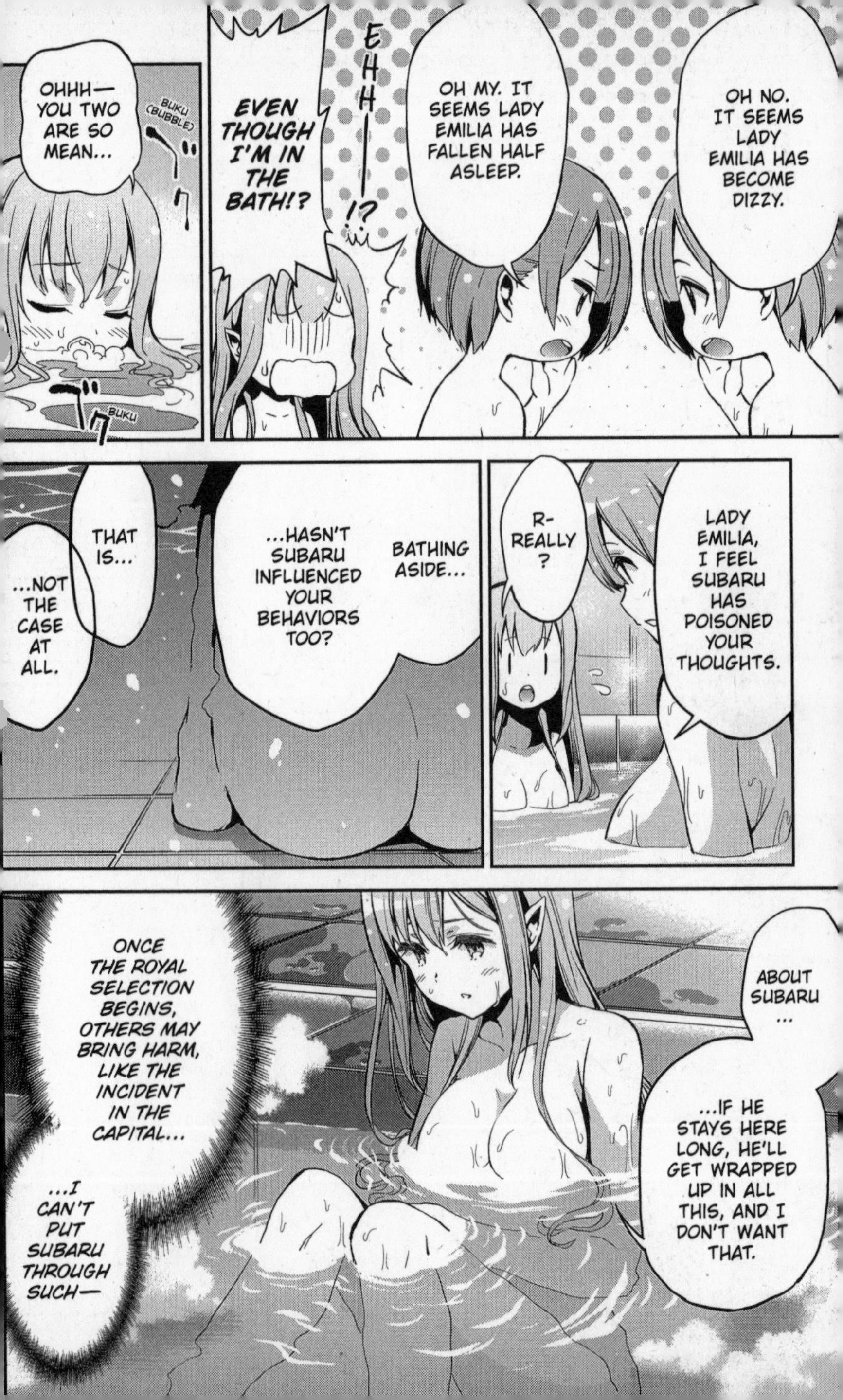
OH NO. IT SEEMS LADY EMILIA HAS BECOME DIZZY.
OH MY. IT SEEMS LADY EMILIA HAS FALLEN HALF ASLEEP.
EHH—!?
EVEN THOUGH I'M IN THE BATH!?
OHHH— YOU TWO ARE SO MEAN...
BUKU (BUBBLE)
BUKU
LADY EMILIA, I FEEL SUBARU HAS POISONED YOUR THOUGHTS.
R-REALLY?
BATHING ASIDE...
...HASN'T SUBARU INFLUENCED YOUR BEHAVIORS TOO?
THAT IS...
...NOT THE CASE AT ALL.
ABOUT SUBARU...
...IF HE STAYS HERE LONG, HE'LL GET WRAPPED UP IN ALL THIS, AND I DON'T WANT THAT.
ONCE THE ROYAL SELECTION BEGINS, OTHERS MAY BRING HARM, LIKE THE INCIDENT IN THE CAPITAL...
...I CAN'T PUT SUBARU THROUGH SUCH—

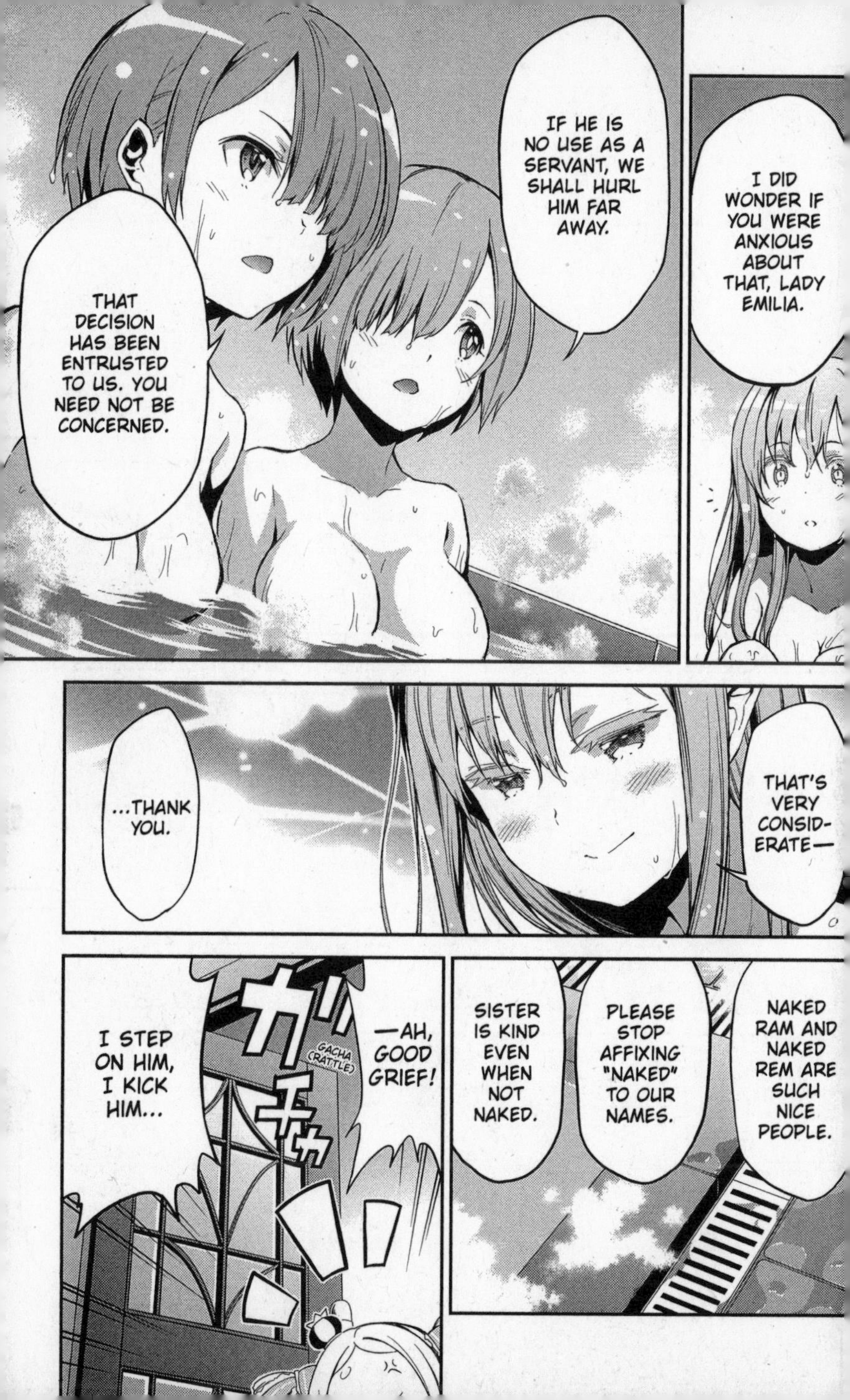
I DID WONDER IF YOU WERE ANXIOUS ABOUT THAT, LADY EMILIA.
IF HE IS NO USE AS A SERVANT, WE SHALL HURL HIM FAR AWAY.
THAT DECISION HAS BEEN ENTRUSTED TO US. YOU NEED NOT BE CONCERNED.
THAT'S VERY CONSID-ERATE—
...THANK YOU.
NAKED RAM AND NAKED REM ARE SUCH NICE PEOPLE.
PLEASE STOP AFFIXING "NAKED" TO OUR NAMES.
SISTER IS KIND EVEN WHEN NOT NAKED.
—AH, GOOD GRIEF!
GACHA (RATTLE)
I STEP ON HIM, I KICK HIM...

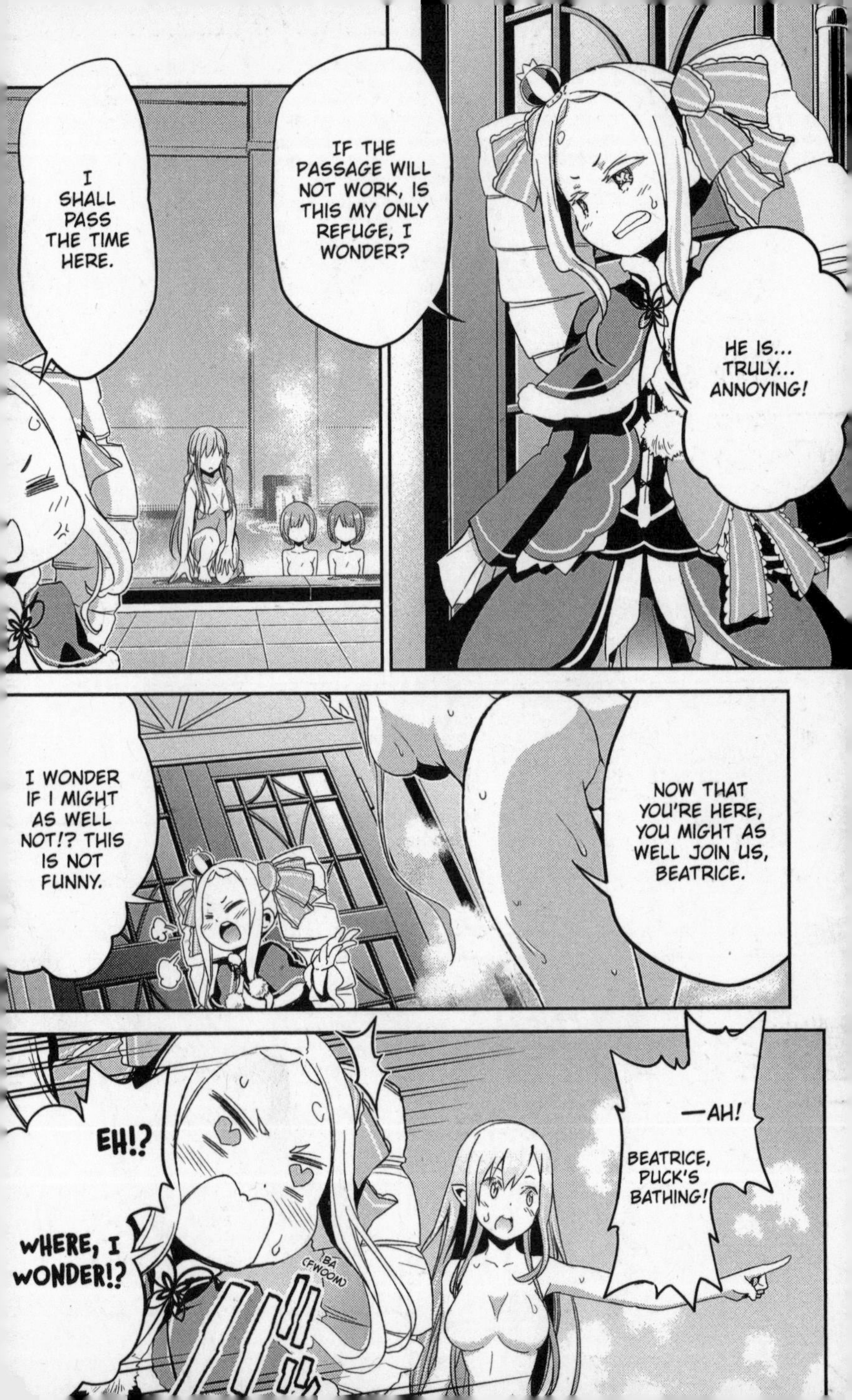
HE IS... TRULY... ANNOYING!
IF THE PASSAGE WILL NOT WORK, IS THIS MY ONLY REFUGE, I WONDER?
I SHALL PASS THE TIME HERE.
NOW THAT YOU'RE HERE, YOU MIGHT AS WELL JOIN US, BEATRICE.
I WONDER IF I MIGHT AS WELL NOT!? THIS IS NOT FUNNY.
—AH!
BEATRICE, PUCK'S BATHING!
EH!?
BA (FWOOM)
WHERE, I WONDER!?

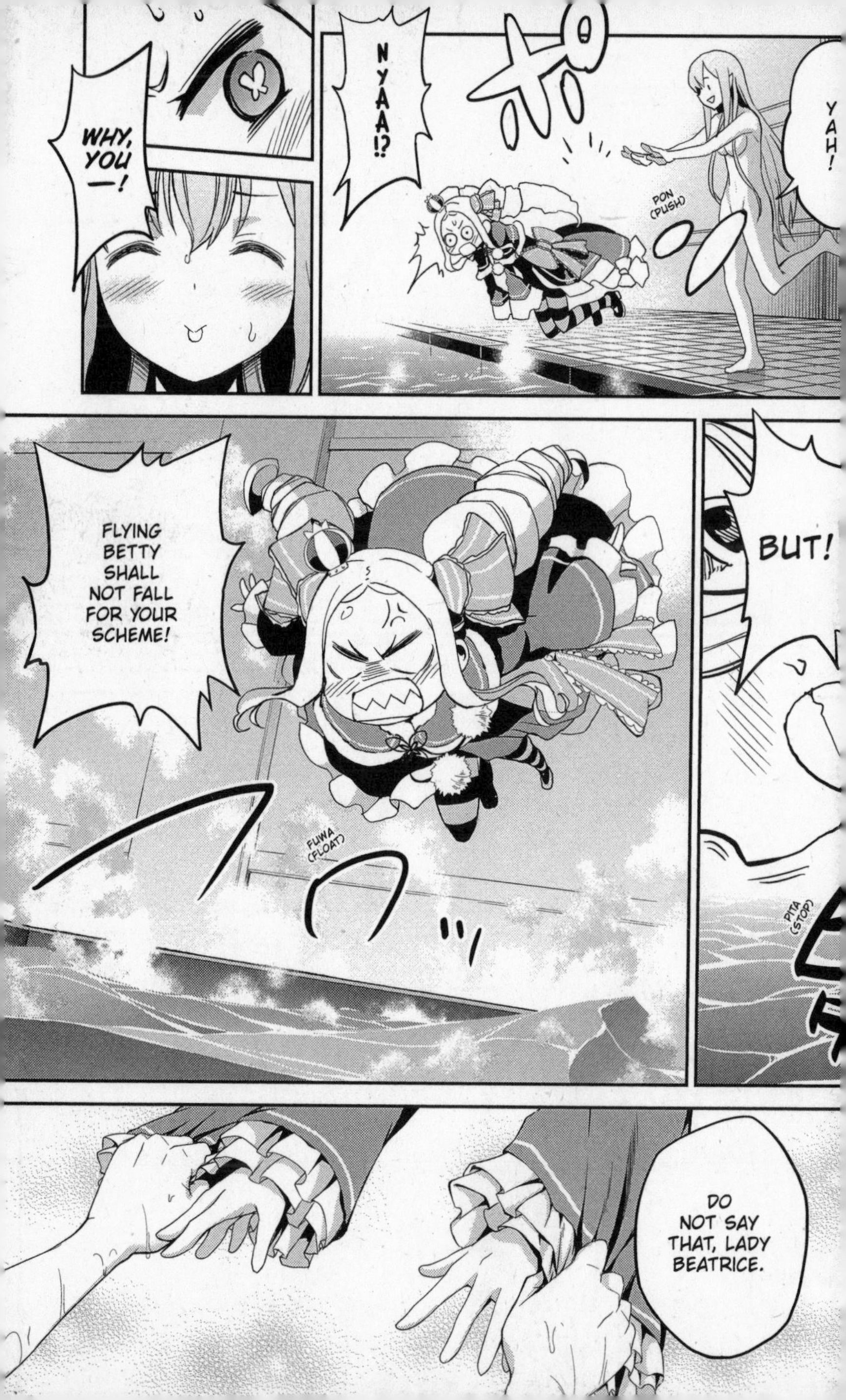
YAH!
NYAAA!?
PON (PUSH)
WHY, YOU—!
BUT!
PITA (STOP)
FLYING BETTY SHALL NOT FALL FOR YOUR SCHEME!
FUWA (FLOAT)
DO NOT SAY THAT, LADY BEATRICE.

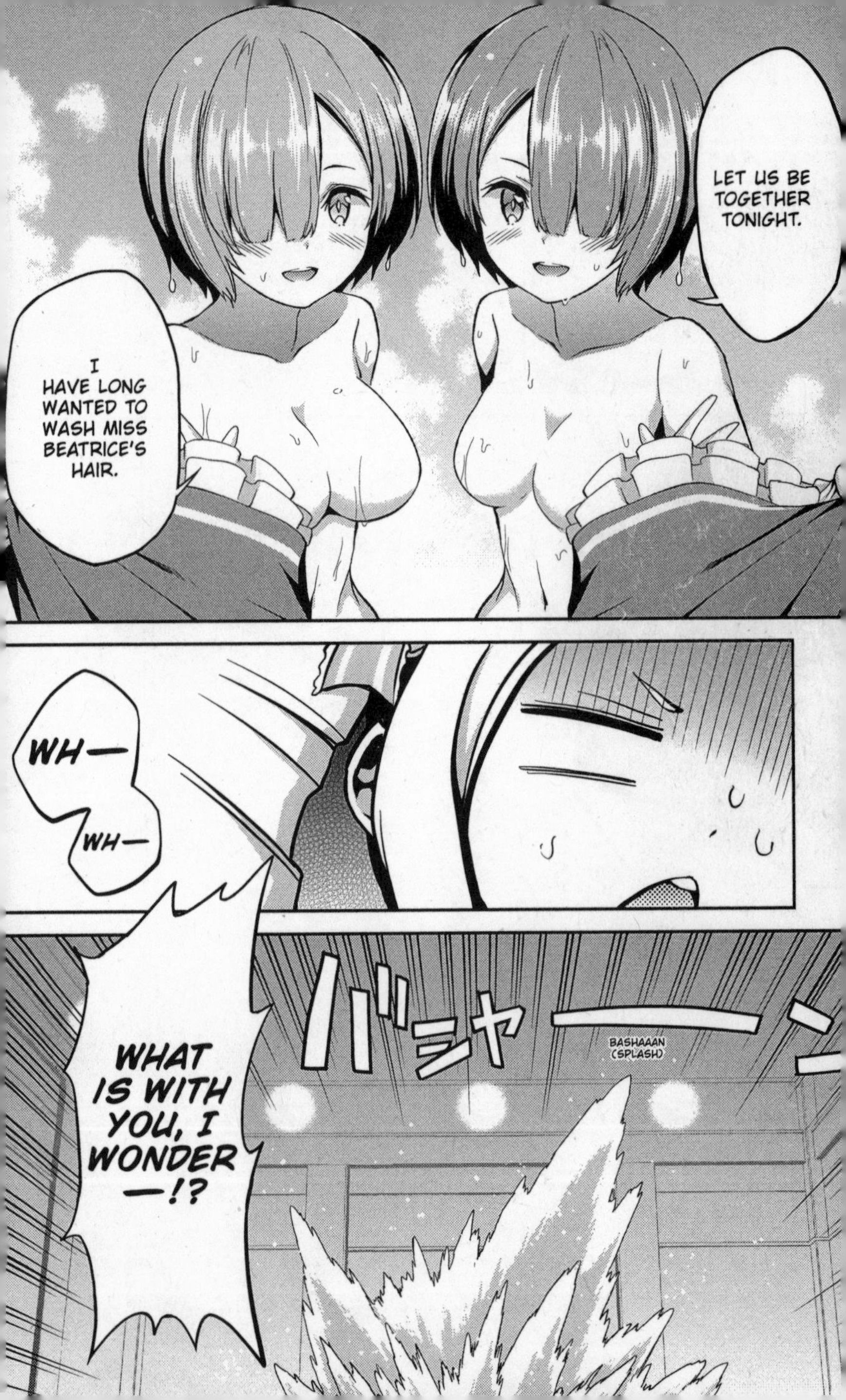
LET US BE TOGETHER TONIGHT.
I HAVE LONG WANTED TO WASH MISS BEATRICE'S HAIR.
WH— WH—
WHAT IS WITH YOU, I WONDER—!?
バシャーーーン
BASHAAAN (SPLASH)

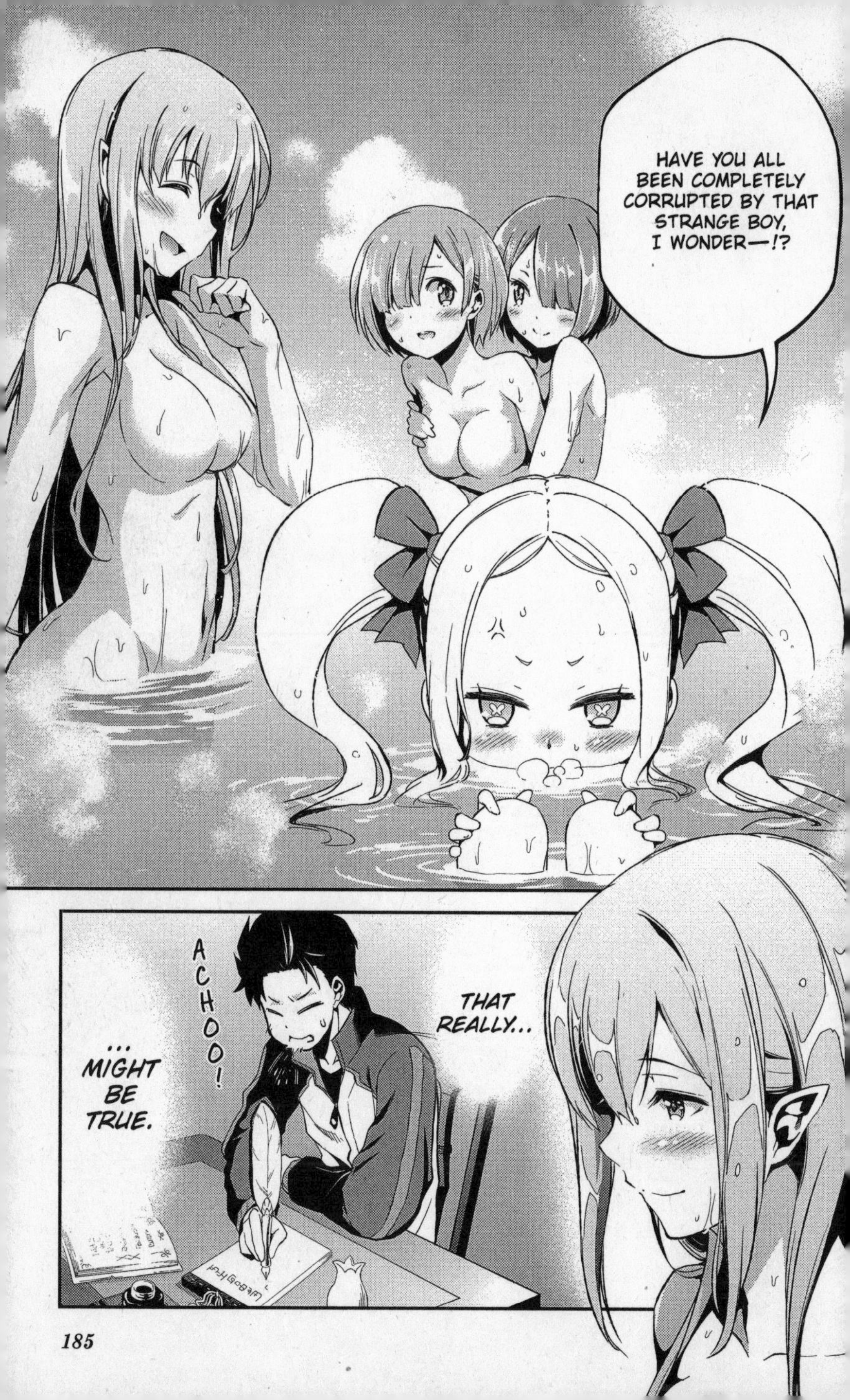
HAVE YOU ALL BEEN COMPLETELY CORRUPTED BY THAT STRANGE BOY, I WONDER—!?
THAT REALLY...
ACHOO!
...MIGHT BE TRUE.

The long-awaited girls-in-the-hot-bath scene!

Everyone already got Subaru and Rozchi hot bath fan service in Volume 2. Personally, I found it a very fun scene to draw.

And here we have the girls' hot bath scene. Just for you!

Actually, I'm not all that great at drawing naked girls, so it was a bit of a hard slog throughout.

Having said that, goodness, Emilia, Rem, and the rest in the nude! Such was the stifling pressure on me, a mix of various feelings as I made my way through the work. I do recall that I couldn't help but have fun drawing them nude.

Nagatsuki-sensei, thank you for having me draw this. I, Fugetsu, have grown as a person accordingly.

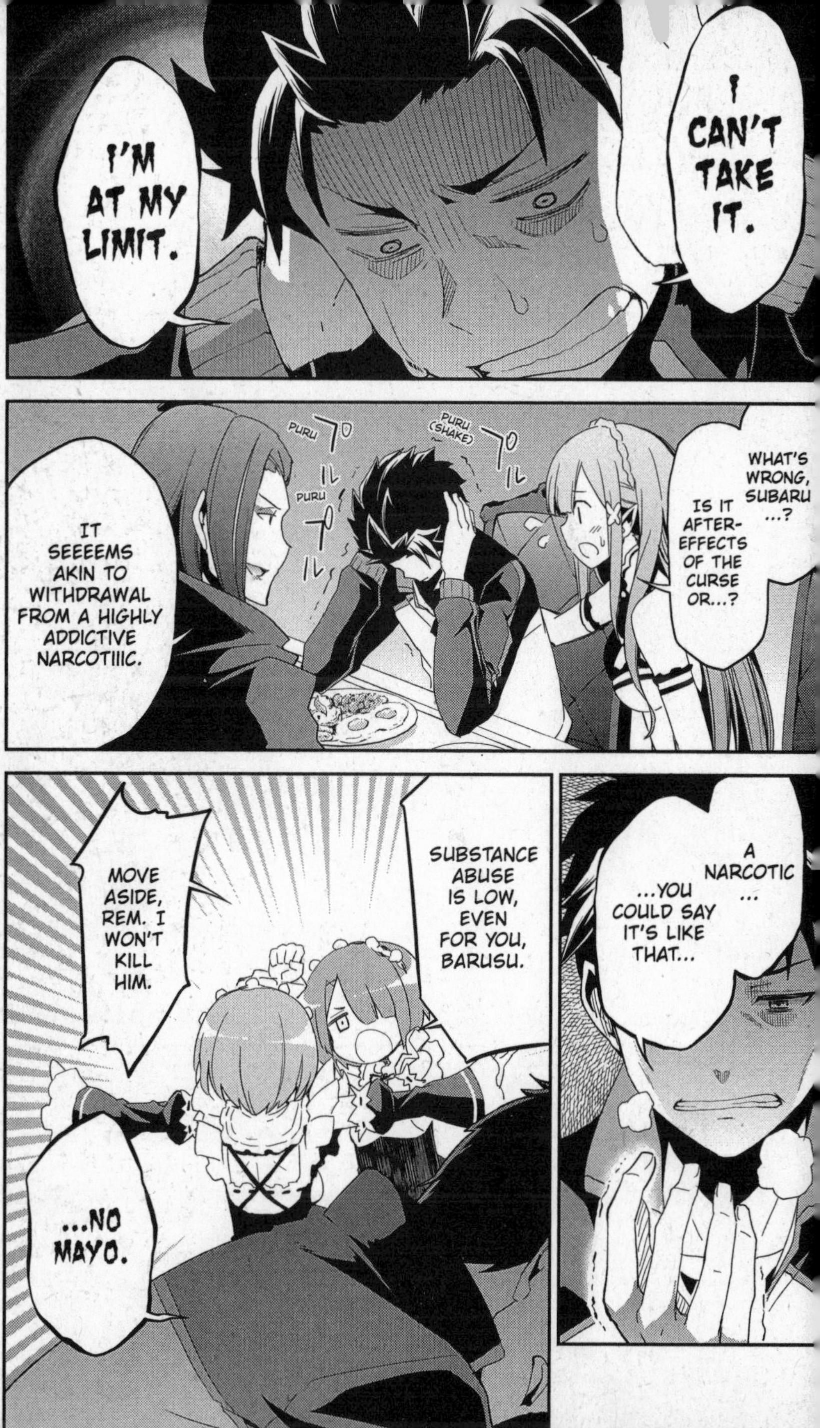
I CAN'T TAKE IT.
I'M AT MY LIMIT.
WHAT'S WRONG, SUBARU...?
IS IT AFTER-EFFECTS OF THE CURSE OR...?
PURU (SHAKE)
PURU
PURU
IT SEEEEMS AKIN TO WITHDRAWAL FROM A HIGHLY ADDICTIVE NARCOTIIIC.
A NARCOTIC...
...YOU COULD SAY IT'S LIKE THAT...
SUBSTANCE ABUSE IS LOW, EVEN FOR YOU, BARUSU.
MOVE ASIDE, REM. I WON'T KILL HIM.
...NO MAYO.

Special Story

The First Mayonnaise Insurrection

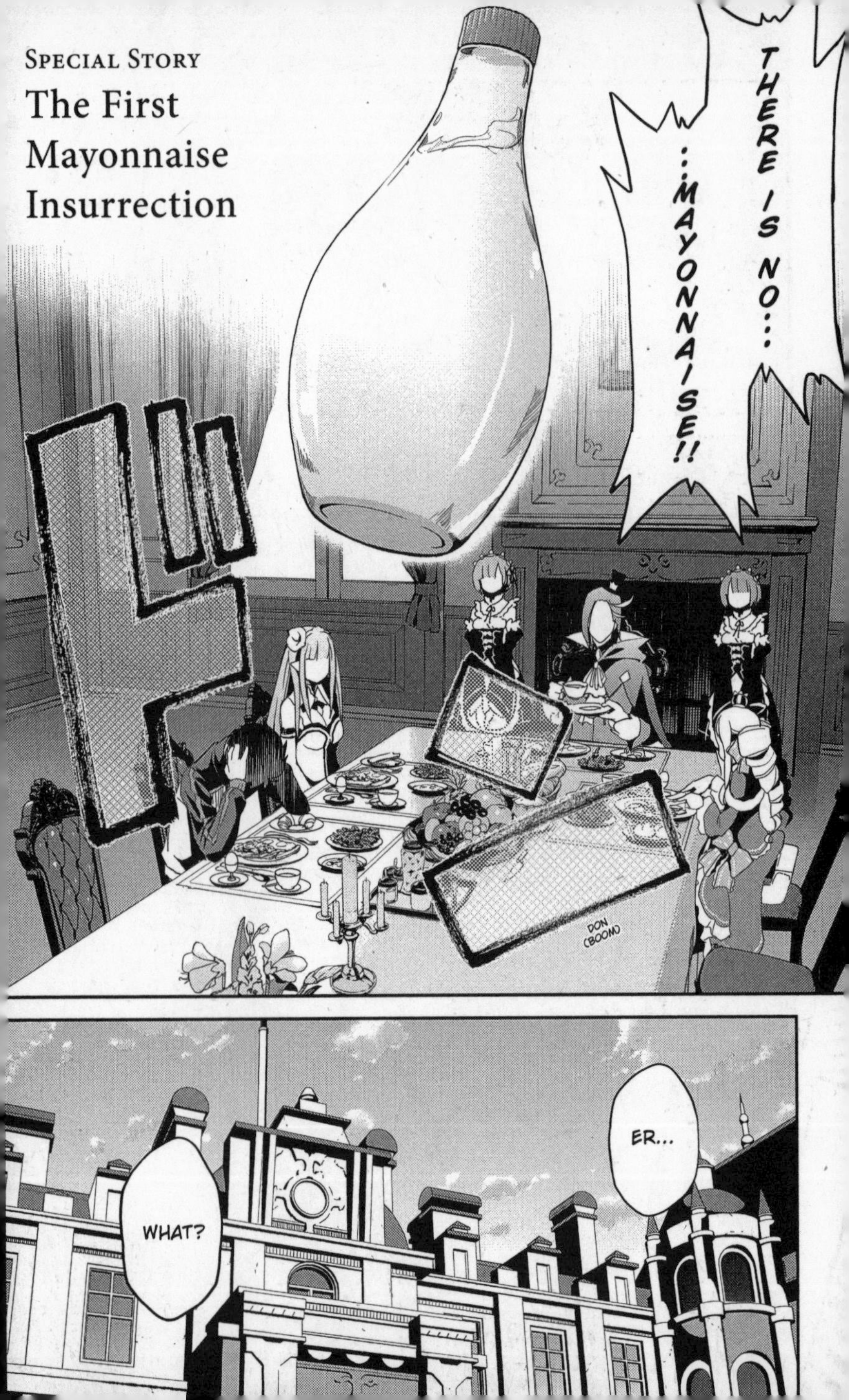

THERE IS NO...
...MAYONNAISE!!
DON
(BOOM)
ER...
WHAT?

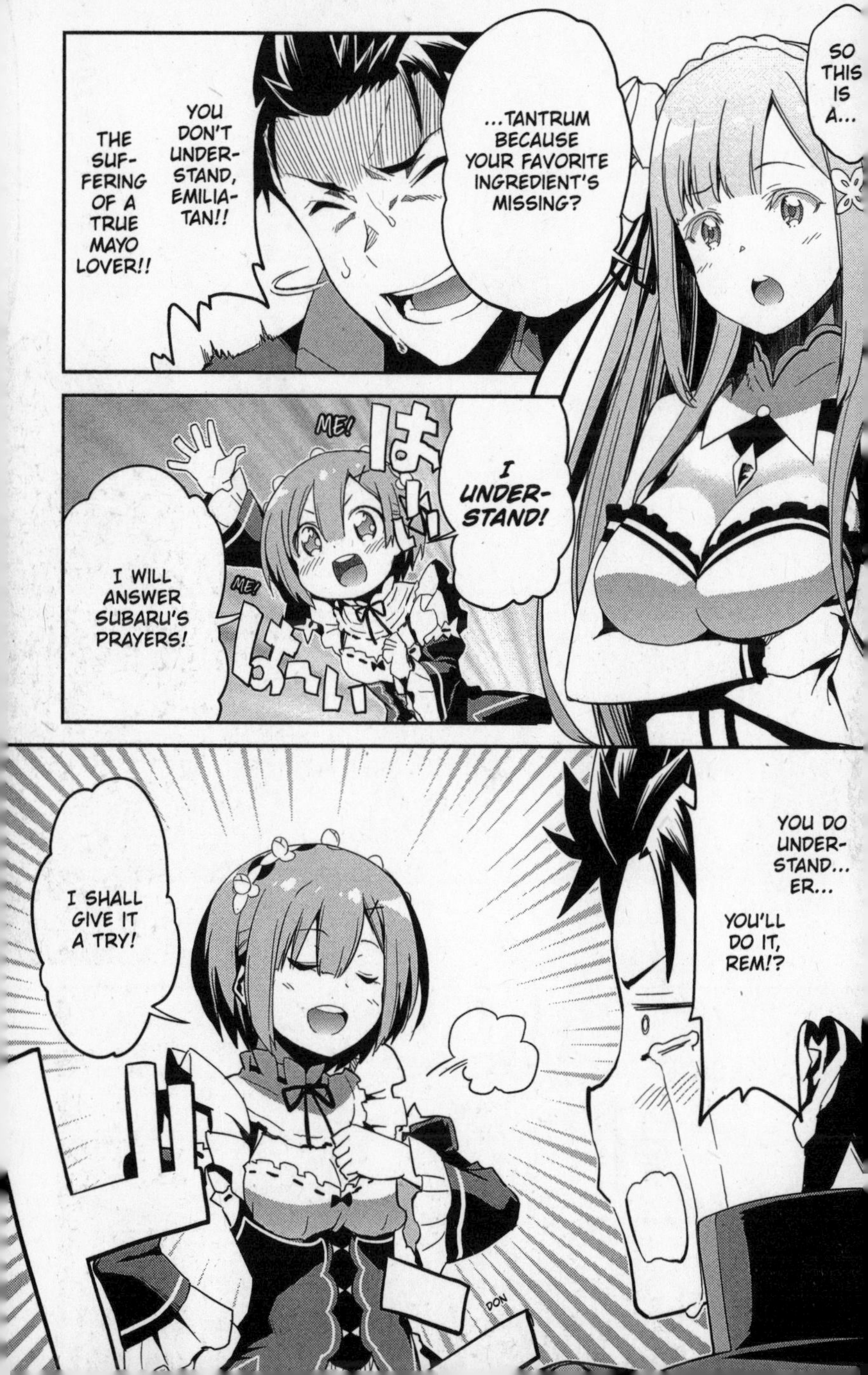
SO THIS IS A...
...TANTRUM BECAUSE YOUR FAVORITE INGREDIENT'S MISSING?
YOU DON'T UNDER-STAND, EMILIA-TAN!!
THE SUF-FERING OF A TRUE MAYO LOVER!!
I UNDER-STAND!
ME!
はーい
ME!
はーい
I WILL ANSWER SUBARU'S PRAYERS!
YOU DO UNDER-STAND... ER...
YOU'LL DO IT, REM!?
I SHALL GIVE IT A TRY!
DON

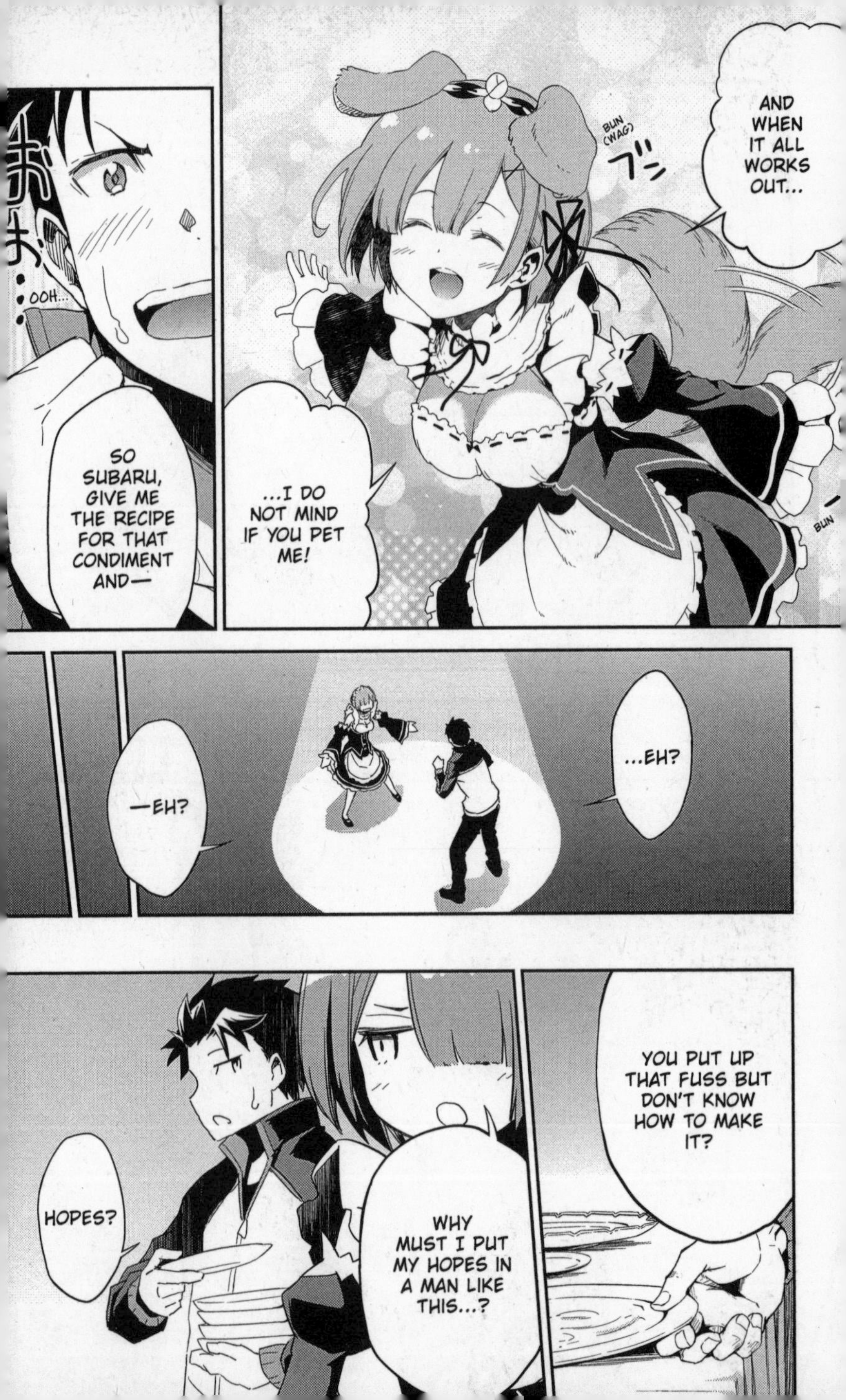
AND WHEN IT ALL WORKS OUT...
BUN (WAG)
ブン
...I DO NOT MIND IF YOU PET ME!
BUN
OOH...
SO SUBARU, GIVE ME THE RECIPE FOR THAT CONDIMENT AND—
...EH?
—EH?
YOU PUT UP THAT FUSS BUT DON'T KNOW HOW TO MAKE IT?
WHY MUST I PUT MY HOPES IN A MAN LIKE THIS...?
HOPES?

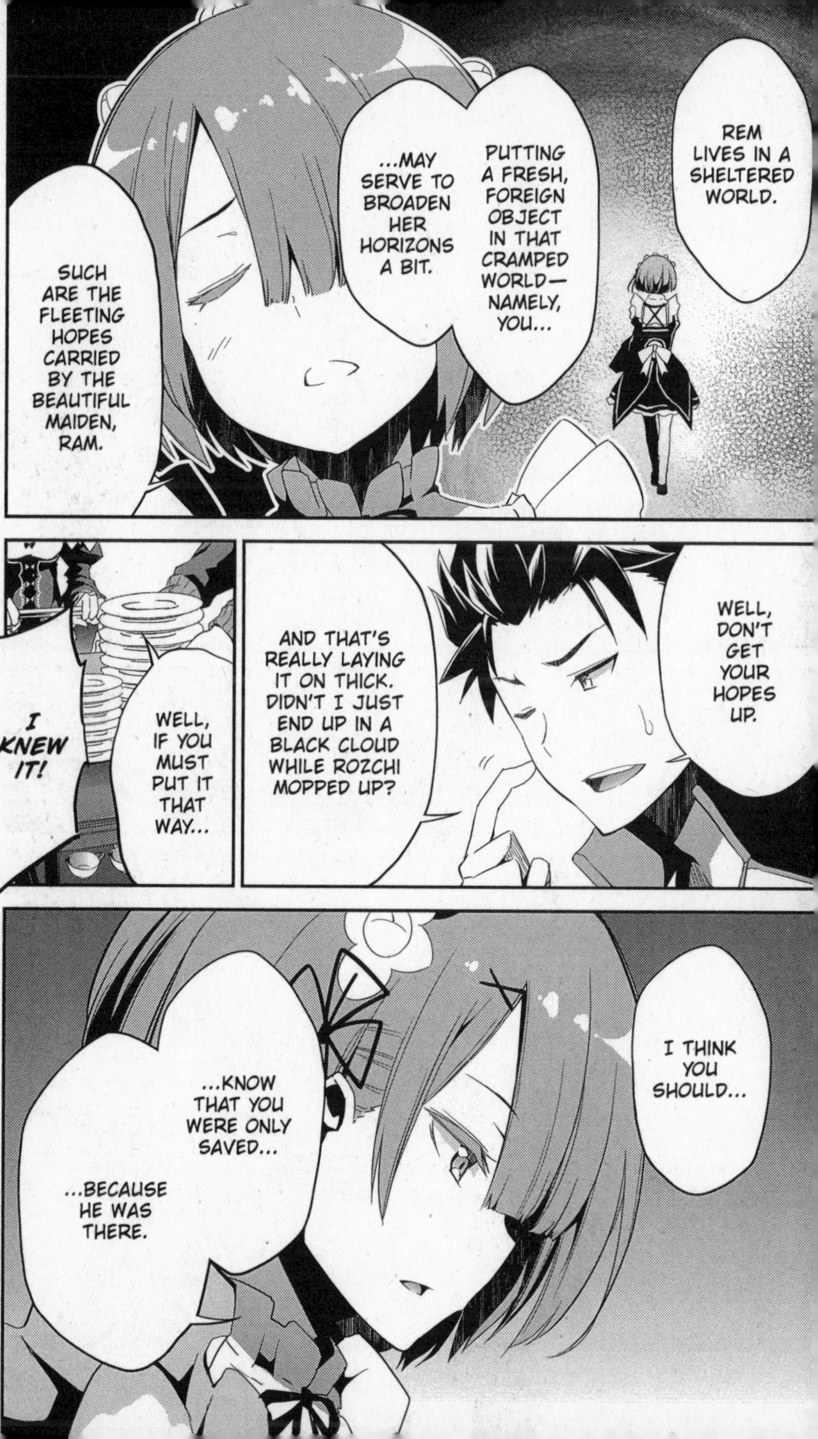
REM LIVES IN A SHELTERED WORLD.
PUTTING A FRESH, FOREIGN OBJECT IN THAT CRAMPED WORLD—NAMELY, YOU...
...MAY SERVE TO BROADEN HER HORIZONS A BIT.
SUCH ARE THE FLEETING HOPES CARRIED BY THE BEAUTIFUL MAIDEN, RAM.
WELL, DON'T GET YOUR HOPES UP.
AND THAT'S REALLY LAYING IT ON THICK. DIDN'T I JUST END UP IN A BLACK CLOUD WHILE ROZCHI MOPPED UP?
WELL, IF YOU MUST PUT IT THAT WAY...
I KNEW IT!
I THINK YOU SHOULD...
...KNOW THAT YOU WERE ONLY SAVED...
...BECAUSE HE WAS THERE.

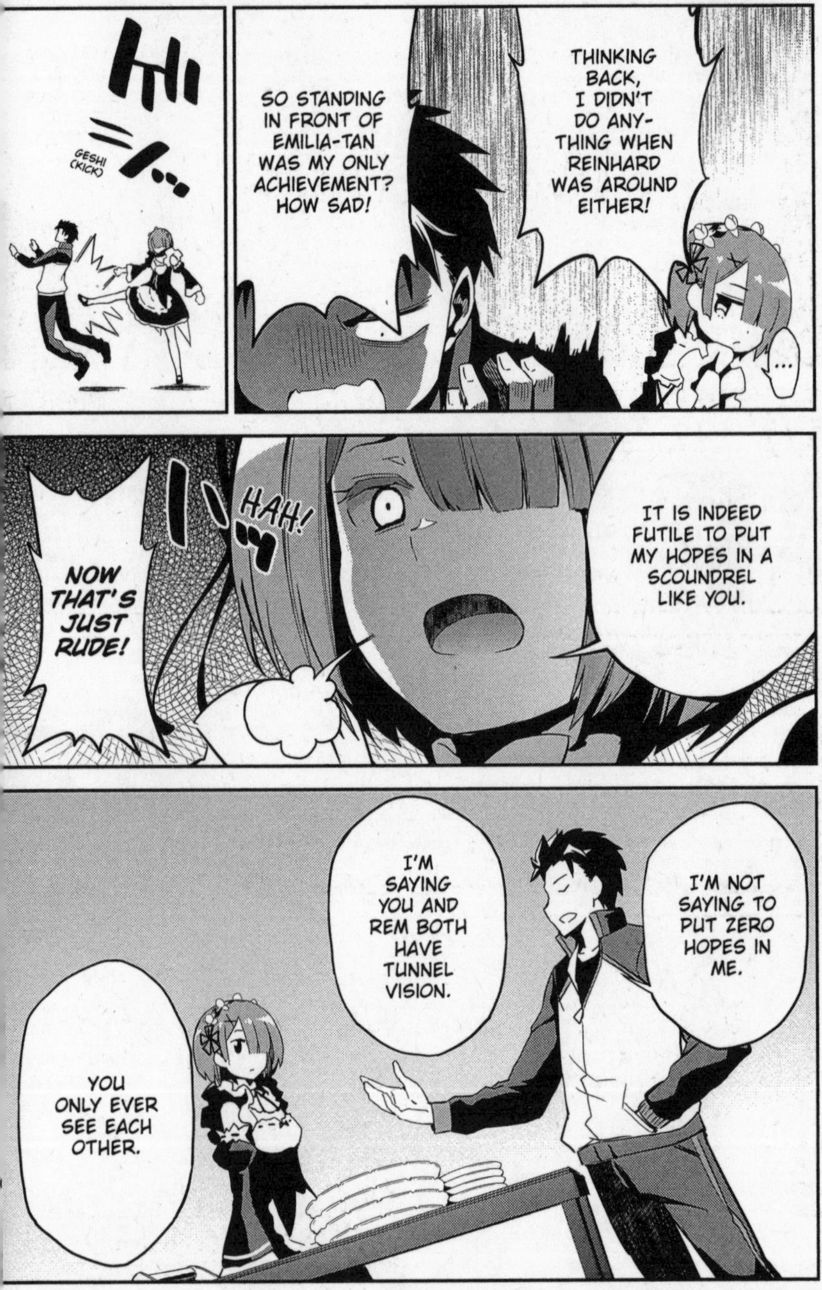
THINKING BACK, I DIDN'T DO ANY-THING WHEN REINHARD WAS AROUND EITHER!
SO STANDING IN FRONT OF EMILIA-TAN WAS MY ONLY ACHIEVEMENT? HOW SAD!
...
GESHI (KICK)
IT IS INDEED FUTILE TO PUT MY HOPES IN A SCOUNDREL LIKE YOU.
HAH!
NOW THAT'S JUST RUDE!
I'M NOT SAYING TO PUT ZERO HOPES IN ME.
I'M SAYING YOU AND REM BOTH HAVE TUNNEL VISION.
YOU ONLY EVER SEE EACH OTHER.

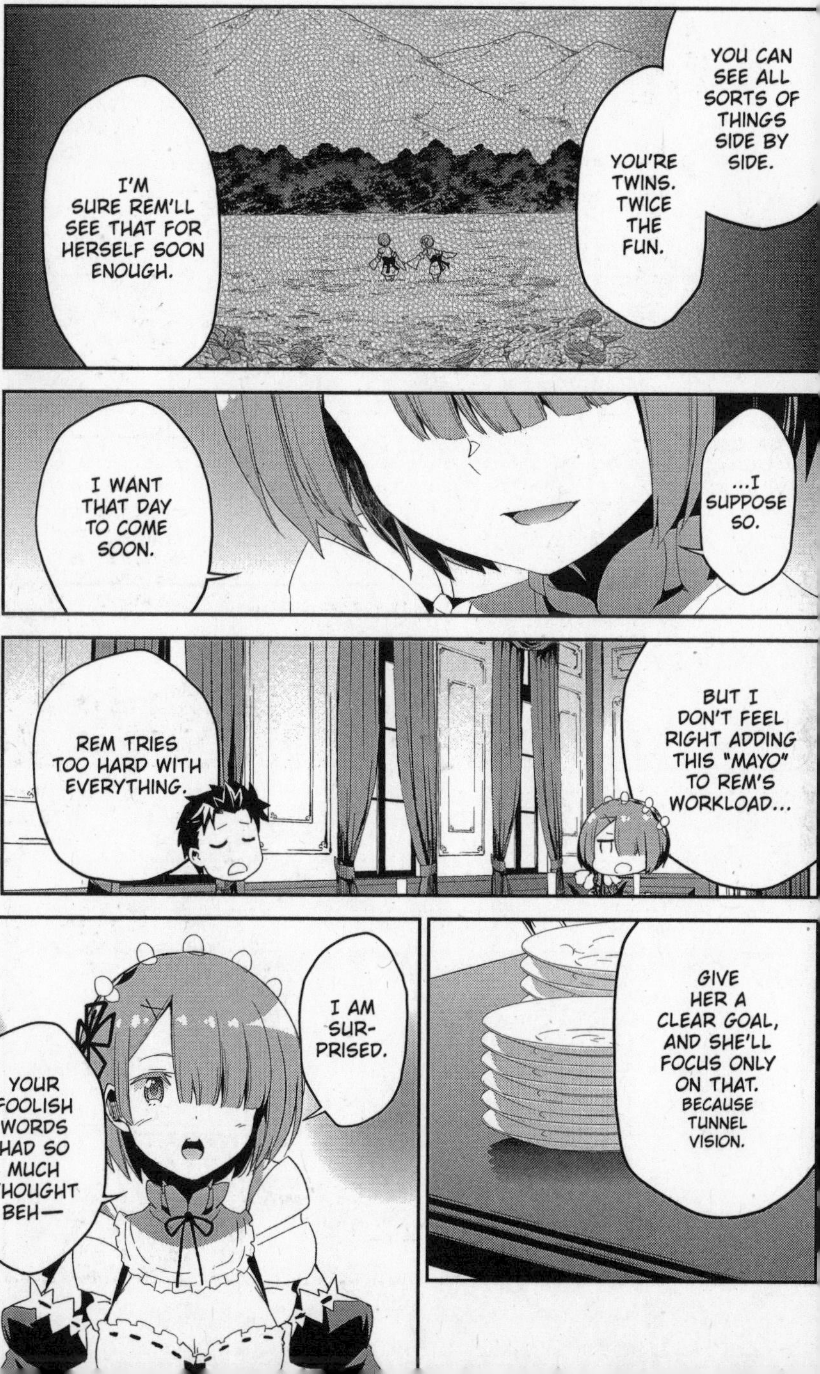
YOU CAN SEE ALL SORTS OF THINGS SIDE BY SIDE.
YOU'RE TWINS. TWICE THE FUN.
I'M SURE REM'LL SEE THAT FOR HERSELF SOON ENOUGH.
...I SUPPOSE SO.
I WANT THAT DAY TO COME SOON.
BUT I DON'T FEEL RIGHT ADDING THIS "MAYO" TO REM'S WORKLOAD...
REM TRIES TOO HARD WITH EVERYTHING.
GIVE HER A CLEAR GOAL, AND SHE'LL FOCUS ONLY ON THAT.
BECAUSE TUNNEL VISION.
I AM SUR-PRISED.
YOUR FOOLISH WORDS HAD SO MUCH THOUGHT BEH—

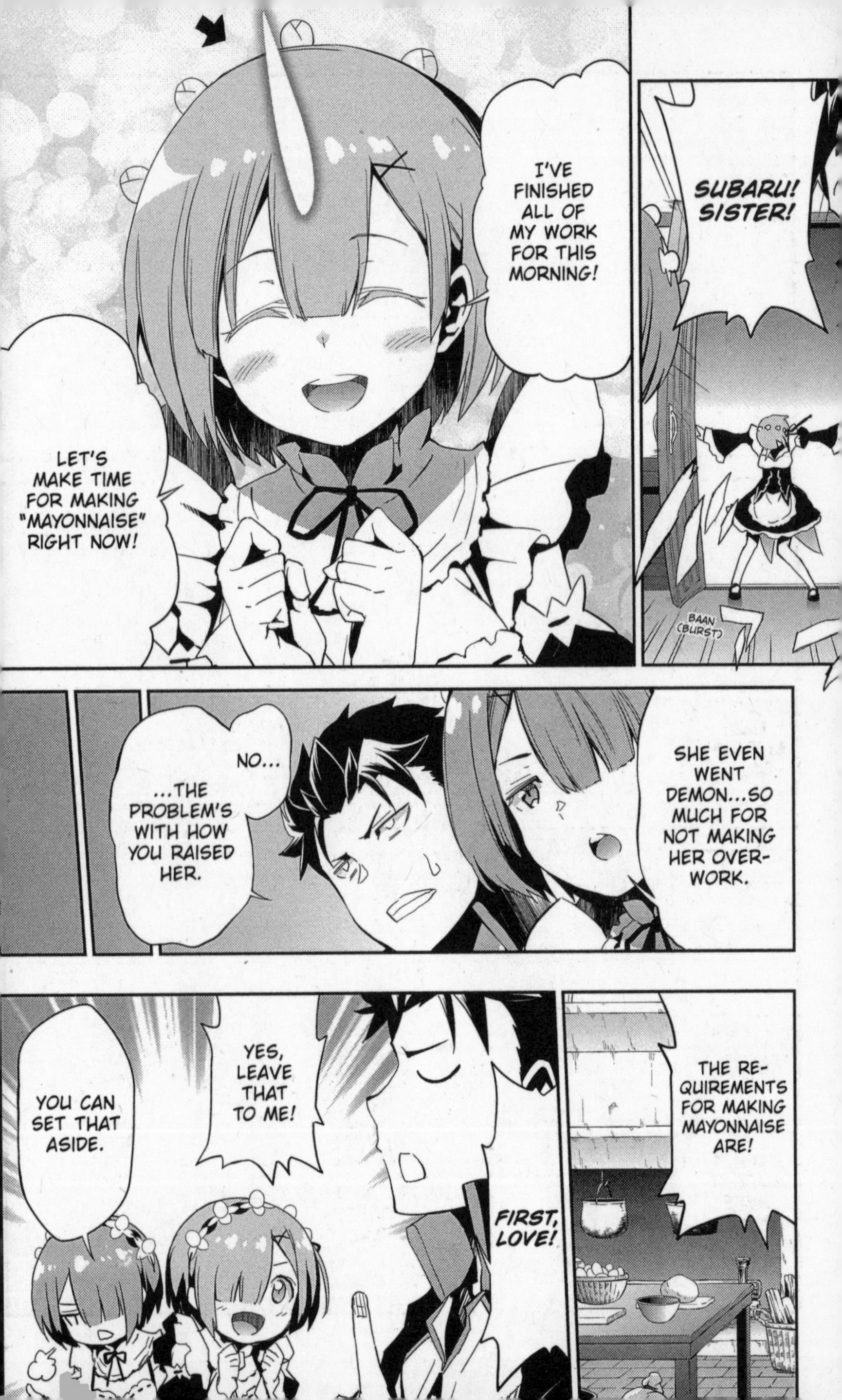
SUBARU! SISTER!
BAAN (BURST)
I'VE FINISHED ALL OF MY WORK FOR THIS MORNING!
LET'S MAKE TIME FOR MAKING "MAYONNAISE" RIGHT NOW!
SHE EVEN WENT DEMON...SO MUCH FOR NOT MAKING HER OVER-WORK.
NO...
...THE PROBLEM'S WITH HOW YOU RAISED HER.
THE RE-QUIREMENTS FOR MAKING MAYONNAISE ARE!
FIRST, LOVE!
YES, LEAVE THAT TO ME!
YOU CAN SET THAT ASIDE.

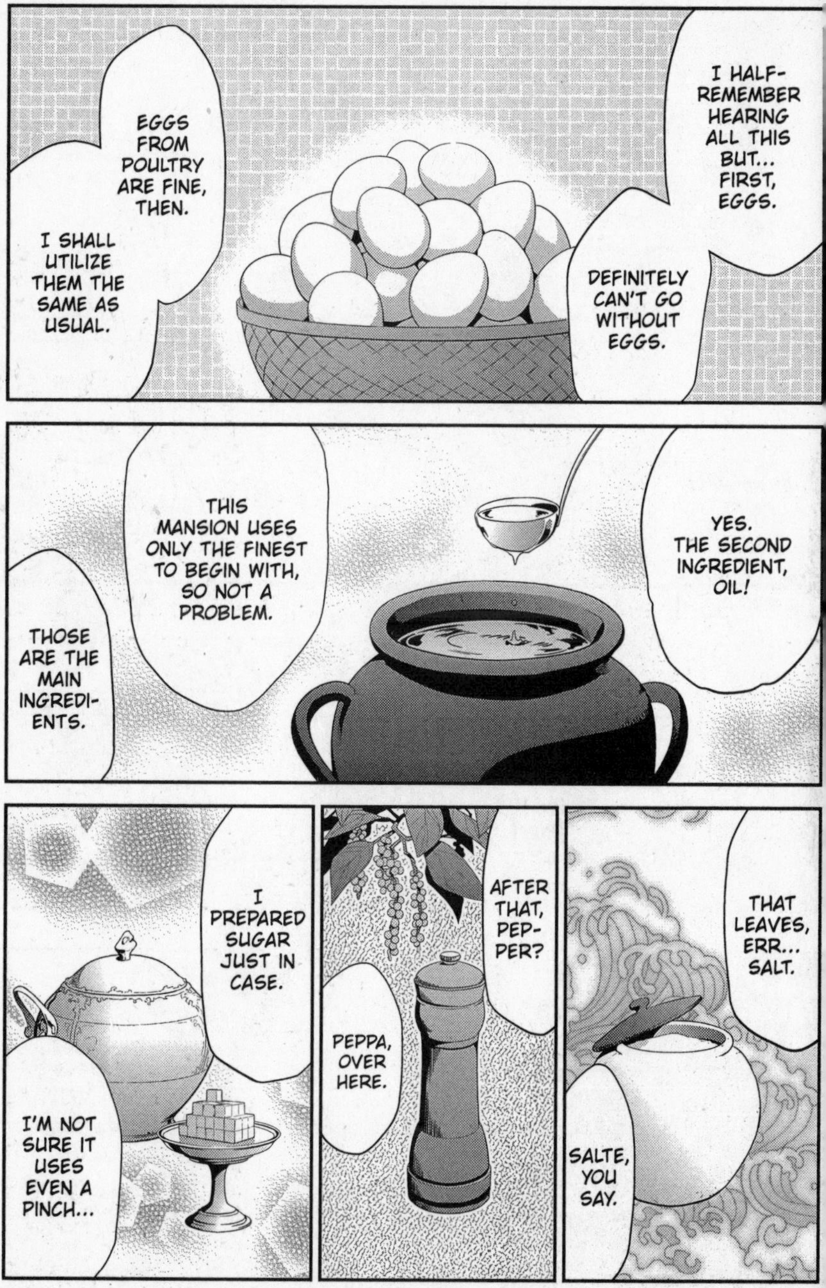
I HALF-REMEMBER HEARING ALL THIS BUT... FIRST, EGGS.
DEFINITELY CAN'T GO WITHOUT EGGS.
EGGS FROM POULTRY ARE FINE, THEN.
I SHALL UTILIZE THEM THE SAME AS USUAL.
YES. THE SECOND INGREDIENT, OIL!
THIS MANSION USES ONLY THE FINEST TO BEGIN WITH, SO NOT A PROBLEM.
THOSE ARE THE MAIN INGREDIENTS.
THAT LEAVES, ERR... SALT.
SALTE, YOU SAY.
AFTER THAT, PEPPER?
PEPPA, OVER HERE.
I PREPARED SUGAR JUST IN CASE.
I'M NOT SURE IT USES EVEN A PINCH...

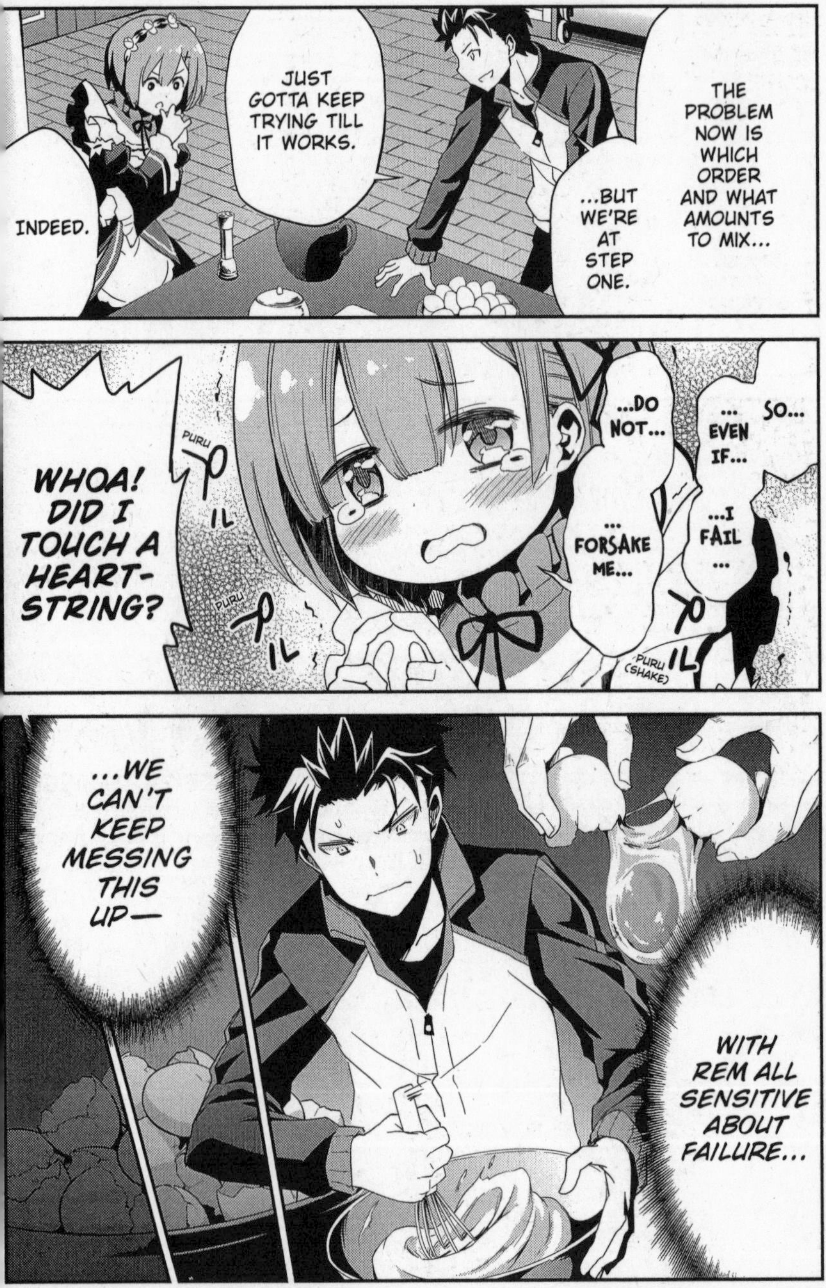
THE PROBLEM NOW IS WHICH ORDER AND WHAT AMOUNTS TO MIX...
...BUT WE'RE AT STEP ONE.
JUST GOTTA KEEP TRYING TILL IT WORKS.
INDEED.
SO...
...EVEN IF...
...I FAIL...
...DO NOT...
...FORSAKE ME...
PURU (SHAKE)
PURU
PURU
WHOA! DID I TOUCH A HEART-STRING?
WITH REM ALL SENSITIVE ABOUT FAILURE...
...WE CAN'T KEEP MESSING THIS UP—

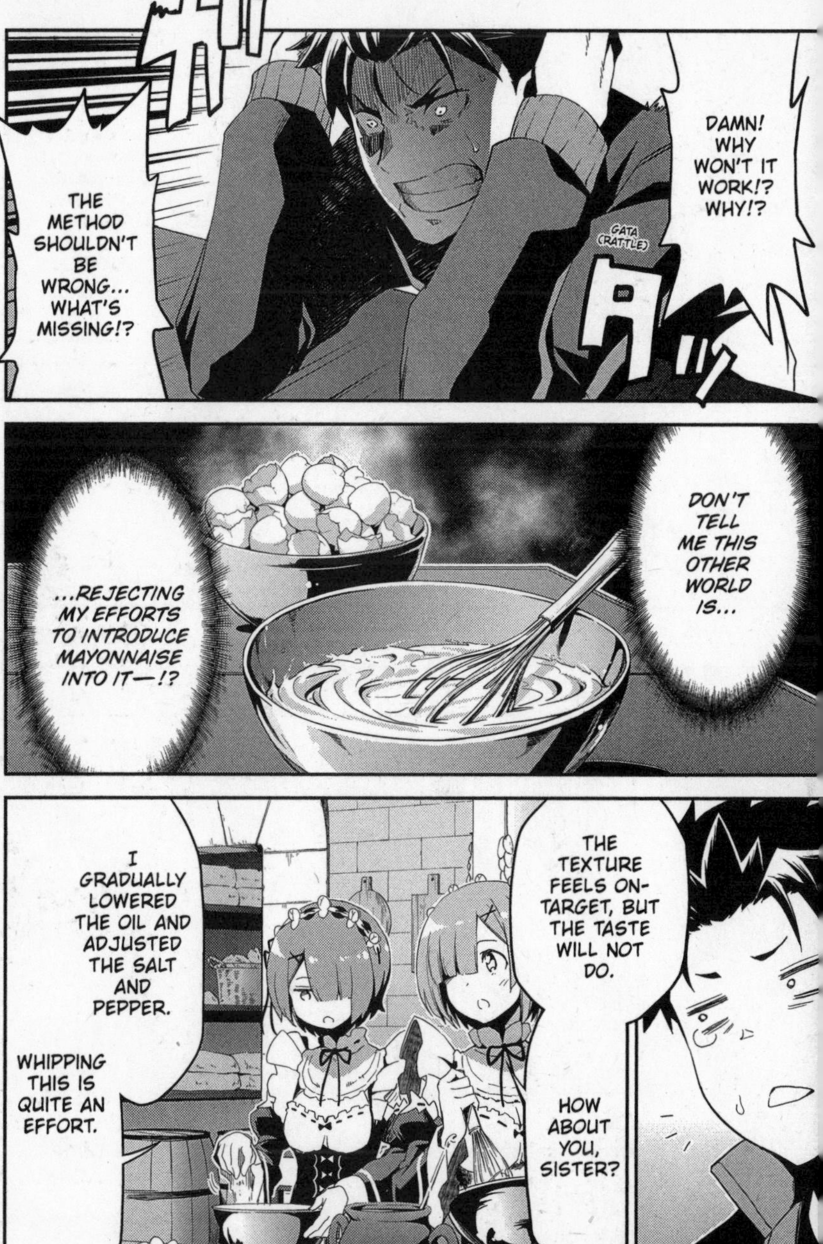
DAMN! WHY WON'T IT WORK!? WHY!?
GATA (RATTLE)
THE METHOD SHOULDN'T BE WRONG... WHAT'S MISSING!?
DON'T TELL ME THIS OTHER WORLD IS...
...REJECTING MY EFFORTS TO INTRODUCE MAYONNAISE INTO IT—!?
THE TEXTURE FEELS ON-TARGET, BUT THE TASTE WILL NOT DO.
HOW ABOUT YOU, SISTER?
I GRADUALLY LOWERED THE OIL AND ADJUSTED THE SALT AND PEPPER.
WHIPPING THIS IS QUITE AN EFFORT.

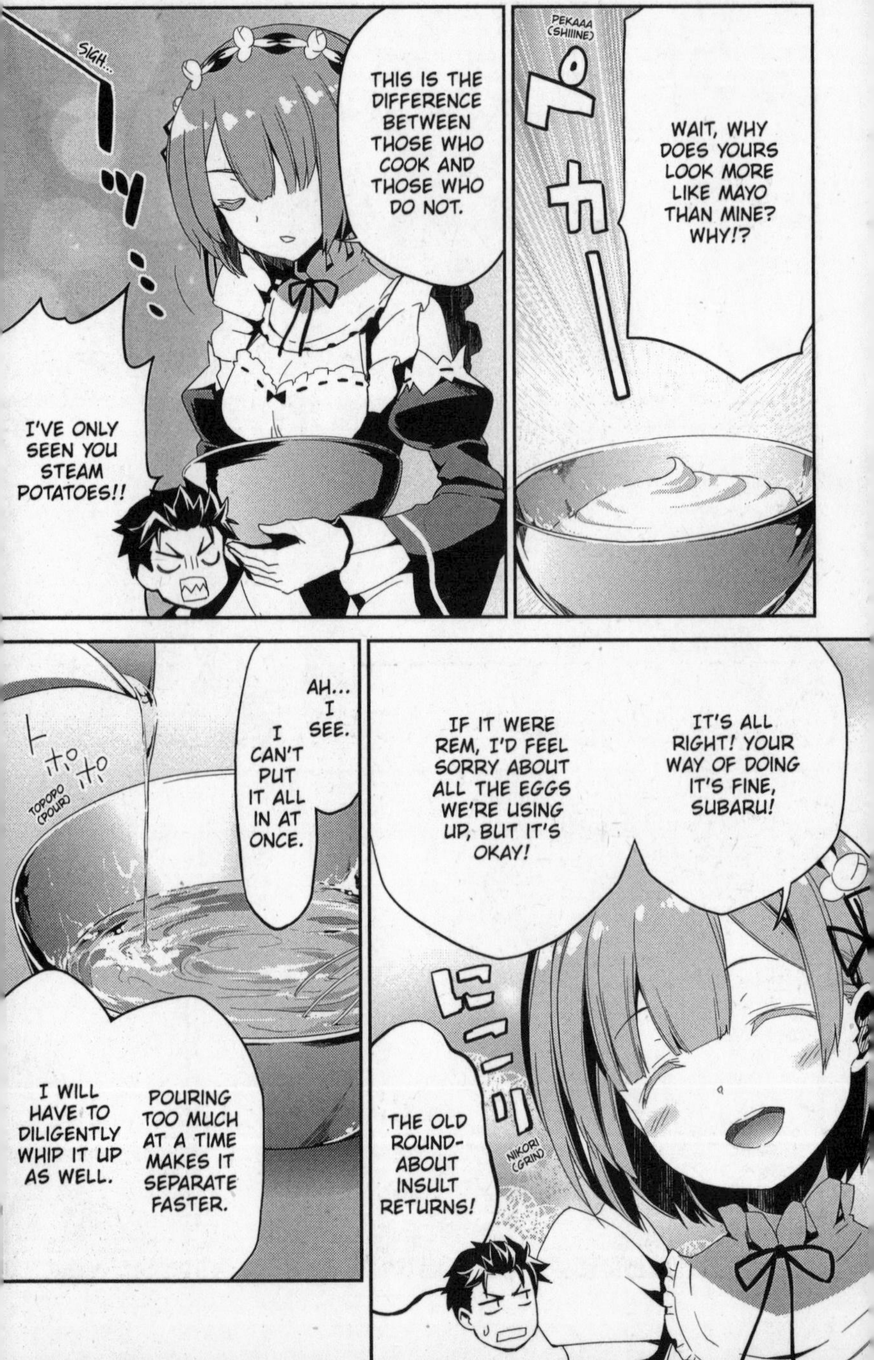

PEKAAA (SHIIINE)
WAIT, WHY DOES YOURS LOOK MORE LIKE MAYO THAN MINE? WHY!?
THIS IS THE DIFFERENCE BETWEEN THOSE WHO COOK AND THOSE WHO DO NOT.
SIGH...
I'VE ONLY SEEN YOU STEAM POTATOES!!
IT'S ALL RIGHT! YOUR WAY OF DOING IT'S FINE, SUBARU!
IF IT WERE REM, I'D FEEL SORRY ABOUT ALL THE EGGS WE'RE USING UP, BUT IT'S OKAY!
NIKORI (GRIN)
THE OLD ROUND-ABOUT INSULT RETURNS!
AH... I SEE.
I CAN'T PUT IT ALL IN AT ONCE.
TOPOPO (POUR)
POURING TOO MUCH AT A TIME MAKES IT SEPARATE FASTER.
I WILL HAVE TO DILIGENTLY WHIP IT UP AS WELL.

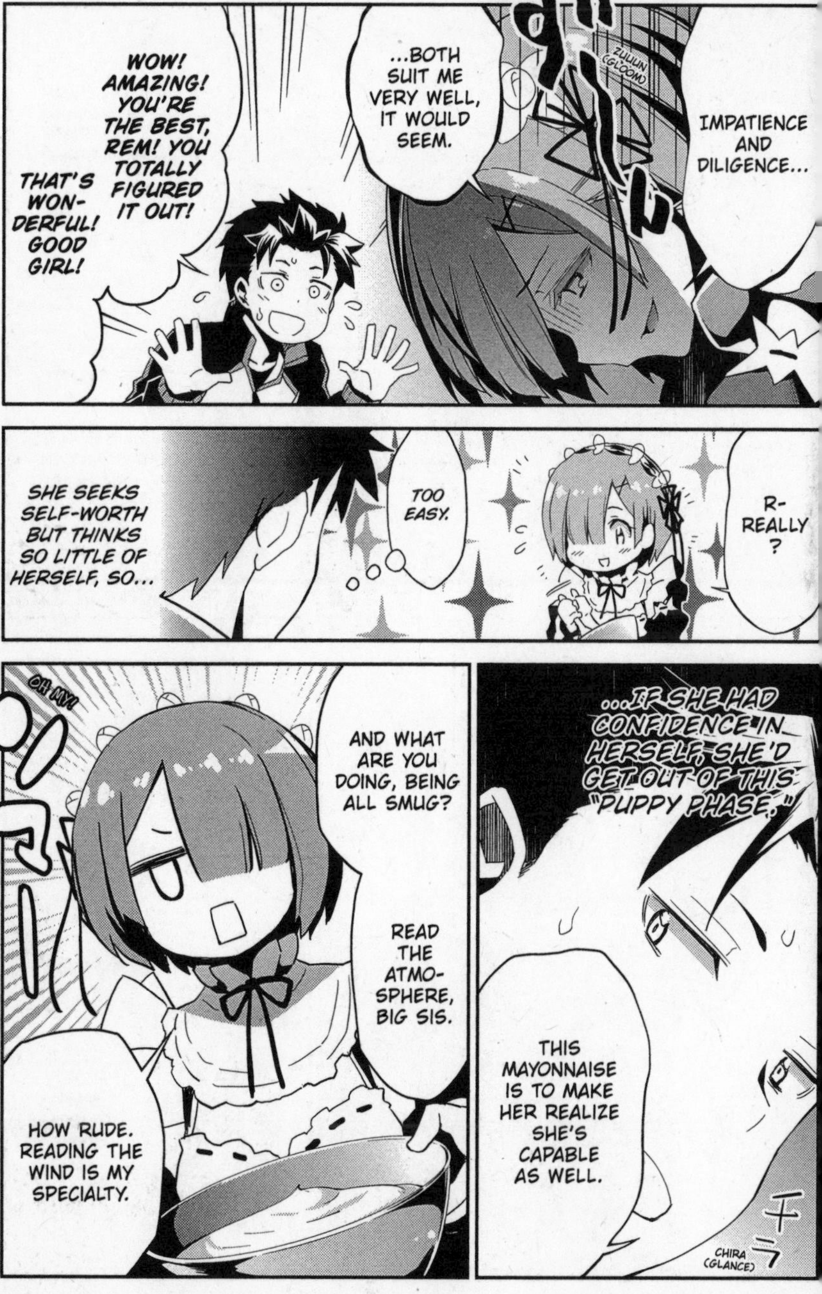
IMPATIENCE AND DILIGENCE...
ZUUUN (GLOOM)
...BOTH SUIT ME VERY WELL, IT WOULD SEEM.
WOW! AMAZING! YOU'RE THE BEST, REM! YOU TOTALLY FIGURED IT OUT!
THAT'S WON-DERFUL! GOOD GIRL!
R-REALLY?
TOO EASY.
SHE SEEKS SELF-WORTH BUT THINKS SO LITTLE OF HERSELF, SO...
...IF SHE HAD CONFIDENCE IN HERSELF, SHE'D GET OUT OF THIS "PUPPY PHASE."
THIS MAYONNAISE IS TO MAKE HER REALIZE SHE'S CAPABLE AS WELL.
CHIRA (GLANCE)
AND WHAT ARE YOU DOING, BEING ALL SMUG?
READ THE ATMOSPHERE, BIG SIS.
OH MY!
HOW RUDE. READING THE WIND IS MY SPECIALTY.

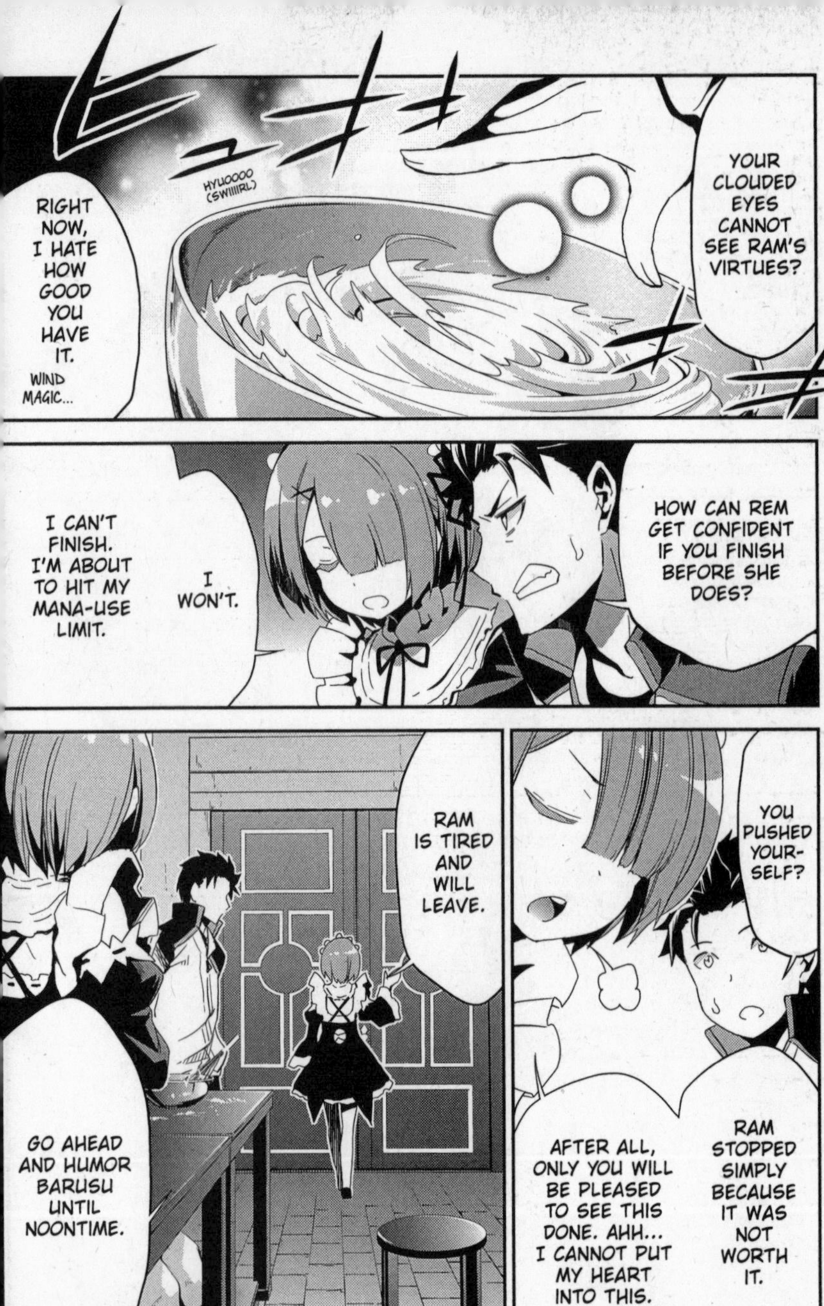
YOUR CLOUDED EYES CANNOT SEE RAM'S VIRTUES?
HYUOOOO (SWIIIIRL)
RIGHT NOW, I HATE HOW GOOD YOU HAVE IT.
WIND MAGIC...
HOW CAN REM GET CONFIDENT IF YOU FINISH BEFORE SHE DOES?
I WON'T.
I CAN'T FINISH. I'M ABOUT TO HIT MY MANA-USE LIMIT.
YOU PUSHED YOURSELF?
RAM STOPPED SIMPLY BECAUSE IT WAS NOT WORTH IT.
AFTER ALL, ONLY YOU WILL BE PLEASED TO SEE THIS DONE. AHH... I CANNOT PUT MY HEART INTO THIS.
RAM IS TIRED AND WILL LEAVE.
GO AHEAD AND HUMOR BARUSU UNTIL NOONTIME.

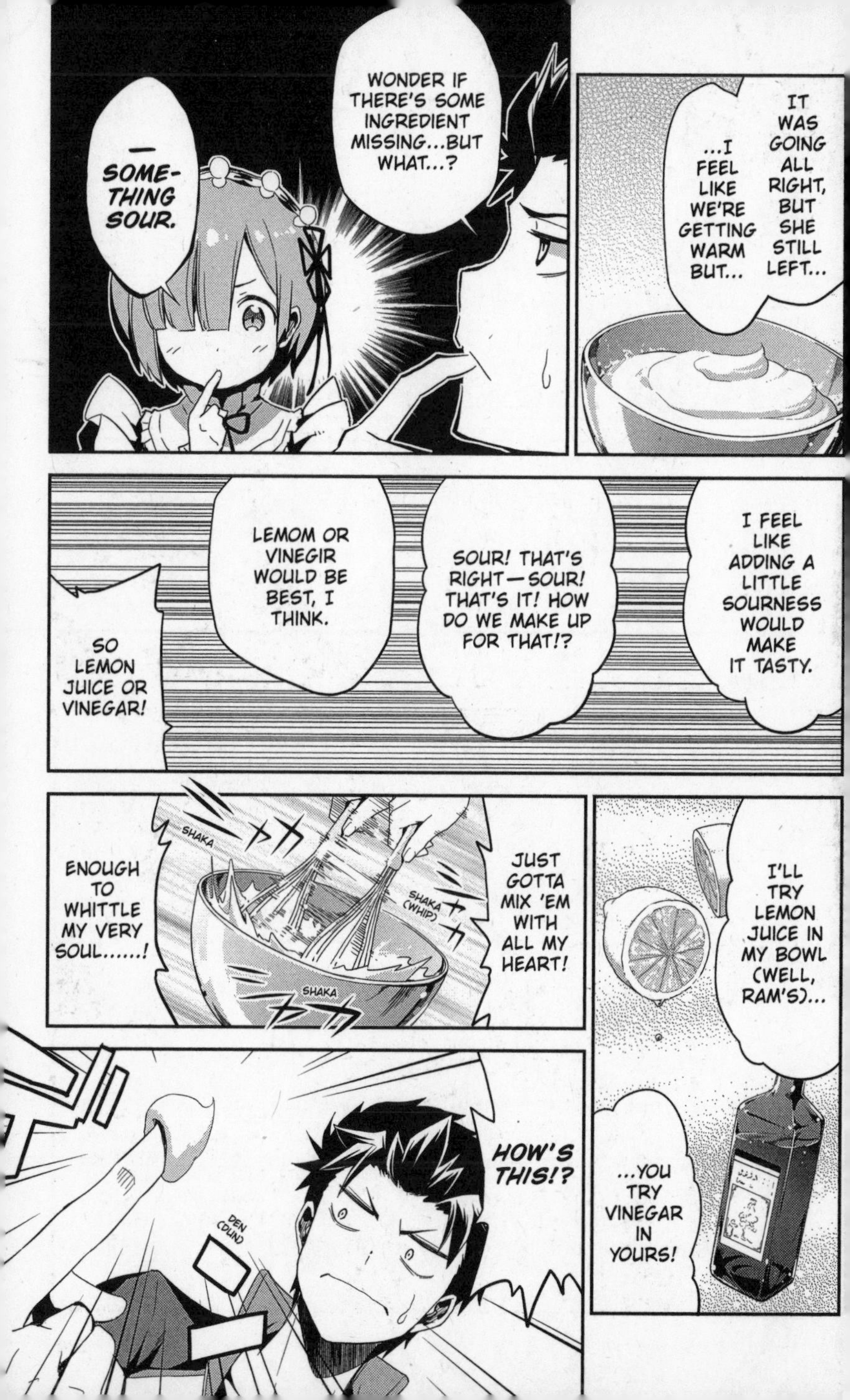
IT WAS GOING ALL RIGHT, BUT SHE STILL LEFT...
...I FEEL LIKE WE'RE GETTING WARM BUT...
WONDER IF THERE'S SOME INGREDIENT MISSING...BUT WHAT...?
—SOMETHING SOUR.
I FEEL LIKE ADDING A LITTLE SOURNESS WOULD MAKE IT TASTY.
SOUR! THAT'S RIGHT—SOUR! THAT'S IT! HOW DO WE MAKE UP FOR THAT!?
LEMOM OR VINEGIR WOULD BE BEST, I THINK.
SO LEMON JUICE OR VINEGAR!
I'LL TRY LEMON JUICE IN MY BOWL (WELL, RAM'S)...
...YOU TRY VINEGAR IN YOURS!
JUST GOTTA MIX 'EM WITH ALL MY HEART!
SHAKA
SHAKA (WHIP)
SHAKA
ENOUGH TO WHITTLE MY VERY SOUL......!
HOW'S THIS!?
DEN (DUN)

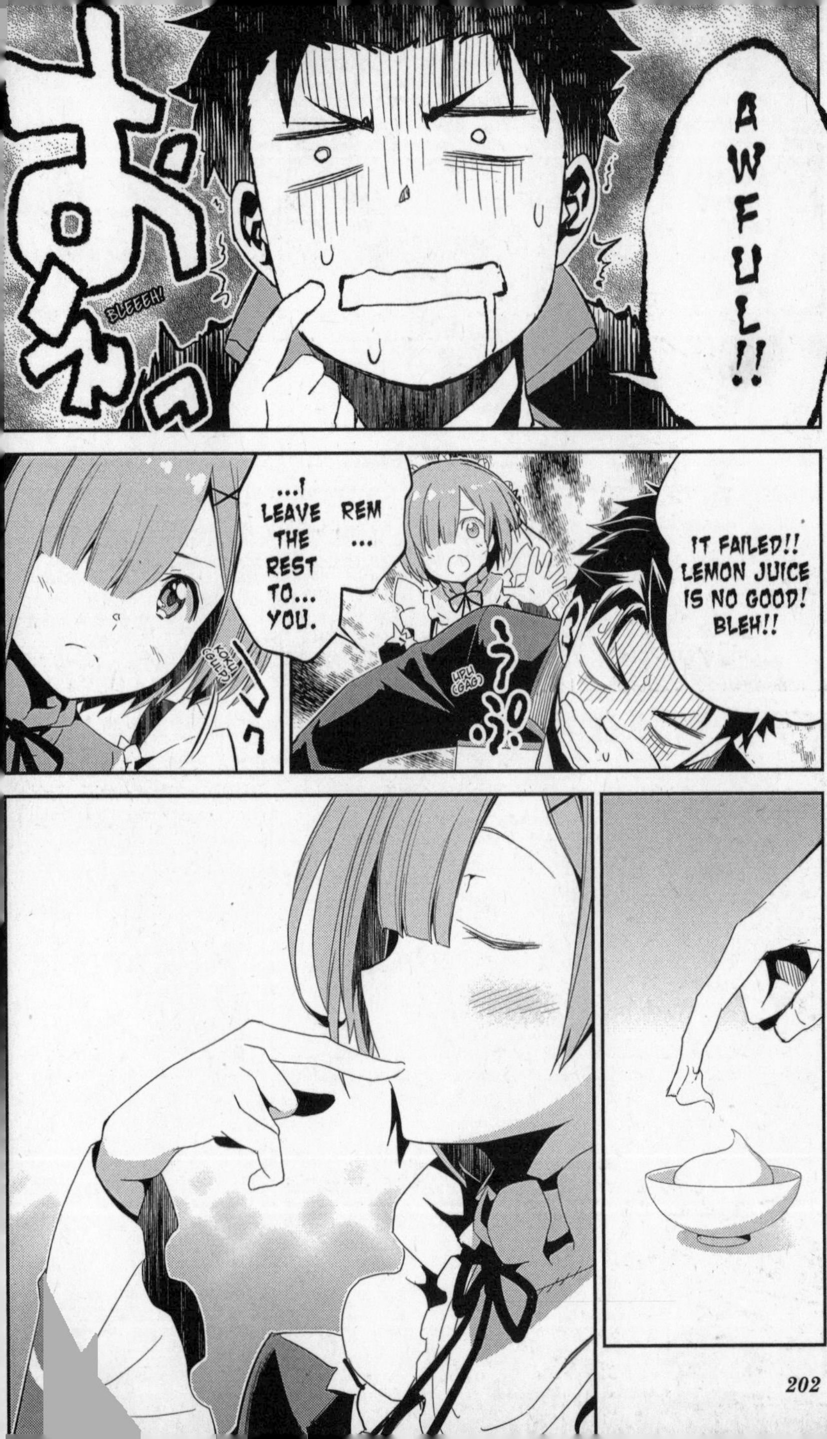
AWFUL!!
BLEEEH!
IT FAILED!! LEMON JUICE IS NO GOOD! BLEH!!
UPU (GAG)
REM ...
...I LEAVE THE REST TO... YOU.
KOKU (GULP)

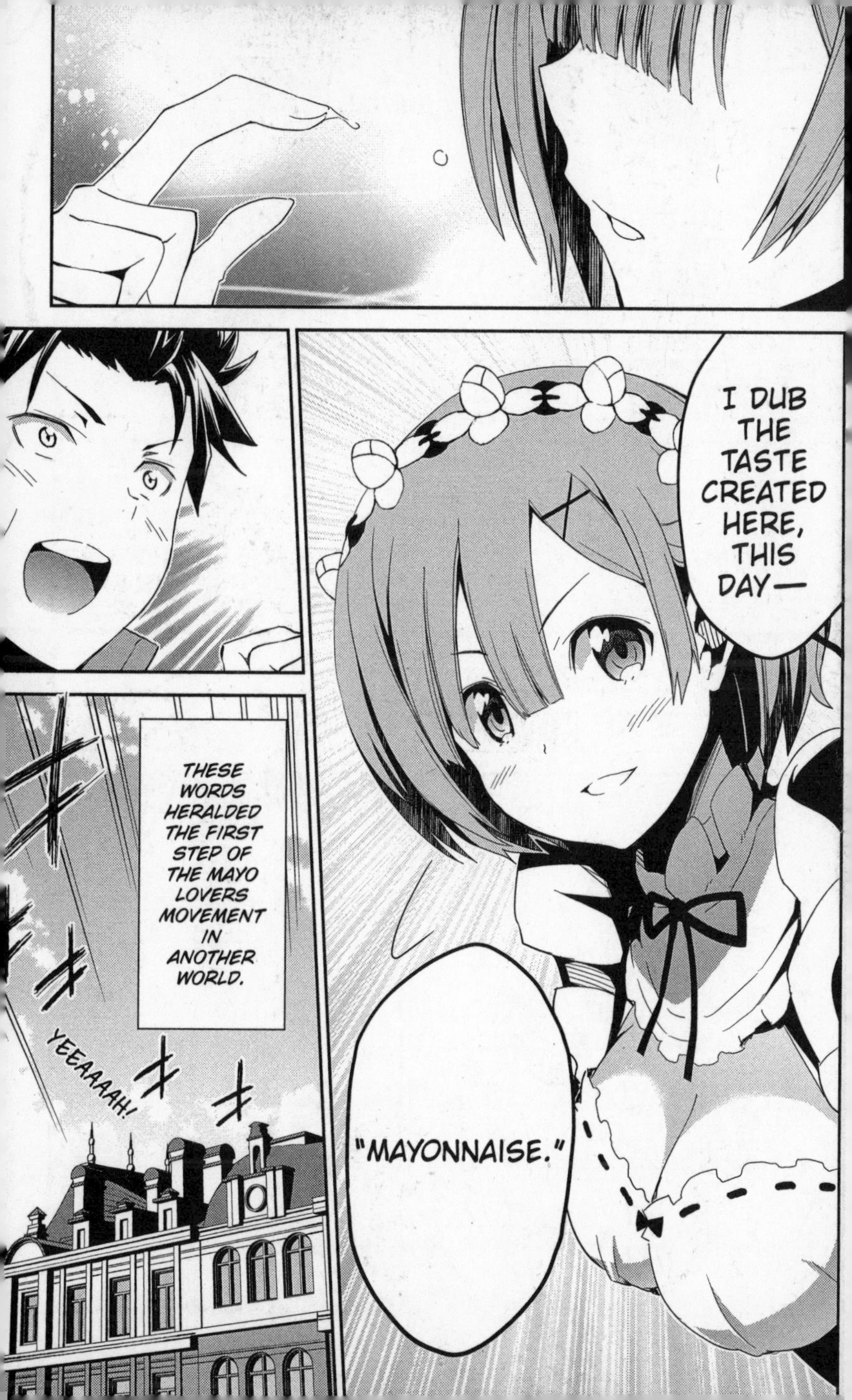
I DUB THE TASTE CREATED HERE, THIS DAY—
"MAYONNAISE."
THESE WORDS HERALDED THE FIRST STEP OF THE MAYO LOVERS MOVEMENT IN ANOTHER WORLD.
YEEAAAAH!

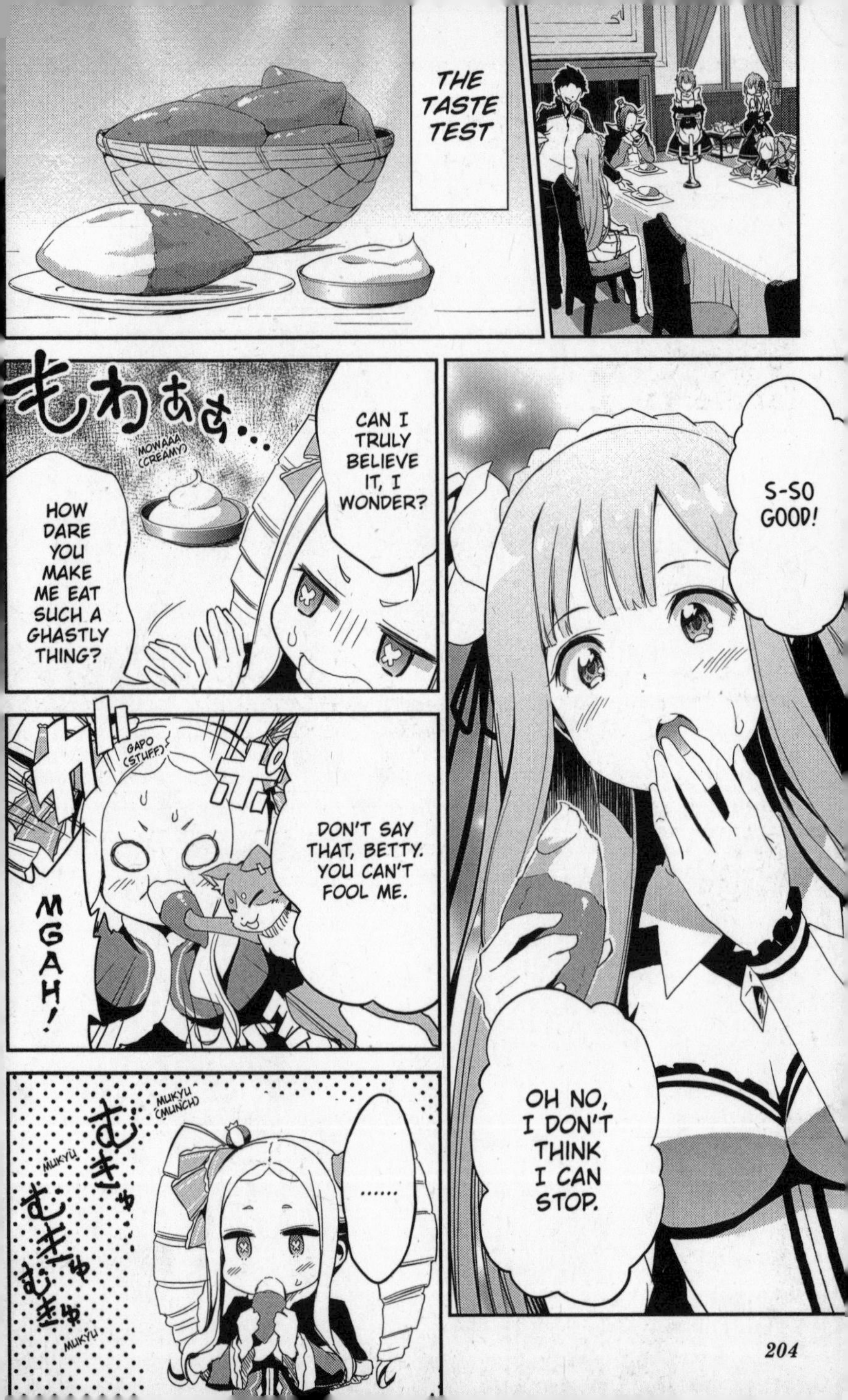
THE TASTE TEST
S-SO GOOD!
OH NO, I DON'T THINK I CAN STOP.
CAN I TRULY BELIEVE IT, I WONDER?
もわぁぁ…
MOWAAA (CREAMY)
HOW DARE YOU MAKE ME EAT SUCH A GHASTLY THING?
DON'T SAY THAT, BETTY. YOU CAN'T FOOL ME.
ガポ
GAPO (STUFF)
MGAH!
......
むきゅ
MUKYU (MUNCH)
むきゅ むきゅ
MUKYU
MUKYU

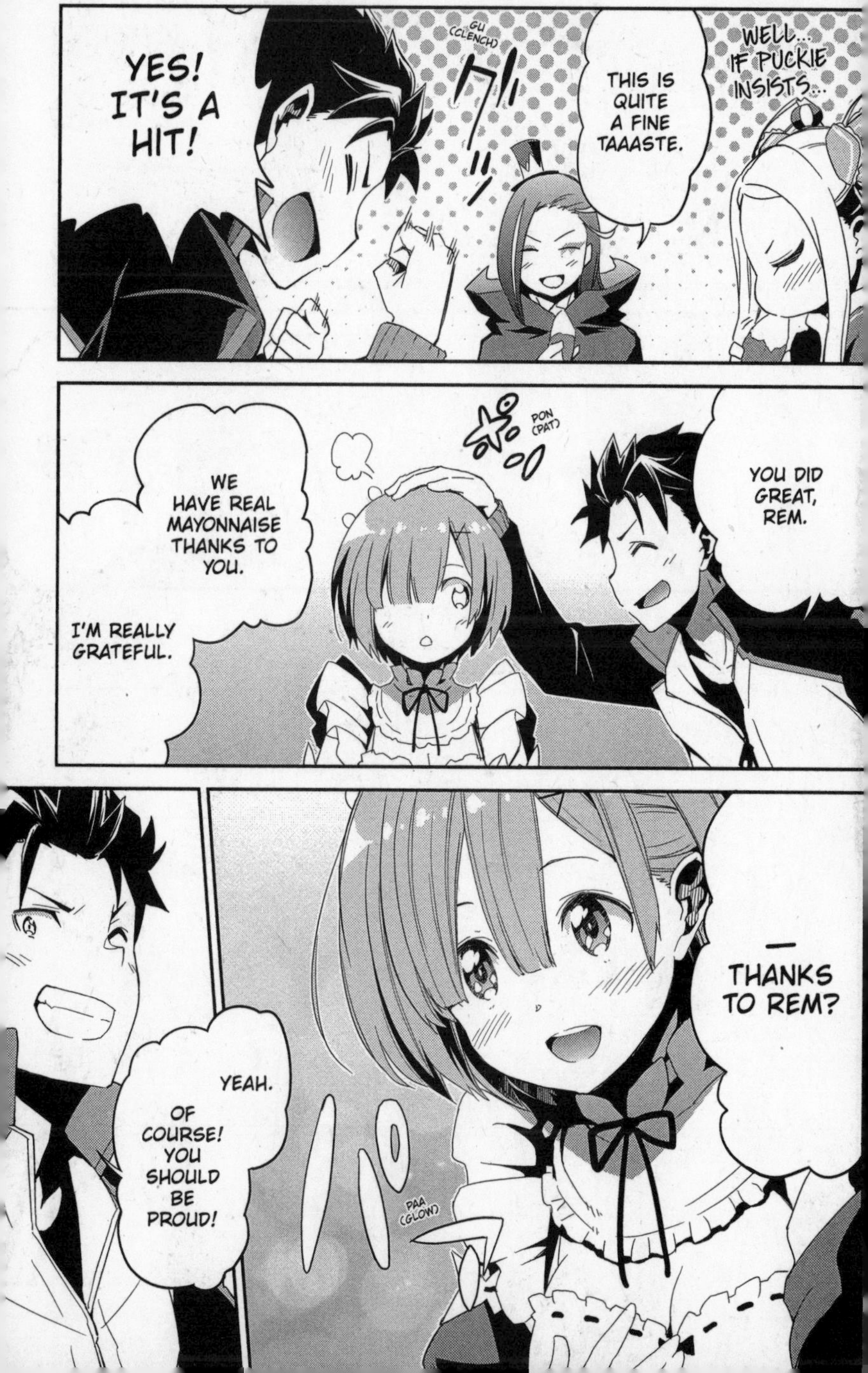
WELL... IF PUCKIE INSISTS...
THIS IS QUITE A FINE TAAASTE.
GU (CLENCH)
YES! IT'S A HIT!
YOU DID GREAT, REM.
PON (PAT)
WE HAVE REAL MAYONNAISE THANKS TO YOU.
I'M REALLY GRATEFUL.
— THANKS TO REM?
PAA (GLOW)
YEAH.
OF COURSE! YOU SHOULD BE PROUD!

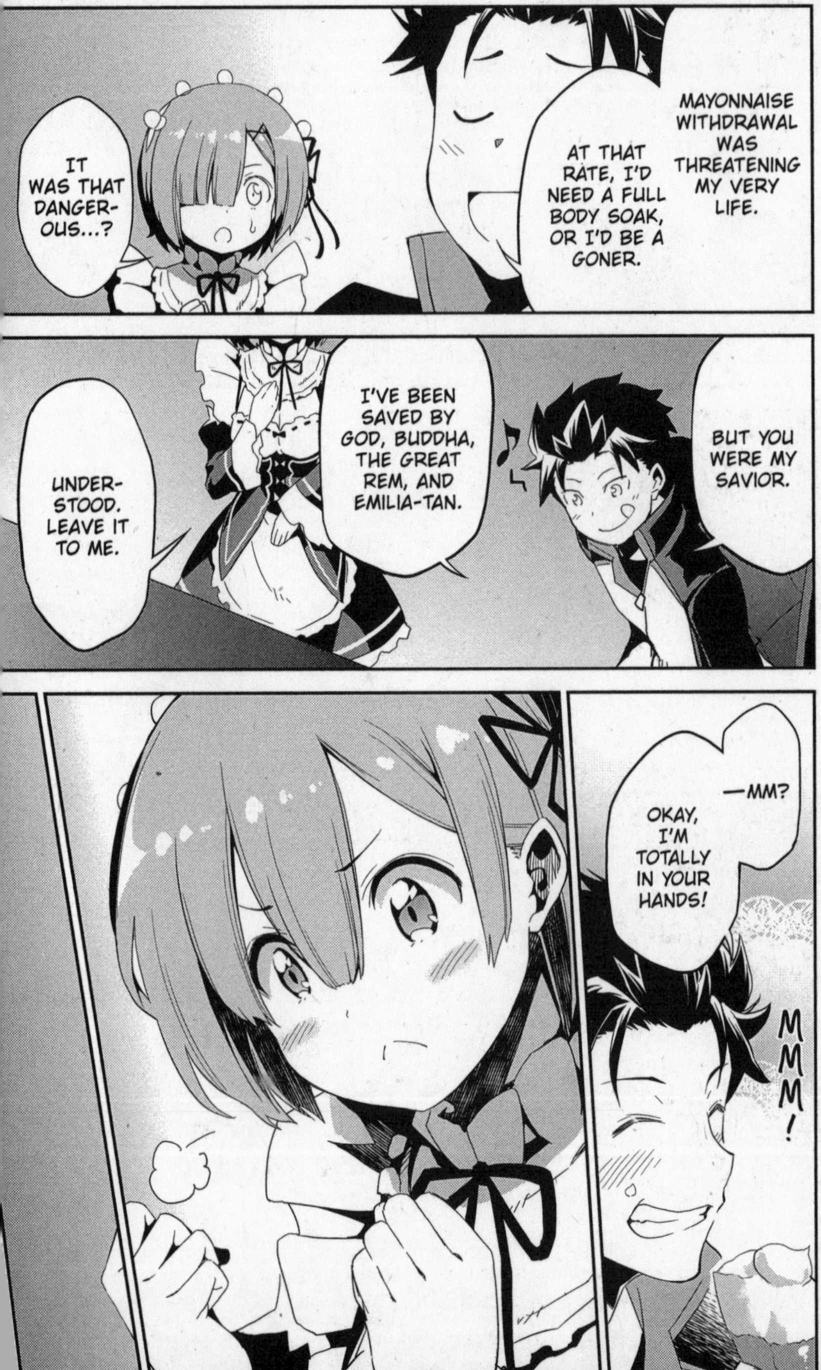
MAYONNAISE WITHDRAWAL WAS THREATENING MY VERY LIFE.
AT THAT RATE, I'D NEED A FULL BODY SOAK, OR I'D BE A GONER.
IT WAS THAT DANGER-OUS...?
BUT YOU WERE MY SAVIOR.
I'VE BEEN SAVED BY GOD, BUDDHA, THE GREAT REM, AND EMILIA-TAN.
UNDER-STOOD. LEAVE IT TO ME.
MMMM!
—MM?
OKAY, I'M TOTALLY IN YOUR HANDS!

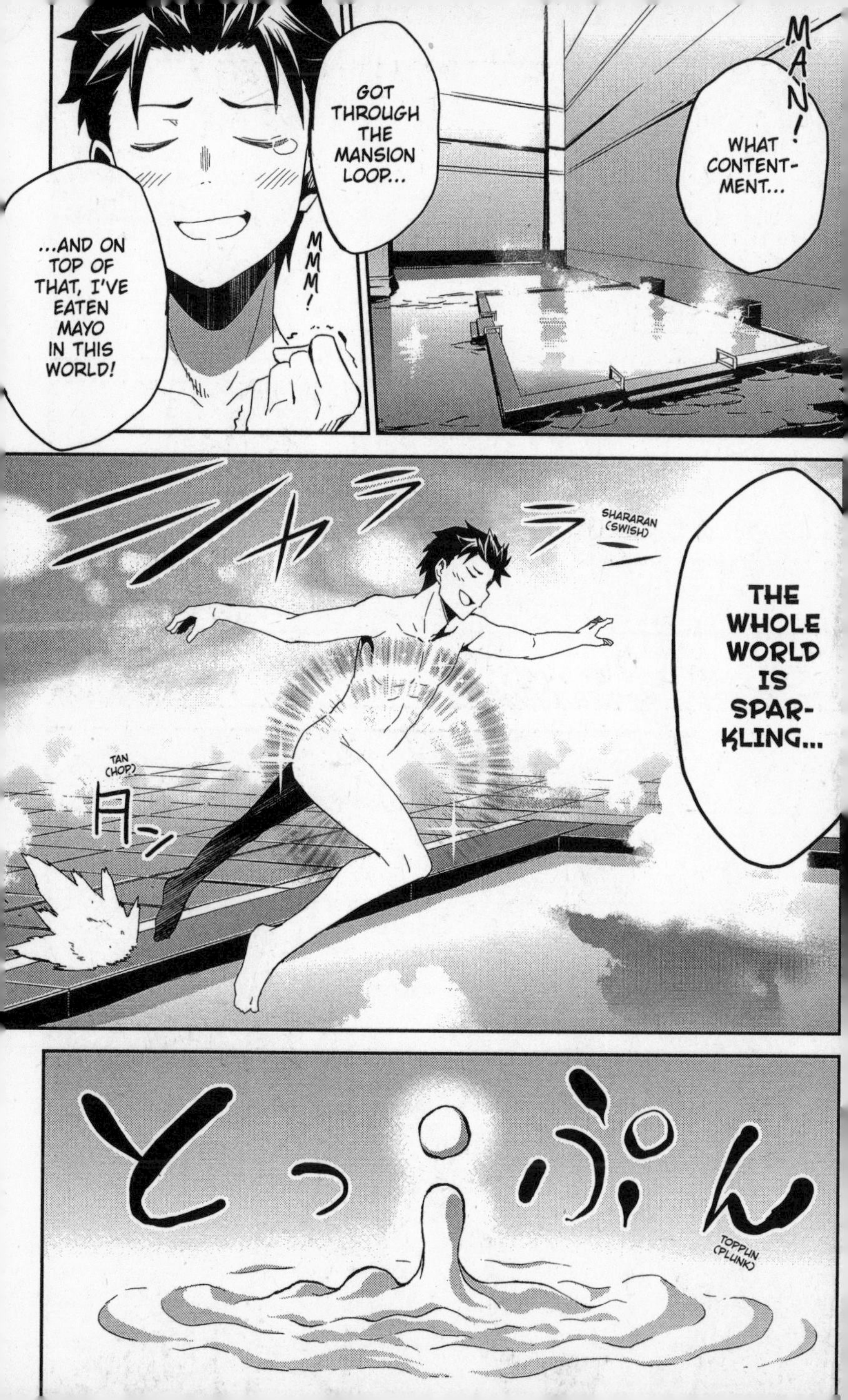
MAN!
WHAT CONTENT-MENT...
GOT THROUGH THE MANSION LOOP...
MMM!
...AND ON TOP OF THAT, I'VE EATEN MAYO IN THIS WORLD!
THE WHOLE WORLD IS SPAR-KLING...
SHARARAN (SWISH)
TAN (HOP)
とっぷん
TOPPUN (PLUNK)

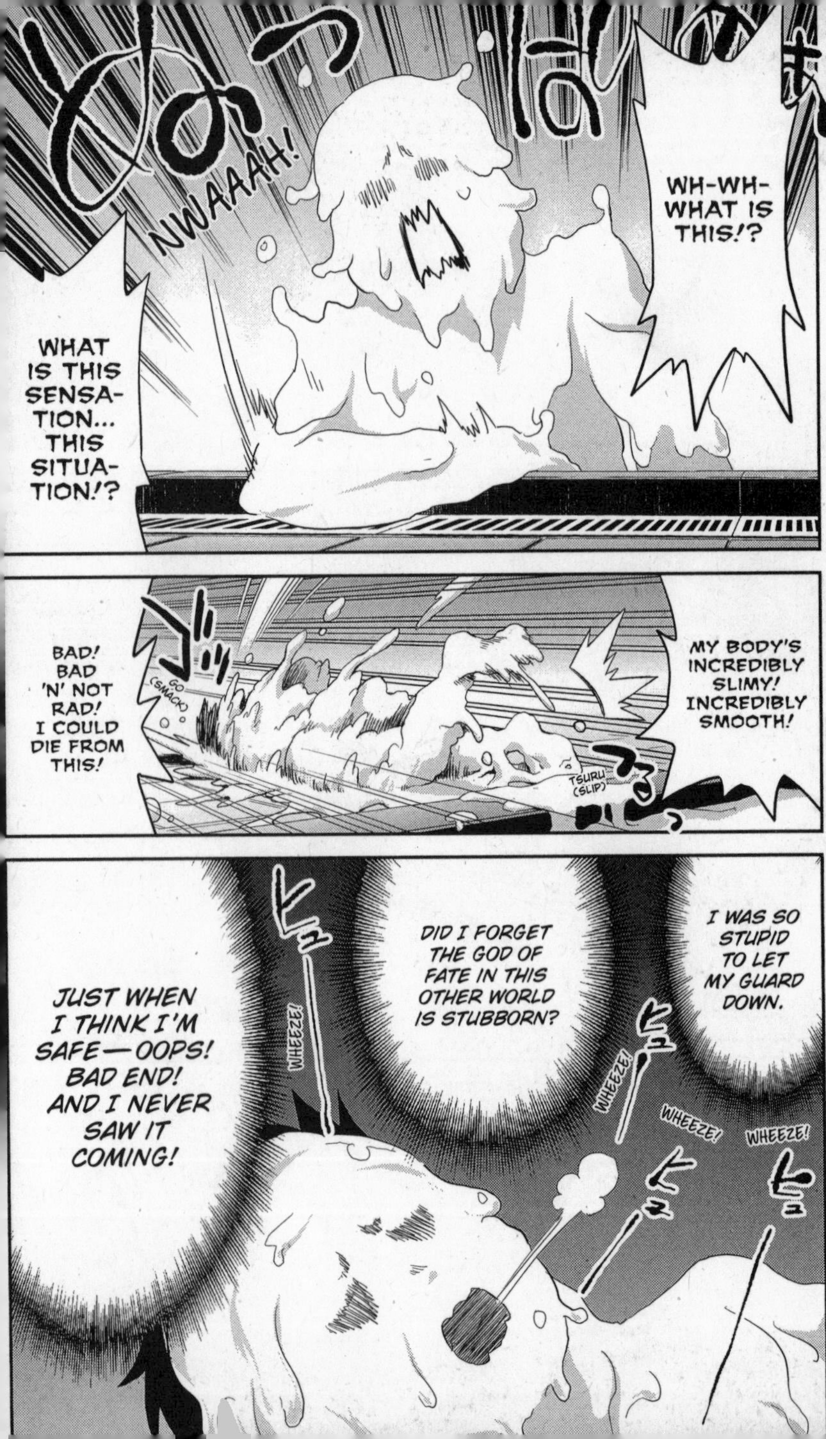
WH-WH-WHAT IS THIS!?
NWAAAH!
WHAT IS THIS SENSATION... THIS SITUATION!?
MY BODY'S INCREDIBLY SLIMY! INCREDIBLY SMOOTH!
TSURU (SLIP)
GO (SMACK)
BAD! BAD 'N' NOT RAD! I COULD DIE FROM THIS!
I WAS SO STUPID TO LET MY GUARD DOWN.
DID I FORGET THE GOD OF FATE IN THIS OTHER WORLD IS STUBBORN?
WHEEZE!
WHEEZE!
WHEEZE!
WHEEZE!
JUST WHEN I THINK I'M SAFE—OOPS! BAD END! AND I NEVER SAW IT COMING!

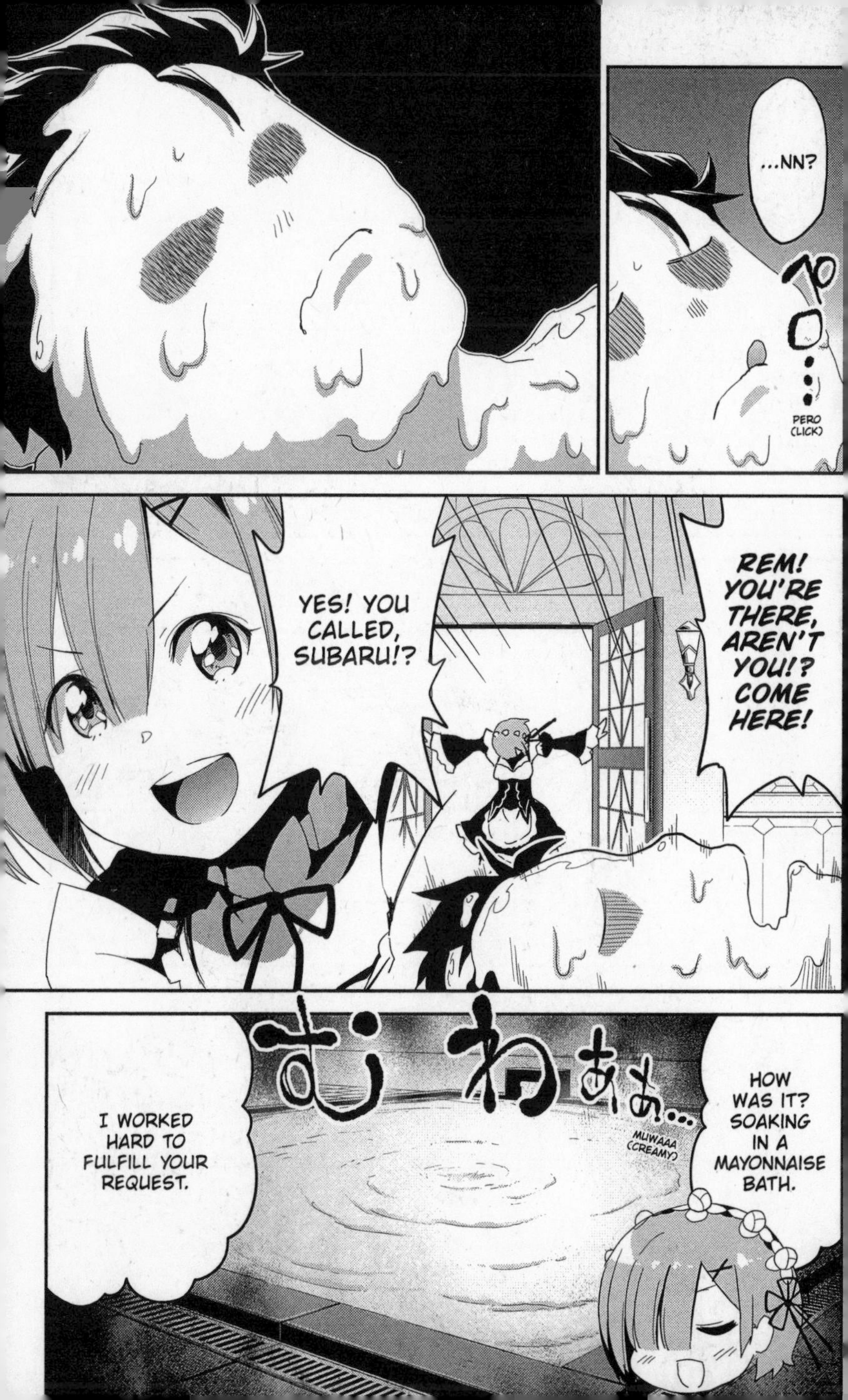
...NN?
ペロ…
PERO (CLICK)
REM! YOU'RE THERE, AREN'T YOU!? COME HERE!
YES! YOU CALLED, SUBARU!?
HOW WAS IT? SOAKING IN A MAYONNAISE BATH.
むわぁぁ…
MUWAAA (CREAMY)
I WORKED HARD TO FULFILL YOUR REQUEST.

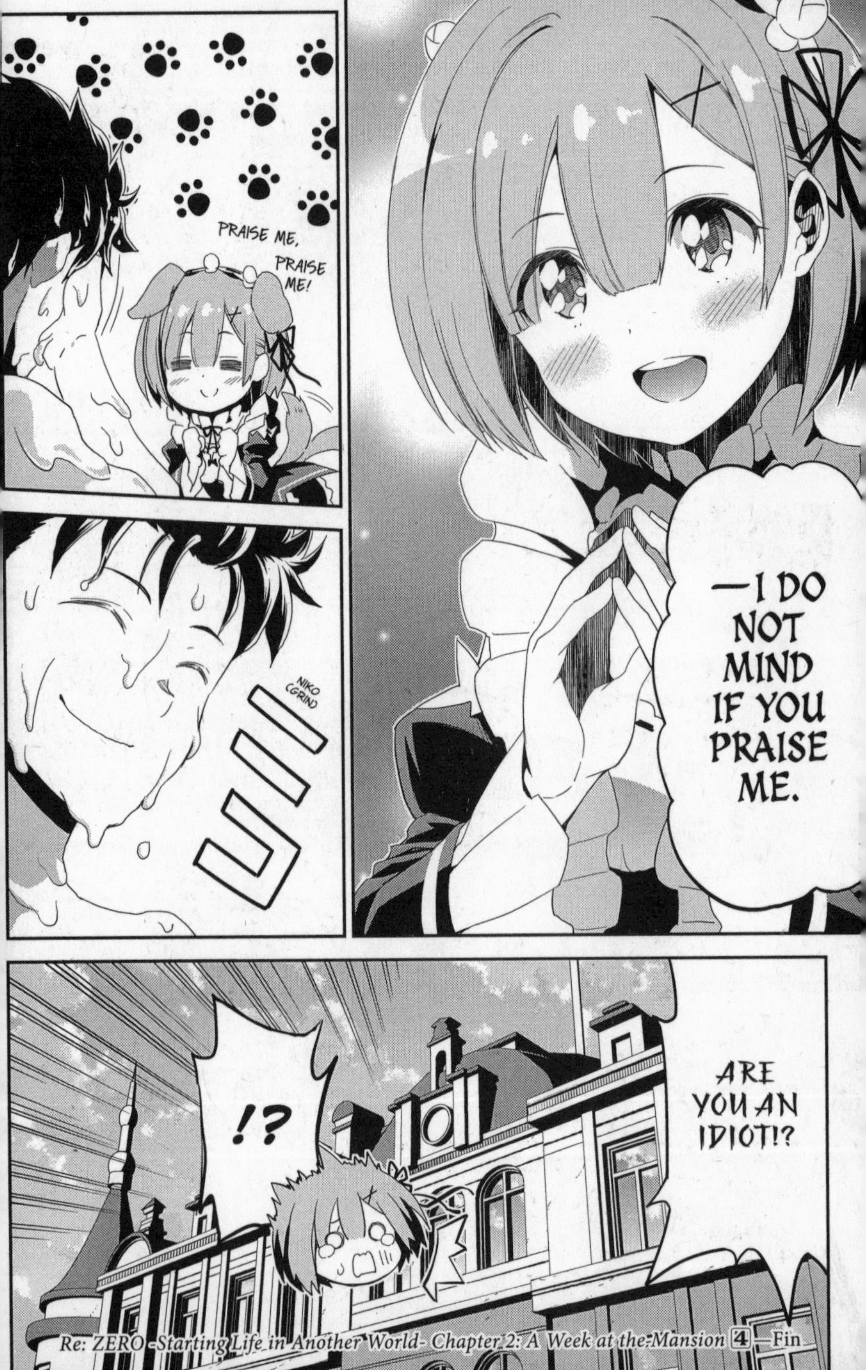
—I DO NOT MIND IF YOU PRAISE ME.
PRAISE ME, PRAISE ME!
NIKO (GRIN)
ARE YOU AN IDIOT!?
!?

Re: ZERO -Starting Life in Another World- Chapter 2: A Week at the Mansion 4 —Fin

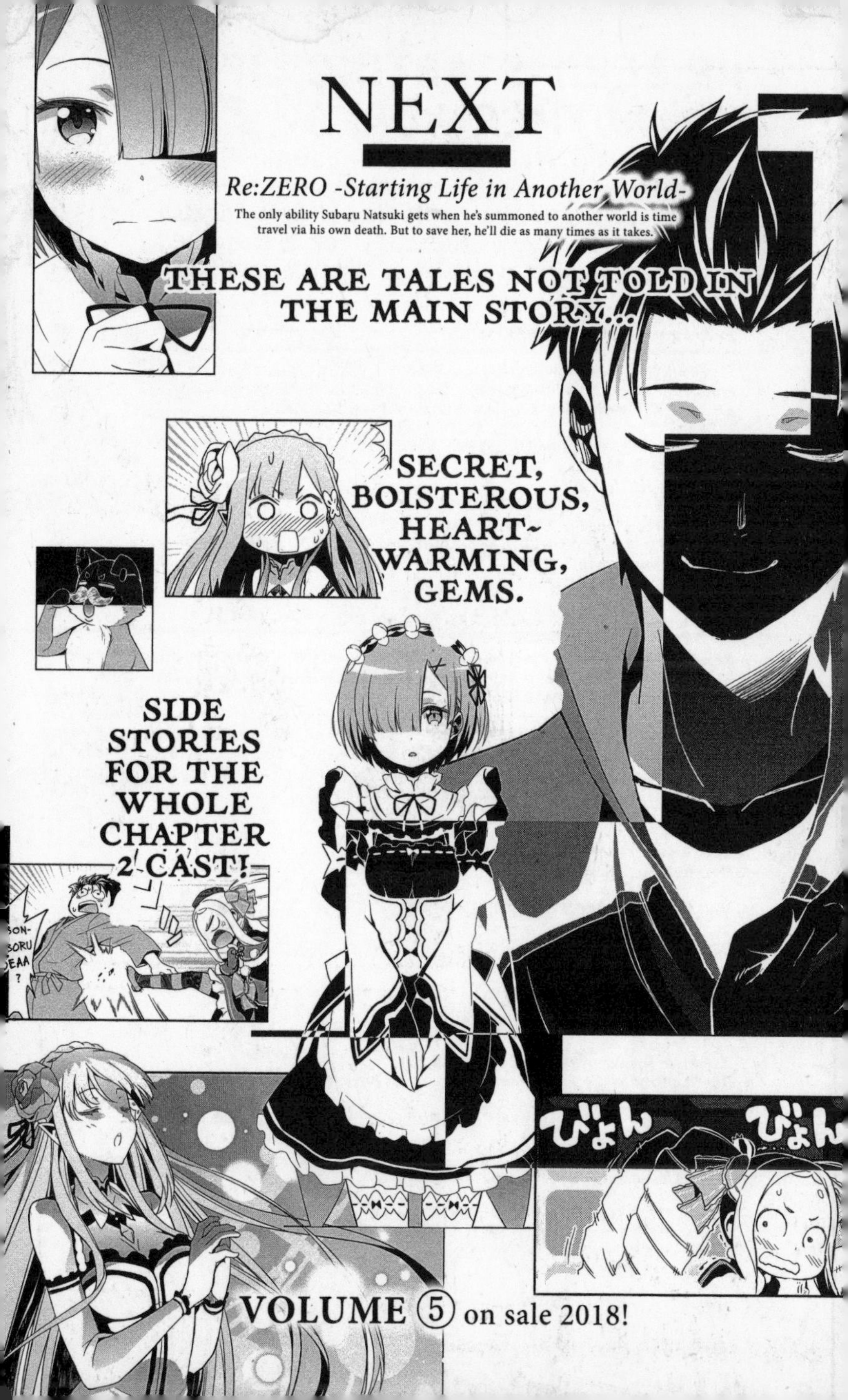
NEXT
Re:ZERO -Starting Life in Another World-
The only ability Subaru Natsuki gets when he's summoned to another world is time travel via his own death. But to save her, he'll die as many times as it takes.
THESE ARE TALES NOT TOLD IN THE MAIN STORY...
SECRET, BOISTEROUS, HEART-WARMING, GEMS.
SIDE STORIES FOR THE WHOLE CHAPTER 2 CAST!
びょん
びょん
VOLUME ⑤ on sale 2018!

RE:ZERO -STARTING LIFE IN ANOTHER WORLD- 4
Chapter 2: A Week at the Mansion

Art: **Makoto Fugetsu**
Original Story: **Tappei Nagatsuki**
Character Design: **Shinichirou Otsuka**

Translation: **ZephyrRZ**
Lettering: **Anthony Quintessenza**

RE:ZERO KARA HAJIMERU ISEKAI SEIKATSU DAINISHO YASHIKI NO ISSHUKAN-HEN Vol. 4
© Tappei Nagatsuki 2014
Licensed by KADOKAWA CORPORATION
© 2017 Makoto Fugetsu / SQUARE ENIX CO., LTD.
First published in Japan in 2016 by SQUARE ENIX CO., LTD. English translation rights arranged with SQUARE ENIX CO., LTD. and Yen Press, LLC through TUTTLE-MORI AGENCY, Inc.

English translation © 2017 by SQUARE ENIX CO., LTD.

Yen Press
1290 Avenue of the Americas
New York, NY 10104

Visit us at yenpress.com
facebook.com/yenpress
twitter.com/yenpress
yenpress.tumblr.com
instagram.com/yenpress

First Yen Press Edition: December 2017

Yen Press is an imprint of Yen Press, LLC.
The Yen Press name and logo are trademarks of Yen Press, LLC.

The publisher is not responsible for websites (or their content) that are not owned by the publisher.

Library of Congress Control Number: 2016936537

ISBNs: 978-0-316-41411-1 (paperback)
       978-0-316-44784-3 (ebook)

10 9 8 7 6 5 4 3 2 1

BVG

Printed in the United States of America